The
Hebrew Letters

The
Hebrew Letters

Channels of
Creative Consciousness

Rabbi
Yitzchak Ginsburgh

Linda Pinsky Publications

a division of Gal Einai
Jerusalem

Printed in Israel
First Edition 1990
Second Edition 1992

This book has previously been published as
The Alef-Beit: Jewish Thought Revealed through the Hebrew Letters

edited by Rabbi Avraham Arieh Trugman
and Rabbi Moshe Yaakov Wisnefsky

For information address:

USA: Gal Einai Institute, Inc.
        PO Box 41
        Cedarhurst, NY 11516-9862,
        tel/fax (toll-free): (888) 453-0571

Israel: Gal Einai
        PO Box 1015
        Kefar Chabad 72915
        tel.: (02) 996-1123; fax: (02) 996-2111

E-mail: inner@inner.org.

Web: www.inner.org

Gal Einai publishes and produces books, pamphlets, audiocassettes and
videocassettes by Rabbi Yitzchak Ginsburgh. To receive a catalog of our
products in English and/or Hebrew, please contact us at any of the above
addresses, email orders@inner.org, or visit www.inner-store.org.

Dedicated in honor of
our beautiful granddaughters

Marley Alexandra
(מלכה פריידא)
and
Jordan Sarah
(ירדנה שרה)
Medina

May they be a source of pride
and joy to us and Klal Yisrael

Michael and Susan Roth

Credits:

project coordination	Moshe Schlass
transcription	Rabbi Dovid Rubin
	Rabbi Moshe Miller
documentation	Michael Elzafon
	Rabbi Moshe Miller
editing	Mordechai Rosner
calligraphy	Ezra Benjamin
word processing	Rachel Trugman

Special thanks to Rabbi Avraham Arieh Trugman for the hundreds of hours he spent painstakingly nurturing the book from its infancy into its present form.

Table of Contents

Preface

This book grew out of a series of lectures on the mystical significance of the letters of the Hebrew alphabet by Rabbi Yitzchak Ginsburgh. In it are discussed many basic as well as advanced concepts in Jewish thought.

The structure of the book is based on the Ba'al Shem Tov's teaching that each letter exists in three dimensions: *Worlds, Souls,* and *Divinity.* "Worlds" refers to the physical/human, dimension, "Souls" to the Jewish spiritual dimension, and "Divinity" to the G-dly dimension [in the classic Kabbalistic texts (the teachings of the Arizal) these three dimensions are called *Vessels, Sparks,* and *Lights*]. Since each of these dimensions is reflected in each letter's three facets—its shape, its name, and its numerical value—we can distinguish nine separate categories of meaning for each letter:

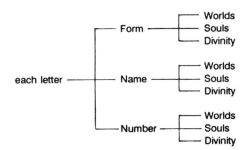

We have preceded our detailed treatment of these nine categories for each letter with (1) a kernel-phrase which synopsizes the basic essence of the letter, (2) a general introduction to the letter, and (3) a summary chart of the discussions to follow. These are intended to help the reader sustain his orientation throughout the ensuing discussion.

Furthermore, before focusing on the individual letters, there is an introduction which expounds on the underlying concepts of language and the role of letter-meditation in Judaism. This introduction contains a wealth of advanced, "theoretical" material the reader need not feel obligated to tackle before proceeding to the body of the work.

At the end of the book we have provided several appendices and a glossary to aid the reader with unfamiliar concepts, although these are generally defined when they first appear in the text.

Following this is section of notes. The purpose of these notes is twofold: First, we have attempted to supply some rudimentary documentation for the many concepts presented in the book. In this way the advanced reader can trace the ideas to their sources for further elucidation of the concepts.

Secondly, we have attempted to clarify some of the concepts presented in the body of the text where this was felt necessary. If the reader comes across a difficult passage in the text, he should first check the notes to see if they shed any light. If not, he should research the references and seek elucidation at the feet of qualified scholars. The works cited in the appendix "Suggestions for Further Reading" should also prove helpful.

The following stylistic conventions have been adhered to throughout the book:

1. G-d is spelled without the "o" in the middle. Since this a holy word, Jewish custom is not to spell it in full except in actual sacred texts.

2. We have referred to the Tetragrammaton (G-d's four-letter Name) as it is generally referred to in Chassidic and Kabbalistic texts: "the Name *Havayah*." The word "*Havayah*" is both a rearrangement of the letters of the holy Name and the Hebrew word for "existence" or "being," serving to indicate the relation of this holy Name to the verb "to be." In the Hebrew, this Name is indicated as 'ה or הוי'. Other Names of G-d are similarly altered slightly, both in Hebrew and English, as a sign of respect.

3. We have translated both the Names *Elokim* and *Havayah* as "G-d." When both appear in the same verse, we have italicized the word "G-d" that corresponds to the Name *Havayah*, a convention for which there is some precedent.

4. We have transliterated Hebrew words according to their Sefardic pronunciation. Although both the Ashkenazic and Sefardic systems are holy, the Sefardic seems to be presently more universal.

5. We have opted to use the half-cross (⊥) rather than the full cross to indicate addition, and the dot (·) rather than the "x" to indicate multiplication.

*   *   *

As with our previous and planned (G-d willing) publications, it is our express wish that the present work inspire the reader to delve ever deeper into the ocean of Torah, and thereby enrich his life and the lives of others.

May we soon see the fulfillment of the *Mashiach*'s promise to the Ba'al Shem Tov as quoted in the Introduction.

Gal Einai Publications
Jerusalem
Erev Shavuot, 5750

Introduction

On Rosh HaShanah of the year 5507 [1746 C.E.] I performed, by means of an oath, an elevation of soul, as known to you, and saw wondrous things I had never seen before. What I saw and learned there is impossible to convey in words, even face to face.... I ascended from level to level until I entered the chamber of the Mashiach, where the Mashiach learns Torah with all the Tanaim and tzadikim and also with the seven Shepherds.... I asked the Mashiach: "When will the Master come?" And he answered: "By this you shall know: When your teaching will become public and revealed in the world, and your wellsprings burst forth to the farthest extremes—that which I have taught you and you have comprehended—and they also shall be able to perform unifications and elevations as you, then all of the 'shells' will cease to exist, and there shall be a time of good will and salvation."

I stood in wonder and great distress as to the length of time necessary for this, when could this be?! But from what I learned there—three potent practices and three Holy Names, easy to learn and explain—my mind settled and I thought that possibly by means of these, men of my nature will be able to achieve levels similar to mine.... But I was not given permission all my life to reveal this.... But this I may inform you and may G-d help you, your way shall ever be in the presence of G-d and never leave your consciousness in the time of your prayer and study. Every word of your lips intend to unite: for in every letter there are Worlds, Souls, and Divinity, and they ascend and connect and unify with each other, and afterward the letters connect and unify to become a word, and [then] unify in true unification in Divinity. Include your soul with them in each and every state. And all the Worlds unify as one and ascend to produce an infinitely great joy and pleasure, as you can understand from the joy of groom and bride in miniature and physicality, how much more so in such an exalted level as this. Surely G-d will be your aid and wherever you turn you will succeed and reach greater awareness. "Give to the wise and he will become ever wiser."

—from a letter by Rabbi Yisrael
Ba'al Shem Tov to his brother-
in-law, Rabbi Gershon of Kitov

ENERGY, LIFE, LIGHT

Each of the twenty-two letters of the Hebrew alphabet possesses three distinct creative powers, which in the teachings of *Chassidut* are termed: energy (כח), life (חיות), and light (אור).

Physical matter, as now understood by modern science, is no more than concentrated energy. In organic matter, the mysterious phenomenon called life becomes manifest. In the mind and soul of higher life-forms, Divine Consciousness, here referred to as light, becomes revealed.

In the creative process, the Hebrew letters appear at each of these three levels: as the energy building-blocks of all of reality; as the manifestation of the inner life-pulse permeating the universe as a whole and each of its individual creatures ("pulsing" every created being, instantaneously, into and out of existence); and as the channels which direct the influx of Divine revelation into created consciousness.

Throughout all of Creation the letters can be envisioned as "standing" as building-blocks, "speaking" with lifeforce (in the secret of "and man became a living soul"—"a speaking spirit"), and "thinking" with meditative power to convey Divine influx.

Creative power	Realm of Manifestation	Role of Letters	Image of Letters
energy	physical matter	energy building-blocks	standing
life	organic matter	life-force	speaking
light	mind and soul	channels of Divine influx	thinking

FIRMAMENT, WATER, LIGHT

The *Zohar* states that "G-d looked into [the letters of] the Torah and created the universe." The Divine act of Creation is referred to by the metaphor of speech, as we say in the beginning of our morning prayers: "Blessed be He who said...and the world came into being." The root אמר, "to say," is an acronym for the first three primary creations: light (אור), water (מים), firmament (רקיע). These represent the three stages in the materialization of the creative seed, as taught by the Arizal: the spiritual origin of the seed in the mind—light; physical manifestation of seed—water; the beginning of conception in the womb—firmament. Light, water, and firmament correspond, in turn, to the three categories defined above: light, life (here viewed as concentrated light)—as in the phrase "living waters," and energy (here, as pregnant "light-life"). The firmament (רקיע), which derives from the root רקע, "to stretch," represents all states of positive tension—energy fields—in nature.

Creative Power	Evolution of Seed	Dimension of Speech
light	spiritual origin	light
life (concentrated light)	physical manifestation	water
energy (pregnant light-life)	beginning of conception	firmament

After each individual act of creation, G-d observed that which He had created and saw it to be good. At the end of the sixth day of Creation, "G-d observed all that He had made, and, behold, it was very good." Thus, "before" Creation G-d looks into the Torah; the act of Creation itself, in each and every "present" moment, is by means of the Divine word; "after" Creation G-d observes His reality to be good. As "there is no good other than Torah," seeing Creation to be good is actually relating created reality "back" to its ideal model—Torah. This act is called, in Kabbalah and *Chassidut*, the process of "clarification." In man's service of G-d, it corresponds to the positive critique of one's deeds, to assure that they remain in tune with and in the light of the teachings of Torah.

In Kabbalah, "before" Creation is the secret of the right eye and "after" Creation is the secret of the left eye. They are the ultimate origins of light and life, respectively. The right eye gazes at the letters of primordial, uncreated reality, as engraved in Torah-"reality", still "nothing" in the sea of Infinite Light. The left eye contemplates created reality in relation to its Torah-model, thereby enlivening it from "the source of living waters" of Torah. The Sages interpret G-d's seeing all to be "very good": " 'good,' refers to the angel of life; '*very* [good]' refers to the angel of death." Death is here understood to serve both as the "antithesis" necessary for the process of "clarification" (whose purpose is to infuse reality with life), and even deeper, the necessary, intermediate stage between the initial state of temporal life and the final, "resurrected" state of eternal life, to be realized on earth in "the future to come."

The mouth, the secret of creation in the "present" moment, whose "breath" represents the continual emanation of energy-matter, is between the two eyes, as the present is between the past and the future. Regarding the position of the head *tefillin*, the Torah instructs that their inscribed words be "a memory between your eyes, so that the Torah of G-d shall be in your mouth." The word "memory" (זכרון) itself, in Hebrew, means "a source of speech" (as in the phrase: בכל מקום אשר אזכיר את שמי אבא אליך וברכתיך, "in that place that I will allow you to *speak* My Name I will come to you and bless you").

So, too, every Jew, whom the Torah commands to emulate G-d, should learn to first see the letters of Torah and their secrets in thought (the sight of the "light" of the right eye), then to speak them with his mouth, and finally to "clarify" them as "rectified" deed (the "life" process of the sight of the left eye).

Time	Act	Organ	Force	Expression
before Creation	looking into the Torah	right eye	light	thought
the act of Creation	speech	mouth	energy	word
after Creation	looking at reality, clarification	left eye	life	rectified deed

LETTERS, WORDS, LIGHT ABOVE ALL

"Two stones build two houses; three stones build six houses; four stones build twenty-four houses; five stones build one-hundred-and-twenty houses; six stones build seven-hundred-and-twenty houses; seven stones build five-thousand-and-forty houses; from here on go and calculate that which the mouth cannot speak and the ear cannot hear."

A stone, in the idiom of *Sefer Yetzirah*, is a letter; a house is a word (or phrase), a specific permutation of letters. Jacob rested his head on stones and thereafter referred to the Temple site-to-be as a "house" (not as Abraham, who called it a "mountain," nor as Isaac, who called it a "field").

Meaning "rests" (hovers) above individual letters, yet "resides" (lives) within words. While meaning is "resting" above the letters/stones, only their energy level, as the building blocks of Creation, is known. Meaning, in general, lives within the completed permutation of a word. Moreover, the unique essence of meaning related to the specific choice of a word (and to no other, though meaning can generally be conveyed by various choices of words) shines above the word, "inspiring" its components (permutation of letters) uniformly. This phenomenon is referred to in *Chassidut* as the "light above all," to be explained.

The awareness of general meaning is the secret of Jacob's dream. The stones, previously beneath his head, come to life and merge to become one, as lifeforce from the head of Jacob permeates them with meaning. Upon awakening he experiences, in awe, the light of the unique essence of Divine meaning inherent in the word. The essence of meaning had been totally unconscious to his own "head" before and during his inspired "dream," the process of permuting letters into words. The innate "style" of the root of his own Soul in Divinity ("*Jacob* called it 'house' ") had never been revealed.

Within the limitations of the scope of this book, we hope to inspire the serious student to "rest" (orient) his head on the Hebrew letters. If one's heart is sincere and true to G-d he will then merit, as our father Jacob, to experience, first in a "dream" as it were, the letters permuting to form words, and finally "awaken," in one's unique style of expression, to the full, awesome consciousness of the House of G-d.

Means of Expression	Focus of Letters	Progressive Revelation of Meaning	Image of Meaning in Relation to Means of Expression	Representation in Jacob's Story
letters	letter as letter; energy	potential meaning	resting—"hovering"—above	resting his head on stones
words	letter as part of word; life	actual meaning	residing—"living"—in	the dream
rhetoric, style	letter as unit of context, light	essence of meaning	light-above-all, "inspiration"	waking to unique soul-style

THE WISDOM OF ADAM AND BEZALEL

Letters build and enliven reality much as the encoded "letters" of DNA build and define the characteristics of the living body. In particular, the twenty-two letters of the Hebrew alphabet are reflected in the number of chromosomes in human seed. The twenty-two male chromosomes together with the twenty-two female chromosomes define forty-four characteristics of the offspring, the secret of the letters דם (=44), "blood," of אדם, "man." The additional two sex chromosomes of father and mother combine to define only one characteristic of the offspring, its sex, the secret of the letter א (=1) of אדם, the union of the higher (male) and lower (female) waters (in the secret of light, *water*, and firmament, discussed above), as will be explained in the discussion of the letter *alef*.

Adam, the first man, was uniquely gifted with the insight (wisdom) to recognize and call every being by its proper name. "And from the ground, G-d formed every animal of the field and every bird of the heavens, and He brought them to Adam to see what he would call them, and what Adam called every living creature, that was its name." Other than man, no created consciousness, even that of the angels above, possessed the ability to call by name. Our Sages teach that after Adam named all creatures, G-d asked him to call Him by Name. Immediately Adam recognized the Name *Havayah* as befitting G-d.

The Hebrew name of every being is the Divine power (or, specifically, the permutation of individual Divine forces, the letters of the name) responsible for and active in its continual recreation "something from nothing," as explained in *Tanya*. In particular, the Hebrew name of each creature is the channel through which lifeforce and consciousness descend from the spiritual root of the creature's soul above to its physical body below. In relation to G-d, His Name is the power—inherent in Him and given to us—to reveal Him below.

Of even deeper significance, one's name contains the secret of one's mission on earth. The two last words of the phrase "and what Adam called every living creature, *that was its name*," reads: הוא שמו, literally, "he is his name," which numerically equals the name *Mashiach* (משיח, 358). Every living creature possesses a spark of *Mashiach*, a spark entrusted with the power to fulfill its mission, to bring redemption to its "portion" on earth. In the Jewish soul this spark is active; in the soul of every other living being the spark is passive, awaiting the "fertilization" of a Jewish soul. Adam, when calling names, had not yet sinned. At this time he was the "potential" prototypical Jew. Had he withstood the temptation of sin, he would have fully actualized his potential, in himself and for all generations to come. His name אדם stands for אדם־דוד־משיח, Adam-David-*Mashiach*, as taught by the Arizal. Only he was able to recognize the individual spark of himself, the spark of the *Mashiach*, as it were, latent in every living being. This is the secret of our Sages' report that in the act of calling names, Adam actually "mated" with ("knew" in the sense of "fertilized") every living creature.

Bezalel, the artisan of the Tabernacle, G-d's "house" during our sojourn in the desert, "knew how to permute letters through which were created heavens and earth." His name, Bezalel (בצלאל), means "in the shadow of G-d." "To shadow" means "to emulate." So did Bezalel, through the knowledge of the power of the letters and their permutations, emulate G-d in the act of Creation, whose ultimate purpose is that all of Creation become a "house" for G-d (as will be explained in the secret of the letter *beit*).

Likewise, one of the meanings of Adam's name (אדם) is "I will be like," as in the verse אדמה לעליון, "I will be like the One on High." (This phrase numerically equals צלם אלקים, "the image of G-d" with which Adam was created.) This "likeness" to G-d, similar to that of Bezalel, refers to his ability to "know" reality by name, as though through the eyes of G-d, the Creator. This is in order to draw down (by means of each creature's name) into the experience of Creation the awareness of the Omnipresence of G-d, whose creative letters, words, and Names never "leave" them, as taught in *Chassidut*.

These two great souls, Adam and Bezalel, whose wisdom and knowledge focused around the secrets of the letters, their permutations, and names, are closely related. Numerically, Adam (אדם)=45, which is the triangle of 9 (i.e. the sum of all numbers from 1 to 9). 9 is the numerical value of the letter *tet* (ט). Bezalel (בצלאל)=153, the triangle of 17. 17 is the *gematria* of טוב, "good" (as will be explained in the secret of the letter *tet*). Nine is also the "middle point" of 17. Together, ט and טוב equal 26, the value of the name *Havayah*. 45⊥153=198=22·9, the product of the twenty-two letters of the Hebrew alphabet and the nine Hebrew vowels (which themselves correspond to the nine "reduced" values of the twenty-two letters), as taught in Kabbalah. The "ordinal" value of Bezalel (בצלאל) is 45, the precise "normative" value of Adam (אדם).

Bezalel's primary involvement in his works of craftsmanship was with physical energy-matter. This is at the general level of Worlds, to be discussed below. Nonetheless, the conscious purpose of the construction of the Tabernacle was, as the Torah instructs: "And they shall make for Me a Sanctuary, and I will dwell in their midst." Bezalel's "creation" served, from its very outset, to reveal Divine Light in the world, the general level of Divinity, to be explained. This was the "idea" he implanted in each of his works of art. For this reason, the Temple, built by the hands of the *tzadikim*, is considered to be a greater "creation" than that of heavens and earth, as created by the hand of G-d.

Adam, in general, drew the full experience of life into "every living creature" by calling it by name. Life relates to the level of Souls, to be explained. In particular, the life of "every living creature" (including the souls of non-Jews) is at the level of "Souls in Worlds"; the soul of Israel, however, which began to appear in Adam's own soul, before the sin, but which was first fully integrated by Abraham, the first Jew, is the true (state of life and) level of Souls.

Level		Expression	Soul
Divinity		intention in construction of Tabernacle	Bezalel
Souls ⌐	Souls *per se*	—Souls of Israel	—(Abraham)
		calling Creation by name	Adam
⌐	Souls in Worlds	—life of every living creature	
Worlds		construction of Tabernacle	Bezalel

SIGNS OF WONDER

The word for "letter" in Hebrew (אות) also means "sign" or "wonder." A wonder is a revelation of Divine light. Wonders of nature are revelations of "Divinity in Worlds," to use the general terminology of "Worlds, Souls, Divinity" (in "interinclusion," level in level), to be explained in greater depth and detail below.

The wondrous sign at the level of Souls is the secret of the "holy sign of the covenant," אות ברית קדש, the sign of circumcision stamped on the body of every Jewish male eight days from birth. (A Jewish female is "born circumcised," possessing "the holy sign" within herself from the moment of birth.) In *Sefer Yetzirah* the twenty-two letters are called עשרים ושתים אותיות היסוד, "twenty-two letters of foundation." In Kabbalah, the power of Foundation (*yesod*) relates to the sign of circumcision, the *brit*, which, when guarded in sanctity, serves as the key to open the secret teachings of the letters of Torah to one's inner mind and heart. In particular, the *brit* is the covenant between G-d and the *body* of every Jew—Divinity in Worlds (body) of Souls (the Jew).

Foundation, *yesod*, is also the power in the soul to relate and connect to other souls and beings. By being connected to each letter of Torah, one obtains the power to productively (as in the act of procreation, the act associated with the *brit*) relate and connect to every soul of Israel (for, ultimately, the letters of Torah and the souls of Israel are one). The reverse is also true: through genuine, loving relationships to one's fellow Jews one strengthens his bond to the letters of the Torah.

Supernatural wonders—miracles—are revelations of letters at the level of Divinity. When they appear as the intervention of the Hand of G-d and His Providence in the course of nature, they are at the particular level of Worlds in Divinity. When they appear as the power of the souls of the great *tzadikim* of every generation to change nature by the force of decree inherent in their service of prayer ("the *tzadik* decrees and G-d fulfills"), they are at the level of Souls in Divinity. When they appear as the experience of the miracles inscribed in the primordial Torah (such as the splitting of the Red Sea) rehappening, as it were, before our very eyes— thereby revealing to us that all of reality is in fact nothing other than the reality of Torah—they are at the level of Divinity in Divinity. Their revelation to us depends upon the אות ברית קדש, "the holy sign [letter] of covenant" between G-d and Israel.

Level	Manifestation of Letters as "Signs of Wonder"
Divinity —Divinity —Souls —Worlds	miracles —miracles of the Torah —miracles of the *tzadikim* —miracles of Divine Providence
Souls	circumcision
Worlds	wonders of nature

FORM, NAME, NUMBER

Each letter possesses three different representations: form (תמונה, "picture"), name (שם), and number (חשבון).

In Kabbalah, the form or visual structure of the written letter (its מכתב, "script") is its representation in the world of Action (עשיה), the lower of the three general classes of created worlds.

The letter's name (its מלוי, "full spelling"; each letter is "pregnant" with one, two, or three other letters which, together with it, serve to express it fully), its meaning (in Hebrew the name of each letter has definite, multifold meaning), together with its sound and other phonetic properties (מבטא), is its representation in the world of Formation (יצירה, the realm of emotion, including emotive intelligence).

The letter's number, understood as the abstract set of all sets of phenomena of that order (number), is its representation in the world of Creation (בריאה, the realm of pure intelligence). Here, number represents the pure abstract thought (מחשבה) of each letter, stripped of the external thought sensations of visuality and audibility. At this level, the word for "number" (חשבון) derives from the root חשב, "to think." חשבון implies the ability to calculate and, in particular, the ability to "assess" or measure reality properly, as in חשבון הנפש, the "reckoning" or "assessment" of the soul. To "think" numbers is to recognize the ratio-relationships (each number is in fact the ratio of $1:n$) and symmetry in nature.

World	Representation of Letter	Experience
Creation (abstract intelligence)	number, "measure"	thought
Formation (emotion & emotive intelligence)	name	sound
Action	form	script

In the Divine world of Emanation (אצילות), above the three lower worlds of Creation, Formation, and Action, the Divine Sources of these three representations invert. (Divinity in general "sees" reality "upside down.") The inner, middle, and outer dimensions of the "vessels" (sources of lower phenomological appearances) of the world of Emanation correspond to form (ספיר, "brilliance"), name (ספור, "tale") and number (מספר), respectively. The three terms "brilliance," "tale," and "number" are three meanings or "senses" of the general term *sefirah* (ספירה) in Kabbalah.

The root of *sefirah* is ספר, "book." The three meanings of *sefirah* correspond to the three "books" with which G-d created the world, as taught in *Sefer Yetzirah*, explained below. They also correspond to the three "books" opened on the Day of Judgment (*Rosh Hashanah*): the book of the righteous ("brilliance"), the book of the intermediate ("tale"), and the book of the wicked (the potential *ba'al teshuvah*, returner to G-d) ("number").

The experience of the world of Emanation is one of selflessness (בטול) above thought (the world of Creation), emotion (the world of Formation), and behavior (the world of Action). Here, number is the most external power, latent in the true state of selflessness, to *differentiate* between phenomena and experiences. Name is here the latent power to *infuse* phenomena and experiences with meaning and the conscious sense of purpose. The brilliant light of "formless" form is the particular ability of each letter (or the "vessel" of each *sefirah* in the world of Emanation) to channel and *crystallize* the revelation of Divine light in a specific manner.

Dimension of the Vessels of Emanation	Representation of Letter	Power	The Three Meanings of ספירה, *sefirah*	The Three Books opened on *Rosh HaShanah*
inner	form	to crystallize Divine revelation	brilliance ספיר	Book of the Righteous
middle	name	to infuse with meaning and purpose	tale ספור	Book of the Intermediate
outer	number	to differentiate between phenomena	number מספר	Book of the Wicked

Even higher, in the "mind" (consciousness) and "crown" (superconsciousness) of the Divine world of Emanation itself, the ultimate source of number, in the sense of the power to "count" all from the absolute One (as will be explained in the secret of the letter *alef*), appears above the dimensions of form and name.

The mind possesses three powers of perception and intellect, the three *sefirot* of chochmah (חכמה, "wisdom"), binah (בינה, "understanding"), and *da'at* (דעת, "knowledge"). Here, number is "counted" by *chochmah*; form "sculptured" by *binah*; name "called" by *da'at* (as in the secret of Adam calling, and thereby "knowing," every living creature by name, as explained above). The "book" (of Creation) of *chochmah* is referred to as סופר, "scribe" or "counter"; the "book" of *binah* as ספר, "book"; the "book" of *da'at* as ספור, "story."

Power of Intellect	Operation Performed	"Book" of Creation
chochmah (wisdom)	count	"scribe" or "counter" (of number) סופר
binah (understanding)	sculpt	"book" (of form) ספר
da'at (knowledge)	call	"tale" (of name) ספור

The "crown" possesses three "heads," which correspond, in the soul, to the three superconscious states of faith, serene pleasure, and will, to be explained below. Here, "counting" is an act of faith; form, an experience of pleasure; name, a statement of will.

Head of the "Crown"	Corresponding Experience
faith	counting (all from the absolute One)
serene pleasure	perceiving form
will	naming

In summation:

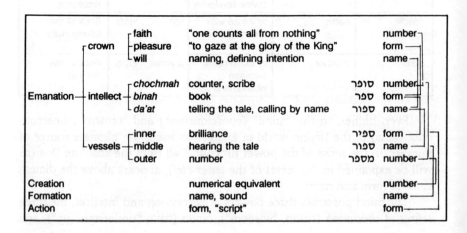

THE "INTERINCLUSION" OF THE EXPERIENCES OF SIGHT, SOUND, NUMBER

Beginning from below, in the world of Action (עשיה), one's consciousness first relates to visual conceptualization. Sound and number also possess visual structure as in musical notation (or, in Torah, the signs of cantillation) and geometric representations of algebraic expressions (as the plenitude of "triangles," "squares," etc. apparent in the mathematical structure of Torah). In general, visualization helps one toward insight into the practical applications of concepts (the world of Action), concepts which otherwise would remain abstract in nature. In Kabbalah we are taught that the Ashuritic script of the Hebrew letters used in the Torah scroll, though generally relating to secrets of all worlds, in particular pictures the inner truth of the world of Action.

Relative to our physical experience, the sense of hearing sound and meaning (in Hebrew, "to hear" means "to understand") is nonetheless more spiritual than that of sight. At Sinai, when these two senses merged, as is said: "And all the people saw the voices..."; "hearing sight" nonetheless transcended "seeing sound," as explained in *Chassidut*. In ordinary terms, "hearing sight" is the experience or perception of harmony (as in music) and balance—grace—in the object of one's vision. Mathematical expressions also possess music; the eloquence of a mathematical demonstration possesses both visual as well as musical beauty. The spiritual force of the word is its power to arouse—"move"—the emotions of man, in the secret of the world of Formation. While sight may "attract," hearing "moves."

The "ten intangible *sefirot*" are, most literally, "ten intangible numbers" (*sefirah* is identical with "number" or "counting" in Hebrew). Numbering in Torah is based upon the decimal system. Whereas each of the twenty-two letters possesses a unique form and sound (name), the corresponding numbers are basically ten with additional construct forms. (Only in the "ordinal numbering system" [מספר סדורי] of the letters, from one to twenty-two, is the number of each letter apparently unique, not reflecting the modulus of ten.) Thus, in general, the numbers associated with the letters allude to a higher, amorphous power, which enters into and finds expression through the means of the letters. Ten resides within twenty-two, in the secret of "ten intangible *sefirot* and twenty-two letters of Foundation," the thirty-two pathways of wisdom of *Sefer Yetzirah*. When expressed mathematically, both form and sound (name) turn into numbers and thereby disappear from the realm of the tangible. Intangibility is the general state of the world of Creation, "something from nothing," whose state of "something" is yet formless and nameless.

World	Perception	Level	Interinclusion		Sensation
Creation	intangibility	number	name	"computerized" sound	clings
			form	"computerized" form, numerical analysis of letter form	
Formation	acoustic conceptualization	name	number	eloquence of mathematical demonstration	moves
			form	harmony and balance, grace	
Action	visual conceptualization	form	number	geometric representation of algebraic expression and eloquence of mathematical demonstration	attracts
			name	musical notation, Torah cantillation	

Thus we see that each level of form, name, and number "interincludes" within (i.e., is present in as a particular aspect of) the other two. "Interinclusion" (התכללות) is fundamental to all truth, as expounded in Kabbalah and *Chassidut*. We have already seen several examples of the principle of interinclusion in relation to the three categories of Worlds, Souls, Divinity. We shall now discuss these most basic three categories in greater depth, and demonstrate how they interinclude and integrate with the concepts of form, name, and number.

WORLDS, SOULS, DIVINITY

The Ba'al Shem Tov, the founder of *Chassidut*, in his famous letter quoted above, initiates us into the awareness of the Hebrew letters (in each of their three representations of form, name, and number) at three general levels of consciousness: Worlds, Souls, and Divinity.

"Worlds" implies the range of all phenomena, whether physical or spiritual, as we perceive them. At the level of Worlds one sees himself as a physical (or spiritual) creature amongst creatures, no different, in essence, than an animal, vegetable, or stone. The positive element of Worlds-consciousness is to "put down" one's ego, in true submission to one's Creator, as will be explained below.

"Souls" implies the sense of creative consciousness (close to the sense that this or similar idioms are used by many of the most outstanding proponents of quantum physics). Here, one interacts with Creation—the reality of the world depends on me and I depend on the reality of the world.

"Divinity" implies the one, true Reality behind and, ultimately, the source of both yet unrectified created consciousness and the quasi-reality it appears to create. Ultimately, the Souls of Israel are one with G-d and "partners" with Him in the act of Creation. In regard to Bezalel, the "creation" of *tzadikim* is even more praiseworthy than that of heavens and earth, for in it the purpose of all Creation is realized—"a dwelling place for the Holy One Blessed be He below." Thus, the "clarified" Creation of Souls of Israel is, in truth, more real than real.

A further way to understand the meaning of Worlds, Souls, Divinity—all in the experience of man in relation to G-d:

At the level of Worlds, one searches for one's Creator, who "hides" within His Creation. The great disciple and successor of the Ba'al Shem Tov, the Maggid of Mezeritch, explains the secret of Creation as G-d playing "hide and seek" with Souls, whose initial consciousness is in a state of "exile," at the level of Worlds.

At the level of Souls, one serves G-d in a state of total commitment to walk in His ways as revealed (commanded) in the Torah. Here, one merits to become a "servant" of G-d, whereas at the previous level of Worlds, one had not yet found the Master nor His explicit directive for rectified behavior.

At the level of Divinity, one experiences "being" (an actual part of) G-d, in the sense of being a "son," whose very essence derives from that of his father, as taught in *Tanya*.

At the level of Worlds, one searches for G-d in each of the Hebrew letters. Each letter appears as a hint or "clue" where to find Him. At the level of Souls, each letter addresses the soul, telling one how to better serve G-d. At the level of Divinity, each letter reveals an essential link (the secret of the *brit*) between G-d's very Essence and the Souls of his children, Israel.

Level	Consciousness	Dynamic	Role of Letter
Divinity	G-d, clarified	being a part of G-d	link between G-d and the soul
Souls	creative	serving G-d	instruction in service
Worlds	creature	searching for G-d	hint or clue where to search

IDENTIFICATION OF SELF AT EACH LEVEL

Let us now attempt an analysis of the steps of meditation and service, centered on letter consciousness, as outlined in the letter of the Ba'al Shem Tov:

First, "include your soul" (identify yourself) at the level of Worlds, by considering yourself a part of created nature, no different, in essence, than an ant or a rock. When not performing G-d's Will, one is actually lower (last, in the six-day account of Creation) than all other creatures: "A gnat precedes you," for the gnat is never disloyal to its Divine intention in Creation.

Thereafter, the Jew appears as "first in Creation" and even "before" being "first": "The thought of Israel preceded everything [even the manifestation of the Divine Will to create]." The source of the souls of Israel is the Divine consciousness active in His decision to create, as it were: "In whom did He take counsel [whether or not to create the world], with the souls of the *tzadikim* [Israel]." After the initial contraction of Infinite Light to produce the "spatial" dimensions of reality to be, the root of the soul, Divine consciousness, descends as a "measuring rod" to determine and differentiate actuality from "chaotic" potential. The soul continues to descend, from world to world, until eventually it enters a physical body below. Here is the true epitome of its being. Here it manifests true "free will" (just as G-d possesses Absolute "free will") and is entrusted with the task of rectifying all reality.

The innate sense in the soul of the ultimate purpose inherent in and dependent upon the realization of its task, the "filling of the earth with the knowledge of G-d as waters cover the sea," is the soul's inclusion in (identification with) Divinity.

Level	Consciousness
Divinity	part of G-d
Souls	rectifier
Worlds	creature

PAST, PRESENT, FUTURE

The "including" of oneself at each of the three levels of Worlds, Souls, and Divinity can also be understood as the full experience of the secret of time at three levels:

"Worlds" is the "local" (as this term is used in modern physics) sense of causal relation apparent in nature. As the present and future are here defined by the past, it is, in general, the sense of the past. "Souls" is the "non-local" sense of the continual present, above the natural co-ordinates of time and space. "Divinity" is the absolute future hidden but "ready" (in Hebrew, "future" means "ready") in the soul's meta-present.

The absolute future is "conceivable" only in the simple faith of the soul. The super-temporal present of the soul is its innate sense of pleasure and serenity. The "run" of time and space, defined by the past, is reflected in the will of the soul ("will," רצון, is cognate to "run," רוץ). Faith (אמונה), pleasure (תענוג), and will (רצון) correspond to the three "heads" of *keter*, the superconscious, as taught in *Chassidut*. In the terminology of Kabbalah they are referred to as "the unknowable head" (רישא דלא אתידע), "the head of nothing" (רישא דאין), and "the head of Infinity" (רישא דאריך, literally, "the head of the long [face]"), respectively. Each "head" is the source of a particular level of consciousness in all of the revealed powers of the soul. Each "head" "lives" in a particular state of "time."

Level	Time	Level of the "Crown"	Name
Divinity	future; absolute	faith	The Unknowable Head
Souls	present; continuous being	serene pleasure	The Head of Nothing
Worlds	past; casual relation	will	The Head of Infinity

ASCEND, CONNECT, UNIFY

The Ba'al Shem Tov continues to teach that "in every letter there are Worlds and Souls and Divinity, and they ascend and connect and unify with each other." The three verbs: "ascend and connect and unify" correspond themselves to the three levels of Worlds, Souls, and Divinity. Worlds, when rectified, "ascend" (the word "ascend," עולים, is close to the word עולם, "world"); Souls "connect"; Divinity "unifies" all.

At the level of Worlds, one experiences himself as being "below" or "down." All of one's effort is set upon ascent from one's initial, relative state of physicality to that of spirituality. This consciousness characterizes all "spiritual searchers." At the level of Souls one senses the primary need for the connection of all souls of Israel as an organic one. Only when connected together do the Souls become the Throne of G-d on earth. "Connection" is a "horizontal" consciousness, for all souls are essentially equal. "Ascent" is a "vertical" consciousness, the will to climb and achieve ever higher states of awareness.

At the level of Divinity one experiences G-d's Absolute will to dwell below, to reveal Himself universally, through the means of the souls of His People Israel. The experience of Divinity and true unification is thus essentially a downward flow.

"Afterwards the letters connect and unify to become a word." Here, only two verbs are used: "connect and unify." In the following phrase, "and [then] unify in true unification in Divinity" only one verb, "unify," appears. From this we learn that, in particular, there are three stages of meditation: meditation of the secrets of individual letters; meditation on the dynamic process of letters combining to form meaningful words; and, in the terminology of *Tanya*, meditation on the "light above all" which spontaneously appears around the total structure of a finished word.

This three-stage process of meditation itself progresses, relatively, in the secret of the sequence of Worlds, Souls, and Divinity. The meditation upon individual letters incorporates all levels of Worlds, Souls, and Divinity, but, nonetheless, relative to the subsequent states of the three-part total meditation, it reaches awareness of Worlds-Souls-Divinity in Worlds. The second part of the total meditation, the meditation of letters combining to form meaningful words, relatively at the general level of Souls, is, in particular, connecting to Souls and Divinity (Worlds here disappear into Souls) in Souls. The meditation of the "light above all" is at the level of Divinity itself.

Level	Verb	Vector	Subject of Meditation	Sequence
Divinity	unify	downward	rhetoric, style	Divinity
Souls	connect	horizontal	letters forming words	Souls-Divinity in Souls
Worlds	ascend	upward	individual letters	Worlds-Souls-Divinity in Worlds

Subsequently, "you shall include your soul with them in each and every state" is the drawing down of all of the above levels, including Divinity itself, to fully integrate with the experience of Souls.

"And all the worlds unify as one and ascend..." draws down Divinity (unification), through the means of Souls, to effect the absolute refinement and ascent of Worlds, to experience, in themselves, the true Unity of G-d.

SUBMISSION, SEPARATION, SWEETENING

The consummate experience of unification is one of "infinitely great joy and pleasure," as that of "groom and bride." This is the ultimate experience of "sweetening" (המתקה), which follows the inclusion of one's own soul "in each and every state," the experience of "separation" (הבדלה, in the sense of the unique, "separate" power of the Jewish soul to "know" all), and the experience of submission (הכנעה) which characterizes the state of the soul during the devoted effort of the meditation process itself. These three— "submission, separation, sweetening"—the most fundamental sequence of experiential categories in Divine service (in the terminology of the Ba'al Shem Tov, as received by him from the prophet Achiah), themselves correspond ultimately to the three relatively "objective" categories of Worlds, Souls, and Divinity.

Level	Service
Divinity	sweetening
Souls	separation
Worlds	submission

POINT, LINE, AREA

"Give to the wise and he will become ever wiser." This verse, with which the Ba'al Shem Tov concludes the revelation of the way to *Mashiach* (the secret of the "three potent practices and three Holy Names," as "enclothed" in the service of ever-deepening awareness of Worlds, Souls, and Divinity) is the guideline of our present book. The information herein, structured in accord with this basic teaching of the Ba'al Shem Tov and as expanded by his successors to this present day, is meant to "open an opening" and inspire the reader to first make devoted effort to integrate its ideas and subsequently search for new insight into the letters, words, and verses of Torah. Insight inspires insight. The experience of true insight is one of total submission and commitment to live by the Will of the Master of Wisdom. Thus all genuine insight into Torah arouses one's will to commit itself, in love, to the Will of G-d, the Giver of Torah.

Our present work begins its exploration into the depths and intricacies of each letter by relating one kernel idea, a teaching of one phrase, to each letter, and thereafter proceeds to develop, from the central theme of each letter, in two stages, "from the general to the particular." The "general meditation" (התבוננות כללית) exposes the kernel idea, much as a line stretches a point. The "particular" meditation (התבוננות פרטית) relates, step-by-step, to each individual level of Worlds, Souls, and Divinity in each dimension of

form, name, and number, as area broadens the line. The structure of the
"particular" is itself a square (area) of three-by-three equalling nine. Interinclusion, in general, produces area; if the number of members in each of the
interincluded groups is equal, the result is a square. In Kabbalah and
Chassidut, point (נקודה), line (קו), area (שטח) are also referred to as point
(נקודה), *sefirah* (ספירה—as a linear "spectrum" of colors emerging from an
undifferentiated "point" of light), and *partzuf* (פרצוף—a fully developed,
human-like figure or constellation of attributes, interincluded in one
another). Each of the nine particular levels of each letter is an entire meditation in its own right.

Dimension	Development	Correspondence in this Book
point	point	kernel idea
line	*sefirah*	introduction to each letter, "general meditation"
area	*partzuf*	the nine categories "particular meditation"

It should be noted that, in accordance with the principle of interinclusion, each "particular" example at one of the levels of Worlds, Souls, or
Divinity may "convert" to each of the other two by means of either abstrac-
tion or concretization.

SILENCE, CIRCUMCISION, SPEECH

The initial "contact" of the soul with the kernel idea of each letter is the
secret of חש, "silence," as taught by the Ba'al Shem Tov. The integration of
the exposition of this kernel idea is the secret of מל, "circumcision," the intermediate stage between silence and speech. The detailed consciousness of
"particular interinclusion" gives birth to potent (in the sense of the power to
"sweeten" reality) speech, the second level of מל in the secret of חשמל,
chashmal, the "mystery" word of Ezekiel's vision of the Divine Chariot, in
the service of G-d.

Potent speech is one of the secrets of the *Mashiach*. The name *Mashiach*,
משיח, can be read משיח, "a speaker." Every Jew possesses an active "spark
of *Mashiach*," as described above. In order to bring the *Mashiach* into one's
full consciousness, each of us must strive to purify and make potent our
faculty of speech in Torah, prayer, and the communication of love between
us. Potent speech depends upon the integration of the secret of *chashmal*,

"to be quiet ['submission'] until one cuts off one's foreign 'shell' of foreskin ['separation,' the spiritual act of circumcision; the ability to 'know' all] and then to speak words with such great potency as to sweeten ['sweetening,' conversion of evil to good] external reality."

CONCLUSION

Before concluding our introduction let us review the terms of the thirteen major "triplets" of concepts exposed (some of them merely touched upon) above. We list the groups in order of their first appearance. The members of each group are listed in ascending order. Though some of the terms "overlap" from group to group, each assumes unique significance relative to the members of its particular group.

1. energy (כח), life (חיות), light (אור)
2. firmament (רקיע), water (מים), light (אור)
3. letters (אותיות), words (תבות), light above all (אור העולה על כולנה)
4. Worlds (עולמות), Souls (נשמות), Divinity (אלקות)
5. form (תמונה), name (שם), number (חשבון)
6. number (מספר), tale (ספור), brilliance (ספיר)
7. will (רצון), pleasure (תענוג), faith (אמונה)
8. searching (דרישה), serving (עבודה), being (הויה)
9. past (עבר), present (הוה), future (עתיד)
10. ascent (עולים), connection (מתקשרים), unification (מתיחדים)
11. submission (הכנעה), separation (הבדלה), sweetening (המתקה)
12. point (נקודה), line (קו), area (שטח)
13. silence (חש), circumcision (מל), speech (מל)

The thoughtful reader will identify many more such "triplets" hinted at above. One should try to integrate the meaning as well as the feeling of these basic concepts before proceeding along the path of meditation outlined in this book; all for the sake of truly "living" the Hebrew letters in thought, word, and deed.

"Open to Me as the opening of the eye of a needle and I will open to you as the great entrance to the Temple Hall." "Give to the wise and he will become ever wiser."

May this book help spread the wellsprings of Torah and *Chassidut*, deepen our sensitivity to the world and its need for elevation; to souls and their need for connection; to Divinity and His need, as it were, to express to us His Unity in all.

Alef

נוֹשֵׂא הֲפָכִים

Paradox: G-d and Man

Alef: The Paradox of G-d and Man

The *alef* is formed by two *yuds*, one to the upper right and the other to the lower left, joined by a diagonal *vav*. These represent the higher and lower waters and the firmament between them, as taught by the Arizal.

Water is first mentioned in the Torah in the account of the first day of Creation: "And the spirit of G-d hovered over the surface of the water." At this time the higher and the lower waters were indistinguishable; their state is referred to as "water in water." On the second day of Creation G-d separated the two waters by "stretching" the firmament between them.

In the service of the soul, as taught in *Chassidut*, the higher water is water of joy, the experience of being close to G-d, while the lower water is water of bitterness, the experience of being far from G-d.

In Jewish philosophy, the two intrinsic properties of water are "wet" and "cold." The higher water is "wet" with the feeling of oneness with the "exaltation of G-d," while the lower water is "cold" with the feeling of separation, the frustration of experiencing the inherent "lowliness of man." Divine service, as taught by *Chassidut*, emphasizes that in fact the primary consciousness of both waters is the sense of the Divine, each from its own perspective: from the perspective of the higher water, the greater the "exaltation of G-d," the greater the oneness of all in His Absolute Being; from the perspective of the lower water, the greater the "exaltation of G-d," the greater the existential gap between the reality of G-d and that of man, thus the inherent "lowliness of man."

The Talmud tells of four sages who entered the *Pardes*, the mystical orchard of spiritual elevation reached only through intense meditation and Kabbalistic contemplations. The greatest of the four, Rabbi Akiva, said to the others before entering, "When you come to the place of pure marble stone, do not say 'water-water,' for it is said, 'He who speaks lies shall not stand before my eyes.' " The Arizal explains that the place of "pure marble stone" is where the higher and the lower waters unite. Here one must not call out 'water-water,' as if to divide the higher and lower waters. "The place of pure marble stone" is the place of truth—the Divine power to bear two opposites simultaneously; in the words of Rabbi Shalom ben Adret: "the paradox of paradoxes." Here "the exaltation of G-d" and His "closeness" to man unite with the "lowliness of man" and his "distance" from G-d.

The Torah begins with the letter *beit*: בראשית ברא אלקים את השמים ואת הארץ, "In the beginning G-d created the heavens and the earth." The

Ten Commandments, the Divine revelation to the Jewish people at Sinai, begin with the letter *alef*: אנכי ה' אלקיך אשר הוצאתיך מארץ מצרים מבית עבדים, "I am *G-d* your G-d who has taken you out of the land of Egypt, out of the house of bondage." The Midrash states that "higher reality" (עליונים) had been set apart from "lower reality" (תחתונים), for G-d had decreed that neither higher reality descend nor lower reality ascend. In giving the Torah, G-d annulled His decree, He Himself being the first to descend, as it is written: "And G-d came down on Mount Sinai." Lower reality, in turn, ascended: "And Moses approached the cloud...." The union of "higher reality," the upper *yud*, with the "lower reality," the lower *yud*, by means of the connecting *vav* of Torah, is the ultimate secret of the letter *alef*.

ALEF

FORM: A *yud* above and a *yud* below with a *vav* separating and uniting them simultaneously.
The secret of the "image" in which man was created.

Worlds The upper and lower waters with the firmament between them.
In the world:
> The upper atmosphere, the lower atmosphere, the ocean & water table
> Energy waves, the atmosphere, the hydrological cycle

In the human body:
> The respiratory system, the diaphragm, the digestive system
> The skull-water, the membrane, the brain-moisture

Souls Feeling both close to G-d and distant from Him with commitment to Torah and *mitzvot* balancing these emotions.
"Crying is enwedged in my heart on one side, while joy is enwedged in my heart on the other side."

Divinity Transcendent and Immanent Light with the contraction (*tzimtzum*) and impression (*reshimu*) between them.
Man in perfect unity with the Infinite Will of G-d.

NAME: Oxen; thousand; teaching; master.

Worlds Oxen—gross physical reality, the lower animal soul.
Thousand—multiplicity in Creation, the "thousand mountains grazed by the ox."
The yoke of the ox yielding a thousandfold and returning to unity.

Souls "I will teach you wisdom"; the root of the soul is derived from the wisdom of G-d.
Direct insight of Divine truth; to be nothing.

Divinity "Master of the universe."
The Divine "One" revealing itself throughout the plurality of Creation.

NUMBER: One

Worlds First of all countable numbers.
The beginning of process in nature and sequence of worldly events.
One counts "something from something."

Souls "One nation in the land."
The organic unity of all Jewish souls.
One counts "something from nothing."

Divinity "G-d is One": the absolute unity of G-d.
"There is none other besides Him": "One, single, and unique."
One counts "nothing from something."

FORM

In the *Zohar*, the form of the *alef* is seen to represent the "image of G-d" in which man was created: נעשה אדם בצלמנו כדמותנו, "Let us make man in our image as our likeness." The name אדם, "man," is itself a compound of א, corresponding to "our image," and דם, the two-letter root of כדמותינו, "as our likeness." At the level of Worlds, the *alef* is the paradox of man, a created finite being, nonetheless "stamped" by the "image of G-d." At the level of Souls, the *alef* is the paradox of the Infinite Being of G-d contracted yet actively manifest in the soul of man (the Jew living a life of Torah and *mitzvot*). At the level of Divinity, the *alef* is the paradox implicit in the phrase used to describe Moses and other *tzadikim*: "the man of G-d"—man in perfect unity with the Infinite Will of G-d. G-d's Infinite Will is the "image" within Him, the ultimate source of His revealed Will as expressed in the finite-oriented *mitzvot* of Torah. The service of "the man of G-d" is his continual "run and return" between G-d's revealed Will in Torah and *mitzvot* and its source in His Essence in order to manifest more and more of the Source in the revelation. This is referred to by our Sages as "unifying Torah with G-d" and is the secret of the potential *beit*, the letter of Purpose—G-d's "dwelling place below"—residing potentially in the *alef*.

WORLDS

At the most basic, physical level, the firmament is the lower stratum of atmosphere enveloping the earth, the higher water is the vapor and impending rainwater condensed and carried by the clouds above the firmament, and the lower water is the sea and the subterranean water in the earth. At a deeper level the lower water can refer to the entire hydrological system, the firmament to the higher strata of the atmosphere and the higher water to the "waves" of the electromagnetic and other energy fields of outer space.

In the human body, the diaphragm is regarded as the symbol of the firmament, separating—but ultimately organically uniting—the respiratory system, the "higher water" above the diaphragm, and the digestive system, the "lower water" primarily below the diaphragm. In the process of digestion the "lower water" separates and clarifies viable sustenance from waste. The inherent "moisture" of the "higher water," of "the breath of life," serves to "lubricate" all of the limbs of the body.

At a higher level, the firmament refers to the membrane above the brain, which separates the innate "moisture" of the intellect, the "lower water," from the spiritual potential of the superconscious, the "higher water" in the skull.

SOULS

In the service of the soul, the higher water represents the state of joy one experiences when feeling close to one's Creator, ever guided by the goodly eyes of His Providence and embraced by the outstretched arms of His Graciousness. The lower water represents the state of bitterness experienced when feeling distant from one's Creator, a part of the suffering of a yet unrectified and unredeemed world.

"The lower waters cry out: 'We want to be close to G-d,' " just as the higher waters are close to Him. This will come to be only in the time of universal redemption, when "I shall make the impure spirit pass away from the earth."

The *vav* in the middle of the *alef* is that power which initially differentiates between, but ultimately connects, these two states. The letter *vav* represents the force of Torah and *mitzvot*. By commitment to serve G-d through Torah and *mitzvot*, one achieves emotional balance and ultimately becomes able to unite the seemingly antithetical states of feeling close to and simultaneously far from one's Creator. The inherent delight of learning the wisdom of G-d's Torah links one to the higher water of joy, while the sincere submission to accept the yoke of Heaven in the performance of G-d's *mitzvot* links him to the lower water of bitterness. The ideal balance and simultaneous experience of joy and bitterness is expressed in the *Zohar* as "crying is enwedged in my heart on one side, while joy is enwedged in my heart on the other side." The power to enwedge is the power of *da'at* ("knowledge"), the secret of the letter *vav* (between the two *yuds* of the *alef*), the power acquired through commitment to Torah and *mitzvot*.

DIVINITY

Chassidut teaches that G-d's light emanates in two different ways: as Transcendent Light (סובב כל עלמין, "surrounding all worlds") which encompasses all of reality, and as Immanent Light (ממלא כל עלמין, "filling all worlds"), which reveals itself to each individual (or vessel) according to his capability to comprehend. The upper *yud* represents the Transcendent Light whereas the lower *yud* represents the Immanent Light. The *vav* that initially differentiates between but ultimately connects these two Divine lights is the secret of the primordial contraction (*tzimtzum*) of G-d's Infinite Light (which originally contained the roots of both the Transcendent Light and the Immanent Light) together with the impression (*reshimu*) of that light which remains after the contraction. The impression serves to connect these two distinct forms of light, just as the commitment to Torah and *mitzvot* (whose power derives from the impression left on new-born consciousness of having been taught Torah in the womb) connects the two distinct (and apparently antithetical) experiences of joy and bitterness in the soul.

At this most subtle level of Divinity, in the experience of the Immanent Light alone (which, at the level of Souls, is the source of joy—feeling close to G-d), one senses distance from His Absolute Transcendence and thus a certain degree of (sublime) bitterness. One's true joy is only to be "drawn" entirely into the Essence of G-d (לאשתאבא בגופא דמלכא) by means of clinging to His Transcendent Light.

NAME

The word *alef* (אלף) can mean any of the following: "oxen," "thousand," "teaching," "master."

WORLDS

The ox, the most basic animal image, symbolizes worldly reality in general. In the human psyche, the "animal soul" is the level of consciousness that instinctively relates to physical creation: "The animal spirit descends to the earth" (unlike the "spirit of man" which "ascends above," relating, instinctively, to the spiritual).

The number thousand represents the complete manifestation of plurality as reflected in physical creation. A thousand is 10·10·10; each ten is a full spectrum of 10 *sefirot*, as manifest in every aspect of reality. This completeness of the number thousand is alluded to in the verse האלף לך שלמה, "A thousand to you, Solomon"—שלמה, "Solomon," being cognate to שלם, "completion."

The "completion" (i.e. rectification) of plurality (אלף) is its return to unity (אלף). The animal is described as ranging over הררי אלף, "a thousand mountains," devouring their grass daily. This symbolizes the initial rectification of reality by the archetypal pure-animal image via its lower *teshuvah*, i.e. initial arousal to return to G-d after having been totally immersed in the material, as taught in *Chassidut*.

In particular, the *alef* pictures the yoke of the ox. By accepting the yoke, "Many are the yields of the power of the ox." The ox, in plowing the earth, has the innate power to bear a thousand (אלף) yields (and thereafter "devour" them in *teshuvah*) from the one (אלף) potential energy source (as in the law of the conservation of energy) of nature.

SOULS

Wisdom relates to Souls, for it is the soul that is taught and, thereafter, conveys wisdom. The Jewish soul itself is drawn directly from the inner wisdom of G-d, just as the seed is drawn from the brain, the seat of wisdom. For this reason the Torah refers to the Jewish people as G-d's children. As was explained in the discussion of the form of the *alef*, the *vav*, representative of Torah and *mitzvot*, reveals the innate connection of the wisdom-point in our souls—whose innermost property is the sense of selflessness—to G-d's Infinite wisdom. Upon meriting such revelation one's soul itself becomes a source of influx of ever new insight, as expressed by the Ba'al Shem Tov: "The soul of man teaches him."

So did Elihu, one of the major images of the soul of the *Mashiach* in the Bible (his full name, אליהוא בן ברכאל, equals 358=משיח, *Mashiach*) open his address to Job and his three companions: "I am young of days and you are the elders, therefore I feared to express my mind to you. I said, days shall speak and many years shall inform wisdom. Yet verily, spirit is within man and the soul of the Almighty bestows upon him understanding...." The "accumulated knowledge" of "days shall speak and many years shall inform wisdom" is, in general, the secret of the sequence of the letters from *beit* to *tav*. For this reason the time process of Creation begins with the *beit* of בראשית, "In the beginning." In contrast, the direct insight of the spirit within man into the Divine Truth concealed within all of reality, above and unchanged by the process of time, is the secret of the letter *alef*. Elihu concludes his first address with the phrase: החרש ואאלפך חכמה, "Be still and I will teach you wisdom"—"And I will teach you" (ואאלפך) is from the root אלף, *alef*. The verse begins: אם אין אתה שמע לי, literally, "If not [i.e., if you have no answer], you listen to me," but, by a slight change of vocalization: "If you are nothing, listen to me." To be "nothing" is the innermost sense of the wisdom of the Jewish soul, the vessel able to listen and be taught true wisdom, the secret of the letter *alef*.

DIVINITY

Our Sages refer to G-d as אלופו של עולם, "Master of the Universe." The word אחד, "One" (In the verse "Hear O Israel...G-d is One") is interpreted as "א (=1), the Master of the Universe, is one in ח (=8), the seven firmaments and the earth, and in ד (=4), the four directions of the world." In contrast to the plurality which the letter *alef* represents at the level of Worlds, here the *alef* represents the Unity of G-d.

"Not like the ways of men are the ways of G-d. A man shoots an arrow and is not able to retrieve it [in mid-air] but G-d shoots His arrows and has the ability to retrieve them as if they had not left His hand." The image of G-d as archer refers to the inherent ability in His Absolute Unity to create ("shoot" into reality) worlds possessing apparent plurality. The word "arrow" in Hebrew, חץ, means "half," indicating the power to split, as it were, the primordial oneness. The source of unity nonetheless "retrieves" plurality by revealing its inner Divine Unity. איכה ירדף אחד אלף, "How does *one* pursue a *thousand*," is interpreted in Kabbalah as referring to the ultimate power of the letter *alef*: one (unity) pursues (in order to "retrieve") a thousand (plurality)—the secret of the Divine paradox. In the phrase איכה ירדף אחד אלף, the initial letters of the four words (איאא) add up to 13, the value of the word אחד, "one." The final letters (הפדף) total 169=13². 169 also equals the sum of אדם אלף אחד, the three *words* for the form, name and number of the *alef*: "man" (the "image of G-d," in which man was created), "*alef*" and "one," all of which begin with the letter *alef*.

NUMBER

The letter *alef* equals one.

WORLDS

The number one is the beginning of all countable numbers (1, 2, 3,...). This level of one is called "the countable one" (אחד המנוי), the starting point or original cause of all natural process or sequence of worldly events. "Causation" and "evolution" are apparent natural phenomena which derive from the "countable one." The "countable one" is in fact the origin of all laws of nature, as revealed to the mind through its rational process of induction. The silent *alef* within the first word of Torah, בראשית ("In the beginning"), as understood at the level of Worlds, is the "countable one." It is the silence (חש) included within the first audible (מל) letter of Creation, the *beit* of בראשית, the two (ב=2) which begins the process of rational deduction.

The word אמונה, "faith," the *first* power of the soul, can be read א מונה, "*alef* counts": the *alef* (whose numerical value is one) "counts" all reality from one. At the level of Worlds, "counting" reality from one is counting "something from something," as in the phenomena of causation and evolution.

The phenomena of free choice and Divine Providence, which change the meaning as well as the reality of the apparent phenomena of "causation" and "evolution," become fully manifest only from the perspective of the higher levels of "one."

SOULS

The one of Souls is the organic unity of the Jewish people, the fusion of all Jewish souls. This inherent unity first became manifest when the people approached Mt. Sinai. In the phrase ויחן שם, "and they camped there," the word ויחן (lit., "and *he* camped") is written in the singular. Rashi comments: כאיש אחד בלב אחד, "as one man with one heart." This oneness and love was the prerequisite for receiving the Torah. At the time of the giving of the Torah our oneness below served as the vessel to receive G-d's Absolute Oneness, as enclothed in the Divine Will and Wisdom of Torah, making "place" for Him to "descend" into our hearts.

The Torah's command to enter into the Land of Israel is so that we may achieve the continual manifestation of this revelation. Infused with G-d's Oneness through Torah, our purpose is to implant this consciousness in the land. We are referred to as גוי אחד בארץ, "one nation in the land."

גוי אחד, "one nation," equals לב, "heart," as in "one man with one *heart*." The entire phrase גוי אחד בארץ, "one nation in the land," equals $325 = 13 \cdot 25$, the sum of all numbers from 1 to 25, whose "middle point" or "heart" is $13 =$ אחד, "one." Unity at the level of Souls takes place in the heart. (At the level of Worlds, unity is reflected in the function of the liver, while at the level of Divinity, Unity is experienced in the inner eye of the mind.) The "land of Israel" (ארץ ישראל$=832$) itself equals "heart" (לב$=32$) times the value of the Name *Havayah* (26, which in turn equals $2 \cdot 13$).

Here, אמונה, taken in the sense of א' מונה, is the secret of one "counting" all "something from nothing" (not as in relation to the "countable one," at the level of Worlds, which counts "something from something"). The "counter" is himself "uncountable," for he is nothing relative to the "counted" reality. Here the "counter" is the organic one of all the souls of Israel, for "nothing [אין] is the *mazal* of Israel," as taught by the Ba'al Shem Tov. This is the "creative art"—אמנות, from the word אמונה, "faith"—of the soul, the "partner" of G-d in the act of Creation.

Just as the Torah teaches that Divine Providence over the whole world begins from His Contemplation of the Land of Israel, so do the fruits of our consciousness of the Divine One sprout from our unity with the Holy Land. These fruits suffice to provide spiritual sustenance for all the nations of the earth.

DIVINITY

שמע ישראל ה' אלקינו ה' אחד, "Hear O Israel, *G-d* is our G-d, *G-d* is One." G-d's Absolute Oneness is completely unique. It is in no way related either to the countable one, at the level of Worlds, or to organic unity, at the level of Souls. Possessing no rational definition and encompassing all of reality, it can only be expressed as in the verse describing the revelation of Sinai: "You have been shown to know that *G-d* is G-d, there is none other besides Him." The Midrash interprets "one" in the verse "Hear O Israel, *G-d* is our G-d, *G-d* is one" with the phrase: אין כיוצא בו, "there is none other like unto Him." In *Chassidut*, we are taught that this interpretation of "one" refers to the very deepest level of G-d's Essence, the level where He is uniquely differ-ent from all rationally definable "others," and thus can only be conceived of as being "the paradox of paradoxes."

"Hear, O Israel...*G-d* is One" is the all inclusive instruction of Moses to the generation about to enter and settle the land of Israel. It follows the phrase: "a land flowing with milk and honey." The verse שמע ישראל ה' אלקינו ה' אחד possesses 25 letters; its middle (13th) letter is the א of אלקינו, "our G-d," which equals אמונה, "faith" (102). אמונה is the secret of א' מונה "*alef*, one, counts," as explained above. At the level of Divinity, counting all from one, the Absolute One of "*G-d* is One," is counting "nothing from something," for all of reality, including its inherent creative power, is in truth "nothing" in relation to His Absolute Something. This is the secret of "the perspective from Above" (דעת עליון), whereas creation "something from nothing" is the consciousness of "the perspective from below" (דעת תחתון), as taught in *Chassidut*. Here all of "counted reality" is no more than the "nothing" of abstract numbers, while the "counter" is absolutely "uncountable," for his Reality and Oneness is not that of number, inconceivable to the number-oriented consciousness of all Creation.

Beit

נִתְאַוָּה הקב״ה לִהְיוֹת לוֹ דִירָה בַּתַּחְתּוֹנִים

Purpose: G-d's Dwelling Place Below

Beit: Purpose—G-d's Dwelling Place Below

The letter *beit*, from the word בית, "house," refers to G-d's house: "My house will be called a House of Prayer for all peoples." The Midrash states that the Divine motivation for creation was that the Holy One, Blessed Be He, desired a dwelling place in lower reality. The fulfillment of this desire begins with the creation of man, a Divine soul enclothed in a physical body, and proceeds with the multiplication of man, to "conquer" the whole world and make it the kingdom of G-d.

The Torah precedes the detailed description of the Tabernacle and its vessels with the statement of its ultimate purpose: "They shall build me a Temple [מקדש] and I will dwell in them." Not "in *it*," the Sages explain, but "in *them*"—in each and every Jew. "Dwelling in them" is, in essence, the revelation of Divinity in the people of Israel, ever present but often "shadowed," as in the time of exile and destruction of the Temple. The innate sanctity of the people of Israel, the "sanctuary of G-d," when revealed and linked to that of the land of Israel, causes the Holy Land to expand and eventually encompass all the earth (lower reality): "the land of Israel will in the future spread out to all of the lands of the earth."

Beit is numerically equal to the word *ta'avah*, "desire" or "passion" (בית=412=תאוה). In general, *ta'avah* connotes a negative human property. However, in several places *ta'avah* denotes the positive passion of the *tzadik*, the righteous man. One passage in Proverbs states: "He will fulfill the passion of the *tzadik*," and a second says: "the passions of *tzadikim* are only good." The *ta'avah* of G-d, the "*Tzadik* of the world," is altogether above reason and logic. At this level one cannot ask "why." As expressed by the Alter Rebbe: "About passion, there is no question." As G-d is the Essence of good so His passion is "only good."

"With whom did the Holy One, Blessed Be He, take counsel whether or not to create the world? With the souls of the *tzadikim*." The "souls of the *tzadikim*" refers to all Jewish souls, as is said: "All of your people are *tzadikim*." G-d's connotation as "the *Tzadik* of the world" refers to the absolute origin and unity of the Jewish soul in His very Essence. When the soul descends to be enclothed in the finite consciousness and experience of a seemingly mundane body, its task is to become the *tzadik* below in true emulation of its Source, the *Tzadik* Above. This is accomplished through the refinement and purification of passion, *ta'avah*, to become "only good."

The *Tzadik* above dwells in the House built for Him by the *tzadik* below.

Here, the deepest passion of the Creator reaches fulfillment. The large *beit*, the first letter of the Torah and the beginning of Creation, expresses this ultimate purpose, as is said: "The final deed arose first in thought." In the first word of the Torah, בראשית, the three "servant" letters—the prefix *beit* and the two suffix letters, *yud* and *tav*—spell בית, "house" (equivalent to the full spelling of the letter *beit*). The root of בראשית, ראש, means "head." Thus the most "natural" permutation of בראשית thus reads: ראש בית, "the head of the house." One permutation of the letters ראש is אשר, "happiness." When the *tzadik* draws G-d, the "Head," into His House, it becomes a house of true and eternal happiness.

The drawing down of the "Head" to dwell in His "House" below, in true happiness, is the secret of "blessing" (ברכה) which begins with the letter *beit*. Our Sages teach that the big *beit* of בראשית begins Creation, and the Torah as a whole, with the power of blessing. G-d blesses His creation, which He creates with the attribute of lovingkindness, the attribute of Abraham, as will be explained in the letter *hei*. Abraham, the first Jewish soul, is subsequently entrusted with the Divine power of blessing, the big *beit* of Creation, as is said: והיה ברכה, "And you shall be [the bestower of] blessing." Afterwards, at the time of his circumcision, he was given the small *hei* of Creation, the power to draw down and manifest the Divine blessing of happiness in the smallest detail of reality.

The Priestly Blessing is composed of three verses. The number of words progress in the order 3, 5, 7, with equal differences of two, *beit*. The number of letters progress in the order: 15, 20, 25, with equal differences of five, *hei*. Words represent full, or large consciousness, whereas letters represent particular, or small consciousness. The power to bless "fullness" is the power of the *beit*, as is said: "And full with the blessing of G-d." The power to draw down the blessing to the smallest detail of reality is that of *hei*.

This service of Abraham, and all Jews after him, leads to the fulfillment of the ultimate intention of Creation, the realization of Israel's power of blessing, that the domain of the King (the "Head of the House") extend to encompass all of reality and, thereby, bestow true happiness to all.

BEIT

FORM: Three connected *vavs* with an opening on the left, the "northern side."

Worlds "Evil begins from the north."
Man's ability to choose between good and evil.
The animal soul's three positive character traits and the evil inclination.
The open north side symbolizes the attribute of courage and might.

Souls The open north side symbolizes the "fear of heaven."
"All is in the hands of heaven except for the fear of heaven."
The *Mashiach* will close the open side—The integration of free will and Omniscience.
Speaking Torah—revealing the innate spark of *Mashiach*.

Divinity Closed Sides—Divine revelation—"You"—in mind, heart, and action.
Open Side—Divine concealment—"He"—in the hidden heart—the darkness above the light.

NAME: House

Worlds A physical house.
One's metaphysical "house"—his relationship to reality.
The whole of Creation is a "house" in relationship to G-d.
Superconscious pleasure—"A man without a house is not a man."

Souls The feminine aspect of the soul represented by the house.
"A man's house is his wife."
The soul as a house for G-d—the daughter of the priest.
The power of pregnancy.

Divinity G-d's desire to make for Himself a dwelling place in lower reality.
The House of Immanence and the House of Transcendence.

NUMBER: Two

Worlds The beginning of manifest plurality.
The dualistic nature of Creation.
Hierarchic complexity.

Souls The soul is described as "the second to the King."
Joseph: the Prism effect—the revelation of mind.
Mordechai: the Time effect—the revelation of heart.

Divinity Divine power of Self to contain two opposites.
Concealment of Divine essence and revelation of His light.
Concealment and revelation of light to lower and higher states of consciousness.
The Torah begins with a large *beit*.
The Name *Havayah* and the Name *Elokim*.
"The two companions that never separate."

FORM

The *beit* is composed of three connected *vavs* resembling a square, yet open on the left side. From the perspective of Torah, the top line of the square faces east, the right side faces south and the bottom side faces west. The open side faces north.

WORLDS

At this level the shape of the letter *beit* represents man's struggle with evil. The natural, animal soul of the Jew is itself a mixture of good and evil. Its three innate positive characteristics—"modesty, mercy, and kindness"— can be seen to correspond to the three *vavs* of the letter *beit*. The evil inclination, the soul's negative character, corresponds to the open north side. From this side G-d allows, as it were, evil temptation to enter the world. So it is said: מצפון תפתח הרעה, "evil begins from the north," meaning that Israel's enemies will attack from the north. In Kabbalah, the north corresponds to the property of *gevurah*, "might." The spiritual source of the north is itself the power to overcome and conquer its lower manifestation, the "open north" of this world. G-d gives the soul the power to conquer its evil inclination, as our Sages teach, "Who is courageous [גבור, from גבורה, "might," the north]? He who conquers his evil inclination." The power to be "courageous" is given to the soul at birth, the moment it enters this world and first confronts the "open north." This power is conveyed by means of an oath: "Be a *tzadik* and don't be a *rasha* [wicked man], and even if the whole world says to you, 'you are a *tzadik*,' consider yourself a *rasha*." "Consider yourself a *rasha*" means to always face the reality of the "open north" with the courage and conviction to conquer it, with the help of G-d. Each year on one's Hebrew birthday this power "shines" most strongly, and so this is the day most potent to arouse consciousness to one's latent "powerhouse."

So, too, the Jewish people as a whole is given the power from Above to conquer its enemies. The birthday of the Jewish people is the day of its exodus from Egypt, the release from servitude to the conventions and restrictions of society by the powerful Hand of G-d. This is commemorated annually at the Seder, bringing us into full consciousness of G-d's power, both from without and from within, to redeem us.

SOULS

"All is in the hands of heaven except the fear of heaven." The open side of the *beit*, the north, represents the power of fear in the soul, as well as that of might. Fear is understood in *Chassidut* to be the ultimate motivation of acts of might. The open side of the *beit*, the battleground of free will, at the deeper level of consciousness and emotion of the Divine soul, corresponds to the service of the soul to achieve the fear of heaven. To achieve fear is the essential "act" of the soul, the manifestation of its inherent power of free will. From the open side of the *beit* is born the following letter, the *gimel*, whose "run" symbolizes free will, as will be explained.

Our Sages teach that the *Mashiach*, who will consummate the work of Creation, will be the one to close the fourth side of the letter *beit*. The *beit* will thus be transformed into a final closed *mem*, as will be more fully explained in the discussion of the form of the letter *mem*. The *Mashiach* will reveal that though free will is true from the perspective of the soul (the secret of the open side of the *beit*), G-d's omniscience permeates all of reality (the secret of the closed *mem*), and thus, paradoxically, free will and omniscience exist simultaneously. The truth of free will is one and the same as the truth of the Divine soul of Israel, an actual part of G-d. The truth of omniscience is the truth of the Infinite Essence of Divinity. The ultimate secret of this integrated consciousness is that the free will of the soul is itself the free will of G-d, for in the time of the *Mashiach* the consciousness of Souls and that of Divinity will merge. The *Mashiach* will reveal the inner dimension of the Torah, which will act as a catalyst uniting, in consciousness, Souls and Divinity.

The written Torah begins with the *beit* of בראשית, "In the beginning," and the oral Torah ends with the closed *mem* of בשלום, "in peace." The juxtaposition of the two letters spell the word בם in the command to continually be occupied in learning and speaking the words of Torah, ודברת בם, "and you shall speak *in them*." By speaking "in them," from the written beginning to the oral end, one reveals his innate "spark of the *Mashiach*," the power to connect the consciousness of free will, ('ראשית יראת ה) בראשית, "the beginning of wisdom is the fear of G-d"), and that of total Omniscience, בשלום (למרבה המשרה ולשלום אין קץ), "to increase reign and peace without end," the all-encompassing Kingdom of G-d revealed on earth).

DIVINITY

There are times when G-d reveals His Presence to us, and there are times of concealment. In times of revelation we are aroused to address G-d directly as "You." In times of concealment we refer to Him as "He." The two words, אתה, "you" and הוא, "He," are composed of four distinct letters, תאוה, "passion," numerically equivalent to בית, the letter *beit*, as explained above. Written in full, אתה הוא equals 418, equivalent to חית, the letter *chet*, this being the secret of the life-dynamic of running upward towards the unknown "He" and returning downwards with impregnant conscious-ness of "You."

The visible lines of the *beit* symbolize levels of Divine revelation, while the missing north implies concealment of Divine Presence. In a deeper sense, every conscious revelation itself possesses a hidden, superconscious level of concealment. The three visible lines of the *beit* correspond to the three general levels of revealed consciousness: mind, heart, and action. The horizontal lines of mind and action, "heaven" and "earth," are connected by the vertical line of the heart, emotion (the "motion" of the soul between heaven and earth), to the right. The invisible left, the concealed "left heart," hints at the service of the Levi (the secret of the left, in Kabbalah) to reach the superconscious concealment above all revelation, as is said: "the Levi serves [the level of] He."

Just as darkness exists below light, in the sense of concealment of light from consciousness, so darkness exists above light, in the sense of the abso-lute consciousness above all possible revelation of light. In this world our relation to this higher darkness is only through simple faith. In the future we shall come to know this darkness just as we know light. Then the dark-ness itself will "shine" with brilliance incomparable to that of any known light. This is an even deeper understanding of the open side of the *beit*: in the future, it will be simultaneously open (unknown and dark) and closed (known and light) as the final *mem*—both aspects at the level of Divinity.

NAME

The word *beit* (בית) means "house."

WORLDS

As an extended image, the house represents man's general frame of reference in his relation to the world. The word בית, "house," is derived either from the root בנה, "to build," or בוא, "to come." Through education and life experience man builds his house and enters into it in order to attain a balanced and stable relationship to reality. On a deeper level, all of reality is a house in relation to G-d, i.e. G-d's Divine frame of reference in relation to His own manifestation of Self. The first word of the Torah, בראשית, spells ראש בית, "the Head of the house." The intention of Creation, the Divine act of building, is that the head, the secret of the letter *alef*—the revelation of G-d's Absolute Unity—comes into His house, the letter *beit*.

Through permuting the letters ראש to spell אשר, the word בראשית becomes בית אשר, "the house of happiness." Man's happiness and satisfaction in life greatly depends upon possession of and dwelling in a house: "A man without a house is not a man." Just as certain conscious and subconscious character traits "fit" one's clothing and thereby become manifest, even deeper properties of soul—especially superconscious pleasure (אשר)—"fit" one's house and thereby become manifest as happiness.

SOULS

Each soul possesses both a masculine and a feminine aspect. The feminine aspect of the soul and, in general, the woman in Judaism, is symbolized by the house. The *beit* stands for blessing: "Whoever is without a wife is without blessing." On the holiest day of the year, *Yom Kippur*, the High Priest, in his Temple service, first atones "for himself and for his house." The Sages teach: ביתו זו אשתו, " 'his house' is his wife." An unmarried High Priest is not qualified to perform the service of *Yom Kippur*. Atonement, the complete rectification of the soul and the ultimate blessing from Above (the power of the priest, in general, is that of blessing the people "in love") depends upon the union of man and wife, the two parts of the same soul.

In relation to G-d all souls are feminine, as the bride of the Song of Songs. In particular, the Jewish soul is referred to as בת כהן, "the daughter of the priest." Here the priest symbolizes G-d. The word בת, "daughter," is closely related to בית, "house." In בת, the נ of בן, "son," falls from the root, just as בית relates to בנה, "to build," as noted above. The power "to build" inherent in woman is the power of pregnancy. In the consciousness of the soul this is the property of *binah* (בינה "understanding"), which represents the mother in Kabbalah. Thus, the daughter, בת, is in fact the potential mother, this being the source of her endearment in the eyes of her husband. בתי, "my daughter," connotes the endearment of husband to wife in the Song of Songs. When the Jewish soul below manifests itself as "the daughter of the priest" in relation to G-d, the Divine Presence, symbolized by the letter *yud* (י) descends to dwell within the soul (בת), thus forming the word בית, "house."

DIVINITY

At the level of Divinity, the house symbolizes the ultimate purpose of all reality: to become a dwelling place below for the manifestation of G-d's presence. "Not as Abraham who called it [the Temple site] 'a mountain,' nor as Isaac who called it 'a field,' but as Jacob who called it 'a house.'" Upon awakening from his Divinely inspired dream, Jacob said, "How awesome is this place; this is none other than the House of G-d, and this is the gateway to Heaven." "Awesome" is the Divine attribute corresponding to Jacob in the beginning of the *Shemoneh Esrei* prayer: "the G-d of Abraham, the G-d of Isaac, and the G-d of Jacob, the Great, Mighty and *Awesome* G-d...." "Awesome" indicates the revelation of Divine Essence as manifest by the power of the Infinite to enter the finite. He of whom is said, "verily the heavens and the heavens of the heavens cannot contain Me, nor can this House," nonetheless enters into His finite house.

The name of G-d in Jacob's phrase "the House of G-d," is *Elokim* (אלקים, numerically equivalent to הטבע, "nature"), that level of Divinity which permeates and reveals itself in nature. In other verses, the Temple is referred to as בית ה', "the House of *Havayah*." In Rabbinic usage, the *House* (the Temple) is referred to as either בית הבחירה, "the Chosen House" (literally, "the House of Choice," from the verse, "and it shall be the place that G-d shall choose to make His Name dwell there") or בית המקדש, "the House of Sanctity" (from the verse, "And they shall make for Me a sanctuary and I will dwell in their midst"). "The House of *Elokim*" refers, in particular, to the secret of "The Chosen House," the place of the manifestation of the union between the choice, free will, of G-d and that of man, as discussed above. This is the revelation of G-d's ultimate Immanence. "The House of *Havayah*" refers, in particular, to the secret of "The House of Sanctity," for sanctity and holiness imply separation and transcendence, as taught in *Chassidut*. The two names "House of *Elokim*" and "House of *Havayah*" (בית אלקים ⊥ בית ה') together equal 36 times 26 (26 being the value of *Havayah*), indicating that ultimately the experience of all souls (as contained within the 36 archetypal souls, the 36 *tzadikim* of every generation) in the Holy Temple, House of G-d, will become that of *Havayah*—"*Havayah* is our G-d, *Havayah* is One."

NUMBER

The letter *beit* equals two.

WORLDS

Plurality begins with two. This is reflected in the Rabbinic principle of Torah exegisis: מעוט רבים שנים, "the minimal level of plurality is two," i.e., since the Torah text always intends to be explicit, an unqualified plural term is understood to mean two.

In particular, two represents the dualistic nature of physical reality: energy and mass, day and night, sun and moon, male and female, etc. At the higher levels of Souls and Divinity the phenomenon of dualism is manifest in the Torah-defined categories of good and evil, pure and impure, holy and profane, and the like. In general, all created reality possesses two interdependent dimensions, form and matter. The inherent dualism in Creation is indicated by the opening letter of the Torah, *beit*.

On the second day of Creation, the waters, initially one on the first day of Creation, were separated by the firmament into two—the higher waters and the lower waters, as explained above. From this we understand that division into two is primarily a consciousness of two categories, one "higher" and the other "lower." The (unconscious) "nature" of the "higher" is to descend to the "lower" (as in physics, for example, higher "energy levels" descend to lower "energy levels"), while the aspiration and conscious desire of the "lower" (as the crying of the lower waters), is to ascend or "return" to the "higher." Until the time of the giving of the Torah, G-d decreed that the "higher" shall not descend to the "lower" nor shall the "lower" ascend to the "higher." With the giving of the Torah, however, this decree was nullified, and the *beit* of Creation (the ב of בראשית, the first word of the account of Creation) became the *alef* of Torah (the א of אנכי, "I," the first word of the giving of the Torah).

Thus, plurality is essentially a state of hierarchy (beginning with the consciousness of "higher" versus "lower") with its intrinsic complexity, whereas unity is essentially a state of equality (*"one* day") with its intrinsic simplicity.

SOULS

In the phrase משנה למלך, "the second to the King," the word "second," משנה, is a permutation of the word נשמה, "soul." The King is G-d, the secret of the letter *alef*, as explained above. The soul is G-d's "second in command." The King takes counsel with his "second," as taught by our Sages: "In whom did G-d take counsel [whether or not to create the world]? With the souls of the *tzadikim*"—i.e., the souls of all Israel, for "Your people are all *tzadikim*." Subsequently, the King appoints His "second" to assume active control over His domain.

Two souls served as "second to the king" in the Bible. Joseph was second to Pharoah, the king of Egypt, and Mordechai was second to Ahasuerus, the king of Persia. In Kabbalah and *Chassidut* we are taught that even a non-Jewish king is (unconsciously) connected Above to the Kingdom of Heaven (the *sefirah* of *malchut* in the world of *Atzilut*, Divine emanation) which reflects itself in the workings of his own kingdom, as is said: "The kingdom of earth is like the kingdom of Heaven." Each king and kingdom below relates to its unique source in the kingdom Above. In the *Zohar* we find that the source of Pharoah is "in him all of the higher lights become revealed [אתפריעו 'become revealed,' from פרעה, 'Pharoah']." The Arizal, in the name of the Sages, interprets אחשורוש, Ahasuerus, as אחרית וראשית שלו, "the end and the beginning are His." *Malchut* is often symbolized as a "prism" through which the lights of the higher *sefirot* are concentrated and shine into the lower worlds. This is the source of Pharoah, and Joseph is his "second" to reveal this property. *Malchut* is also the origin of time, as we say: "G-d is King, G-d was King, G-d will be King for ever and ever." This is the source of Ahasuerus, and Mordechai is his "second" to reveal this property. The "prism" effect of *Malchut* is basically a revelation to the mind (whose essential quality is the perception of light), while the "time" effect of *malchut* ("the commemoration of Purim will never cease from the Jewish people") is primarily a consciousness of heart (in command of the circulatory system, comparable to the flow and cycle of time, whose "heartbeat" defines the basic unit of time). Thus, relatively, Joseph and Mordechai correspond to "higher" and "lower" categories in the function of "second to the king," the fundamental secret of two.

DIVINITY

Within Himself, G-d contains two antithetical states, as it were. In general, these two states are the simultaneous concealment of G-d's Essence and revelation of His light, or—at a lower level—the revelation of light to higher states of consciousness and the concealment of light to lower states of consciousness.

The opening *beit* of the Torah is large, hinting at the paradox of two at the level of Divinity. These two are the secret of the two Divine Names *Havayah* and *Elokim*, the two Names used together in the phrase "the House (בית) of G-d," as explained above. From a higher perspective, *Havayah* is the Name referring to G-d's Transcendent, concealed Essence, whereas *Elokim* is the Name which refers to His Immanent, revealed light. From a lower perspective, *Havayah* is the Name of Divine revelation to higher states of consciousness, whereas *Elokim* is the Name which denotes the Divine power to conceal the revelation of G-d's ever present light from lower levels of consciousness.

In the first account of Creation only G-d's Name *Elokim* appears, whereas in the *second* account—the detailed account of the creation of Adam and Eve (the essential two at the level of souls)—the two names *Havayah* and *Elokim* appear together. The Name *Elokim* is in the plural, and—in accordance with the Rabbinic principle mentioned above, מעוט רבים שנים, "the minimal level of plurality is two"—itself hints at the interinclusion of two levels in Self. *Elokim* (אלקים) equals כלי הו״י, "the vessel of *Havayah*" (60⊥26=86), thus containing within itself the property of "vessel" together with the included light of *Havayah*. The two letters י־ה in אלהי־ם are actually the first two letters of *Havayah* inverted in order. They are referred to as "the *two companions* that never separate," the secret of the continual union of "father" (wisdom) and "mother" (understanding). In *Havayah*, father precedes "mother," whereas in *Elokim* "mother" precedes "father," in the secret of "All that Sarah says to you, listen to her voice." Thus, *Havayah* is primarily the power innate in Abraham, whereas *Elokim* is primarily the power of Sarah, whose inherent plurality is the power to bear many children, the rectification of the original *two*, Adam and Eve, by total devotion to the Divine, as taught in Kabbalah and *Chassidut*.

Gimel

שָׂכָר וָעֹנֶשׁ

Reward and Punishment

Gimel: **Reward and Punishment**

Our Sages teach that the *gimel* symbolizes a rich man running after a poor man, the *dalet*, to give him charity. The word *gimel* is derived from the word גמול, "giving." גמול in Hebrew means both the giving of reward as well as the giving of punishment. In Torah, both reward and punishment have the same ultimate aim—the rectification of the soul to merit to receive G-d's light to the fullest extent.

Reward and punishment imply that man is free to choose between good and evil. (The teaching of the *gimel* thus refers back to that of the open left side of the *beit*, from which it is born, as explained above.) The Rambam (Maimonides), in particular, places great stress upon free choice as being fundamental to Jewish faith. According to the Rambam, the World to Come, the time of reward, is a completely spiritual world, one of souls without bodies. On this point the Ramban (Nachmanides) disagrees and argues that since complete freedom of choice exists only in our physical world, the ultimate rectification of reality—the reward of the World to Come—will also be on the physical plane. Kabbalah and *Chassidut* support the opinion of the Ramban.

This is alluded to by the leg of the letter *gimel*, which expresses the running of the rich man to bestow good upon the poor man. Running, more than any other physical act, expresses the power of will (רץ, "running," from רצון, "will") and freedom of choice. In running, the leg is firmly in contact with the earth; through an act of will, the soul directly affects physical reality. The final reward, the ultimate revelation of G-d's Essential light, will thus justly be bestowed upon the soul in the very same context as its life's endeavor, the physical world.

The Torah says: "today [in this world] to do them," from which the Sages infer: "tomorrow [in the World to Come] to receive their reward." Only "today" do we possess the opportunity to choose between good and evil. And so in accordance with our choice do we, ourselves, define the reward and punishment of "tomorrow." Just as evil is a finite phenomenon, so is punishment. Not so good and reward, which are truly infinite. The *gimel* of "today" is the secret of "better one hour of *teshuvah* and good deeds in this world than all the life of the world to come." The *gimel* of "tomorrow" is the secret of "better one hour of serenity in the world to come than all of the life of this world."

GIMEL

FORM: A *vav* with a *yud* as a "foot."
A person in motion.

Worlds The running of the rich to the poor, the full to the empty, inherent in nature.

Souls The run and return of the soul between its Divine source and physical abode.
The hand of Jacob grabbing the heel of Esau.
The constant progression of the Jew.

Divinity The expansion and contraction of the Infinite Light in the process of Creation.

NAME: Camel; bridge; weaning; benevolence.

Worlds The camel's journey through the desert of this world.
The camel symbolizes the angel of death.
A bridge; the connecting force inherent in nature.
Primordial matter and Divine wisdom.

Souls The soul nursing from its Source.
The process of weaning through which a person learns to be independent.

Divinity G-d's continual bestowal of lovingkindness and the weaning of the *tzimtzum*.
The obligation to emulate G-d by giving to others.

NUMBER: Three

Worlds Numerical symbol of stability and balance.
Equilibrium between the three primary elements of Creation: air (אויר),
water (מים), and fire (אש).

Souls Three Fathers: Abraham, Isaac, and Jacob.
Three divisions of Jewish souls: *kohanim* (priests), *leviim* (levites), and Israelites.
The *segol* and the *segolta*.

Divinity Three parts of the Torah: The Five Books of Moses, the Prophets, and the Writings.
"Three bonds are bounded together: Israel, Torah, and G-d."

FORM

The *gimel* is composed of a *vav*, representing an erect man, with a lower *yud*, a foot in motion.

WORLDS

The foot of the *gimel*, symbolized by the *yud*, is the ability to give a part of oneself to another. The letter *yud*, the smallest yet most compact and concentrated of the letters, represents a point of essential self, a seed of reproduction. Its lower position, as the foot of the *gimel*, is the secret of actual giving to another. In Kabbalah, we are taught that the head symbolizes receiving; the body, integrating with oneself; the feet (including the *brit*), giving to another. When the *yud* of the *gimel*, the rich man or male, is given to the *dalet*, the poor man or female, the *dalet* becomes an impregnated *hei*. This explains the sequence of these three letters: the *gimel*, the rich man, *running* after the "static" *dalet* (as a door, merely able to turn on its hinges, to open or close), the poor man, in order to fill his needs, the *hei*.

At the level of Worlds, the run of the rich to the poor, the full to the empty, is engraved in the laws of nature. Water (the masculine power of *chesed* [lovingkindness and charity]) runs down to fill the lowest, empty basin. Higher energy states run to lower energy states. In living creatures, parents bear and thereafter care for and feed offspring. The *gimel* gives life, the pulse of "run and return," fully to become manifest in the letter *chet*, the letter of life, as will be explained.

SOULS

As explained above, the *gimel* is in a state of motion, primarily downward, to infuse the previously lifeless body with life: "And He blew into his nostrils the breath of life, and man became a living creature." The bestowing of life is the secret of reward and punishment, the inherent pleasure and pain of life itself. The inward life-pulse is the experience of good and pleasure descending from one's benevolent source. The outward pulse is the experience of the pain of confinement within the lower physical domain and the passion to become freed from its imprisonment and return to one's source. Here, the *yud*, the foot of the *gimel* running towards the lifeless *dalet* to enliven it, is the secret of the "heel" of the soul's root which descends from its source Above to take hold of and breathe life into the body, the physical "heel." This is the secret of Jacob (יעקב, *yud*-"heel"), whose hand (יד, from ייד, *yud*), at birth, took hold of Esau's heel, as taught in Kabbalah and *Chassidut*.

The dynamic motion of life, the secret of the *chet* born from the *hei* impregnated by the *gimel* (in the secret of the relation: 3 [*gimel*] ⊥ 5 [*hei*] = 8 [*chet*]), alternates in direction. First it runs upward to its spiritual source and then it returns downward to enliven its physical abode, the body. Every living creature possesses the dynamic motion of "run and return." The vital force of the Jewish soul is unique in that its "run and return" transcends the limitations of nature. Whereas the "run" of all other creatures is each to its particular source in the scaled revelation of G-d's Immanent Light in nature, the "run" of the soul of Israel is to its truly Divine Source, G-d's Transcendent Light, infinitely above the lifeforce manifest in nature. Even angels are referred to as "standing"—static—in contrast to the ever "walking" of the Divine soul: "And I shall make you 'walkers' amongst those 'standers.' " The ever-progressing ("walking") "run and return" of the Jewish soul is the secret of the ongoing "travelling" of the first Jew, our father Abraham: "And Abraham travelled [continually], walking and travelling to the south." "The south" symbolizes G-d's Infinite Transcendent Light, the goal of Abraham's upward run, as well as the attributes of *chochmah* (wisdom) and *chesed* (lovingkindness), the specific attributes of soul whose light he brought down in the return from his Source.

The downward run of the *gimel*, first bestowing life and sparking the dynamic of "run and return" (the *chet*), reflects its power and source in the service of the soul to return and descend from the peak of its upward run, in order to fulfill G-d's Will below. The effect of this service, the impact of the soul's "return" on this world, though in direct proportion to the aspiration of the "run," is nonetheless greater than all expectation, for in its return the soul is infused with additional power from the Inner Essence of its Source, unobtainable in virtue of its upward run alone. Thus, the external reality of the *gimel* sparks life while its inner reality fulfills life.

DIVINITY

The directions of the "run and return" of the Divine light and lifeforce itself are opposite to those of the soul. The "run" is downward toward Creation, the primary direction of the *gimel*, while the subsequent "return" is upward into Self. The downward run is the secret of the foot of the *gimel*, as explained above. The upward return is the secret of the elevation and inclusion of the extension of the *gimel* with its lower foot into its "head," the *yud* at its top. The downward run is the secret of the *gimel* of גדולה, "greatness" (the attribute of Abraham), the ultimate motivation of all true acts of kindness, as explained in *Chassidut* (itself synonymous with the *sefirah* of *chesed*, "lovingkindness"). The upward return is the secret of the *gimel* of גבורה, "might" (the attribute of Isaac), the power to return to one's source. The balance of these two complimentary motions of the Divine light insures stability throughout Creation. The "run" of the Divine light brings Creation into existence. The "return" allows for Creation to experience self-consciousness, the prerequisite for free choice.

The most fundamental concept of Torah directly related to the meaning of the letter *gimel* (גימל) is "acts of kindness," (גמילות חסדים, whose initial letters, *gimel* and *chet*, manifest the relation between *gimel* and *chet* discussed above). In the phrase גמילות חסדים, חסד implies bestowing kindness, whereas גמילות implies the removing of such bestowal (as in the meaning of "weaning" of the *gimel*, as will be explained in the following section). This seeming paradox of the phrase גמילות חסדים, at the level of Divinity, refers to G-d's bringing all of reality into Creation ("run") and simultaneously removing Himself, as it were, from Creation ("return"), just as a parent stands by his child in support, yet simultaneously removes himself from him in order to teach him to walk.

NAME

The word *gimel* (גימל) means "camel," "bridge" (in Aramaic), "weaning," and "benevolence."

WORLDS

The English word "camel" derives from the name of the Hebrew letter *gimel*. The camel symbolizes the motion of travelling through the desert, the journey of life on earth. Carrying the burdens of life as well as its rewards, the camel stores within itself the waters of kindness necessary to exist in the dry desert. The camel brings life into the lifeless desert but, on the "other side," symbolizes in Kabbalah the angel of death, who emerges from the desert. For the *tzadik*, mundane existence alone is death. This is symbolized by the camel. Rebecca fell off the camel when she first saw Isaac, her destined soul mate and personification of Divine purpose in life.

In Aramaic, the word *gamla* (גמלא) means "a bridge," which symbolizes the connecting forces inherent in nature, such as electricity, magnetism, and gravity. A bridge resembles the "hunchback" of a camel, a link between the *gimel* and the (form of the) *chet*, the sole letter which possesses a "hunchback" (חטוטרת)—a bridge between its two components, the two previous letters, *vav* and *zayin*. As explained above, the lifeforce emanating from the *gimel* becomes manifest in the *chet* as "run and return." The bridge connects the two alternating motions. In nature, certain forces appear to be two but are in fact two manifestations of a single force, as electricity and magnetism. Other forces, such as gravity, appear to be unique. These phenomena would be symbolized by a double hunchback or a single hunchback camel.

Through interchanging the letters of the root גמל one derives the word גלם, "primordial, formless matter," whose numerical value, 73, equals that of חכמה, *chochmah* ("wisdom")—the basic power of Creation: "You have made all of them with wisdom." In the *Zohar*, the word *chochmah* is read as כח מה, "the power of 'what,'" i.e., of formless matter (of which one asks the question, "what?"). *Chochmah* corresponds to the *yud* (י) of G-d's Name *Havayah*, which together with גלם spells גימל, *gimel*.

SOULS

The word *gamul* (גמול) means "a nursing infant," alluding to the soul
receiving nourishment from its Source. Paradoxically, it also means "to
wean." These seemingly opposite concepts of nursing and weaning, giving
of oneself to another and subsequently removing oneself and one's gift, are
a reflection of reward and (constructive) "punishment," at the level of
Souls. In fact, this apparent duality is manifest in all productive relationships, where giving is for the sake of establishing independence in the receiver. The comparison of the soul to a nursing infant is found in Psalm 131:
נפשי כגמל עלי אמו, "my soul [is like] a child nursing on his mother." Some
commentaries interpret the word גמל in this verse to mean "a weaned
child." According to both interpretations the metaphor expresses the total
trust of the soul in G-d. The nursing and weaning process from Above, as in
the consciousness of the mother, reflects itself in the child as the trust in his
mother and, thereafter, his own sense of independence. As explained above,
the "reward and punishment" of the *gimel* becomes the "run and return" of
the *chet*. Here, the "reward" of nursing and the "punishment" of weaning
become the "run" of trust and the "return" of mature independence.

The relation of the *gimel* to the *chet*, at the level of Souls, is most
beautifully and succinctly expressed by King David in Psalm 119: גמל על
עבדך אחיה, "Bestow kindness on your servant, I shall live"—"bestow kindness" (גמל) being cognate to *gimel*, and "I shall live" (אחיה) deriving from
the root of *chet*.

DIVINITY

The Torah commands us to walk in the ways of G-d, to emulate His Divine attributes and, in particular, His acts of lovingkindness, as is said: והלכת בדרכיו, "And you shall walk in His ways." "Walking," as well as giving of oneself, is the teaching of the letter *gimel*, as explained above. We further find in the Talmud:

> " 'After G-d your G-d you shall walk': Is it possible for man to walk after the Divine Presence, of which it is said, 'G-d your G-d is a consuming fire'? But [it means, rather,] to walk after the attributes of the Holy One, Blessed be He: just as He clothes the naked, as it is said, 'And G-d made for Adam and his wife garments of skin and clothed them,' so you clothe the naked; the Holy One, Blessed be He, visited the sick, as is said, 'And G-d appeared to him [Abraham, who was ill after his circumcision] in the plane of Mamre,' so you visit the sick; the Holy One, Blessed be He, consoled mourners, as is said, 'And it was after the death of Abraham and G-d blessed [i.e., comforted] his son Isaac,' so you console mourners; the Holy One Blessed be He buried the dead, as is said, 'And He buried him [Moses] in the valley,' so you bury the dead."

G-d continuously performs the greatest act of lovingkindness by recreating, from nothing, all of reality, and sustaining each and every one of His creatures. Since in ultimate truth He is all, His very creating us—and thereafter providing us with all of our needs—is actually giving us a part of Himself. To give of oneself is the ultimate act of lovingkindness, as symbolized by the form of the letter *gimel*. The secret of the *tzimtzum*, His contraction and concealment of His own infinite light, corresponds to the element of "punishment" in the secret of the *gimel*, here for the sake of establishing the sense of independent existence in all created beings. The more continuously we merit to perform sincere acts of lovingkindness, emulating G-d and walking in His ways, so do we become "partners" with Him in the process of continual re-creation.

NUMBER

The letter *gimel* equals three.

WORLDS

In general, the number three represents stability and equilibrium: "The world [i.e., the level of Worlds] stands on [i.e., is supported and sustained by the merit of] three things [i.e., three realities at the level of Souls]: on [the study of] Torah, on service [i.e., the Temple service, and, in general, the service of prayer] and on acts of lovingkindness." Just as the House of Israel stands on the merit of the three Patriarchs, as will be explained at the level of Souls, so do these prototype souls permeate nature itself, in order to sustain it. In nature, souls appear as אור חוזר, "returning light," and so we find that the three pillars of Torah, service, and acts of lovingkindness in the above *mishnah* correspond to the three Patriarchs in reverse order: Jacob, Isaac, Abraham. In nature, equilibrium exists between the three primary elements of Creation: air, water, and fire. Air derives from the root of "Torah," the middle line; fire derives from "service," as the Temple sacrifices which are called "fires," the left line; water derives from acts of lovingkindness, which, like water, descends and gives of itself to those below it, the right line. These elements correspond to the three Hebrew letters א (אויר, "air"), מ (מים, "water"), and ש (אש, "fire"), the three principle letters of Creation, as explained in *Sefer Yetzirah*.

The fourth element, earth, is not included in the analysis *Sefer Yetzirah*, for in relation to the three active, "rich" elements, earth is "poor" and passive, thus corresponding to the following letter, *dalet*.

SOULS

The three divisions of the Jewish people—*kohanim* (Priests), *leviim* (Levites), and Israelites—derive from the three primal soul roots of our people, the three patriarchs, Abraham, Isaac, and Jacob, respectively.

The state of equilibrium and harmony created by the unified effort of these three divisions of souls is primarily manifest in the Temple, where, simultaneously, the *kohanim* perform the rites of sacrifice, the *leviim* sing, and the Israelites observe the sacrifice while reading verses from the Torah. Here is revealed the spiritual harmony of the whole universe in microcosm. G-d calls us His עם סגלה, "chosen people." The term סגלה, "chosen," comes from the word סגול, *segol*, the name of the Hebrew vowel composed of three dots in the form of a triangle: ֶ The dot to the upper right corresponds to the property of kindness, that to the upper left to the property of might, and that between them below to the property of mercy. These three attributes are identical with those represented by the prototype souls of the Patriarchs, and thereafter manifest in the three divisions of the Jewish people.

In the cantillation notes of the Torah, the סגולתא, *segolta*, also from סגלה, is likewise composed of three dots, only here the middle dot appears above those to the right and the left: ֒. These three dots correspond to the roots of kindness, might, and mercy as they appear in the mind and the supermind. The root of Jacob, mercy, is the middle point of the crown of the superconscious (which reveals itself as knowledge). The right point is that of wisdom, the root of Abraham, and the left point is that of understanding, the root of Isaac.

DIVINITY

At the level of Divinity, the number three represents the three divisions of the written Torah—אורייין תליתאי, "the triple Torah": the Five Books of Moses, the eight books of the Prophets, and the eleven books of the Writings. (The "base" of the arithmetic progression of 5, 8, 11 is 3. Extrapolating, the progression begins from 2, corresponding to the two Tablets of the Covenant, received by Moses at Sinai, the origin of the Written Torah.)

This is alluded to in the verse in Proverbs: הלא כתבתי לך שלישים במעצות ודעת, "Have I not written to you *excellent things* in counsels and knowledge." The word שלישים, "excellent things," comes from the word שלש, "three." The triple nature of the Torah reflects its eternal strength, as is said: והחוט המשולש לא במהרה ינתק, "a string braided from three strands will not easily be severed." The inherent structure of Torah is a property of Divinity, for ultimately "Torah and G-d are one."

Another triplet at the level of Divinity is the bond that exists between Israel, the Torah, and G-d. This is expressed in the *Zohar* by the well-known dictum: תלת קשרין מתקשרין דא בדא, ישראל באורייתא, ואורייתא בקב"ה, "three bonds are bonded together: Israel to Torah and Torah to G-d." Before Creation, these three were one. After Creation the soul of Israel must re-establish its essential bond to G-d through its connection to Torah.

In fact, there are three independent bonds, as taught by the Lubavitcher Rebbe *shlita*: the bond of Israel to Torah, the bond of Torah to G-d, and the direct bond of the Divine Essence of the souls of Israel to G-d (as manifest in moments of true self-sacrifice for G-d, above our "consciousness" of Torah).

Dalet

דְּלֵית לָהּ מִגַּרְמָהּ כְּלוּם

Selflessness

Dalet: **Selflessness**

The *dalet*, the poor man, receives charity from the rich man, the *gimel*. The word *dalet* means "door." The door stands in the opening of the house, the *beit*.

In the *Zohar*, *dalet* is read as דלית לה מגרמה כלום, "that has nothing of her own." This expresses the property of the lowest of the Divine Emanations, the *sefirah* of *malchut*, "kingdom," which has no light other than that which it receives from the higher *sefirot*. In man's service of G-d, the *dalet* characterizes *shiflut*, "lowliness," the consciousness of possessing nothing of one's own. Together with the awareness of one's own power of free choice, one must be aware that "He gives you the power to achieve success," and not to think, G-d forbid, that one's accomplishments are "My power and the strength of my hand." Any achievement in this world, particularly the performance of a *mitzvah*, the fulfillment of G-d's will, depends upon Divine aid. This is especially true in one's struggle with his evil inclination, whether it be manifest as external passion, stubborn resistance to accepting the yoke of Heaven, or laziness, apathy, and the like. As our Sages teach: "If not for G-d's help he [man] would not have been able to overcome it [the evil inclination]."

The Talmud describes a situation where one man is carrying a heavy object and another man appears to be helping him by placing his hands under the object, when in truth the first man is carrying all the weight. The second man is referred to as "a merely apparent helper." So are we, explains the Ba'al Shem Tov, in relation to G-d. Ultimately, all of one's strength comes from Above. Free choice is no more than the expression of one's will to participate, as it were, in the Divine act. One merely places one's hands under the weight carried exclusively by G-d.

"For to You, G-d, is kindness, for You pay man in accordance with his deed." The Ba'al Shem Tov observes: Just payment in accordance with one's deed is not an act of kindness (חסד), but rather one of judgement (דין)! He answers: כמעשהו, "in accordance with one's deed", can be read "as though the deed is his." Thus G-d's ultimate kindness is His enclothing the "undeserved" reward in the guise of deservedness, so as not to shame the receiver. The Name of G-d in this verse is אדנ-י, the letters of which also spell דינא, "judgement," implying the Divine guise of judgement, through which G-d's kindness (חסד) is most fully expressed. The *Zohar* reads *chesed* (חסד) as חס ד', "having compassion [on] the *dalet*," i.e. he who possesses nothing of his own.

In regard to an arrogant person G-d says: "I and he cannot dwell together." The door to G-d's house allows for the humble of spirit to enter. The door itself, the *dalet*, is the property of humility and lowliness, as explained above. The *dalet* is also the initial letter of the word דירה, dwelling place, as in the phrase דירה בתחתונים, "[G-d's] dwelling place below." Thus the full meaning of the *dalet* is the door through which the humble enter into the realization of G-d's dwelling place below.

DALET

FORM: Two lines forming a right angle, with a corner point.
A man bent over.
Three levels of *bitul*.

Worlds   The corner point: Consciousness of the ego.
Bitul HaYeish.
Every creature's unconscious awareness of its continual re-creation by G-d.

Souls   The vertical line: selflessness.
Bitul Bimtziut; "Standing crowded."
Collective consciousness; willingness to sacrifice one's life for one's people.

Divinity   The horizontal line: submergence of the soul in its Divine Source.
Bitul Bimtziut Mamash; "Prostrating wide."
Letters being surrounded by white parchment.
Willingness to sacrifice one's life for G-d.

NAME: door; poor man; lifting up—elevation.

Worlds   Door—*bitul*, the entrance way to truth.
The servant who refuses to go through the door of freedom.

Souls   True lowliness of the soul.
The moon as a symbol of the soul.

Divinity   The elevation of the soul by G-d into Himself.
"I will exalt you G-d for you have lifted me up."
Not belonging.

NUMBER: Four

Worlds   Four elements of the physical world: fire, air, water, and earth.
Solid, liquid, gas, combustion.
Hydrogen, carbon, nitrogen, oxygen.
The four physical forces: gravity, electromagnetic, strong, weak.
Man, animal, vegetable, and inanimate objects.
Four seasons of the year; Four directions.
The four worlds: *Atzilut, Beriah, Yetzirah*, and *Asiyah*.

Souls   Four matriarchs: Sarah, Rebecca, Rachel, and Leah.
Jacob's four wives: Rachel, Leah, Bilhah, and Zilpah.
The four sons and the four cups of wine of the Seder.
The four expressions (levels) of redemption.
Four feet of the Divine Throne: Abraham, Isaac, Jacob, and David.
Father, mother, son, daughter: the first commandment of the Torah: "be
fruitful and multiply."

Divinity   Four letters of G-d's Name.
Four components of the Torah text.
Four basic levels of Torah interpretation.

FORM

The form of the *dalet*, a man bent over, symbolizes the state of *bitul* (בטול), "self-nullification." The three components of the letter *dalet*, two lines and a corner point, represent three different levels of *bitul*.

WORLDS

At the level of Worlds, *bitul* manifests itself as the conscious effort to nullify one's ego. Nullification of ego depends upon one's feeling of indebtedness to G-d for each and every breath of life and bodily movement. One must continually say to oneself, "I deserve nothing," for, in truth, all is a gift from Above. "Give Him that which is His, for you and yours are His. And so does David say, 'for all is from You, and from Your hand we have given to You.' " (From a deeper perspective David's statement reflects his state of *bitul* at the levels of Souls, as will be explained below, in the discussion of the name of the *dalet*).

This level of *bitul* is called *bitul hayeish* (בטול היש), "nullification of one's 'somethingness.' " "Somethingness" refers to the experience of existing independently of one's Creator. This level of *bitul* is represented by the corner point of the *dalet*. At the level of the "universal unconscious," every aspect of Creation possesses, in truth, a "spark" of *bitul hayeish*, as taught in *Chassidut*, for otherwise it would cease to exist. Its "spark" can only become conscious through the service of Jewish souls, who in igniting their own spark of Divinity in love and fear of G-d, ignite simultaneously the spark of consciousness of continual recreation—"something" from "nothing"—as well as the ultimate dependency of the created on the Creator, in the many objects around them.

SOULS

The second level of *bitul*, *bitul bimtziut* (בטיל במציאות), is a state of true selflessness, or total absence of self-consciousness. This is represented by the vertical line in the letter *dalet*. *Bitul bimtziut* exists potentially in the soul of every Jew, in contrast to *bitul hayeish* which exists potentially in every created being, as explained above.

One of the ten miracles witnessed in the Temple was that even though the congregants stood crowded together, each one found, at the time of prostration, four empty cubits of space around him. In *Chassidut* we are taught that the two states of "standing crowded" and "prostrating wide" correspond to the two states of *bitul* at the levels of Souls and Divinity, respectively. The *bitul* of the souls crowded together (the "crowd" representing the inherent unity of the souls) is *vertical* in nature. Therefore it corresponds to the vertical line of the *dalet*, as stated above.

"Standing crowded" is "returning" from one's normal state of individual consciousness to the true "collective consciousness" of the People of Israel. This inner act of return—to be embraced by one's people—purifies otherwise impure souls. For this reason we find that all Jews are considered by *halachah* (Jewish Law) to be pure when coming to Jerusalem and the Temple to celebrate together the three annual festivals of the Torah.

Conscious willingness to sacrifice one's life for one's people derives from this level of *bitul*.

DIVINITY

The miracle itself of "prostrating wide," the revelation of Divinity, is in a horizontal position. It is thus represented by the higher, horizontal line of the *dalet*. In prostration one totally merges with G-d. This is referred to as *bitul bimtziut mamash*, "*absolute* selflessness," the soul merging completely with its Divine Source. From the "collective consciousness" of the Jewish People one enters into the even higher state of Divine consciousness, "audible" only to the united soul of Israel: "Hear O *Israel, G-d* is our G-d, *G-d* is One."

In the Torah text, the "erect" letters themselves correspond to the level of "standing crowded." Each letter corresponds to a Jewish soul. As the Torah, in general, relates to the level of Divinity, the *halachah* requires that each letter be surrounded by pure white parchment. Thus in truth, the Souls, in their Divine Source, the Torah, are in a state of "prostrating wide," each soul merging with the "white" Transcendent Light that encompasses it.

Conscious willingness to sacrifice one's life for G-d derives from this level of *bitul*.

NAME

The word *dalet* (דלת) means "door"; "a poor man"; "lifting up"—"elevation."

WORLDS

In discovering a truth about the physical world, a scientist must experience some level of *bitul hayeish*, for *bitul* alone is the "doorway" to truth. *Bitul* produces a "cavity" in the self, an opening and "vessel" for truth to enter.

In Torah, a Hebrew servant goes free after six years of servitude. If, however, he desires to remain in servitude, he must have his ear pierced with an awl against a door. Instead of walking through the door to freedom and reliance on G-d, he chooses to rely on the sustenance of his mortal master.

For any aspect of Creation other than the Jewish soul, this servitude may be the maximal level of conscious *bitul* attainable. Of the Jewish People, however, G-d says: "They are my servants"—"and not servants to servants." Thus, for a Jew this level of *bitul* alone is not only inadequate but reprehensible. The piercing of the ear against the door symbolizes the Jew's lack of comprehension (the inner hearing of the ear) of what the door is meant to mean to him.

His decision made, the Hebrew servant serves his mortal master until the Jubilee year, the year which corresponds in Kabbalah to the *sefirah* of *binah*, "understanding," the inner rectification of the hearing of the ear. For it is in the Jubilee year that all ears hear the great *shofar*-blast of freedom from all forms of foreign servitude and return to their true Source.

SOULS

"The poor man possesses nothing of his own" (דלית ליה מגרמיה כלום).

The experience of poverty, compared with one's initial physical orientation of consciousness, is *bitul hayeish*, the *dalet* at the level of Worlds. When the experience of poverty extends to encompass one's entire consciousness, it becomes *bitul bimtziut*, the *dalet* at the level of Souls. The first state ("poverty" in the sense of of *bitul hayeish*) is similar to the experience of a physically poor person "overcome" by the reality of his poverty, his lack of physical possessions. The second state ("poverty" in the sense of *bitul bimtziut*) can be compared to a rich man, whose wealth includes both physical as well as spiritual possessions (such as wisdom and rectified character traits), yet who nonetheless experiences the existential "poverty" of possessing *nothing*, and even more so, *being* nothing, without G-d. Not only does G-d continually recreate and sustain him (the sense of *bitul hayeish*) but he is truly nothing apart from G-d (the sense of *bitul bimtziut*). This is the state of existential poverty personified in the Torah by King David, who though blessed with all the riches of kingdom, nonetheless continuously felt himself as a "miscarriage," the essence of whose very life is not his.

King David is symbolized by the moon, which possesses no light of its own, only that which it receives from the sun. This consciousness of the moon, as it were, in *receiving* light from the sun is still in the state of *bitul hayeish*, at the level of Worlds. The level of the moon in *shining* light to the earth is a reflection of *bitul bimtziut*, and is therefore a symbol of the Jewish soul. Of the new "birth" of the moon each month, it is said: "David, the King of Israel, is alive forever."

DIVINITY

Included in the name *dalet* is the meaning "to lift up," as expressed in the verse: **ארוממך ה' כי דליתני**, "I will exalt you G-d for you have lifted me up." This meaning corresponds to the third and highest level of *bitul*: *bitul bimtziut mamash*, the epitome of all spiritual ascent, the actual merging of the soul with G-d.

By lifting us up into Himself, G-d gives us the power to "raise" Him, as it were. This is the ultimate secret of the above quoted verse: "I will *exalt* [i.e., raise] You G-d—for you have lifted me up." This act of "raising" G-d means our ability to ever increase the revelation of G-d's Infinite Transcendence within the confinement of finite Creation. *Chassidut* explains that wherever transcendent light is revealed (paradoxically) within the confines of Creation, it appears, as it were, to be in a state of ascent, ever rising "above and away." This is so for it does not "belong" to the consciousness of Creation, but it is truly "out" of the grips of all such consciousness. "Not belonging" is, in general, the secret of the letter *dalet*, here corresponding to G-d's Transcendent Light, which can only be revealed to us in a state of "not belonging"—"I will exalt You G-d."

NUMBER

The letter *dalet* equals four.

WORLDS

There are many ways to translate the traditional understanding of the physical world as being composed of four elements—fire, air, water, earth—into the language of modern science. One interpretation is that the matter of our physical world assumes one of four states: solid (earth), liquid (water), gas (air), active combustion (fire). Another understands the "four elements" to correspond to the four basic chemical elements of hydrogen ("water" in its purest abstract sense), carbon (the combustive element in coal and the "fire" of life—organic matter), nitrogen (crucial to the power of growth inherent in the earth), and oxygen (air's "viable" substance, its "breath" of life; while four-fifths of its mass is actually "earth"—nitrogen). The atomic numbers of these four elements are 1, 6, 7, and 8, which total 22, corresponding to the 22 letters of the Hebrew alphabet. Yet other interpretations relate the "four elements" to subatomic phenomena, or to the four forces known to modern physics (gravity, electromagnetic, strong, weak).

Many more fours are reflected in nature: man, animal, vegetable, inanimate, the four seasons of the year, and the four directions of the compass (Modern physics has discovered that "right" and "left," "south" and "north," are physically definable concepts, and not arbitrary, as previously believed by scientists.).

In Kabbalah we are taught that the totality of reality can be divided into four worlds: the world of *Atzilut* (אצילות, "Emanation"), the world of *Beriah* (בריאה, "Creation"), the world of *Yetzirah* (יצירה, "Formation"), and the world of *Asiyah* (עשיה, "Action"). Each of these four worlds possesses the entire spectrum of ten *sefirot* which develop into five (sometimes six) complete (i.e., mature) *partzufim* (פרצופים, "figures"), each of which in turn possesses the entire spectrum of ten *sefirot* (the "triangle" of four [1⊥2⊥3⊥4] equals 10).

SOULS

The Jewish people was born of four matriarchs: Sarah, Rebecca, Rachel, and Leah. Jacob was married to four wives—Rachel and Leah and their two maidservants, Bilhah and Zilpah—who gave birth to his twelve sons. The Torah speaks of four types of sons: the wise son, the wicked son, the simple son, and the son who does not know how to ask, as told in the Haggadah of Pesach. Each son must be educated in accordance with "his way," as is said: "Educate the youth in accordance with his way, even when he grows old he will not stray from it." Education is initially entrusted to the mother, though later becoming the *mitzvah* of the father. Furthermore, at the Seder we drink four cups of wine in commemoration of the four expressions of redemption from Egypt (and all subsequent states of exile).

The three patriarchs, Abraham, Isaac and Jacob, together with the fourth prototype-soul of the Jewish people, David, constitute the four feet of the Divine Throne. They are the prototypes of lovingkindness, might, beauty (mercy), and kingdom, respectively. The fourth level, kingdom (מלכות), the basic secret of the *dalet*, completes the Divine Throne, which, in general, is the symbol of the Kingdom of G-d on earth.

The first (and thereby foremost) *mitzvah* of the Torah is "be fruitful and multiply." To fulfill this *mitzvah* one must give birth to at least two children, a son and a daughter. This quartet—father, mother, son, and daughter—is the primary manifestation of four at the level of Souls. They themselves correspond to the four letters of the Name *Havayah*, which, in turn, correspond to the four worlds, etc.

DIVINITY

The Name *Havayah* is composed of four letters. Our Sages refer to it as "the Name of four letters." "Before the creation of the world He and His Name were alone." Subsequently, as it were, in the process of emanation and creation of all reality, each letter of the four-letter Name is seen to correspond to an individual stage. The *yud* represents the initial contraction of G-d's infinite light, resulting in the "appearance" of one origin-point of Creation. The first *hei* represents the expanse of this point at the level of Divine "thought." The *vav* represents the downward force connecting the expanse of "thought," the concealed worlds, to that of "speech," the revealed worlds, which is represented by the final *hei* of G-d's Name.

The Torah text possesses four components (in descending order): cantillations (טעמים), vowels (נקודות), crowns (תגין), and letters (אותיות). The two lower levels are revealed in the Torah script, the two higher levels are concealed, as it were, in the white of the Torah parchment. All four components are alluded to in the verse: "The concealed things [the first two letters of the Name *Havayah*, corresponding to the cantillations and vowels] are for G-d our G-d, while the revealed things [the two final letters of the Name *Havayah*, corresponding to the crowns and letters] are for us and our children," as taught in the *Zohar*.

There are four basic levels of Torah interpretation (in ascending order): the literal (פשט), allusion (רמז), allegory (דרוש), and secret (סוד).

These phenomena of four in Torah directly correspond to the four letters of G-d's Name. Indirectly, each of the above sets of four, both at the level of Worlds and the level of Souls, ultimately derive from the Divine Name.

Hei

מַחֲשָׁבָה, דִּבּוּר, מַעֲשֶׂה

Expression: Thought, Speech, Action

Hei: Expression—Thought, Speech, Action

The name of the letter *hei* appears in the verse הא לכם זרע, "*Take* for yourselves seed." "Take" (הא) expresses revelation of self in the act of giving of oneself to another. Giving to others in the form of self-expression is the ultimate gift of self. In the secret of the letter *gimel*, the rich man gives of himself to the poor man in the form of charity. The highest form of charity is when the giver is completely concealed from the receiver, in order not to embarrass him, as is said, "the concealed gift subdues anger." Here, in the secret of the letter *hei*, the gift itself is the relation and expression of self, drawing the receiver into the essence of the giver.

Joseph, the speaker of the verse "take for yourselves seed," corresponds to the *sefirah* of *yesod*, whose function is to express self in the form of giving seed, as explained in Kabbalah. When Joseph first gave grain to his brothers, they were unable to recognize him, similar to the *dalet* in relation to the *gimel*. Upon his revelation to his brothers (and thereby to all of Egypt), his giving became that of the *hei*. Instead of grain (בר) he now gave seed (זרע).

The soul possesses three means of expression—"garments," in the terminology of the Kabbalah and *Chassidut*: thought, speech, and action. The higher garment, thought, is the expression of one's inner intellect and emotions to oneself. The process of the intellect and emotions becoming conscious through thought is similar to giving oneself (the essentially unconscious domains of the soul) to another (one's state of consciousness). The two lower garments, speech and action, express oneself to others.

The three lines which compose the form of the *hei* correspond to these three garments: the upper horizontal line to thought; the right vertical line to speech; the unattached foot to action.

The horizontal line symbolizes a state of equanimity. The continuous, horizontal flow of thought is the contemplation of how G-d is found equally in every place and in every thing. In relating to one's fellow Jew, one must realize that each of us possesses an innate inner point of goodness, and that all Jews are equal in essence. This realization, the horizontal high plane of one's consciousness in relation to another, sets the "scene" for all individual, personal relationships.

The origin-point of speech, the right vertical line of the *hei*, is directly connected to the line of thought and thereafter descends to express one's thoughts and inner feelings to others. The root of the word "speech" in Hebrew, דבר, means "leadership," as in the expression דבר אחד לדור ולא שני דברים לדור, "There is one leader in a generation, not two leaders in a generation." Leadership implies hierarchy, relative positions of up and down, and thus is represented by a vertical line. The King, and likewise every leader, rules through his power of speech, as is said: באשר דבר מלך שלטון, "By the word of the King is His sovereignty."

The separation of action, the unattached left foot of the *hei*, from thought, the upper horizontal line, reflects a deep truth about the nature of action. "Many are the thoughts in the heart of man, yet the advice of G-d shall surely stand." The servant of G-d experiences the existential gap between his thoughts and deeds. Often he is unable to realize his inner intentions. Other times he is surprised by unexpected success. In both cases he feels the hand of G-d directing his deeds. The gap is the experience of the Divine Nothing, the source of all Creation in deed: something from nothing.

We have now reached the culmination of the sequence represented by the three letters *gimel, dalet,* and *hei,* the process of giving of oneself to another. The gift, represented by the foot, the unattached segment of *hei,* when fully integrated in the receiver, becomes his own power of action and giving of himself to others. Even more, now he fully realizes that the ultimate effect and potency of his deeds are in truth the act of Divine Providence.

HEI

FORM: Three lines; the two lines of the *dalet* together with an unattached left foot.

Worlds   Three dimensions of physical reality:
Width—horizontal line,
Length—vertical line,
Depth—unattached foot.
There is a dimension of reality beyond initial sensory perception.
"We will do and understand."

Souls   Three garments ("servants") of the soul:
Thought (meditative or involuntary)—horizontal line,
Speech (from the heart or from the lips)—vertical line,
Action—unattached foot.
The *beinoni*, who masters his "servants."

Divinity   Three Divine manifestations:
Essence—horizontal line,
Transcendent Light—vertical line,
Immanent Light—unattached foot.

NAME: To be broken; to take seed; behold—revelation.

Worlds   Breaking of the vessels and the resulting plurality of Creation.
The teacher breaking the brilliance of his comprehension for the sake of the student.
Broken existence resulting in unified existence.

Souls   Impregnating reality with the souls of Israel.

Divinity   Divine revelation—"Beholding" G-d.
Ultimate revelation of the *Mashiach*.
Small *hei*: potential Divine revelation.

NUMBER: Five

Worlds   Symbol of division.
Five origins of speech in the mouth.
Five fingers of the hand.
Five visible planets in the solar system.
The five vanities in the opening verse of Ecclesiastes.

Souls   Five levels of the soul.
Five times "Bless G-d, my soul" in Psalms 103 and 104.
Five voices of the joy of bride and groom.

Divinity   Five Books of Moses.
Five voices at the giving of the Torah.
Five times "light" in the first day of Creation.
Five final letters.
Five redemptions.

FORM

The *hei* is composed of three lines, the two lines of the *dalet* together with an unattached foot.

WORLDS

The three lines of the *hei* correspond to the three dimensions of physical reality: breadth, height, and depth. The dimension of depth is represented by the unattached left foot of the *hei*. The fact that this component is unattached to the rest of the letter, and resembles the point of a *yud* in comparison to the two lines or *vavs* of the *hei*, can be viewed as hinting at a third coordinate running through the page, or plane, upon which the letter is inscribed. The experience of depth, the "third dimension," on our plane of normative consciousness, should remind us that even in our physical world there is a dimension of reality beyond our initial sensory perception.

One's initial state of thought (the upper, horizontal line of the *hei*, as explained above) reflects the "breadth" of one's consciousness. The ability of thought to delve into the depths of reasoning and cognizance, to "hear" (*derher* in Yiddish) reality as it "really" is, depends upon the linking power of the "action" coordinate—depth—to that of thought—breadth. This is the secret of Israel's pronouncement, before receiving the Torah (speech/height here serving to raise action to affect thought): "We will do and [thereafter and thereby] understand."

Even at the level of Worlds, it is active experimentation that enables the scientist to achieve deeper awareness of physical truth.

SOULS

As explained above, the three lines of the *hei* correspond to the three "garments" of the soul: thought, speech, and action. A "garment" is a means of expressing otherwise inexpressible states of cognizance and emotion.

The "garments" are also referred to as the "servants" of the soul, for they serve to reveal the ten inner powers of the soul, the three powers of intellect and the seven powers of emotion. "This world was created with the letter *hei*," for this is the world whose consciousness, at the level of Souls, is one of service. Our service of G-d, the realization of His Will, the *mitzvot* of the Torah, takes place at the "servant" level of our souls—thought, speech and action—as taught in *Tanya*. The *beinoni* ("intermediate man") of *Tanya*, whose service of G-d reflects the basic nature of "this world," is the one who is able to master the "servants" of his soul. The true *tzadik*, who tastes even now of the World to Come, is the one who has mastered the inner powers of his soul.

"The World to Come was created with the letter *yud*," the manifestation of the ten (*yud* equals ten) inner powers of soul which reflect the ten Divinely emanated *sefirot*. These manifest themselves fully in the life of the *tzadik*. The *hei* equals five, for though the "garments" or "servants" of the soul are three, thought and speech both divide into two dimensions of "depth," related to the effect of action on them, whereas action itself does not divide. The two levels of thought are deep, meditative thought versus involuntary flow of consciousness or light, imaginative thought. The two levels of speech are "words from the heart" versus "words from the lips," whose ultimate Divine origin is the difference between the "Ten Command-ments" of Torah and the "Ten Sayings" of Creation, as will be explained in the letter *yud*. In the written, two dimensional form of the *hei*, this phenom-enon is indicated by the fact that the two line segments corresponding to thought and speech are twice as long as that corresponding to action.

By our thoughts, words, and deeds of Torah and *mitzvot*, the "gar-ments" of our souls "serve" to become "garments" of the Divine Soul, as it were, the ten *sefirot* of *Atzilut* (the Divine "world" of Emanation). Just as the garments of the soul are one's means of self-expression, so, through the ful-fillment of Torah and *mitzvot*, do we express and reveal the Divine Self to the eyes of all.

DIVINITY

At the level of Divinity the three components of the letter *hei* correspond to the three Divine Manifestations: "He fills all worlds, He surrounds all worlds, and all is naught before Him."

"He fills all worlds" refers to G-d's Immanent Light, as hinted at by the unattached lower foot of the *hei*. The finite revelation of Immanent Light to each and every created being, to each in accordance with the capacity of its vessel to receive, appears separate from its absolutely Infinite Source. Nonetheless, at the "infinite point" of its hidden dimension of depth, it touches and unites with its Source.

"He surrounds all worlds" refers to G-d's Transcendent Light, which, though uniformly present throughout all of reality, appears to "surround" it, for the vessels of reality are unable to comprehend its brilliance. In our experience of the infinite nature of this light we see it as touching its Absolute Source. In the experience of its hovering above us we sense it as descending from its Source to relate to our finite state. This is represented by the right vertical line of the *hei*, which visibly touches its source, the upper horizontal line, and thereafter descends below. Descent on the *right* represents entrance into the *spiritual* consciousness of lower beings, whereas the *left* symbolizes the dominion of *physical* sensation. This teaches us that G-d's Immanent Light is meant to be perceived even by the physical senses of man, whereas His Transcendent Light can only be perceived by man's inner spiritual senses.

"And *all* is naught before Him" refers to G-d's Essence. Its revelation to us is represented by the upper horizontal line of the *hei*. The horizontal state implies equality, as explained above. Here, "*all*" (including the Transcendent and Immanent Lights themselves) is equally "naught" in the presence of ("before") the Essence of G-d.

NAME

The word *hei* (הא, also written הי or ההה) means "to be broken"; "to take seed"; "behold"—"revelation."

WORLDS

In the verse ואני דניאל נהייתי ונחלתי ימים, "And I, Daniel, was broken and became sick for many days" (subsequent to Daniel's vision of the trials and tribulations of exile and holocaust awaiting the Jewish people), the root הי, *hei*, means "to be broken." The Kabbalah tells of the primordial catastrophe, "the breaking of the vessels." In order to convey his thoughts to an uninitiated pupil, a teacher may be forced to "break" the coherent brilliance of his own comprehension of a most sublime truth into a multitude of small, seemingly disordered and unrelated pieces of information. So too, Divine Unity appears to "shatter" itself into plurality in order to create our physical state of being and bestow us with freedom of choice between good (unity) and evil (apparent plurality).

So, the meaning "to be broken" (הי) is closely related to the root היה, "to be" or "to become." This is hinted at in the second verse in the Torah: "And the earth *was* chaos...." Here, the verb "to be" appears for the first time in the Torah (whose beginning is the account of Creation). "Chaos" (תהו, *Tohu*) refers to the primordial world where "the breaking of the vessels" occurred, as taught in Kabbalah. The next two appearances of the root "to be" are in the third verse of Torah: "And G-d said '*Let there be* [יהי] light,' *and there was* [ויהי] light." The Torah continues: "And G-d saw the light as good, and G-d separated between the light and the darkness." Darkness is the "context" in which plurality appears to exist. Light is the revelation of unity, as is indicated by the fifth, concluding verse of the first day of Creation: "And G-d called the light day...*one* [not 'first,' as noted by the Sages] day." From broken being derives, ultimately, unified being. This is the very secret of the act of Creation.

SOULS

Joseph said to the Egyptians, toward the end of the years of famine: הא לכם זרע וזרעתם את האדמה, "Take for yourselves seed, and sow the earth." Here, *hei* (הא) means "to take," specifically in reference to seed, as explained above.

Our Sages teach us that Joseph forced the Egyptians to circumcise themselves, thereby intending to impregnate all of reality—as then reflected by the pervasive and flourishing Egyptian culture—with Jewish souls. Unfortunately his intention was not realized, for the Egyptians were not a fitting vessel for such revelation. Instead, his very act infused ("gave suck to," in the terminology of Kabbalah) the Egyptians with additional power to subjugate and bitterly enslave the Jewish people. Joseph's attempt was "premature" and thus failed and even backfired. The moral of the story is: don't "play around with" Jewish souls. This refers even to a great *tzadik* at the level of Joseph, whose intended purpose was only good. One must not "force the end" by means other than those revealed to us as G-d's Will in Torah. Through "merit" in Torah we are able to achieve the "speeding up" of the end, as taught by the Sages.

The premature attempt to bring about the end is likened to miscarriage, instead of good-timely birth. The form of the letter *hei* symbolizes the stable state of pregnancy, as taught in Kabbalah. The suspended left vertical line corresponds to the fetus within the womb of the horizontal and vertical lines. The embryo begins "to be" with the gift of the male seed ("take...seed"). The embryo of the soul is the "depth" of rectified action, first "broken" from the co-ordinate of thought, as discussed above. It develops over a period of nine months, but sometimes the process can be (stably) speeded up to the beginning of the seventh month, as in the case of the birth of Moses, the redeemer of Israel. In the Exodus, Moses took Joseph's bones ("bones" [עצמות] means "being" [עצמות] in Hebrew), thereby fulfilling, in a rectified state, Joseph's instruction: "Take...seed," for one's seed is, in truth, an indivisible part of one's very being (bone), as taught in *Chassidut*.

DIVINITY

Hei, short for the word הנה, "behold," expresses Divine revelation, as in the verse הנה אלקינו זה קוינו לו, "*Behold* this is our G-d that we have been waiting for." This verse refers to the ultimate revelation of G-d upon the arrival of the *Mashiach*. The word קוינו, "we have been waiting," comes from the root קו, "a line," and as the verb form is here in the plural, it hints at the three lines which compose the letter *hei*. Our "waiting" is not passive, but rather the active effort of filling the three "lines" of our consciousness, thought, speech, and action, with the G-dliness of Torah and *mitzvot*.

Though the sound of the name of every letter, when properly understood, is onomatopoeic, this phenomenon is most obvious with regard to the letter *hei*, which, even in English, expresses the astonishment of a new revelation.

In the story of Creation, the word בהבראם, "upon their being created," is written with a small *hei*. The Midrash explains that the letters בהבראם when rearranged spell באברהם, "with [the attribute of] Abraham." The Divine attribute represented by our father Abraham is the lovingkindness through which the world was created, as is said "the world is built with lovingkindness." Lovingkindness is the means through which G-d's presence is ultimately revealed. This is the secret of the small *hei*, the "potential" Divine revelation impregnant within all of Creation. When, at the age of ninety-nine, G-d commanded Abraham to circumcise himself (only after he had achieved the maximal spiritual level obtainable being uncircumcised, unlike the premature attempt of Joseph to circumcise the totally unworthy Egyptians), He gave him the letter *hei*, thereby converting him from אברם, Abram, to אברהם, Abraham. G-d's giving to Abraham His power of *hei*, Divine revelation, in fact infused him with the power of procreation of the Jewish soul, G-d's "image" on earth, the power of the Infinite, as taught in *Chassidut*. Abraham's G-d-given *hei* was his power to impregnate Sarah with Jewish seed, to be born as Isaac at their respective ages of one hundred and ninety (the two letters *kuf* and *tzadik*, which spell the word קץ, "end"). Isaac's name means "laughter" and "delight" due to the supernatural revelation—*hei*—of the Divine.

NUMBER

The letter *hei* equals five.

WORLDS

The number five represents the power of division. Division ("breaking," as explained in the name of the letter *hei* at the level of Worlds) into five states of plurality, facilitates expression, as in the five origins of speech in the mouth: throat, palate, tongue, teeth, and lips, and in the five fingers of the hand.

The five visible planets of the solar system: Saturn, Jupiter, Mars, Venus, and Mercury, correspond to five powers that combine to influence physical phenomena on earth. These five (ה) planets, together with the two (ב) luminaries, the sun and the moon, and the twelve (ל, the twelfth letter of the alphabet) constellations of the Zodiac, combine to spell the word הבל, "vanity," as is said in the opening, all inclusive, verse of Ecclesiastes: הבל הבלים אמר קהלת הבל הבלים הכל הבל, "Vanity of vanities, says Ecclesiastes, vanity of vanities, all is vanity."

For the Jew, of whom it is said "there is no *mazal* [causal influence of heavenly bodies] for Israel," the worldly influence of the planets, etc., is in truth vain, for we are directly connected to the true Unity behind and above all states of apparent division and plurality. Nonetheless, if one allows "vanity" to enter his consciousness and deeds, he makes himself vulnerable to the "vain" influences of nature. This actually occurs from the moment of birth, as is said, "the inclination of the heart of man is evil from birth." The Divine soul of Israel, above all vanity, begins to shine its light and power from the moment of circumcision (or, in the female, from birth itself, for the Jewish woman is "born circumcised"), and thereafter matures sufficiently to be able to *overcome* all vanities at the age of *bar-* (or *bat-*) *mitzvah*.

SOULS

At the level of Souls, the number five corresponds to the five different levels of the soul, as taught by the Sages, and elucidated in Kabbalah and *Chassidut*: the lower soul (*nefesh*, נפש) relates to behavior and action; the spirit (*ruach*, רוח) to the emotions; the inner soul (*neshamah*, נשמה) to the mind; the "living one" (*chayah*, חיה) to the bridge between the first flash of conscious insight and its superconscious origin; the "single one" (*yechidah*, יחידה) to the ultimate unity of the soul in G-d, as manifest by pure faith, absolute devotion, and the continual readiness to sacrifice one's life for G-d.

In Psalms 103 and 104, King David repeats the phrase ברכי נפשי את ה', "My soul, bless G-d," five times. These five times correspond to the drawing down and implanting the consciousness of Divinity in the five levels of the soul ("to bless" in Hebrew, means to draw down and implant, as explained in the letter *beit*). The numerical value of ברכי נפשי את ה' (1099) exactly equals that of the sum of the five names of the soul: נפש, רוח, נשמה, חיה, יחידה. (In the phrase ברכי נפשי את ה', *nefesh* is used as the general name through which all of the particular levels of the soul reveal themselves.)

In Jeremiah, the joy of groom and bride is expressed by five voices: "The voice of joy and the voice of gladness, the voice of the bridegroom and the voice of the bride, the voice of them that shall say 'Praise the G-d of Hosts...' " Even at the time of union, marriage, the full expression of joy is represented by the number five, in order to insure the purpose of marriage, the drawing down of individual souls into the world, as in the secret of "take...seed" explained above.

DIVINITY

The revelation of the Torah, though absolutely one with G-d, nonetheless requires particular, explicit expression of G-d's Will to man, and thus was given with five voices and is divided into the Five Books of Moses. The giving of the Torah to the Jewish people is referred to as G-d's marriage to Israel.

Our Sages teach that whoever gives joy to groom and bride, whose joy is expressed by five voices, merits the Torah, which was given with five voices. In the first day of Creation the word אור, "light," appears five times. Light is the beginning of rectified (i.e., unified) being, subsequent to the initial, dark, "broken" state of being, as explained above.

As the Torah is referred to as light (in the verse תורה אור, "the Torah is light"), this phenomenon alludes to the five books of the Torah, whose ultimate purpose is to rectify all of Creation in Divine Unity.

The Hebrew alphabet possesses five final letters: מנצפך. They allude to five "ends," or redemptions from the darkness of our exile within the consciousness of plurality to the light of the final awareness of G-d's Absolute Unity. We are taught that the first four ends, alluded to by the letters ךףןם, have already become (partially) manifest in the redemptions of the past. The final end, the secret of the final *tzadik*, awaits the coming of the *Mashiach*. Then will be the consummate revelation of the *tzadik* of Israel—"And your People are all *tzadikim*"—as one with "The *Tzadik* of the World," G-d. The letter *tzadik* is the fifth letter from the *end* of the alphabet, just as the *hei* is the fifth letter from the beginning (or, *hei* and *tzadik* transform in *atbash*). The final *tzadik*, the fifth final letter, as the secret of the redemption to come, is most beautifully alluded to in the verse מכנף הארץ זמירות שמענו צבי לצדיק, "From the end [i.e., wing or corner] of the earth we have heard songs, the desire of the *tzadik*..." The word **מכנף**, "from the end," is composed of the first four letters which possess final forms. "We *have* heard songs," in the past tense, indicates that their revelation (song) has already been heard in the redemptions of the past. "The desire of the *tzadik*," **צבי לצדיק**, means that our ultimate desire is the consummation of the secret of the final *tzadik* ("the end of the [word] earth," מכנף הארץ, itself—the word ארץ being short for the phrase אור זרע לצדיק, "light is implanted in the *tzadik*").

Vav

התְקַשְּׁרוּת וְהִתְחַבְּרוּת

Connection

Vav: **Connection**

In the beginning of Creation, when Infinite Light filled all of reality, G-d contracted His Light to create hollow empty space, as it were, the "place" necessary for the existence of finite worlds. Into this vacuum G-d drew down, figuratively speaking, a single line of light, from the Infinite Source. This ray of light is the secret of the letter *vav*. Though the line is singular in appearance, it nonetheless possesses two dimensions, an external as well as an internal force, both of which take part in the process of Creation and the continuous interaction between the creative power and created reality.

The external force of the line is the power to differentiate and separate the various aspects of reality, thereby establishing hierarchical order, up and down, within Creation. The internal force of the line is the power to reveal the inherent interinclusion of the various aspects of reality, one in the other, thereby joining them together as an organic whole. This property of the letter *vav*, in its usage in Hebrew, is referred to as *vav hachibur*, "the *vav* of connection"—"and." The first *vav* of the Torah—בראשית ברא אלקים את השמים ואת הארץ, "In the beginning G-d created the heavens *and* the earth"—serves to join together spirit and matter, heaven and the earth, throughout Creation. This *vav*, which appears at the beginning of the *sixth* word of the Torah, is the twenty-second letter of the verse. It alludes to the power to connect and interrelate all twenty-two individual powers of Creation, the twenty-two letters of the Hebrew alphabet from *alef* to *tav*. (The word את is generally taken to represent all of the letters of the alphabet, from א to ת. Our Sages interpret the word את in this verse to include all of the various objects of Creation present within heaven and earth).

In Biblical Hebrew, the letter *vav* also possesses the function of inverting the apparent tense of a verb to its opposite—from past to future or from future to past (*vav hahipuch*). The first appearance of this type of *vav* in the Torah is the letter *vav* which begins the twenty-second word of the account of Creation, "*And* G-d said...." This is the first explicit saying of the ten sayings of Creation: ויאמר אלקים יהי אור ויהי אור, "*And* G-d said [the verb 'said' being inverted from the future to the past tense by the *vav* at the beginning of the word—'And']: 'Let there be light,' and there was light." The phenomenon of light breaking through the darkness of the *tzimzum*, the primordial contraction, is itself the secret of time (future becoming past) which permeates space.

In the Divine service of a Jew, the power to draw from the future into the past is the secret of *teshuvah* (repentance and returning to G-d) from love. Through *teshuvah* from *fear*, one's deliberate transgressions become like errors; the severity of one's past transgressions becomes partially sweetened, but not completely changed. However, when a Jew returns in *love*, his deliberate transgressions become like actual merits, for the very consciousness of distance from G-d resulting from one's transgressions becomes the motivating force to return to G-d with passion even greater than that of one who had never sinned.

Every Jew has a portion in the World to Come, as is said: "And all your nation are *tzadikim*; forever they will inherit the land." The power of *teshuvah* to completely convert one's past to good, is the power of the *vav* to invert the past to the future. This transformation itself requires, paradoxically, the drawing down of light from the future to the past.

Drawing the future into the past in the Divine service of man is the secret of learning the inner teachings of the Torah, that aspect of the Torah which is related to the revelation of the coming of the *Mashiach*. Rashi explains the verse in the Song of Songs: "May he kiss me with the kisses of his mouth, for your love is better than wine" as alluding to the sweet teachings that will be revealed by the *Mashiach*. When a person intently studies the secrets of the Torah, he draws from the future into the past, in order to strengthen himself to return in complete *teshuvah* from love and thereby convert his past into future.

VAV

FORM: A vertical line.
A pillar.
A man standing upright.

Worlds   Twelve pillars of Creation—the twelve lines of a cube. The twelve tribes.
Seven pillars of Creation—six directions and time. The seven shepherds.
One pillar of Creation—the future. *Mashiach.*
The connecting rods in the Tabernacle.

Souls   Complete stature of man—standing on earth with head reaching up towards
heaven.
The Jewish people standing together.
The "Golden Path" in the service of G-d.
The torso in relation to the hands, feet, and *brit.*

Divinity   The pillar of Truth.
Consistency of the middle pillar.
Divinity piercing through the middle point of every Creation.

NAME: A Hook.

Worlds   The connecting hooks of the pillars in the Tabernacle—concealment and
revelation.
The axis of symmetry and the equilibrium between symmetry and asymmetry.

Souls   The power which links together the souls of Israel.
The points of will to do G-d's Will engraved in the heart of every Jew.
The axis which connects the good points present within every Jew.

Divinity   The connecting link between the separate Laws—engraved letters of Divine
essence—of the Torah.
The force of connection between the Divine sparks inherent throughout
reality.

NUMBER: Six

Worlds   Six Days of Creation, and their six corresponding Divine forces active in
creation.
Six letters of the word בראשית, "In the beginning."
Six *alefs* in the first verse of the Torah.
Six-millennium duration of the world.
Six directions of the physical world.

Souls   Six wings (states of love and fear in the soul) of the fiery angels.
"Give truth to Jacob."

Divinity   Six orders of the *Mishnah.*
The six "wings" of the *Magen David.*
Six cubits—the dimensions of the Tablets received by Moses at Mt. Sinai.

FORM

The *vav* is a verticle line representing a pillar or a man standing upright.

WORLDS

"The world stands on pillars." The pillars, a symbol of support, hold Creation together. In the Talmud we find three opinions as to their number: twelve, seven, or one. As generally understood when relating varied opinions of the Sages to physical phenomena, each opinion refers to a different aspect of reality. Or even deeper: each opinion describes a different model of the universe.

In *Sefer Yetzirah* we are taught that the twelve pillars of Creation, referred to as the "twelve diagonally inclined borders," correspond to the twelve peripheral lines of an ever-expanding cube (universe), from an initial single point of *tzimtzum*. They, at the level of Worlds, correspond to the twelve tribes of Israel, at the level of Souls. The word "tribe" in Hebrew means "staff," similar to a pillar of support.

The model of seven pillars corresponds to an ever-expanding universe of six spacial pillars, the six directions of three-dimensional space, together with the "real" past, half the coordinate of time, the fourth dimension. At the level of Souls, these seven pillars correspond to the seven "shepherds" of Israel: Abraham, Isaac, Jacob, Moses, Aaron, Joseph, and David.

The model of one pillar is the secret of the ultimate dependence of all reality on the potential, hidden half of the fourth dimension, the future. From this perspective, all stands on the future. In Hebrew, the word "future" (עתיד) means "ready." At the level of Souls, this is the secret of the soul of the *Mashiach*, "ready" to come throughout time (from its very beginning, and even before...), the ever-supported "fallen one," as will be explained in our discussion of the letter *nun*.

In the Tabernacle, constructed by Moses in the desert, there were long rods running through all the boards on three of its sides, connecting and holding them together. The structure and components of the Tabernacle directly correspond to the secrets of Creation. Inspired by Moses, Bezalel, the chief craftsman of the Tabernacle, "knew how to permute letters through which heavens and earth were created." In particular, the rods manifest the connecting force of the letter *vav*.

SOULS

The *vav*, a single erect line, symbolizes the upright stature of man standing on earth with head reaching towards the heavens. So too, all Jewish souls stand together, as a single man, in their service of G-d. This is similar to the "standing crowded together" mentioned earlier in relation to the form of the letter *dalet*.

The Rambam, in dealing with the rectification of one's character traits in the service of G-d, speaks of the "middle path," which seeks to avoid the extreme manifestation of any particular emotive attribute, and leads to a life of moderation and constant consideration of one's fellow man. This ideal state of man is in truth the return to G-d's initial intention in His creation of man, as said in Ecclesiastes: אשר עשה האלקים את האדם ישר והמה בקשו חשבונות רבים, "that G-d has made man *upright*, but they have sought out many schemes." The word ישר means both "upright" as well as "straight," and hints at the saying of our Sages: איזו היא דרך ישרה שיבור לו האדם, כל שהיא תפארת לעושיה ותפארת לו מן האדם, "Which is the *straight* way that a man should choose? That which is beautiful to its doer and beautiful from the perspective of man." The straight middle path corresponds to the attribute of *tiferet* ("beauty"), that beauty which, as the inner power of the "line" descibed above, serves to manifest the interinclusion and harmony between all of the emotive powers of the soul. This is the secret of the letter *vav*, as taught in Kabbalah. (Its number, six, corresponds to the six emotive properties of the heart: lovingkindness, might, beauty, victory, thanksgiving, fulfillment [foundation]. Beauty [*tiferet*] is the all-inclusive "middle" attribute of these six, like the human torso from which emerge the hands, feet, and *brit*.)

DIVINITY

The *vav*, at the level of Divinity, represents the middle pillar—the "pillar of truth"—which pierces through the middle point of all of reality. Truth is defined as the constant middle, which expresses itself as the power to support two apparent opposites simultaneously. "Truth is one and only one." The ultimate Truth is the unity of Torah in G-d. From this point of origin Truth descends through the "middle" of all emanated and created worlds.

The structure of the *sefirot*, the emanations of G-d's light in the process of Creation, is made up of three lines or channels. The right, the side of lovingkindness, and the left, the side of severity, may possibly degenerate into external manifestations, whereas the middle remains constant in its inner manifestation of *bitul* to the will of G-d. This channel or "pillar of truth" runs through all worlds and all beings.

Every created being, even an inanimate object, has a "Divine" middle point of truth. One's perception of this middle point of truth is his being in tune, so to speak, with that being or object. By simultaneously running through all the middle points of reality, the Divine power of the letter *vav* connects and unifies all of reality, ultimately to include our own human consciousness in this Unity, by reaching and touching all of our powers of perception.

NAME

The word *vav* (וו, also spelled ואו or ויו) means "a hook."

WORLDS

In the Tabernacle, the microcosm of all Worlds, the hooks used to connect the pillars to the curtains were called ווי העמודים, "the *hooks* [*vavs*] of the pillars."

This phrase, ווי העמודים, is actually repeated six times (the numerical value of *vav*) in the account of the Tabernacle. (Two instances are in the Torah-portion *Terumah*, where the construction of the Tabernacle and its vessels is commanded, and four are in the portion *VaYakhel*, where their construction is carried out. In each portion, the word ווי is the sixth word of the verse it appears in first).

The curtains of the Tabernacle represent the power of concealment that exists between worlds, each higher world "hiding itself" behind a "curtain" from the lower world. The pillars stand for manifest revelations of light channelled downward from world to world. The hooks—*vavs*—serve to connect the two powers of concealment and revelation.

Thus, while the form of the *vav* depicts the pillars themselves (the power of explicit revelation), the name *vav* refers to the hooks connecting the two seemingly opposite powers of concealment and revelation. Nonetheless, the hooks relate in particular to the pillars, "the hooks of the *pillars*," rather than to the curtains, for the ultimate purpose of linking concealment to revelation is for the sake of continued, ever deeper, revelation. Concealment is merely a means towards an end—revelation—as taught in *Chassidut*. The final revelation enters a world or a frame of reference that could only have come into being and remain in a stable state of existence in virtue of the power of concealment.

The *vav* as pillar and the *vav* as hook are actually the secret of the two *vavs* in the full spelling of the letter *vav*: וו. The initial *vav*, corresponding to its form, is the pillar, or the *sefirah* of *tiferet* ("beauty"). The second *vav*, the "filling" of the first *vav*, thus giving it name, is the hook (of the pillar), or the *sefirah* of *yesod* ("foundation," "connecting"). At the level of Worlds, the pillar represents the "axis" around which harmony and symmetry (beauty) are revealed throughout nature. The hook represents the power of connection and equilibrium between the symmetrical and asymmetrical states inherent in nature.

SOULS

At the level of the innermost point of the heart, all Jewish souls are connected and one. This innermost point of the heart, the essential point of consummate will to serve G-d, is equally present within every Jew. The function of the hook, the name of the letter *vav*, becomes apparent when the initially amorphous will to serve G-d begins to assume form and definite direction, based upon the realization of one's specific task in the service of G-d. As differentiation (concealment of one from another) begins within the individual hearts of Jews, the power of the hook keeps them linked together, all conscious of the common goal (revelation).

Just as we all possess the common potential of essential will in the innermost point of our hearts, so every Jew is full of actual points of good: "Even the wicked amongst you are as full of *mitzvot* as a pomegranate [is full of seeds]." The form of a pomegranate resembles the sphere of the planet earth, itself a symbol of the People Israel: " 'and you [Israel] shall be for Me a desired land [i.e., earth],' says G-d." Just as the earth revolves around its axis, so the axis of the "earth—Israel" is the power that runs through and connects all of the actual points of good present within every Jew. This axis may be understood to be the power of the letter *vav* as the pillar of good around which the beauty of the people becomes manifest. However, upon the deeper realization that the unique character of the good points of different individuals initially serves to differentiate one from the other, the power to connect the good points of different individuals (often the good thoughts of one join to the good deeds of another, resulting in one integral good, as taught in *Chassidut*) is the secret of the hook to reveal the pillar of the common goal of all good (Divine Revelation) through the curtain of apparent differentiation.

DIVINITY

Rabbi Shalom Dov Ber of Lubavitch would frequently recite the verse in Psalms: ברוך אתה ה' למדני חוקיך, "Blessed are You, G-d; teach me [i.e., reveal to me] Your Laws," and interpret "Your Laws" as "the engraved letters of Your Essence present throughout all reality" (חוק, "law," comes from the root חקק, "to engrave"). These engraved letters of Divine Essence correspond, at the level of Divinity, to those essential points of will (to fulfill G-d's Will—His Law) engraved in the heart of every Jew, at the level of Souls. The engraved letters, the "Law" of Divine Will, became audible (and visible) at the time of the giving of the Torah. As our Sages teach, we then perceived G-d's command from every direction and dimension of Creation: "I am *G-d* your G-d...." The Ten Commandments themselves were first pronounced as one Word. No differentiation between the individual laws of the Torah was then apparent. As the Laws assume individual garb and appear to become separate from one another, the power of the letter *vav* is what reveals their innate common Essence and Purpose.

The sparks of Divinity that enliven every aspect of Creation correspond to the actual points of good present within every Jew. The power of the letter *vav* is what manifests the "continuum" of these sparks, in essence, and as "released" or "redeemed" from moment to moment, in the continual rectification of Creation.

NUMBER

The letter *vav* equals six.

WORLDS

The first word of Creation, בראשית, is read in the *Zohar* ברא שית, "He created six" (שית in Aramaic is equivalent to ששה in Hebrew, "six"). The most obvious phenomenon of six in relation to Creation is the fact that the world was created in six days, as is said: את ה' עשה ימים ששת השמים ואת הארץ, "*Six* days did G-d make the heavens and the earth." The *Zohar* interprets: "each day performed its action." Each day corresponds to a unique Divine force active in the creative process and primarily manifest in the acts of creation on its day.

The word בראשית itself possesses six letters. In the first verse of the Torah, בראשית ברא אלקים את השמים ואת הארץ, "In the beginning G-d created the heavens and the earth," there are six *alefs*, which correspond to the six millennia (*alef* means "a thousand") of the endurance of our present state of reality, as taught by the Sages. The six millennia themselves are a projection of the six days of Creation, as is said: אלף שנים בעיניך כיום אתמול, "A *thousand* years in Your eyes are as a day of yesterday," a day of Creation.

Three-dimensional physical space is composed of ו' קצוות, "six extremities": right, left, front, back, up, and down. According to the basic orientation of Torah, front corresponds to east, thus defining right, left, and back as south, north, and west, respectively. The six days of Creation relate to south, north, front, up, down, and west, the same order as that of the traditional shaking of the *lulav* and *etrog* on *Sukot*, as taught in Kabbalah.

SOULS

In prophetic vision, Isaiah saw the fiery angels or *serafim* as each possessing six wings:

שרפים עומדים ממעל לו, שש כנפים שש כנפים לאחד, בשתים
יכסה פניו, ובשתים יכסה רגליו, ובשתים יעופף. וקרא
זה אל זה ואמר קדוש קדוש קדוש ה' צבאות מלא כל הארץ כבודו.

> "*Serafim* stood above Him, each one had *six* wings—with two he covered his face, and with two he covered his feet, and with two he flew. And one called to another and said: 'Holy Holy Holy is G-d of Hosts, the whole earth is full of His glory.'"

In general, wings symbolize the two primary emotive powers of the soul: love and fear. The *Zohar* teaches that *mitzvot* performed without love and fear, though infinitely significant and potent in themselves, do not possess the "wings" necessary to fly upward to Heaven (i.e. to reveal their Divine origin). The two wings that cover the face of each angel correspond to the manifestations of love and fear, "born" from meditation. The covering of the face represents the attribute of "holy shame" in the face of G-d. The two wings that cover the feet of each angel correspond to the innate qualities of love and fear that exist in every soul. The covering of the feet represents the attribute of "walking humbly with your G-d." The two wings of flight itself correspond to the experience of Divinely-inspired love and fear that are given from Above to one who has sincerely served G-d with love and fear to the maximal, though limited, level of his soul's initial state of consciousness. These G-d-given emotions serve to elevate the soul to infinitely higher states of consciousness, as the flight of the *serafim*.

In the verse "Give truth to Jacob," the Divinely inspired experiences of love and fear are referred to as the "stamp of truth" with which G-d "certifies" one's own initial manifestations of love and fear. All experience from below is temporal and unstable by nature, and thereby untrue. G-d-given emotions are eternal and stable by nature, while, simultaneously, infinitely powerful. This is the secret of the seal of Truth given by G-d to Jacob (Jacob representing the initial temporal emotions manifest in the soul from below), as taught in *Chassidut*. The secret of the word "truth," אמת, is 21^2, אהיה אשר אהיה, "I shall be that which I shall be" (the Divine Name אהיה, "I shall be," equals 21). Each 21 is in turn the "triangle" of six $(21=1 \perp 2 \perp 3 \perp 4 \perp 5 \perp 6)$. For this reason, the letter *vav*, whose numerical value is six, is referred to as "the letter of truth."

DIVINITY

"The Torah of G-d is perfect, restoring the soul. The testimony of G-d is sure, making wise the simple. The statutes of G-d are right, rejoicing the heart. The commandments of G-d are bright, enlightening the eyes. The fear of G-d is pure, enduring forever. The judgements of G-d are true and are righteous all together."

Our Sages teach that these six phrases, all relating to the intrinsically Divine nature of Torah and Its Ways (the Torah *of G-d*... the testimony *of G-d*...) hint at the basic structure of the Oral Torah—the six orders of the *Mishnah*. The Oral Torah, in a certain way even more so than the written Torah, links the essence of the Jewish soul to the Will of G-d. This is the ultimate manifestation of *vav hachibur*. G-d's Name appears as the second of the five words of each of the six phrases. In Kabbalah we are taught that each of the five-word phrases corresponds to the five fingers of the right hand. The Divine Name corresponds to the second finger, the finger upon which the bride accepts her betrothal ring, whose function is to "point" at Divine revelation.

The consummate structure of six (as in the form of a *Magen David*, the outer area of whose six "wings" equals, and therefore folds onto, the area of its inner hexagon), reflected by the six orders of the *Mishnah*, finds its source in the dimensions of the Tablets given to Moses at Sinai. They were cubes measuring six handbreadths in each direction. "Inscribe them [i.e., the words of Torah] on the tablet of your heart." Then "the heart of the wise teaches his mouth"—from G-d to the tablet of the heart to the word of the mouth—the six orders of the Oral Torah.

Zayin

אֵשֶׁת חַיִל עֲטֶרֶת בַּעְלָה

The Woman of Valor

Zayin: **The Woman of Valor**

The Maggid of Mezeritch, the successor of the Ba'al Shem Tov, teaches that the verse "A woman of valor is the crown of her husband" alludes to the form of the letter *zayin*. The previous letter, *vav*, portrays the *or yashar* ("straight light") descending from G-d into the worlds. The *zayin*, whose form is similar to a *vav*, though with a crown on top, reflects the *or yashar* of the *vav* as *or chozer* ("returning light"). *Or chozer* ascends with such great force that it reaches a higher state of consciousness than that of the revealed origin-point of the *or yashar*. When reaching the initially superconscious realm of *keter* (the crown), it broadens its awareness to both the right and the left. In truth "there is no left in that Ancient One [the level of *keter*], for all is right." This means that the awe of G-d (left) at this initially superconscious level is indistinguishable, in its nature to cling directly to G-d, from the highest manifestation of the love of G-d (right).

The experience of *or chozer*, subsequent to the consummation of the creative process inherent in *or yashar*, the creation of man on the sixth day, is the secret of the seventh day of Creation—Shabbat. The Shabbat Queen who, in general, signifies woman in relation to man—"the woman of valor is the crown of her husband"—has the power to reveal in her husband his own superconscious crown, the experience of serene pleasure and sublime will innate in the day of Shabbat.

"Who is a good [literally, *kosher*] woman? She who does her husband's will." *Chassidut* explains that the word "does" also means "rectifies," as said in the completion of the account of Creation (the seal of the seventh day, Shabbat): "that which G-d created to do"—"to do" in the sense of "to rectify" (thus implying that G-d has given us the task to consummate the rectification of His Creation), as explained by the Sages. Thus the "*kosher* woman" is she who rectifies her husband's will by elevating him to ever new awareness of previously superconscious realms of soul.

ZAYIN

FORM: A *vav* whose head extends in both directions and thus appears as a crown. Scepter of a King.

Worlds   Rulership manifested in the world.
"Natural" selection.

Souls   "A woman of valor is the crown of her husband."
Sarah: the soul's experience of Shabbat and Kabbalah.
The election of the Jewish people.

Divinity   Shabbat, Kabbalah.
Returning light spreading, at its peak, to the left—fear, and to the right—love.
Becoming a vessel for G-d's blessing and sanctity.

NAME: Weapon—sword; ornament or crown; species—gender; to sustain.

Worlds   Weapon—a sword.
Conflict as an inherent property of physical nature.

Souls   Species or gender; the union of husband and wife.
Man is the crowning ornament of Creation.
G-d's three crowns, two of which He gives to His children.

Divinity   G-d sustaining the world.

NUMBER: Seven—"All sevens are dear."

Worlds   Maximal compactness.
The seventh day of Creation—Shabbat.
Seven weeks of counting the Omer.
Seven consecutive months in which fall the three Festivals.
The sabbatical year; The jubilee year, after $7 \cdot 7$ years.
The seventh millennium.
Seven fruits of Israel; Seven seas; Seven heavens.
Seven chambers of Paradise.

Souls   Seven lamps of the menorah; seven categories of Jewish souls.
Seven shepherds of Israel: Abraham, Isaac, Jacob, Moses, Aaron, Joseph, and David.
Seven circuits, seven blessings, and seven days of celebration of groom and bride.
Seven Rabbinic *mitzvot*.

Divinity   Seven "eyes" of G-d watch over all Creation.
Seven lower *sefirot*.
Tishrei, the seventh month:
Rosh HaShanah and Yom Kippur, the revelation of Divine Providence,
Sukot—Seven clouds of glory,
Simchat Torah—Seven Hakafot.

FORM

The form of the *zayin* resembles both a golden scepter and the crown on the head of a king.

WORLDS

In general, the scepter of a king symbolizes rulership and the extension of the king's power throughout his domain. In particular, the king extends his golden scepter to his subject to whom he wishes to show special favor and acceptance, as in the story of King Ahasuerus and Queen Esther: "All the king's servants and the people of the king's provinces know that whoever, whether man or woman, shall come to the king into the inner court who is not called, there is one law for him, namely to be put to death, except to the one who the King shall hold out his *golden scepter*, that he may live.... And so it was that when the King saw Esther the queen standing in the court, she aroused favor in his eyes; and the king held out to Esther the *golden scepter* that was in his hand. So Esther drew near and touched the top of the scepter."

On the plane of physical reality, with its laws of nature, the extension of the scepter to an individual creation can be understood as the manifestation of Divine Providence in "selecting" an individual or species to endure and prosper in nature, while simultaneously rejecting another individual or species, sentencing him to death or extinction. This phenomenon, secularly referred to as "natural selection," is in truth the extension of the scepter of the King, the Creator, to that creation which arouses favor in His eyes. As no created consciousness can comprehend the thoughts of the Creator nor fathom His ways in the workings of nature, the process of natural selection often appears to hide the Hand of G-d continuously involved in the perfecting of nature. Much remains a mystery and riddle to our senses: "How great are your workings, G-d; your thoughts are infinitely deep"—"For My thoughts are not your thoughts, nor My ways your ways." The mystery itself is intended to draw us closer to the experience of awe in the presence of the Omniscient and Omnipotent King.

SOULS

As explained above, the verse: "A woman of valor is the crown of her husband" alludes to the form of the letter *zayin*. The woman, the secret of Shabbat, reveals the superconscious serenity and will of her husband's soul. On Friday night, before saying *Kiddush*, we recite the twenty-two concluding verses of the book of Proverbs (acrostically arranged alphabetically, from *alef* to *tav*), in praise of the "woman of valor." The opening verse, "A woman of valor who shall find, she is far more precious than pearls," refers, in particular, to the first Jewish woman, our mother Sarah, as taught by the Sages. In the saying explained above, "Who is a good woman? She who does her husband's will," "a good [literally: *kosher*] woman" (אשה כשרה) can be read: "a woman like Sarah" (אשה כשרה). G-d told Abraham to listen and follow her advice and instruction: "everything that Sarah says to you, listen to her voice." From this verse the Sages learn that Sarah was greater than Abraham in prophecy. Sarah here appears as Abraham's crowning ornament, just as the Shabbat, the seventh day, crowns the six days of the week.

The last word of the verse, בקלה, "to her voice," permutes to spell קבלה, "Kabbalah." The six weekdays are the secret of (i.e. are rectified by) *halachah*, the process of ever "going" in G-d's Way. The *halachah* is the power of Abraham, as is written: "And Abram traveled, going and traveling southward." South corresponds to the first, all inclusive, day of Creation, as explained above in the discussion of the number of the letter *vav*. The first day of Creation relates to the *sefirah* of *chesed*, "lovingkindness", the particular attribute of Abraham: "*chesed* to Abraham."

Shabbat is the secret of Kabbalah, the crowning power of Sarah in relation to Abraham. Whereas the *or yashar* (straight light) of Abraham is always returning to the beginning of Creation in order to start anew the ongoing process of rectification, the *or chozer* (returning light) of Sarah is ever conscious of the Shabbat-to-come (the secret of the future), whose source is ultimately before the secret of Creation—the superconscious crown above Creation, the origin of the souls of Israel. For this reason, Sarah's insight and prophecy, above that of Abraham, manifested itself in her ability to distinguish between Jewish and non-Jewish souls. (She commanded Abraham to drive out Hagar together with her son Ishmael, and G-d affirmed her judgement.) Similarly, though a non-Jew is permitted to observe many of the *mitzvot* of Torah (in addition to the seven *mitzvot* he is obliged to observe), if he keeps Shabbat he is liable to death. Here the Divine scepter, the secret of the letter *zayin*, "selects" His chosen one, the souls of Israel.

DIVINITY

"And G-d blessed the seventh day and sanctified it, because in it He rested from all His work that G-d had created 'to do.' " G-d's resting on the seventh day, Shabbat, is the secret of the phenomenon of *or chozer* (returning light), experienced throughout Creation upon the conclusion of the creative process of *or yashar* (straight light), as explained above. The awakening of all of Creation to return to its Divine source is the true manifestation of Divinity *within* Creation and the consummate state of "arousal from below." By this awakening on Shabbat the world becomes a fitting vessel for the revelation of G-d's Infinite blessing ("and G-d blessed the seventh day") and His elevation of the world to unite with His own transcendent sanctity ("and He sanctified *it*"). The average value of the two words ויברך ("And He blessed") and ויקדש ("And He sanctified") equals seven times the value of בטול, "selflessness," that attribute most intrinsically identified with the state of the soul's Divine service on Shabbat, as taught in *Chassidut.*

$$
\begin{aligned}
&\text{ויברך} = \ \ 238 \\
&\text{ויקדש} = \ \underline{\ 420\ } \\
&658 \div 2 = 329 = 7 \cdot 47; \ \text{בטול} = 47
\end{aligned}
$$

Becoming a fitting vessel for Divine revelation is the secret of Kabbalah, which means "to receive," the secret of Shabbat, as explained above. The opening prayers of Shabbat eve are called *Kabbalat* Shabbat, "receiving Shabbat." In them we say השתחוו לה' בהדרת קדש, "Bow down to G-d in sacred splendour," whose initial letters spell קבלה, "Kabbalah," backwards (in the secret of *or chozer*).

The epitome of "arousal from below" in the soul is the revelation of one's own transcendent state of love and fear of G-d: love and fear at the level of the crown, the superconscious. The love is represented by the extension of the crown of the *zayin* to the right, and the fear by its extension to the left, as explained above. The love, to the right, is one's becoming a fitting vessel for G-d's infinite blessing (ויברך), whereas the fear, to the left, is one's becoming a fitting vessel for the experience of uniting with G-d's transcendent sanctity (ויקדש).

NAME

The word zayin (זין) means a "weapon," especially "a sword." A sword is considered an ornament in certain halachic contexts. Conceptually, all ornaments derive from the all-encompassing ornament of the head—the crown. The "crowns" (תגין, tagin) above the letters are referred to by the Sages as זייני, "zayins."

The two-letter root of zayin, זן, means "species" or "gender," as well as "to sustain."

WORLDS

The sword, the prototype weapon of war, symbolizes the conflict inherent in physical reality. Though it does not initially seem so, conflict—like all natural phenomena—is purposeful and constructive. Through the seemingly external necessity to confront one's enemy in battle, and often to even physically wrestle him (as did Jacob with the archangel of Esau), previously opposite attributes subconsciously merge, thereby elevating one to a higher state of existence.

When seen superficially, the inherent conflict within the world appears to be the "law of the jungle" or the "survival of the fittest." In truth, all wrestling within nature is controlled by the Divine scepter, as explained above, and ultimately both "winner" and "loser" combine to reach ever higher states of consciousness. This is the secret of evolution from the perspective of Torah.

The first iron sword was produced during the seventh (the numerical value of zayin) generation of mankind, the generation of Lemech (the descendant of Cain, who killed his brother Abel), by his son Tuval-Cain. According to tradition, Lemech himself mistakenly first killed his ancestor Cain and then his own son Tuval-Cain, the seventh generation from Cain. This was in fulfillment of G-d's promise to Cain that revenge would be taken against him in the seventh generation. Though the lineage of Cain became extinct with the Flood (according to the Midrash, the descendants of Cain actually degenerated—"de-evolved"—into monkeys), nonetheless its last remnant, Naamah, Tuval-Cain's sister, merged with the lineage of Seth (who was born "in place" of Abel) for, according to the Sages, she was Noah's wife.

SOULS

The initial letters of זכר, "male," and נקבה, "female," spell זן, "species" or "gender." Thus in both its form and its name, the letter *zayin* represents the relation of man to wife, man recognizing that his wife is his crown. When man and wife do not merit to assume their proper roles of mutual support in relation to one another, the "duet" degenerates into a "duel."

The meaning "ornament" or "crown" alludes to the soul, as the crown of Creation. The "artistic" instinct and desire of the soul is to make "crowns" for G-d through the words of prayer and acts of goodness. Our Sages teach us that each day when we say, קדוש קדוש קדוש ה' צבקות, מלא כל הארץ כבודו, "Holy Holy Holy is G-d of Hosts, the whole world is full of His glory," we make three crowns for G-d. G-d keeps one crown and returns two to us. This is indicated by the phenomenon that after the first word קדוש, "Holy," there is a line separating it from the two subsequent expressions of קדוש. The two crowns given to Israel are in virtue of our declaring נעשה ונשמע, "we will do and [then] we will hear [understand]," the statement prerequisite for our receiving of the Torah. The first word, נעשה ("we will do"), corresponds to the revelation of our infinite unconditional love for G-d (the "irrational" willingness to do His will, regardless of how He will choose to express it), the secret of the extension of the crown of the *zayin* to the right. The second word, ונשמע ("and we will hear"), corresponds to the revelation of our innate power of contraction, awe, in order to become a fitting vessel to experience ("to hear" G-d's Sanctity, the secret of the extension of the crown of the *zayin* to the left.

DIVINITY

Of all the hundred blessings a Jew is required by the Sages to say every day, the one explicit in Torah is *Birkat HaMazon* (ברכת המזון), the blessing after meals: "When you have eaten and are satiated, then you shall bless *G-d your G-d*...." The hundred daily blessings express the secret of the hundred *sefirot* interincluded at the level of *keter*, the crown, as taught in Kabbalah and *Chassidut*. *Birkat HaMazon*, the origin in Torah of all blessing, is thus the crowning ornament of the crown itself.

Birkat HaMazon begins: ברוך אתה ה' אלקינו מלך העולם **הזן** את העולם כלו בטובו, "Blessed are You, *G-d* our G-d, King of the Universe, who *provides* (הזן) for the whole world in His goodness...." The word הזן is the seventh word of the blessing (ז=7). The first blessing, originally composed by Moses himself, concludes, as well, with the word זן: ברוך אתה ה' **הזן** את הכל, "Blessed are You, *G-d*, who *provides* for all." According to the Ashkenazic text, this blessing actually possesses נז (=57) words.

The Sefardic text and that of the Arizal add to the first blessing of *Birkat HaMazon* the verse from Psalms which most clearly states G-d's continual expression of benevolence to sustain all of His Creation: פותח את ידך ומשביע לכל חי רצון, "You open up Your Hand and satisfy the desire of every living thing." This verse contains seven words. The middle word, **ומשביע**, "and satisfies," derives from the same three-letter root as the number seven, שבע. In Kabbalah we are taught of several secret Divine Names hinted at in the letters of this verse, the most important of which is פאי, the initial letters of the first three words **פותח את ידך**, which equals 7 times 13. (7·13=91=אמן, "amen." אמן, in its sense of "craftsman," relates to the workings of the Divine Hand, as in the phrase **מעשה ידי אמן**, "the working of the hands of the craftsman.") Sustaining is thus the secret (the "craft" or "art") of the continual opening of the Divine Hand to extend His scepter of benevolence to every one of His creatures.

NUMBER

The letter *zayin* equals seven. The number seven possesses unique significance in Torah, as is said: "all sevens are beloved."

WORLDS

On a plane, seven is the number of "maximal compactness": six equal objects perfectly surround a seventh in the middle. (Six coins, for example, fit perfectly around a seventh coin of the same size.) The six days of Creation, together with Shabbat, the seventh, on which G-d rested and thus consummated and elevated the entire creative process, constitute the basic rhythm and cycle inherent in Creation. Every week defines a complete, self-contained cycle. Our Sages teach that on Shabbat one's mental attitude should be as though "all your work is done." On Shabbat one stands in the middle of complete, perfectly compact reality.

The cycle of seven repeats itself continually in ever-growing spirals of time, days, weeks, months, years, cycles of years, and millennia:

The seven weeks of counting the *omer*—"and you shall count for yourselves from the day after the Shabbat [i.e., *Pesach*] from the day you brought the omer of wave offering; seven complete Shabbats [i.e., weeks] shall there be"—is the period of time from the day after the Exodus from Egypt until the giving of the Torah, fifty days later, at Sinai.

The three festivals of the Torah—*Pesach, Shavuot* and *Sukot*—all fall within the seven months, beginning from *Nisan*, the New Year of months, until *Tishrei*, the New Year of years.

The *Shmitah*, or Sabbatical year, is the culmination of the seven-year cycle in Torah: "Six years you shall sow your field and six years you shall prune your vineyard and gather its fruit. But on the seventh year there shall be a complete Shabbat for the land, a Shabbat for G-d; you shall neither sow your field nor prune your vineyard." Besides the resting of the land on the seventh year, all produce becomes "ownerless," giving everyone an equal chance to share the bounty of the land. On the seventh year all debts become void.

Land returns to its original owner on the fiftieth or Jubilee year, after the culmination of seven times seven years.

The consummation of the six thousand years of this world, discussed in the number of the letter *vav*, will be the "Great Shabbat" subsequent to the Messianic era, a time of "all Shabbat and rest for eternal life."

Among the other important sevens of the Torah in relation to Worlds, are the seven fruits of Israel, the seven seas, the seven heavens, the seven chambers of Paradise, and so on.

SOULS

"The candle of G-d is the soul of man." The seven candles of the *menorah* in the Temple, correspond to the seven archetypal levels of souls of Israel.

The first category of souls are those who serve G-d with "love as water" (the experience of ever drawing nearer and "clinging" to G-d). The second category of souls serve G-d with "love as fire" (ecstatic, impassioned love). Others serve G-d primarily through Torah study; others are driven by the motivation to overcome evil and do good; others through humble acknowledgment of G-d's loving Providence; others with the uplifted spirit in the performance of G-d's Will befitting a king ("all Israel are princes"); and others with the sense of lowliness before G-d, ever returning to Him.

On the festival of *Sukot* we invite into our *sukah* seven spiritual guests, the ultimate sources of the seven archetypes of Jewish souls. These are the seven shepherds of Israel: Abraham, Isaac, Jacob, the three patriarchs; the two brothers Moses and Aaron, the giver of the Torah and the High Priest of Israel; Joseph, our sustainer throughout the seven-year famine in Egypt as well as the years to come; and King David, the ancestor of all future kings of Israel including the *Mashiach*.

The number seven appears in the wedding ceremony several times: the bride circles the groom seven times; seven blessings are recited; the celebration of the wedding is continued over a period of seven days, each day with renewed festive gatherings and the recitation of the same seven blessings.

The seven Rabbinic *mitzvot* complete the 613 mitzvot of Torah to 620, the numerical value of כתר, "the crown." The Sages (representative of all souls of Israel) are the "woman of valor" who is "the crown of her husband [G-d]"—the secret of the letter *zayin*.

DIVINITY

"There are seven eyes of G-d that traverse the entire earth." This meta-phor portrays G-d's Providence as "contracted" and revealed through the means of the "eyes" of the seven lower *sefirot*, which, in the soul of man, correspond to the seven attributes of the heart, the seven ways of serving G-d discussed above. G-d sees us through the Divine Sources of our own ways of serving Him.

The greatest revelation of Divine Providence occurs in the seventh month of the year, *Tishrei*. "*Tishrei*" (תשרי) exactly equals seven times עין, "eye" (910=7·130). The word *Tishrei* itself means "to look," as in the verse: תשורי מראש אמנה, "*see* from the head of faith." Just as our true sight is from our "head of faith" in G-d, so His Providence is from His "head of faith," his essential bond to us, His children.

Tishrei begins with G-d's judgement of each of His creations from *Rosh HaShanah* to *Yom Kippur*. These days of *teshuvah* are followed by the seven days of dwelling in the *sukah*, symbolic of the seven clouds of glory which accompanied and protected Israel throughout our forty-year sojourn in the desert. The four species (the three myrtle branches, two willows, one palm branch and one *etrog*, adding up to seven in all) are "shaken" to the six directions of physical space and then brought to the heart, the center of the seven emotive *sefirot*, the "middle point" in relation to the directions of space. On the seventh day of *Sukot*, *Hoshanah Rabbah*, seven *hakafot* or circles are made around the *bimah* of the synagogue. Finally, on *Simchat Torah*, the twenty-second day of *Tishrei* from *Rosh HaShanah* (the culmina-tion of the revelation of the twenty-two letters of the *alef-beit*), the entire process of *teshuvah* and revelation of Divine Providence reaches its consum-mation with seven joyous *hakafot* of dancing with the Torah.

Chet

רָצוֹא וָשׁוֹב

The Life Dynamic: Run and Return

Chet: The Life Dynamic—Run and Return

Chet is the letter of "life" (חיים, from the root חיה, whose most important letter is *chet*). We are taught in *Chassidut* that there are two levels of
life: "essential life" (חי בעצם) and "life to enliven" (חיים להחיות). G-d Himself, as it were, is in the state of "Essential life." His creative power, continually permeating all of reality is "life to enliven." So in the Jewish soul: the
essence of its root, at one with G-d, possesses the state of "essential life."
The reflection of the light of the soul which shines below to enliven the
body and its physical experience is at the level of "life to enliven." The second level of life, life as we know it in general, manifests itself as pulsation,
the secret of "run and return."

According to the Arizal, the letter *chet* is constructed by combining the
two previous letters, *vav* and *zayin*, with a thin bridge-shaped line, referred
to as the *chatoteret* ("hunchback"). The new energy effected by the union of
the *vav*—or *yashar*—and the *zayin*—or *chozer*—is the secret of "hovering"
or "touching yet not touching." The image of "hovering" appears at the very
beginning of Creation: "And the spirit of G-d was hovering over the water."
The word "hovering" (מרחפת) is the eighteenth (=חי) word in the Torah. It
is the first word in the Torah which is numerically a multiple of twenty-six,
the value of the Name *Havayah* (מרחפת=728=26·28). Twenty-eight is the
numerical value of כח, "power." Thus, the full secret implied by the numerical value of the word "hovering" is "the power of G-d." In Kabbalah, this
word is, in particular, the secret of the Divine power to resurrect the 288
fallen sparks that "died" in the process of the "breaking of the vessels"
(מרחפת being a permutation of מת רפ"ח, "288 have died"). The Sages teach
us that the "Spirit of G-d" here referred to is in fact the soul of *Mashiach*
(שם חי משיח:, "the living name").

"Hovering" is symbolized in Torah "as an eagle arouses her nest and
hovers over her young," as taught by the Maggid of Mezeritch. In order not
to crush her young and their nest, the eagle hovers over her nest when feed-
ing her young, "touching yet not touching." The eagle here is a metaphor for
G-d in relation to His children Israel in particular and to the totality of His
Creation in general. Were G-d to either fully reveal His ultimate Presence or
withdraw His power of continual re-Creation, the world would instantaneously cease to exist.

Therefore, by "hovering" over created reality, G-d continues to sustain
and nourish His Creation while simultaneously allowing each creature or, in

the terminology of Kabbalah, each vessel, the ability to grow and develop "independently." The letter *chet* thus hints at the delicate balance between the revelation of G-d's Presence to us (the *vav* of the *chet*) and the concealment of His creative power from His Creation (the *zayin* of the *chet*).

This state of hovering, "touching yet not touching," is the beginning of the phenomenon of "life to enliven." "Touching yet not touching" from Above thereafter reflects itself as "run and return" in the inner pulsation of every living creature. "And the living creatures run and return like the appearance of lightning." "Do not read *chayot* [חיות, 'living creatures'] but *chayut* [חיות, 'lifeforce']."

The *chatoteret*, that sublime thin line that connects the two components or motion of the "life to enliven," itself points upward. It hints at "He who lives at the summit of the world," G-d's "Essential Life." In truth, His Essence paradoxically fills and sustains all created reality while simultaneously hovering high above the level of the hovering lifeforce itself, unfathomable and beyond all human perception.

CHET

FORM: A *vav* on the right, a *zayin* on the left, with a thin, "hunchback" bridge (*chatoteret*) connecting them above.

Worlds A gateway: the power to enter a higher energy level and exit therefrom.
The ascent of all worlds on Shabbat and their subsequent descent after Shabbat.
(At the level of Souls: the power to enter the mysteries of one's own soul and thereafter return to worldy consciousness.)
(At the level of Divinity: the power to enter the mysteries of the Torah and thereafter return to the consciousness of one's task on earth.)

Souls The union of "three partners in man": father (*vav*), mother (*zayin*), and G-d (*chatoteret, chupah*).
The marital dance.

Divinity "G-d lives at the summit of the world"—the *chatoteret*.
G-d hovering over Creation.
The union of G-d's immanence, transcendence, and the Jewish people.

NAME: Fear; Life—whose full expression is love.

Worlds Loving G-d with one's physical body.
Lifeforce of the body.

Souls Loving G-d with one's soul.
Lifeforce of the soul.
The heartbeat of the *tzadik*.

Divinity Essential unity with G-d.
Lifeforce of life itself.
Resurrection of the dead.

NUMBER: Eight

Worlds Eight vertices of a cube.
Three-dimensional plurality.
"G-d is one in the seven heavens and the earth."

Souls The eighth day—the day of circumcision.
The eight days of *Chanukah*—"The candle of G-d is the soul of man."
The circumcision of the foreskin of the lips on (*Zot*) Chanukah.
The circumcision of the foreskin of the ears on the eighth day of *Sukot*.
The circumcision of the foreskin of the heart on *Yom Kippur*, the eighth day of the High Priest's separation.

Divinity Gateway to infinity.
G-d's Transcendent Light.
Origin of the Jewish soul and its descent through the seven heavens to earth.

FORM

The form of the *chet* is the product of the two letters preceding it: a *vav* on the right, a *zayin* on the left with a thin bridge connecting them above.

WORLDS

The form of the letter *chet* resembles a gateway. Through a gateway one enters and exits. One enters into an inner realm or chamber, a deeper state of awareness, a truer level of experience. One exits to return to one's previous, stable state of existence, infused with the light of one's new experience.

At the level of Worlds we find a plenitude of phenomena where an object or particle (especially the sub-atomic elementary particles of quantum mechanics) enters a higher energy level only thereafter to return to a lower energy level. A more spiritual example: before Shabbat, all created worlds begin to ascend (each world to that above it, to an altogether higher spiritual-energy level). After Shabbat the worlds descend to their original "space," infused with new lifeforce for the coming week.

(At the higher levels of Souls and Divinity the gateway symbolizes the power to enter into the inner mysteries of one's own soul [Souls] and the secrets of Torah [Divinity]. Subsequently, one must exit and return to one's original low-energy state in order to perform one's task on earth, inspired by new insight.)

The *Zohar* teaches that the ability to exit is greater than that to enter. The ascending light represented by the *zayin* on the left of the *chet* is the ability to enter. The descending light represented by the *vav* on the right of the *chet* is the ability to exit. "He who knows only to enter but not to exit better not to enter."

SOULS

The union of the *vav* and the *zayin*, by means of the *chatoteret*, in the form of the letter *chet*, alludes to the secret of conception of new life, the basic meaning of the name *chet*.

"There are three partners in man: the Holy One Blessed Be He (alluded to by the *chatoteret*), his father (the *vav* of the *chet*), and his mother (the *zayin* of the *chet*)." G-d (the secret of "Essential Life," as explained above) draws together and unites father and mother, groom and bride ("life to enliven"). This is the secret of the wedding canopy, the *chupah* (חפה, read: ח' פה, "[the power of] the *chet* is here"), under which the groom and bride enter into the covenant of marriage.

By dividing the *pei* of *chupah* (חפה) into its two numerical components, *lamed* and *nun* (in the secret of the expression: פנים אל פנים, "face to face"), the word *chupah* becomes the two word phrase: חן לה, "grace unto her." This alludes to the power of the *chupah*, whose impression remains throughout marriage, to effect the holy balance (whose manifestation is the state of "looking face to face," as explained in *Safra d'Tzniuta*, "The Book of Modesty," the deepest section of the *Zohar*) of bride and groom, continuously finding favor one in the eyes of the other. The *nun* of חן ("grace") is the secret of the son, the "heir to the throne," (as will be explained in the letter *nun*) born from the marriage of groom and bride as pictured by the *chet*.

The holy balance of marital relation in Torah, whose outer manifestation is the laws of family purity, is the secret of the "dance" back and forth, as taught by the Ba'al Shem Tov, in interpretation of the verse: "then shall the maiden be joyous in dance." In the "*mitzvah*-dance," the groom and the bride take hold of a sash or kerchief, which, in a true state of ecstasy, arches upward, pointing at "He who lives at the summit of the world." This ability of souls to regularly, in proper rhythm, enter and exit (dance back and forth) as it were, in relation to one another, constantly augments the essence of the marital covenant.

DIVINITY

As explained above, the *chatoteret*, bridging the two more tangible components of the *chet*, the *vav* and the *zayin*, points upward to "He who lives at the summit (רומו) of the world." The word for "summit," רום, also means "exalted." Exaltation is, in truth, a revelation of Divinity which permeates all worlds, though at every point of reality the light of the "exalted one" appears to ascend and disappear into the "summit," as taught in *Chassidut*. G-d's "Essential Life" (חי בעצם), though absolutely transcendent on the one hand, nonetheless permeates all of reality ("the world") with a sense of Divine exaltation. This sense serves to elevate all lower forms of life to the "Life of all life," Blessed be He.

"G-d, You are my G-d, I will exalt you and give thanks to Your Name, for You have done wonders, counsels from afar in true faithfulness." "Counsels from afar" is interpreted to mean promises from the times of old; "in true faithfulness" to the time when all will become realized and fulfilled. "In true faithfulness" (אמונה אמן—two forms of the same root) implies the absolute bond and covenant of marriage between G-d and the souls of Israel. "Faithfulness" (אמונה) is the secret of the bond of the bride to groom, the *zayin* of the *chet*; "True" (אמן) is the secret of the bond of the groom (G-d's Immanence) to bride, the *vav* of the *chet*. "Counsels from afar" (עצות מרחק) is the secret of *chatoteret* of the *chet* pointing upwards at the "Exalted One" (G-d's Transcendence), the *"far* encompassing Light" in the terminology of *Chassidut*.

NAME

The word *chet* (חית) means both "life" (חיות), and "fear" (as in חתת
אלקים, "the fear of G-d"). Life and fear are related, as stated in Proverbs:
יראת ה' לחיים, "Fear of G-d to [i.e., is the source of] life."

The experience of life begins with an experience of fear, the "shock" of
"becoming alive," the experience of the first "life pulse." Thereafter one's
consciousness expands into full life-consciousness. As one's awareness of
life grows, one senses more and more *good* throughout reality, as expressed
in the verse: "See, I have placed before you today life and good...." Perceiving good is the basis of an optimistic attitude towards life in general. Placing
one's emphasis on the perception of evil around him, the basis of pessimism,
derives from a general experience of reality more inclined to death than to
life, as the verse continues: "...and death and evil."

The experience of life arouses the power of attraction to the essential
good inherent in life, thereby converting the initial point of fear into the full
expression of love. Love, ultimately the love of G-d, the Absolute Good, is
thus the final expression of the experience of life, the secret of the *chet*. The
Torah teaches us to love G-d "for He is your life." This love is manifest on
three levels, corresponding to Worlds, Souls, and Divinity. Each level begins
from an initial point of fear, "shocking" the "vessel" at that level into a state
of pulsation, life.

WORLDS

The first level of loving G-d, as experienced at the level of Worlds, is
that love which derives from the full consciousness of the lifeforce inherent
in physical reality, particularly the life of one's own body. For the Jew, the
full experience of the lifeforce flowing through all the limbs of his body
(חיי הגוף) relates to the state of serving G-d with each and every bodily
movement and breath.

In Psalms, King David proclaims: "All my bones [i.e. limbs] say 'G-d,
who is like unto you...' " and "Every soul [or 'breath'] shall praise G-d, Hallelujah."

In the first verse, the Name *Havayah*, which corresponds to G-d's attribute of Infinite mercy over all of His Creation, is used. This implies that
every bodily movement should express ("say"), with full consciousness,
G-d's Mercy responsible for one's ability to move and "working" through the
limbs of one's body. The second verse uses the two-lettered Name, *yud-kei*

(י-ה, the first two letters of the Name *Havayah*), the Name of Divine Wisdom in Kabbalah. This implies that the act of breath, in particular, entails the experience of G-d's Wisdom in Creation.

In *Chassidut* we are taught that the physical experience of loving G-d can actually result in increased heartbeat and breath, similar to the physical experience of loving another individual.

SOULS

The second level of loving G-d derives from the full experience of the lifeforce inherent in the soul itself, חיי הנשמה, "Life of the Soul." At this level one's continual service of G-d manifests itself as ever-increasing awareness and concern for the spiritual well-being of other souls, connected in essence to one's own soul. The true, unselfish experience of another soul depends upon one's ability to abstract the experience of one's own soul from that of the body, as explained in *Tanya*. Here, the concept of "body" includes one's "self-image" at all levels of experience. One's self-image must be transcended in order to truly relate, in love, to another soul, as expounded by the present Lubavitcher Rebbe, *shlita*.

Just as the lifeforce innate in the body is in a continual state of "run and return," so too, the spiritual lifeforce connecting the souls of Israel, in their communal service of G-d, is in a state of "run and return." This is so because all Jewish souls constitute one organic whole, whose heart and other vital organs correspond to the *tzadikim* of the generation. The heartbeat of the *tzadik* impresses itself upon other souls of the generation who might otherwise be unable to experience this level of love. The conscious recognition of this dependency on the *tzadik* is referred to as being "face-to-face" with the *tzadik*. If this truth be unconscious, one is referred to as being "back-to-back" with the *tzadik* yet, nonetheless, receiving the potential of this level of love through the means of the *tzadik*'s soul.

DIVINITY

The third and highest form of loving G-d entails the ultimate experience of G-d Himself as being the חיי החיים, "Life of life." Though the previous levels of life reflect the Presence (and Goodness) of G-d, only at this level is the Divine Presence fully revealed. Life itself must live in G-d. If not, even the spiritual experience of the life of the soul can degenerate into the experience of physical life alone, and further degenerate into more and more mundane experiences of mere "reflections" of life until ultimately falling into death, the opposite of life. The "Life of life" keeps life alive. Moreover, not only does the "Life of life" save life from falling into the pit of death, but in it is the power of G-d to resurrect the dead from the grave.

Having achieved perfect awareness that all forms of life and lifelessness are equally dependent upon the One Essential "Life of life," the prophet or Sage receives, from the Hand of G-d, the "key of resurrection." "Even the smallest of you is able to resurrect the dead," is said of the *Tanaim*, the Sages of the Oral Torah. The power to enliven is manifest in the mouth, as the words of the "living Torah" become alive when uttered by the mouth of the Sage (and, so too, every Jew truly devoted to Torah). So do we find in relation to Elijah, after he resurrected the son of the Tzarfit woman: "Now I know that the word of G-d is true *in your mouth*." This is also the secret of the *chupah* (חפה), explained above, the lifeforce of the letter *chet* (ח) as revealed through the mouth (פה).

NUMBER

The letter *chet* equals eight.

WORLDS

In physical three-dimensional space, the number eight appears as the number of vertices of a cube. A vertex, a point, is dimensionless. The cube possesses, as well, twelve lines (of one dimension) and six sides (surfaces, of two dimensions). The numbers of these three lower-dimensional levels of the three-dimensional cube—8, 12, 6—total 26, the numerical value of G-d's Essential Name *Havayah*. The number twenty-six itself reduces (by summing its two digits) to eight, thus indicating that the essence of the cube is defined by its eight vertex-points. Eight here appears as the number which reflects the Divine Essence in physical reality.

The eight points of the three-dimensional cube correspond to the four points that define a two-dimensional square or the two points that define a one-dimensional line. Two, four, and eight are the first three powers of two (after $2^0=1$, the zero-dimensional point itself). So, a four-dimensional "cube" is defined by sixteen ($=2^4$) points and a five-dimensional "cube" by thirty two ($=2^5$) points, etc. The exponential series of 2^n is basic to nature. Just as two was explained to represent the origin of plurality in Creation, so 2^n represents the evolution and development (successive "interinclusion") of pluralistic phenomenology throughout nature. Eight is thus understood to represent three-dimensional plurality.

The word *echad* (אחד, "one") is interpreted to read: "G-d is one (א=1) in the seven heavens and the earth (ח=8) and the four directions of the earth (ד=4)." Here, eight represents the plurality of the dimension of "height" in particular (the initial "sensation" of "dimension" in three-dimensional reality, as explained in *Chassidut*). The division of eight into seven (heavens) and one (earth) corresponds to the phenomenon that seven of the eight points of the cube are visible at once, whereas the eighth remains concealed, as taught in Kabbalah.

The *dalet* ($=4$) of *echad* begins the "return" of plurality towards the direction of unity. From an even deeper perspective, just as the product of two negations becomes positive, so, in Torah, "a plurality after a plurality comes to diminish," as though the product of two pluses becomes a minus (in ultimate truth, anything other than the middle zero point of a linear coordinate is "negative" relative to absolute unity). Thus every even ("finite") power of two (as four, the *dalet* of *echad*, $4=2^2$) implies a "return" to unity, whereas every odd ("male") power of two (as eight, the *chet* of *echad*; $8=2^3$) implies a "surge" ahead in the pluralistic process of Creation. Every even power of two is itself a square (a perfect unit), whereas every odd power of two is a double-square (as two itself, the origin of plurality).

SOULS

The Torah prescribes that the circumcision of a male child take place on the eighth day from birth. These eight days must always include at least one Shabbat, the seventh day, which corresponds to the experience of perfect harmony within nature. The eighth day of circumcision represents the power of the soul to contact that light which totally transcends nature. Through circumcision the Jew is given the power, throughout his life, to overcome all of the obstacles nature may seem to place in the face of his service of G-d.

The eight days of *Chanukah* commemorate one of the greatest expressions of the Jewish soul to overcome the obstacles of nature. Spiritually, the Hellenistic adversity to the Jewish Way was the battle of secular philosophy, based on superficial understanding of nature, against the Divine insight of Torah, as directly perceived by the innermost point of the Jewish soul. The revelation of the Transcendent Light inherent in the soul and the ability to be triumphant in the face of adversity are central themes in our lighting candles during the eight days of *Chanukah*. On *Chanukah* we light a total of thirty-six candles ($1\bot2\bot3\bot...\bot8=36$), corresponding to the thirty-six *tzadikim* (the *tzadik* is the secret of the power inherent in circumcision, as explained in Kabbalah and *Chassidut*) of the generation, from whom all of the souls of the generation receive inspiration and might.

By intently observing (contemplating) the *Chanukah* candles and remembering the miracle, one's mouth is spontaneously opened to give thanks and praise to G-d, as we say in the *HaNeirot Halalu* prayer after lighting the candles. This is referred to as "the circumcision of the foreskin of the lips," through the means of the rectification of the eyes, a process which takes eight days.

The Torah speaks of four foreskins of the body (physiological/psychological barriers in the way of true expression): the foreskin of the flesh; the foreskin of the lips; the foreskin of the ears; the foreskin of the heart. Each foreskin must be circumcised on the eighth day. The foreskin of the flesh is circumcised on the eighth day from birth; the foreskin of the lips on the eight days of *Chanukah*, especially on the last day—*Zot Chanukah* (the eighth day of *Chanukah* is called "this is *Chanukah*," for on it all of the eight days combine, as it were, in consummate revelation); the foreskin of the ears on the eighth day of *Sukot*—*Shmini Atzeret-Simchat Torah* ("The joy of the Torah," when heard and comprehended fully); the foreskin of the heart on *Yom Kippur* (the eighth day that the high priest was separated from his home in order to prepare for the service of the most Holy Day of the year), the culmination of *teshuvah*, the circumcision of the heart to return to G-d.

Thus the secret of eight reveals itself in four "directions," the secret of the *chet* (ח=8) and *dalet* (ד=4) of *echad* (אחד), the "return" of eight, through four, to one (א=1).

DIVINITY

At the level of Divinity, the number eight alludes to the absolute Infinity of G-d. This level of Infinity is the same as the secret of "He who lives at the summit of the world," alluded to through the *chatoteret* of the letter *chet*, as explained above. Whereas at the level of Souls, circumcision gives one the power to overcome obstacles, at this level awareness of G-d's true Infinity links one, in covenant, to His very Essence.

When linked to Infinity, overcoming obstacles, even death, the secret of resurrection, becomes self-evident and "second nature." When absolutely connected to the Infinite One, there can in truth be no obstacle.

From this level of sacred covenant, the souls of Israel are drawn. From the "summit of the world" the souls descend from their ultimate source in the Essence of G-d, through seven heavens until reaching earth, the physical body. This is the secret of the conception of a Jewish child, as symbolized by the letter *chet*.

אחד היה אברהם, "Abraham was one." The first Jew, and, by virtue of inheritance—in addition to the dictum: "The deeds of the fathers are signposts for the children"—all Jews after him, fully integrated and expressed in his life the secret of the Divine *One*. The root of the Jewish soul in the very Essence of G-d is the secret of the *alef* of אחד, "one." The "journey" of the soul in its "becoming" ("a part of the Creator becomes created")—its descent through seven heavens to earth until entering a physical body—is the secret of the *chet* of אחד, "one."

The Sages teach us that upon the culmination of the soul's descent to this world, at the moment of birth, it is "sworn in" to be a *tzadik*. The function of this oath is to "satiate" it (שבע, "to swear" as well as "to satiate") with Divine Power to overcome all of the obstacles of life. The experience of the oath itself, upon the culmination of the journey of eight, infuses the soul with consciousness of its essential bond to the Infinite, from which perspective there can, in truth, be no obstacle in the way of fulfilling G-d's Will on earth.

Tet

טוּבְיָה גָּנִיז בְּגַוֵּיה

Introversion: The Concealed Good

Tet: Introversion—the Concealed Good

The *tet* (ט) is the initial letter of the word טוב, "good." The form of the *tet* is "inverted," thus symbolizing hidden, inverted good—as expressed in the *Zohar:* טוביה גניז בגוייה, "its good is hidden within it." The form of the letter *chet* symbolizes the union of groom and bride consummating with conception. The secret of the *tet* (numerically equivalent to nine, the nine months of pregnancy) is the power of the mother to carry her inner, concealed good—the fetus—throughout the period of pregnancy.

Pregnancy is the power to bring the potential to actualization. The revelation of new, actual energy, the revelation of birth, is the secret of the next letter of the *alef-bet*, the *yud*. The *yud* reveals the point of "Essential Life" as realized in the secret of conception of the *chet* and carried, impregnant, in the *tet*.

Of the eight synonyms for "beauty" in Hebrew, טוב—"good"—refers to the most inner, inverted, and "modest" state of beauty. This level of beauty is that personified in Torah by Rebecca and Bat Sheva, who are described as טובת מראה מאד, "very *beautiful* [goodly] in appearance."

At the beginning of Creation, the appearance of light is termed "good" in G-d's eyes: "And G-d saw the light was good." Our Sages interpret this to mean "good to be hidden for the *tzadikim* in the Time to Come." "And where did He hide it? In the Torah, for 'there is no good other than Torah.' "

The Ba'al Shem Tov teaches that the "Time to Come" refers also to each and every generation. Each soul of Israel is a potential *tzadik* (as it is said: "and your people are *all tzadikim*"), connected to the goodly light hidden in Torah. The more one actualizes his potential to be a *tzadik*, the more goodness he reveals from the Torah "womb."

In the first verse of the Torah—"In the beginning G-d created the heavens and the earth"—the initial letters of את השמים ואת הארץ ("the heavens and the earth") spell אהוי״ה, G-d's "hidden Name" in Creation, according to Kabbalah. The numerical value of this name is seventeen, the same as that of the word טוב, "good." The word *tzadik* (צדיק) equals $12 \cdot 17 = 204$, the total value of the twelve permutations of the four letters of this hidden Name. *Tzadikim*, who are called "good," possess the power of the hidden Name (derived from "the heavens and the earth"), the hidden goodness needed to unite heaven and earth and thereby reveal the inner light and purpose of Creation. Just as the *alef* possesses the power to bear opposites—the power of the firmament to join the higher and lower waters together—so does the *tet* possess the power to unite the upper and lower worlds, "heavens and earth." *Chassidut* teaches that in the service of the soul, this power is manifest in man when he assumes the state of being "in the world yet out of the world" simultaneously. To be "in the world" means to be fully consciousness of worldly reality in order to rectify it. To be "out of the world" means to be fully aware that in truth "there is none other besides Him."

Another connection between light and good is found in the story of the birth of Moses: "And she [Yocheved, Moses's mother] saw him that he was good [טוב]." Rashi quotes the Midrash, which explains that at the birth of Moses a great light filled the room. According to the early *Masorah*, the *tet* in the word טוב of this verse is written extra large. This hints at the Absolute Divine Good entrusted to the soul of Moses, whose life mission was to fulfill the promise of redemption from Egypt and the revelation of Torah at Sinai. The Egyptian exile is compared to a womb in which Israel was latently pregnant for two hundred and ten years. At Sinai, heaven and earth were united, as discussed in the letter *alef*.

Thus, the full teaching of the *tet* is that, through the service of the soul, all of reality becomes "pregnant" with G-d's Infinite goodness and beauty, thereby bringing harmony and peace to "heavens and earth."

TET

FORM: A vessel with an inverted rim; the *sefirah* of *yesod*; peace.

Worlds Form hidden in matter.
Potential hidden in actual.
Peace among the elements of Creation.
Peace between water and fire in heaven: "He who makes peace on high."

Souls The soul hidden in the body.
Peace among the souls of Israel.
The outer womb: the impure world; the inner womb: the pure aspiration of the soul.

Divinity G-d hidden within His Creation.
Future revelation of universal peace.
G-d's presence impregnant in the world.

NAME: Inclination; staff—snake; below; bed.

Worlds The snake in the Garden of Eden: the liver; innate behavior patterns.
Lower worldly inclinations.
The tendency to lie.

Souls The power to judge properly.
The correct power of imagination.
The twelve tribes of Israel.
The twelve senses.

Divinity The breastplate of the High Priest.
The bed—unity of man and wife in the Presence of G-d.
Torah cantillation.

NUMBER: Nine

Worlds Nine physical materials that form vessels which contract impurity.
Nine levels of peace.
Nine *sefirot* pouring blessing into *malchut*.

Souls The nine months of pregnancy.
The nine positive commandments in the laws of Foundation and Character.

Divinity The numerical symbol of truth and eternity.
Nine blessings of *Musaf* on *Rosh HaShanah*.
Nine blasts of the *shofar*.
Eternal life.

FORM

The *tet* (ט) resembles a vessel with an inverted rim, a vessel containing the blessing of peace. *Tet*, the ninth letter of the *alef-bet*, corresponds to the ninth Divine *sefirah, yesod* ("Foundation"), the *sefirah* symbolizing peace. Peace is the only vessel capable of containing blessing, as our Sages teach: "The Holy One, Blessed be He, found no vessel that could hold blessing for Israel other than peace." To the degree that one is first blessed with peace (as the Priestly Blessing concludes: "...and He shall grant you peace"), so does one become an ever more potent "vessel" to receive "additional" blessing directly from the mouth of G-d (as is said in the verse following the Priestly Blessing: "And they [the *kohanim*] shall place My Name ['Peace,' a Name of G-d] on the People of Israel, and *I* will bless them").

WORLDS

At the physical level, the property of introversion, as illustrated by the *tet*, signifies form hidden in matter or potential hidden in actual. At the level of Worlds, peace, as symbolized by the *tet*, represents the peace that exists between the elements of Creation.

In Torah, the primary example of peace between the elements of nature is the secret of the word שמים, "heaven." Our Sages interpret this word as comprising two elements: אש, "fire," and מים, "water." Heaven—i.e., spiritual reality relative to earthly reality—manifests harmony and peace between the elements of nature. The task of the Jew is to draw down the "days [revelations] of heaven onto earth," to reveal harmony and peace universally. "He makes peace in His heights"—"Michael, the angel of water, and Gabriel, the angel of fire, do not extinguish one another." The two opposite forces of nature, represented by the two archangels, Michael and Gabriel, reside together in peace, for both nullify their individuality in awe before the Creator. This is the level of consciousness characteristic of heaven.

SOULS

Just as, at the level of Worlds, the *tet* symbolizes form as present within matter, so too, at the level of Souls, the *tet* symbolizes the soul as hidden within the body. Throughout the nine months of pregnancy, the mother constantly aspires to the moment of birth, the visible manifestation of fulfillment. Similarly, the souls of Israel aspire mutually to bear a world of truth and good out of the womb-context (the *tet*) of our present world of deceit and suffering. This peace of unity between souls, when striving together for true peace on earth, enables us even in the present to receive the blessing of G-d.

Thus, there exist simultaneously an outer womb and an inner womb. The outer womb is the reality of the present world of deceit and suffering. The inner womb is the common aspiration of the souls of Israel for a world of peace and good. Within this aspiration (the inner womb) the new world (the fetus) nurtures. The new world is, in fact, Worlds at the level of Souls. It is the final fruition of G-d's blessing to Souls: ultimately Souls return to their origin in Divinity and Worlds reach the level of Souls.

The outer womb is the *tet* of טמא, "impure." The inner womb is the *tet* of טהור, "pure." "Who can give [i.e., produce] pure from impure, only One." When the purity of the souls of Israel (in their aspiration for redemption) becomes manifest as ever present within the impurity of the present world, the ultimate power of the "one" becomes known, the power of good (טוב, "good" transforms into אחד, "one," in *atbach*) to unite the "new heaven and new earth," the secret of the *tet*.

DIVINITY

The two states of Divine Transcendence and Immanence both involve an aspect of hiddenness, symbolized by the *tet*. Divine Transcendence implies, from our human perspective, a certain withdrawal from active involvement in worldly affairs. Divine Immanence, though permeating the consciousness of all levels of Creation, must nonetheless be concealed to a large extent so as to endow Creation with a sense of independence and man with free choice.

The root of the word עולם, "world," means "concealment," as in the verse: זה שמי לעלם, "This is My Name forever," which our Sages read: "this is My Name to conceal." "My Name" refers in particular to the blessing of peace which concludes the Priestly Blessing: "...and He shall grant you peace. And they shall place My Name on the people of Israel and I will bless them." From the word שמי ("My Name"), our Sages learn that the word שלום, "peace"—which numerically equals שמי ה', "My name is *Havayah*"— is itself a Name of G-d.

Thus, at the level of Divinity, the *tet* represents the concealment of G-d's essential Name throughout reality. The essential property of the Name is mercy; by emulating G-d's mercy we reveal His Name, and thus actualize the potential (impregnant) Divine peace inherent in Creation.

The root of עולם, "world" (and "forever"), also means "maiden": "Behold the maiden (העלמה) is pregnant and will bear a son, and shall call his name Immanuel ['G-d is with us']." In this verse the word "son," בן, equals 52, while his name, Immanuel, עמנואל, equals 197. This alludes to the "impregnant" secret of the first day of Creation (hidden light—good; union of heavens and earth), whose account in the beginning of the Torah contains 52 words and 197 letters.

NAME

The *tet* (טית) is the basic consonant letter in the words מטה ("staff"), הטיה ("inclination"), מטה ("below"), and מטה ("bed"). The symbol of the staff is related to that of the snake, as in the story of the Divine sign which Moses performed before Pharoah of the staff becoming a snake. According to Kabbalah, the *tet* resembles a snake coiled head into tail.

WORLDS

In the story of the Garden of Eden the three characters are man, woman, and snake. In physiology (and the parallel concepts in psychology) they correspond to brain, heart, and liver; intelligence, emotion, and innate characteristics and habits, respectively. The downward propensity of the snake, when rectified, serves to productively connect us to the physical world. Indeed, the snake was originally intended to be the "great servant of man," as taught by the Sages. But when left unrectified, the snake leads one to self-destruction and to fall below his intended place (exile from the Garden of Eden). "Behaviorism" then rules over man. The inner qualities of mind and heart become enslaved to the habitual characteristics of "first (unrectified) nature."

According to the Sages, the snake has a gestation period of seven years. As taught by Rabbi Pinchas of Koretz, one of the great disciples of the Ba'al Shem Tov, in relation to the tendency to lie, the primordial tendency of the snake, it takes seven years of devoted spiritual labor to uproot and begin to rectify an innate character trait. Another seven years is necessary to recognize and relate to truth, and a final seven years is necessary to fully integrate truth into one's being, until it becomes "second nature." (טבע שני ["Second nature"] = אמת ["truth"] = 21^2 = $[3 \cdot 7]^2$.) The first seven years (snake pregnancy) rectifies the liver; the second seven years, the heart (in relation to liver); the third seven years, the mind (in full, productive control of heart over liver, form over matter).

SOULS

At the level of Souls, the snake represents the power to judge properly. False judgement—guessing—is the inclination of the unrectified power of imagination of the animal soul and the innate property of the primordial snake. The word נחש, "snake," also means "to guess." "Guessing" is one of the magical practices of ancient Canaanite culture forbidden by Torah: ולא תנחשו, "you shall not guess."

In praising the character of the Jewish people, Balaam said: כי לא נחש ביעקב, "for there is no guessing in Jacob." Jacob corresponds to the attribute of truth, true judgement, as is said: "Give truth to Jacob." His son Joseph, the most essential "extension" of Jacob's property of simple truth, personifies the power to rectify imagination and what would otherwise be considered guessing. Joseph said to his brothers (who didn't recognize him): כי נחש ינחש איש אשר כמוני, "For a man like me is surely able to guess."

The ultimate rectification of the guessing nature of imagination, the consummate conversion of imagination into the rainbow of manifestations of "Divine Inspiration" (רוח הקודש), is the task of the *Mashiach*. For this reason we are taught that "*Mashiach*" (משיח) equals "snake" (נחש, 358). He will kill the evil snake and thereupon be given the "princess" (the pregnant maiden discussed above), the consciousness of "Divine Inspiration" in prayer, as taught in the *Zohar*.

The twelve tribes of Israel are referred to as "staffs." The word מטה, "staff," the secret of the letter *tet*, means "inclination." Each tribe represents a unique "sense," as taught in *Sefer Yetzirah*. A "sense" is a specific means through which the soul contacts (in order thereby to rectify) reality. Each "sense" is a definite inclination of soul as how to relate to experience. Whereas all worldly senses are downward in nature, the senses represented by the tribes of Israel are upward, aspiring to ever higher levels of Divine consciousness, in relation to both spiritual and material experience.

DIVINITY

חשן, the breastplate worn by the High Priest in his Temple service, is a permutation of נחש, "snake." The names of the tribes were inscribed upon twelve precious stones affixed to the breastplate. When the King would pose the High Priest a fateful question (such as whether or not Israel should go to war), certain letters of the breastplate would shine. The High Priest, if worthy to receive "Divine Inspiration," would be able to permute the letters—illuminated by virtue of a secret Name of G-d written on a parchment concealed within the breastplate—into a meaningful answer.

The full name of the breastplate, חשן משפט, means "breastplate of judgement." Our Sages teach that its purpose was to rectify the property of judgement in the soul and to atone for false judgement. The breastplate is thus the Divine aid to confront the primordial snake in the soul, kill its evil manifestation, and "clarify" its latent potential.

The *tet* as "bed" (מטה) symbolizes the spiritual as well as physical setting of man and wife uniting for the sake of drawing new souls into the world. This can be understood in relation to all three levels of Worlds, Souls, and Divinity. At the level of Divinity, the *Shechinah,* the Divine Presence of G-d, the third partner in the act of conception, is revealed above the bed of man, as the Sages say in reference to the bed of our father Jacob, the Divine setting of the birth of the twelve tribes of Israel.

The meaning of "inclination" at this level is purely superconsciousness, yet reflected by the musical intonations of speech. In the reading of the Torah this is the secret of traditional Torah cantillation (טעמים, literally "tastes" or "reasons"). The forms of the signs of the various cantillation marks resemble different positions and motions of a (rectified, controlled) snake, as taught in Kabbalah. As the wisdom concealed in the cantillation is superconscious, its revelation awaits the coming of *Mashiach,* as taught by the Sages.

NUMBER

The letter *tet* equals nine.

WORLDS

In Torah, nine physical materials form vessels which contract impurity: metal, wood, skin, bone, cloth, sack, pottery, nitrium, and glass. The first eight of these nine categories are specifically mentioned in the Written Torah. The ninth, glass, is an addition of the Oral Torah, a Rabbinic injunction. Glass, although a physical material, is nonetheless at the relative level of "Souls in Worlds." Glass symbolizes the inner womb of the *tet* within the outer womb, discussed above. Job speaks of a form of glass more precious than gold, for, in a certain sense, glass epitomizes the rectification of physical substance—conveying and even directing (enlarging or reducing the effect of) light. The word זכוכית, "glass," derives from the two letter root זך, "pure" and "refined" (whose reduced numerical value is nine), as in שמן זית זך, "*pure* olive oil" (the "source of light" [מאור] in the Temple). Its numerical value (463) is related to the Ba'al Shem Tov's "meditation for immersion in a *mikvah*," the secret of purity. Prophecy, the ultimate rectification of the "guess" of the snake (referred to as "the coarse skin" of physical consciousness in Kabbalah), is referred to as a glass pane. Moses's prophecy was through אספקלריא המאירה, the "transparent pane," whereas that of all other prophets was through אספקלריא שאינה מאירה, the "translucent pane" (or the indirect, "mirror" vision).

The capacity and conduciveness of the vessels ("wombs") formed of these nine substances to become impure implies their inherent relationship to the categories of purity and impurity in general. When pure, these vessels symbolize nine levels of peace into which may be drawn the blessings of G-d.

In the terminology of the Kabbalah, each vessel is an aspect (i.e. particular sub-*sefirah*) of the *sefirah* of *malchut*, kingdom, the "lower mother." When pure (i.e. not in a state of exile, the exile of the kingdom of Israel), each receives the flow of blessing from the corresponding *sefirah* of the nine *sefirot* above it.

SOULS

The number nine at the level of Souls relates to the nine months of pregnancy. Both the form of the *tet* as well as its number allude to the great wonder of new life being nurtured within the mother's womb. In the truest sense, a woman is the vessel wherein potential becomes actual. Through her, the spiritual blessing of a new soul descends into a physical body of this world.

Nine months of pregnancy are necessary for the complete development of the nine general divisions of body and soul. The three general levels of head, body (above abdomen), and feet (below abdomen) each divide into three. Each of the resulting nine further develops by means of interinclusion, into $9 \cdot 9 = 81$, and thereafter each of the 81 divides into three strata of inner, middle, and outer limbs: $81 \cdot 3 = 243$. An additional five limbs are added by means of the growth process as directed by the "five kindnesses" (hormones) of the body, thus resulting in a total number of 248 limbs. (Originally, Abraham was named Avram [אברם=243]. Subsequently, he was given an additional *hei* [ה=5], the secret of the "five kindnesses"— "kindness to Abraham," and became Abraham [אברהם=248], as the total number of limbs in the body.) These 248 limbs, each of which contains a corresponding power of soul, become true vessels to reveal G-dliness in the world through the performance of the 248 positive commandments of Torah.

The relation of 248 to nine appears in the text of the complete recitation of the *Shema*. To the initial 239 words an additional nine words (six at the beginning and three at the end) are added to the text in order to total 248, corresponding to the positive commandments of the Torah.

This structure of nine (as further divided into six and three) as the basis of 248 can be seen to be reflected in the *Mishneh Torah*, the Code of Maimonides (the Rambam). The Rambam defines the first two categories of Torah-law as "Foundations" and "Character." In "Foundations" there are six positive commandments: to know G-d, to unify Him, to love Him, to fear Him, to sanctify His Name, to obey the prophet who speaks in His Name. In "Character," the first three positive commandments are: to emulate His ways, to cling to those who know Him, to love one's fellow Jew. The two all-inclusive commandments of Torah (each considered by the Sages sufficient to support the entire Torah) are the first (faith-knowledge of G-d) and the ninth (love of Israel). Thus, we can understand that these first nine positive commandments (with their inner subdivision of six and three) according to the order of the Rambam are the true basis for all of the 248 positive commandments of Torah. They correspond to the nine months of spiritual pregnancy (certain, exceptional souls—such as Moses's—only require six months of pregnancy; these are pure "foundation" souls) during which the entire body of the Jew (his 248 limbs—commandments) is formed.

DIVINITY

Nine, in Kabbalah, represents the qualities of truth and eternity, qualities of the Divine. This is symbolized by the arithmetical phenomenon,
unique to the number nine (in a decimal system), that all multiples of nine
remain equal, in their reduced value, to nine (i.e. 2·9=18, 1⊥8=9;
3·9=27, 2⊥7=9 etc.). The reduced value of אמת, "truth," is nine (441→9),
as is that of the words ברית, "covenant" (612→9); אור, "light" (207→9);
שבת, "Shabbat" (702→9), and many other words pertaining to the above
two qualities of truth and eternity.

The silent prayer, the *Amidah*, which contains eighteen (now, nineteen)
blessings on a weekday and seven blessings on Shabbat and holidays, consists, once a year, of nine blessings, at *Musaf*, the additional prayer, of *Rosh
HaShanah*. These nine blessings correspond to the various series of the *shofar*-blasts of *Rosh HaShanah*, which are arranged in sets of nine. The *teruah*,
one of the three sounds of the *shofar*, itself consists of nine short staccato
sounds. This repetitive theme of nine on *Rosh HaShanah* hints at both the
hidden judgement of this awesome day as well as the "pregnant" blessings
awaiting "birth" in the New Year.

Both the Torah-reading and the *Haftorah* of the first day of *Rosh Ha-
Shanah* relate the miracle of pregnancy and birth. Three great women were
"remembered" (for pregnancy) on *Rosh HaShanah*: Sarah (שרה), Rachel
(רחל), and Chanah (חנה). Together their names possess nine letters. The
initial letters of their three names spells (in correct chronological order) the
name of another great woman in Torah, Serach (שרח), the daughter of
Asher (whose name means "happiness," the level of mother, as explained in
Kabbalah and *Chassidut*).

The sum of all four names—שרח, חנה, רחל, שרה—equals nine times
עולם, "world," the secret of the "pregnant world," as discussed above. This
"One emanating from the 'head' of three" is found also in Rabbi Shimon Bar
Yochai's teaching in *Pirke Avot*: "there are three crowns...and the crown of
the goodly name [actually a fourth crown] ascends above them all." The
"woman of valor" is the "crown of her husband," as explained above in the
secret of the letter *zayin*.

Serach was the one to bring to her grandfather, Jacob, the tiding that
his lost son Joseph was still alive. By this she enlivened the spirit of Jacob
himself—ותחי רוח יעקב, "and the spirit of Jacob came to life," as though
spiritually "bearing" her own grandfather. (It was thus as though the soul of
Joseph married the soul of his niece, Serach, to give birth to the soul of his
father, her grandfather, Jacob. The total of their three names—יעקב, יוסף,

שרח [846]—is also a multiple of nine: nine times מזל טוב, *"mazel tov"* [94·9=846]. In "reduced numbering" they equal 45, the "triangle" of nine.) For this she was blessed with eternal life, the Divine secret of nine, as taught by our Sages.

Yud

מְעַט הַמַּחֲזִיק אֶת הַמְרֻבָּה

The Infinite Point

Yud: **The Infinite Point**

The letter *yud*, a small suspended point, reveals the spark of essential good hidden within the letter *tet*. Subsequent to the initial *tzimtzum*, the contraction of G-d's Infinite light in order to make "place" for Creation, there remained within the empty void a single, potential point or "impression." The secret of this point is the power of the Infinite to contain finite phenomena within Himself and express them to apparent external reality. Finite manifestation begins from a zero-dimensional point, thereafter developing into a one-dimensional line and two-dimensional surface. This is alluded to in the full spelling of the letter *yud* (יוד): point (י), line (ו), surface (ד). These three stages correspond in Kabbalah to: point (*nekudah*), spectrum (*sefirah*), figure (*partzuf*). The initial point, the essential power of the *yud*, is the "little that holds much." The "much" refers to the simple Infinity of G-d hidden within the initial point of revelation, which reflects itself as the Infinite potential of the point to develop and express itself in all of the manifold finite phenomena of time and space.

Before the *tzimtzum*, the power of limitation was hidden, latent within G-d's Infinite Essence. Following the *tzimtzum*, this power of limitation became revealed, and paradoxically the Infinite Essence of G-d that originally "hid" the power of limitation now Itself became hidden (not in truth, but only from our limited human perspective) within the point of contracted light.

From within this point of limitation is revealed the secret of the ten *sefirot*, the Divine channels of light through which G-d continually brings His world into being. Ten, the numerical value of the *yud*, is also the number of commandments (literally "statements") revealed by G-d to His People Israel at Sinai. All of the commandments, and in fact every letter of Torah, possess the power of the "little that holds much"; each is a channel for the revelation of G-d's Infinite Light in finite reality.

YUD

**FORM: A "formed" point: a crown above and a "pathway" below.
The smallest of the letters; The only letter suspended in mid-air.**

Worlds The "pathway" of the *yud*; The initial point of space and time.
Natural wisdom: "The wisdom of Solomon."
Direction and purpose: the consciousness of the present moment.

Souls The "body" of the *yud*; The enwedged point.
"The wisdom of G-d" as manifest in the judgement of Solomon.
The power of self-nullification.

Divinity The crown of the *yud* above; The unenwedged point.
"The wisdom of G-d" inspiring and directing Solomon's genius.
Revealed Omnipresence; The beginning and end of every letter (form).

NAME: Hand; to thrust.

Worlds The secret of space; To thrust—the principle of action and reaction.
The wave-nature of radiation.

Souls Intelligence; Friendship.
To acknowledge—to make space for others; Empathy

Divinity G-d's "hand"—the Infinite Will and ability to sustain the Creation.
Charity, physical and spiritual.
"Shaking G-d's Hand": identifying with archtypal souls and Temple service.
G-d's thought—the origin of the Jewish soul

NUMBER: Ten; "The tenth shall be holy"; the decimal nature of reality.

Worlds Ten Divine utterances through which the world was created.
Ten things created on the first day.
Ten things created at dusk at the end of the first Friday.
Ten generations from Adam to Noah and from Noah to Abraham.
Ten kings ruled the whole world; Ten nations given to Abraham.
Ten pure animals; Ten categories of forbidden magic.
Ten battles of Joshua; Ten essential limbs of the body.

Souls The *sefirot*—Spiritual Powers; Ten categories of the souls of Israel.
Ten trials of Abraham; A *minyan* of ten men.
Ten synonyms for prayer; Ten synonyms for song.
Ten cardinal songs sung throughout history.
Ten martyrs of Israel; Ten spiritual functions of the heart.

Divinity Ten Commandments; Ten plagues.
Ten miracles in the Holy Temple; Ten days of repentance.
Yom Kippur—the tenth day; The Divine Name ten times on *Yom Kippur*.
Ten names of *Ruach HaKodesh*; Ten are called "the man of G-d."
Ten verses of Kingdom, Remembrance and Shofar-blast.
Ten synonyms for *teshuvah*.

FORM

The *yud*, the smallest of the letters, is the only letter suspended in mid-air. It symbolizes the point of spiritual force within all the letters of the *alef-beit*. Its shape is a "formed point," consisting of a "pathway" below (corresponding to Worlds), a "body" or "trunk" (Souls) and a "crown" or "thorn" above (Divinity).

WORLDS

The lower "pathway" (שביל) of the *yud* is the secret of the point of the present in four- (or multi-) dimensional reality. Its physical origin is the initial point of space and time, the contracted point of *tzimtzum*, that subsequently expands into the physical universe.

The "pathway" of the *yud* manifests itself in the physical laws of nature. The *yud*, in general, is the secret of the point of insight and wisdom. True natural wisdom is referred to in the Torah as "the wisdom of Solomon," as is said: "...and he spoke of trees, from the cedar tree that is in Lebanon to the hyssop that comes out of the wall; he spoke also of beasts and of birds, and of creeping things and fishes. And there came from all the nations to hear the wisdom of Solomon, from all the kings of the earth, who had heard of his wisdom." This level of wisdom, founded upon the continual consciousness of recreation in the present moment, "attracts" all of the "sparks" of Worlds to return to their source in Israel.

In the service of G-d, the "pathway" is the ability to contract and direct one's energy in a concentrated and purposeful way. Finding the "pathway," one's direction in life, depends upon the ability to subdue one's worldly desires and passions and to humble one's ego. This is the act of contraction, *tzimtzum*, by which one enters into the consciousness of the present moment, the point of "suspended animation"—continual re-creation.

SOULS

The "body" or "trunk" (גזע) of the yud is referred to in the *Zohar* as the "enwedged point," corresponding to the lifeforce present within every created being. Even inanimate beings possess lifeforce, as taught by the Arizal and explained in the *Tanya*.

The "body" and "crown" of the *yud* are referred to as "the wisdom of G-d" possessed by Solomon, in contrast to the natural "wisdom of Solomon," as explained in Kabbalah. The "body" of the *yud* indicates the "wisdom of G-d" as manifest in the judgement of Solomon; the "crown" of the *yud* indicates the Divine inspiration directing Solomon's own genius.

First we are told of King Solomon's Divinely inspired wisdom in the act of judging truly between souls. This wisdom is called "the wisdom of G-d" within him. Thereafter the phrase "the wisdom of Solomon" appears three times (the last time as experienced by the Queen of Sheba). The first, Divine revelation of wisdom in Solomon corresponds to his wisdom at the level of the world of Emanation (*Atzilut*), the origin of Souls. The subsequent three revelations of Solomon's own wisdom reflect his relation to the three lower worlds: Creation (*Beriah*), Formation (*Yetzirah*), and Action (*Asiyah*).

The *yud*, the smallest of letters, suspended in mid-air, represents that state of self-nullification for which every soul must strive in order to begin to comprehend the true service of G-d. "He who is [i.e. feels] small is big and he who is [i.e. feels] big is small." In the Masoretic literature, the letter *yud* is referred to as זעירא, "the small one." זעירא is also the name of one of the Sages of the Talmud, who strived and succeeded to come to the land of Israel and receive there its sublime point of wisdom.

To feel suspended in mid-air is the experience of the point of the earth "hanging" in outer space, as is said: תלה ארץ על בלימה, "He suspends [literally, 'hangs'] the earth on nothingness." The entire phrase, תלה ארץ על בלימה, actually equals the first word of the Torah, the first experience of the soul in contact with the Torah: בראשית, "In the beginning."

The letter *yud* is the common beginning of Israel, ישראל, and G-d's Name *Havayah*, יהו־ה.

DIVINITY

The "crown" or "thorn" (קוץ) of the *yud*, hinting at G-d's Transcendent Light, the supernal crown above wisdom, is referred to in the *Zohar* as the "un-enwedged point." The "enwedged point" is the point of life innate in every created being, as explained above. The "unenwedged" point is light above life. *Chassidut* explains that, in general, there are three levels of Divine influx: light (אור), life (חיות), and energy (כֹה). Light reveals Divinity; life infuses Souls; energy is conserved in Worlds. Divinity is Transcendent Light, indirectly responsible for life yet "un-enwedged" in its consciousness.

The script of every letter begins and ends with a *yud*, just as the number of every letter is in fact a set or continuum of the ever "counting" *alef*. The *alef* itself most visibly begins with a *yud* and ends with a *yud*, the secret of the higher and lower waters, as explained above. The *yud* "travels," as it were, from beginning to end. Thus, in fact, each letter can be seen as the tracing of the pathway of a *yud* in motion. This alludes to the phrase in the *Zohar*: "There is no place empty of His Presence."

A modern illustration: an image on a movie screen is in fact composed of a multitude of points, similar to the multitude of particles which compose any physical body. According to one physical theory, all of the multitude of elementary particles in the universe can be understood as one and the same particle travelling "back and forth" in time. In truth all of the points (or "strings") are one, ultimately the impression of Divine Omnipresence.

NAME

The word *yud* (יוד) means "a hand" or "to thrust."

WORLDS

One of the meanings of "hand" in Torah is "place," as in the verse: ויד תהיה לך מחוץ למחנה, "And a *place* [literally, 'a hand'] shall be for you outside of the camp...." The "camp of Israel" is the well-defined "place" of Souls. "Outside the camp" refers to the state of Worlds below Souls. Just as primordial space was initially created by G-d for the sake of making possible the creation of worlds therein, so does physical space allow for the ability of motion and formation of objects to take *place*. After an entity has taken *place*, it must then be taken in *hand*, in order to direct—"thrust"—its energy in a purposeful way, as explained above in the form of the *yud*.

The "place" ("hand") in the above verse is actually designated to "hold" the waste product of man. In Kabbalah we are taught that the waste product of a higher being becomes the sustenance and lifeforce of a lower being. Thus, the waste of man becomes a source of energy for Worlds. If man digests his food properly, as part of his service of G-d, his very waste will serve to give the nature of Worlds a positive thrust.

The meaning of "to thrust" or "to cast," as in the verse: וידו אבן בי, "and they have cast a stone at me," implies and relates to the various physical laws which control the forces of nature and their "fields" ("places"). The stone symbolizes a particle of nature, as the point of the form of the *yud*. The energy of the field (place) casts it in a definite direction. Thus the name of the *yud* implies the wave nature of the various forms of radiation, whereas its form represents their particle nature.

The two hands of the body hint at the law of nature that for every action there is an equal and opposite reaction, as in the saying of our Sages: "the left hand pushes away and the right hand draws near."

SOULS

"Hand," יד, is used idiomatically in Hebrew to connote the extent of one's intelligence, as in the idiom: "to the ability of the hand of one's mind to grasp." Just as the hand extends itself from the body to catch a physical object, so does the hand of the mind extend itself from its initial boundaries to grasp a new idea.

From the root ידה, "to thrust," derives the meaning הודיה, "to give thanks." After extending one's hand to receive, one must "thrust," in return, one's expression of thanks. הודיה, "to thank," is in turn related to the word הוד, "splendor" or "majesty" (the name of the eighth *sefirah* in Kabbalah), which derives from the meaning הד, "echo." In giving thanks one echoes and reveals the goodly intentions of the giver, previously "hidden" in the act of his giving.

In Hebrew, "to thank" implies the acknowledgment of truth above the initial capability of one's intelligence to grasp. By first acknowledging (upon "sensing" the truth as truth), one widens one's "place" and "hand" to extend out of one's limitations and relate inwardly (if not to grasp entirely) to even the most allusive truth. One makes "room" in one's consciousness for new and varied insights.

In thanks and acknowledgement all ten levels of Souls unite, while with regard to intelligence, each soul is unique.

The word for "close friend" (ידיד) is actually the word "hand" (יד) twice. This can be seen to symbolize friendship as two companions "shaking hands." The extended hand of each friend to his companion is the secret of the extension of the soul's power of *malchut* (kingdom) as personified by King David, whose name (דוד), which is related to the root of ידיד) means "lover" (as throughout the Song of Songs) and numerically equals יד, "hand." The root of the word *malchut* means "the will to take counsel"; "giving one's hand" to another is interpreted (in the book of Ezra) to mean promising to follow his advice. King David empathized and related personally, in friendship, to every Jewish soul, as is seen by the Book of Psalms he composed, the most personal supplications of each and every soul in times of distress. As befitting a righteous King, the *Tanach* relates that King David possessed a close friend, Chushai, through whom he drew his friendship to extend to every one of his subjects, the People of Israel.

DIVINITY

The "Hand" of G-d symbolizes His boundless ability and will to give and sustain all of Creation, as we say three times a day in the daily prayers (as well as in the Grace after Meals): פותח את ידך ומשביע לכל חי רצון, "You open Your hand and satisfy every living being with favor." In Kabbalah, ידך, "Your Hand," is interpreted as יוד ך, "Your [power of] *yud*." Thus, when man engages in acts of charity, whether through financial support and assistance to others, or by spiritual encouragement and companionship, he is in truth emulating G-d Himself, by means of the power of the letter *yud*.

יבא ידיד בן ידיד ויבנה ידיד לידיד של ידיד בחלקו של ידיד ויתכפרו בו ידידים, "The 'companion' [ידיד] son of the 'companion' shall come and build the 'companion' for the 'companion' in the portion of the 'companion' in order to atone for the 'companions.' " This riddle of the Sages is interpreted to mean: "Solomon, the descendant of Abraham, shall come and build the Temple, for G-d, in the portion of Benjamin, in order to atone for Israel." The Sages cite a verse for each of the above six in which it is referred to as a ידיד, "companion." From this we learn that the concept "companion" unifies the souls of Israel and G-d through the means of the specific archetypal souls and the Temple service. Or in other words: through the sense of identification with the archetypal souls of Israel and the devotion to extend oneself and give of one's best in the Temple service, one "shakes hands" with G-d.

We are taught that G-d created the world with one Hand, whereas the Temple is built with two hands, the two hands of the *tzadikim* of Israel, or, even deeper, the two hands of the *tzadik*, linked in true "companionship" to G-d. This secret of "shaking hands" with G-d in the Temple is reflected in many ways, one of which is the status of the *kohanim* in the Temple service. According to one supposition of the Sages, the *kohanim* represent the extension of the Hand of G-d to us (שלוחי דרחמנא). According to the second supposition (and as known: "both are the words of the Living G-d") the *kohanim* represent the extension of the hand of Israel to G-d (שלוחי דידן).

The letter *yud* is the first letter of G-d's Name *Havayah*. In *Chassidut*, the grammatical significance of the *yud* in the Name is interpreted to be the power of Divine Thought, as it were, to continually retain "balance" in the present moment for the sake of re-creation, the spontaneous generation of all of reality. Rashi states: "the *yud* refers to thought," the thought and intention of an act about to be performed.

"Israel ascended in thought." The origin of the souls of Israel is in G-d's primordial thought of Creation. The "small," suspended point of the *yud*, together with the phonetic and grammatical relation of its name to the word

"Jew" (יהודי, from הודיה, "thanks") is taken to indicate that the secret of the soul of Israel ("the smallest of peoples," suspended in mid-air as it were, in relation to the other "well-founded" nations of the earth) is one with the "thought" of the *yud* of the name *Havayah*.

NUMBER

The letter *yud* equals ten. Torah states: "The tenth shall be Holy for G-d." The fact that the number ten is universally accepted as the basis of the number system reflects the intrinsic nature of ten as the consummate expression of plurality. Ten serves to reveal in full the hidden spectrum of plurality inherent in every point of Creation, as well as to bring plurality "back" to a sense of initial and essential unity. We count from one to ten not because we possess ten fingers, but rather we possess ten fingers because of the inherent properties of the number ten.

WORLDS

"Through ten utterances was the world created." In relation to the revealed sanctity of the Ten Commandments given at Sinai, the ten utterances of Creation are considered to be "mundane words." The purpose of the utterances is to establish individual creations possessing self-consciousness, hiding the Creator from the created. The purpose of the Ten Commandments is to reveal the Creator and Redeemer to Israel.

On the very first day of Creation, ten things were created. Likewise at the end of Creation, twilight of the sixth day entering into Shabbat, ten things were created. Before the appearance of our father Abraham, the first Jew, the consciousness of man was confined to the general level of Worlds (or, in particular: Worlds, Souls, and Divinity in Worlds). Thus the ten generations from Adam to Noah and the ten generations from Noah culminating with Abraham are reflections of the secret of ten at the level of Worlds. Abraham first "crowns" the second series of ten at the level of Worlds (as reflected by his great knowledge of the workings of nature, as told by the Sages), and then is taken out of Worlds, as is said: "And He [G-d] took him [Abraham] outside"—"outside the universe." Here he reached the true consciousness of Souls. Afterwards, when the additional *hei* was added to his Name at circumcision, he reached consciousness of Divinity.

Included amongst the many groupings of ten in the Talmud that relate to Worlds are: "Ten Kings ruled over the whole world"; "Ten nations were given to Abraham"; "Ten pure animals are explicitly mentioned in Torah"; "Ten categories of forbidden magical practice in Torah"; "The ten battles of Joshua"; "Ten essential limbs of the body," and so on.

SOULS

In direct correspondence to the ten *sefirot* (the ten Divine attributes reflected in the spiritual structure of the soul of man), the souls of Israel possess ten general categories:

The Heads of the Thousands of Israel:	*keter*—"crown"
The Wise:	*chochmah*—"wisdom"
The Understanding:	*binah*—"understanding"
The Bestowers of Lovingkindness:	*chesed*—"lovingkindness"
The Mighty Ones:	*gevurah*—"might"
The Masters of Torah:	*tiferet*—"beauty"
The Prophets:	*netzach*—"victory"
The Seers:	*hod*—"splendor"
The Righteous:	*yesod*—"foundation"
The Kings:	*malchut*—"kingdom."

The first Jew, Abraham, merited to implant within the consciousness of his own soul the roots of all of these categories of his children-to-be. "With ten trials was our father Abraham tried and he stood firm through them all, to show how great was the love of our father Abraham for G-d." By standing firm through each trial one additional soul-root became manifest in Abraham's soul. These trials were further intended to aid Abraham to elevate himself, level by level, until he, by virtue of his own achievement, reached total awareness of the One G-d. By virtue of Abraham's inner *minyan*, the interinclusion of all ten soul-roots in himself, he was able to reach full consciousness of One.

A *minyan* is the quorum of ten men required for Jewish communal prayer. Ten is the first number whose total number of permutations $(10! = 10 \cdot 9 \cdot 8 \cdot ... \cdot 2 \cdot 1 = 3,628,800)$ exceeds 600,000, the number of archetypal souls of Israel. In *Chassidut* we are taught that Jews upon gathering together express as many spiritual powers as their number of permutations. They unite in every possible order, thus indicating that no one essentially precedes any one else, but rather, there exists a specific order, in which each precedes his companion. In a *minyan*, the origin of each of the archetypal souls of Israel is expressed.

Included among the many groupings of ten in the Talmud that relate to souls are: "ten synonyms for prayer"; "ten synonyms for song"; "ten cardinal songs sung through history"; "ten martyrs of Israel"; "ten spiritual functions of the heart," and so on.

DIVINITY

The Ten Commandments given to us at Sinai are the ultimate statement of G-d's Will. As true revelation of Divinity comes only after evil (that which intentionally hides G-d's Light) is defeated, ten plagues were required in order to defeat the evil "shell" of Pharoah and Egypt before the Ten Commandments could be pronounced.

Ten miracles (revelations of supernatural Divinity) were performed for our fathers in the Temple. Similar to the form of the *yud*, which consists of a "pathway" (Worlds), a "body" (Souls), and a "crown" (Divinity), so too did these ten continuous miracles reveal that the Temple was the one place in the world where the levels of Worlds, Souls, and Divinity were in a constant state of union and interrelation.

Yom Kippur, the tenth day of *Tishrei*, is the culmination of the "Ten Days of Repentance." The High Priest, entrusted with performing the Temple service in the name of all Israel, would pronounce the Ineffable Name ten times on that day. All present, despite the apparent lack of physical space, would bow down in total self-nullification. Miraculously, open space would appear around each prostrating individual. Thus the Temple site itself reflected the secret of the "little that holds much."

Included among the many groupings of ten in the Talmud that relate to Divinity are: "ten names of *Ruach HaKodesh*"; "ten are called 'the man of G-d' "; "ten verses of the Kingdom of G-d, His Remembrance and His *shofar*-blasts, recited in the *musaf* prayer of *Rosh Hashanah*"; "ten synonyms for *teshuvah* corresponding to the ten days of *teshuvah*," and so on.

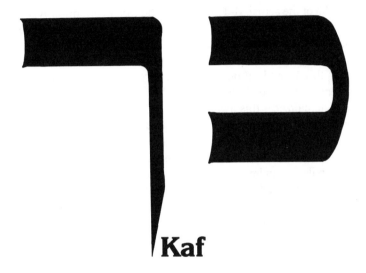

Kaf

כֹּחַ הַפּוֹעֵל בַּנִּפְעָל

The Crown:
The Power to Actualize Potential

Kaf: The Crown—the Power to Actualize Potential

The two letters of the full spelling of the *kaf*, כף, are the initial letters of the two words: כח, "potential," and פועל, "actual." Thus, the *kaf* hints at the power latent within the spiritual realm of the potential to fully manifest itself in the physical realm of the actual. G-d must create the world continuously; otherwise Creation would instantaneously vanish. His potential is therefore actualized at each moment. This concept is referred to as כח הפועל בנפעל, "the power to actualize potential ever-present within the actualized." In *Chassidut* we are taught that this should be one's initial awareness upon awakening. Since the literal meaning of the letter *kaf* is "palm"—the place in the body where potential is actualized—this awareness is reflected in the custom of placing one palm on the other upon awakening, before reciting the *Modeh Ani* prayer: "I thank You, living and eternal King, for you have mercifully restored my soul within me; Your faithfulness is great."

Placing palm on palm is an act and sign of subjugation, similar to the act of bowing before a king. Whereas in bowing one totally nullifies one's consciousness in the presence of the King, in placing palm on palm one enters into a state of supplication and prayer to the King to reveal new will from His supernal crown (Will) to His subjects.

Kaf is also the root of the word כפה, *kipah* (etymologically, the root of the word "cap" in English), the *yarmulke* or skullcap. In reference to the creation of man it is said: ותשת עלי כפכה, "You have placed Your Palm over me." Our Sages refer to Adam as יציר כפיו של הקב"ה, "the formation of the Palms of the Holy One, Blessed be He." The awareness of the presence of the "Palms" of G-d over one's head, in His ongoing creation of him, becomes the cap (*kipah*) on his head. Even higher, the very power to actualize potential manifest in His Palms, as it were, derives ultimately from His crown (the power of will) above His head (i.e. "superational" Will.)

As a verb, *kaf* means "to subdue" or "coerce." We are told in the Talmud that at the time of the giving of the Torah at Sinai, "He suspended [כפה, in the sense of "subdued"] the mountain over them as a barrel." In *Chassidut* it is explained that the Divine motivation manifest in this act was actually one of greatest love for Israel. So much love was revealed by all of the tremendous revelations at Sinai that the people were "coerced," as it were, to respond in acceptance of the yoke of Heaven, in love. The mountain itself appeared to forcefully embrace the people. Here the secret of the *kaf* is the "much" revealed from the "little" point of the *yud*.

KAF

FORM: Three connected lines with rounded corners; the crown on the head of a prostrating king.

Worlds The totality of space surrounding the earth.
The outermost sphere of the universe.

Souls Three connected properties of the crown: faith, sublime pleasure, and will.
The three meanings of *keter*: "wait," "crown," and "encircle."

Divinity Three stages of light before G-d created the world.
The ability of the soul to relate to the Essence of G-d.

NAME: Palm; clouds; power to suppress.

Worlds The power to suppress the forces of nature.
The toil of labor.
The power to rule.
Physical clouds; expression of power.

Souls The power to suppress one's evil inclination.
The clouds surrounding Mt. Sinai—Jewish identity.
Faith despite "dark clouds."
Clean palms—observance of the commandments between man and man.

Divinity The vessel to receive Divine pleasure.
"I have engraved you upon My Palms."
The Clouds of Glory.

NUMBER: Twenty

Worlds Twenty pieces of silver for which Joseph's brothers sold him.
Twenty cubits, the maximum height of a *sukah*.

Souls Twenty *gera*, the full value of a *shekel*, symbolizing the union of two half-*shekels*.
The age to become a soldier and pursue a livelihood.
The twenty years Jacob worked for Laban.

Divinity The twenty *sefirot* of the two countenances of the crown.

FORM

The *kaf* is composed of three connected lines with rounded corners, forming the image of a crown lying on its side, as if resting on the head of the king while in a state of prostration or self-nullification.

WORLDS

Imagining our earth to be the point of the letter *yud* suspended in mid-air, the *kaf* may be seen to represent the visible half-sphere of outer space surrounding the earth. This all-encompassing aspect of space becomes most conscious when observing the horizon, the crown approaching one in a horizontal position. According to the theory of general relativity, the natural, geocentric perspective of man is perfectly tenable from an objective view of reality. Most references in Torah to celestial motion relative to the earth reflect this perspective of celestial spheres surrounding the earth. The highest of the spheres, which corresponds to the secret of the crown relative to physical reality, is vacant of all celestial bodies. Called the "sphere of the daily cycle," its function is to cause all of the lower spheres with their contained bodies to revolve daily around the earth. Though the natural direction of most of the celestial bodies in their orbits around the earth would be from west to east, the sphere of the daily cycle "forces" them to revolve in the opposite direction, from east to west. This continuous heavenly motion is their prostration to the Divine Presence, which, as taught by our Sages, is most revealed in the west.

The mathematically simpler, heliocentric understanding of the solar system, and further envisioning the solar system itself as a tiny speck in motion around a galaxy etc., enhance our experience of the humble wonder of the Psalmist: "When I see Your heavens, the work of Your fingers, the moon and the stars that You have established; what is mankind that You are mindful of him and man that You remember him?" Nonetheless, the sense that our earth is in some mysterious way the center of the universe impresses upon us the realization that G-d, the Creator of the Universe, has chosen us to fulfill His purpose in Creation. The force of this latter impression of heavens on earth is the secret of the letter *kaf*.

SOULS

The three lines of the *kaf* relate to the three properties of the supercon-scious: simple and absolute faith, sublime pleasure in the experience of unity with G-d, and superconscious desire to dedicate one's life to fulfilling G-d's Will. These properties are referred to as "the three heads of the crown," and in turn relate to the three actual meanings of the word for "crown," *keter*. The highest of the heads, simple faith, corresponds to *keter* meaning "to wait," as in כתר לי זעיר, "*wait* for me a little." This implies that faith entails the patience and confidence that G-d's ultimate good in His Divine intention for each individual soul, together with all of Creation will in time be fulfilled.

The second head in the crown, sublime pleasure, relates to the most obvious meaning of keter, "crown." The genuine pleasure of a Jew is the intimate experience of standing in the presence of the Creator and King of the Universe.

The lowest head of the crown, will, relates to *keter* meaning "to sur-round" or "encircle." Every Jewish soul possesses the latent power to decree its will upon reality. This potential is actualized by linking one's own power of will to that of G-d, as taught by Rabban Gamliel: "Make His Will as your will, so that He will make your will as His Will. Nullify your will to His Will, so that He will nullify the will of others to your will."

DIVINITY

Here, the three lines of the *kaf* correspond to the three levels present within G-d's Infinite Light before the beginning of Creation. These three levels, when viewed as a whole, are the ultimate secret of the Divine Crown, above the conscious process of Creation which begins from the initial contraction (*tzimtzum*) of the Infinite Light.

Corresponding to the highest "head" of *keter*, simple faith, as reflected in G-d's very Essence, as it were, is the absolute bond of G-d to the origin of the souls of Israel in the Divine Self.

His sublime pleasure, corresponding to the second "head" of *keter*, is His delight in each individual soul as it is linked by Him to a specific letter of the primordial Torah. Here, G-d "learns" Torah "for its own sake" (לשמה), not yet utilizing the Torah as the blueprint of Creation.

His Will, corresponding to the third "head" of *keter*, is the Will to create, which "appears" (in the terminology of the *Zohar*: "ascends") in the Infinite Light only "after" (time does not yet exist) the two previous levels of G-d's relation to the primordial source of Israel. Within this appearance of Will to create, the Torah "comes into [the Divine] focus" as the blueprint and utensil of Creation.

The form of the final *kaf* (ך) represents the drawing down of these three levels of Divine Superconsciousness—the levels of the Divine Crown—into corresponding levels of the superconscious of Souls. The final *kaf*, as a suffix letter, means "you" or "yours," frequently used in reference to G-d, as in the verse, ארוממך אלקי המלך "I will exalt *You*, my G-d the King." The ability of the soul to relate to the Essence of G-d in the second person—"You"—is its innate power to draw into itself the Divine Crown.

NAME

The word *kaf* (כף) means "a palm" (used also as an image for clouds) and "the power to suppress."

WORLDS

The power to suppress or coerce is apparent throughout nature. As a positive force, man is able to subdue and control natural phenomena for the benefit of mankind. All productive labor is referred to in Torah as the toil of the palms: "The toil of your palms you shall eat, happy are you and goodness is yours." As a negative force, history is full of conflict between nations in struggle over power (the *keter* of the *kaf*). Ultimately this negative, egocentric force will be converted to good when *Mashiach* will selflessly use the power of the *kaf* to "force" (paradoxically: "pleasantly") all people to abide by the Divine statutes of Torah.

The image of clouds, at this level, refers to physical clouds, the impression of the "Palms" of the Creator, as it were, filling the sky. In *Chassidut* we are taught that often when light is reduced, expression of power increases. Thus, a cloudy sky, though reducing the brilliance of natural sunlight, simultaneously emphasizes, as it were, the latent powers of nature. Job 36:32 can be read: "With clouds He covers light, and thereby commands with forcefulness."

SOULS

"Who is the mighty one? He who suppresses his evil inclination." In the *Zohar* and *Chassidut* this power of soul to suppress evil is referred to as *itkafia*, אתכפיא, from the root כף, *kaf*. In the Rabbinic idiom of *Pirkei Avot* quoted above, the word for "suppress" (כובש) can actually be understood to be a compound of כ, the letter *kaf*—in the above sense of אתכפיא, "to subdue"—and בש, "evil."

When Moses ascended Mt. Sinai to receive the Torah, he passed through the clouds: "And Moses entered into the cloud and ascended to the mountain." The word "mountain" in Hebrew, הר, implies brilliance and radiance, as in the five three-letter synonyms for "light" in Hebrew all ending with the two-letter syllable הר: בהר, טוהר, נהר, זהר, צהר. The brilliance is the revelation of G-d to Moses at the summit of the mountain, the revelation of Divinity. Entering into the cloud symbolizes the secret of Moses's self-identification with the souls of all Israel, the impression of Divine Light on created reality.

The ultimate power of Souls is that of simple faith, which becomes ever stronger and pronounced in times of relative darkness—"cloudy" times. The darker and denser the clouds, the greater the darkness, and the more pronounced simple faith, in order to persevere and proceed.

Similarly we find in Psalms: "Who will ascend to the mountain of G-d...the clean of *palms* [כפים] and pure of heart...." "The clean of palms" implies consummate rectification of all *mitzvot* and relationships between man and his fellow, and thus connection of one's soul to the souls of all Israel. G-d's Palms (the clouds) clean man's palms. Entering the clouds is the prerequisite to ascend to the mountain of G-d.

DIVINITY

In Ecclesiastes we find the phrase: מלא כף נחת, "a full palm of satisfaction." The palm, when turned upward, becomes the vessel to receive Divine blessing and sustenance. G-d opens His Hand—the secret of the *yud* at the level of Divinity as explained above—into our open palm, the *kaf*. From our service of G-d (opening our hand to Him) He Himself receives from us "sustenance" and pleasure, "a full palm of satisfaction." So teach our Sages: "Israel sustains her Father in Heaven." The essential satisfaction Above produced by our service below is due to the subjugation and devotion of our will to fulfill His Will. G-d says: "I am most gratified, for I have spoken and My Will has been done." The force inherent in the instruction of G-d's Will to us is His downward-projected palm. By our subjugation and devotion we fill His palm with satisfaction, as it were.

One image for the root of the soul in G-d's Essence is: "Behold, on [My] Palms [i.e., Clouds of Glory] I have engraved you." In prayer we lift up our hearts to our root in G-d, so as to arouse His memory of us and Infinite Mercy: "We shall lift up our hearts to the clouds [i.e., palms, our engraving upon His Palms], to G-d in heaven."

NUMBER

The letter *kaf* equals twenty.

WORLDS

Joseph was sold by his brothers for twenty pieces of silver, with which they purchased shoes. Shoes, the garment of the feet, the lowest part of the physical body, represents enclothement in lower physical desires and passions, as taught in Kabbalah and *Chassidut*. G-d's command to Moses at the burning bush to remove his shoes, "for the place that you are standing on is Holy earth," is interpreted as referring to the spiritual act of stripping off physicality. The selling of Joseph symbolizes the inability to suppress the desire for physical pleasures resulting in the soul being sold into slavery.

In *halachah*, Jewish law, the maximum permissible height of a *sukah* is twenty cubits. This is explained to be due to the fact that the maximum vertical range of eyesight, when looking forward (within relatively close distances) is twenty cubits. This phenomenon relates to the form of the *kaf* as the space of the horizon, discussed above. The *sukah* itself symbolizes the clouds of glory which encompassed and protected us in our sojourn through the desert.

SOULS

The value of a *shekel*, the most basic monetary unit in Torah, is twenty *gerah*. This equality is explicitly stated four times in Torah, corresponding to the secret of the four letters of the Name *Havayah*. The first time is in relation to each Jew's obligation to donate yearly one-half *shekel* for the sake of purchasing the communal sacrifices required for the Temple service. The inner secret and significance of this donation is to atone for both the sale of Joseph and the sin of the golden calf. Every Jew contributes a half *shekel*, ten *gerah* (corresponding to the ten levels of his soul), thereby indicating that only the union of two Jews constitutes the consummate state represented by a full *shekel*.

The second time is in reference to an oath to contribute the value of man to G-d (i.e. for the sake of the Temple service). The third time is in reference to the redemption of the first-born son. The fourth time is in reference to this same law together with that of the redemption of the first-born male offspring of a non-pure animal.

Whereas the word *shekel* (שקל) equals the union of the two patriarchs Abraham and Jacob (יעקב⊥אברהם=248⊥182=430), who in the soul correspond respectively to love and mercy, the word *gerah* (גרה) equals the value of the third patriarch, Isaac (יצחק=208), who corresponds to the attribute of fear and awe of G-d. The word for "twenty" itself (עשרים) equals the value of the letters "pregnant" (i.e., added to the root letters in their full spelling) in the name Isaac (עשרים = 620 = יוד צדיק חית קוף). Thus, עשרים גרה, "twenty *gerah*," is the total value of Isaac (יצחק) spelled in full. This beautiful phenomenon teaches that the primary, small component of our service of G-d is that of fear. Twenty small units of fear (*gerah*) become one full unit of love and mercy (*shekel*).

In Torah, twenty is the age when a Jewish male is enlisted for army service. Furthermore, our Sages teach that the age of twenty is the time to begin to "pursue" a livelihood—the "peaceful" equivalent to war. At the natural level of Worlds, this relates to the verse mentioned above: "The toil of your palms you shall eat...." At the deeper level of Souls, work itself and struggle for self-sufficiency is in truth an act of clarification of Divine sparks—"souls"—imprisoned throughout reality.

This is the secret of the period of twenty years that Jacob worked for Laban. During this period of hard physical labor (in exile from his homeland, the land of Israel)—work of the palms—he succeeded in redeeming those sparks existentially related to ("possessed" by) his own soul, the souls of his wives and the souls of his children.

DIVINITY

In Kabbalah we are taught that only the *sefirah* of *keter* (crown), the secret of the letter *kaf*, "develops" into two "twin" *partzufim* (spiritual countenances), which each contain ten individual *sefirot*. The inner *partzuf, Atik Yomin* ("The Ancient of Days"), corresponds to simple faith and sublime pleasure in the soul. These, in turn, correspond to the two highest levels of the Infinite Light, discussed above, where G-d relates to the source of Israel in Himself and His primordial Torah, as it were, before the "ascent" of His Will to create. The outer *partzuf, Arich Anpin* ("The Long Countenance"), corresponds to superrational will in the soul. This, in turn, corresponds to the appearance of Divine Will to create within G-d's Infinite Light. The word "twenty" itself (עשרים) equals *keter* (כתר, 620).

The 613 commandments of the Torah together with the seven Rabbinic injunctions total 620. The Ten Commandments possess exactly 620 letters, each corresponding to the ultimate root of one, full expression of Divine Will, a *mitzvah*. The seven last letters of the Ten Commandments compose its two last words: אשר לרעך, "which are to your companion." The Sages of Israel are referred to as the "companions" of G-d. These last seven letters thus hint at the seven Rabbinic commands.

The very last, 620th letter of the Ten Commandments is the final *kaf* of לרעך, "to your companion." This corresponds to the last Rabbinic command to be revealed, the *mitzvah* of lighting Chanukah candles. Each letter, *mitzvah*, is a precious stone in the crown of G-d; the final stone of Chanukah is that which consummates the splendor and majesty of the Divine Crown.

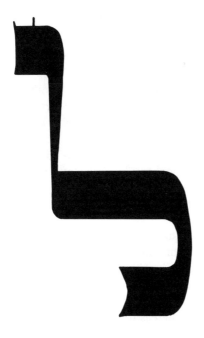

Lamed

מִגְדָּל הַפּוֹרֵחַ בַּאֲוִיר

Aspiration: Contemplation of the Heart

Lamed: Aspiration—Contemplation of the Heart

In *The Letters of Rabbi Akiva*, the full spelling of the letter *lamed*, למד, is read as short for the phrase: לב מבין דעת, "a heart that understands knowledge." The numerical value of this phrase (608) equals "heart" (לב, 32) times "Eve" (חוה, 19), i.e. "the heart of Eve."

In his commentary on the story of the Garden of Eden, the original episode of mankind, Rabbi Avraham Ibn Ezra states that Adam is the secret of the brain; Eve, the secret of the heart; the snake, the secret of the liver. In Kabbalah and *Chassidut* these fundamental correspondences are developed and explained in depth.

Adam and Eve, male and female, are the prototype spiritual forces of giving and receiving. The marital union and gift of male to female relates to the secret of knowledge, as is said: "And Adam *knew* his wife Eve." For this reason Adam and Eve are often seen to represent teacher and pupil. The teacher contracts his intellect into a point (*yud*) in order to convey his teaching to his student, whereas the student nullifies his previous levels of conception to become a fitting vessel for the new, wondrous teachings of his teacher.

In particular, the form of the *lamed* represents the aspiration of the truly devoted pupil to learn from the mouth of the teacher. The literal meaning of the letter *lamed* is "to learn" (or "teach"). The seed of wisdom, alluded to by the letter *yud*, descends from the brain (Adam) to impregnate the full consciousness of the heart (Eve). The heart aspires (upwardly) to receive this point of insight from the brain. This is the secret of the form of the letter *lamed*, the heart ascending in aspiration to conceive and comprehend ("understand knowledge") the point of wisdom, the *yud* situated at the top of the letter *lamed*.

Our Sages refer to the *lamed* as "a tower soaring in air." Three hundred (=10·30, ל·י) laws relate to the secret of this "flying tower." In our study of Torah, the "flying tower" is the expression of our love and devotion to the teachings of the Torah, our aspiration to conceive its inner truth, lifting us above the "gravity barrier" of earthly preoccupation.

We are told that the Ba'al Shem Tov would place the palm of his hand on the heart of a Jewish child and bless him to be a "warm Jew." The palm, the power to actualize potential, becomes manifest—at the inner spiritual level—in רעותא דלבא, the "will [crown, *keter*] of the heart" to conceive and unite with G-d's Will, the teachings of Torah. The *lamed*, the heart, aspires upwardly and connects to the *yud* of Divine insight. This is reflected in the form of the letter *lamed,* a *kaf* reaching upward to a *yud.* This is also the secret of the spiritual sequence hinted at in the letters of the word כלי, "vessel": the power to actualize potential (the palm of the Ba'al Shem Tov, כ) manifest in the aspiration of the heart (ל) reaching upward to conceive the secret of Divine wisdom (י). Throughout Torah the heart symbolizes the primary concept of vessel, the secret of Eve.

LAMED

FORM: A *vav*—whose head (*yud*) looks downward—on a *kaf*.
"A tower soaring in air."
The only letter ascending above the line.

Worlds A three-stage rocket ship soaring into outer space.
Man's aspiration to understand the universe.

Souls A heart of a wise man ascending to comprehend the wisdom of G-d.
Learning in order to teach, learning in order to do.

Divinity Divine inspiration; the higher *Shechinah*.
Prophetic imagination breaking through the limitations of rational intellect.

NAME: To learn; to teach.

Worlds The power to direct and control the animal instinct.
Learning secular skills; empirical knowledge.

Souls The yearning of the soul to learn Torah.
Rectification of the power of imagination.
Simultaneously learning in order to teach and learning in order to do.

Divinity Learning about the Essence of G-d.
Creating new heavens and earth.

NUMBER: Thirty.

Worlds Thirty days of the month.
Malchut is acquired through thirty attributes.
Thirty-*shekel* value of an adult woman.
The menstrual cycle.

Souls The thirty *tzadikim* in whose merit the world stands.
Thirty generations from Abraham to the destruction of the First Temple.

Divinity Thirty levels of Kingship.
Thirty categories of *tzadikim* in the World to Come.

FORM

The form of the *lamed* is unique in that it is the only letter of the alphabet that ascends above the "upper bound" line of the script of the letters. For this reason, our Sages refer to it as "a tower soaring in air." The *lamed* is composed of three letters: a downward looking *yud* which forms the head of a *vav* which stands, in turn, erect upon a *kaf*.

WORLDS

With a little imagination (*lamed*, in general, is the secret of the rectification of the power of imagination), the form of the letter *lamed*, the "flying tower" of Torah, can be seen as a three-stage rocket ship taking off into space. First, the ascending rocket ship semicircles the earth, the secret of the form of the letter *kaf* (of the *lamed*), as explained above. The first stage then drops off leaving the *vav* with a *yud* on top. The *vav-yud* breaks through the gravity barrier ascending directly into outer space, upon which the second stage of the rocket drops off, leaving only the cabin with its contained souls-astronauts—the *yud* of the *lamed*.

The *lamed*, at this level, characterizes man's desire and aspiration to understand the nature of the world he lives in. This "mother" instinct in the heart of man strives to know "mother nature"—Eve, "the mother of all life." The ever-soaring quest into the heights of understanding the universe is symbolized by the "flying tower."

Just as the *yud* is the smallest of letters so the *lamed* is referred to as the "biggest" of letters. "Thinking big" can relate to all worldly affairs—and especially to aspiring to understand and eventually "conquer" the secrets of nature.

SOULS

The humble and sincere heart of the wise man continually aspires to ascend higher and higher in his comprehension of the wisdom of G-d and His Torah. The power to nullify all previous preconceptions, together with the tremendous desire for knowledge and truth, are the two prerequisites necessary in order to pierce the barriers of man's innate physical, emotional, and mental limitations.

One of the great teachers of Kabbalah before the revelation of the *Zohar*, Rabbi Avraham Abulafia, explains that the heart (לב) is the secret of two *lameds* face to face: ל ל . The *beit* of לב equals two; thus לב can be read: "two *lameds*." The two *kafs* of the *lameds* form the heart itself, while the two *vavs* represent the two blood vessels leading to and from the brain.

The *lamed* to the right is the secret of "one who learns in order to teach." The *lamed* to the left is the secret of "one who learns in order to do." Though the brilliance and scope of the mind of the teacher is "infinitely" above that of the pupil, nonetheless the true teacher contracts his own intellect in order to "learn with" his student. (In Yiddish, "to teach" is "to learn with." In Hebrew, "to teach" is the *piel* [intensive] form of the verb "to learn.") Whereas in teaching, the art of "learning with" the student is revealed, in doing (the *mitzvot* of Torah), the art of "learning with" the objects of nature one contacts—although present—is concealed. Thus, teaching is the revealed "learning" of one soul with another soul (Souls with Souls); doing is the concealed "learning" of Souls with Worlds.

DIVINITY

Whereas at the level of Worlds and Souls the *lamed* signifies aspiration from below, at the level of Divinity it symbolizes Divine inspiration hovering and descending into the world from above. This hovering, as that described in relation to the letter *chet*, is similar to a mother's devotion to her children. Whereas the *chet* is the source of life (inherent in the wisdom of Torah, "touching yet not touching" the mind and heart of man), the *lamed* is the source of knowledge (complete integration of *chochmah*, *binah*, and *da'at* in the heart). In Kabbalah the "hovering mother" image of the *lamed* is referred to as the "higher *Shechinah*," the source of Divine inspiration to those who truly aspire to know and serve G-d.

The three components of the *lamed*—the *yud*, *vav* and *kaf*—correspond in general to the three levels of Divinity, Souls, and Worlds, respectively.

The *yud* at the peak of the *lamed*, bent slightly, as if looking down, is the secret of the teaching of the Sages: "In every place that you find the greatness of G-d, there you will find His humility." G-d has no need to reveal greatness to Himself; the King's leaving His "private domain" to display greatness to His subjects (absolutely incapable of comprehending His Transcendent Essence) is His truest expression of humility. The lowered head of the *lamed*, the "greatest" of the letters, symbolizes the humility of the "King of the Universe."

NAME

The word *lamed* (למד) means both "to learn" and "to teach."

WORLDS

In the verse: "And after him was Shamgar son of Anat, and he slew six hundred Philistine men with an ox goad, and he also delivered Israel," the word for "goad" or directing rod, מלמד, is derived from the root למד, *lamed*. The deeper sense of מלמד הבקר, "an ox goad," is the power to direct and control animal instinct. One who possesses such power is able, as was the judge Shamgar, to slay the evil instinct represented by the Philistines, the animal desire to cast off yoke, as explained in *Chassidut*. We are further taught in *Chassidut* that directing—literally, "teaching"—the ox (i.e. animal soul; often the parable is that of whipping a horse) implies first teaching him to recognize that he is an ox and then "whipping him" out of being an ox.

In relation to man's instinctive aspiration to understand and control nature, the "ox goad" can be understood as "the learning process related to the ox," i.e. nature, and the resultant development of technology. The initial mentality of the ox is to grasp and relate to physical reality as the ultimate "something." The true, Torah-oriented "teacher" of the ox, מלמד הבקר, elevates the initial mentality of Worlds to recognize the presence of Souls (the ox—Worlds—thereby becoming conscious that he is only an ox) and then Divinity (thus "whipping" the ox "out" of being an ox).

SOULS

Learning Torah for the sake of fulfilling its directive, in order to rectify one's soul, is the most all-inclusive of *mitzvot*. It serves as the foundation and catalyst in motivating performance of all other *mitzvot*, as our Sages teach: תלמוד תורה כנגד כולם, "learning Torah is equal to them all."

Learning Torah not only sharpens the intellect, in the sense of logical analytical reasoning, but it also rectifies one's initially unrectified power of imagination. The process of rectification follows the three stages of "submission, separation, and sweetening" taught by the Ba'al Shem Tov. This service endows one with the "wings" necessary to break through the inherent limitations of logic and rationality, and ultimately to draw down the blessing (the ב of לב) of Divine inspiration.

"He who learns in order to teach [הלומד על מנת ללמד] is granted the ability to learn and teach; he who learns in order to do is granted the ability to learn, teach, guard, and do."

In *Chassidut* we are taught that teaching a beginner, previously uninitiated to the wonder of Torah and *mitzvot*, is the greatest of all "deeds." Thus when one learns intending to become qualified to initiate others into Torah and *mitzvot*, he is simultaneously "learning in order to teach" and "learning in order to do" at the very highest level.

DIVINITY

"And all of your children are 'students of G-d,' and great is the peace of your children." The phrase "students of G-d" (למודי ה') is interpreted to refer both to the state of learning directly from the mouth of G-d, as it were, and to the devoted study of G-d Himself (in contrast to the study of the Divine Law of Torah, for the sake of the rectification of Souls and Worlds), i.e., the deep teachings of *Chassidut*. The latter—particularly the teachings of *Chabad Chassidut*—are meditations on G-d Himself without any conscious intention to "utilize" the "results" of the meditation for the sake of any particular rectification, but rather exclusively to cling to Him.

On the verse "...and great is the peace of your children," our Sages teach: "don't read 'your children' but 'your builders.' " The "students of G-d," who learn the revealed and hidden dimensions of Torah "directly from the mouth of G-d" (i.e. ever conscious of G-d's continual giving of the Torah to Israel), and are primarily involved with its transcendent mysteries (the study of G-d Himself), are true "builders"—rectifiers of reality. The letters of the Torah they learn are so potent as to actually create "new heavens and new earth"—"new" in the sense of being perfectly "transparent" to G-d's Infinite Light.

NUMBER

The letter *lamed* equals thirty.

WORLDS

In the Jewish calendar, a "full month" possesses thirty days. In Hebrew there are two words for month: חדש, literally, "new [moon]," and ירח, "moon." The moon and its cycle of birth, apparent death and spontaneous rebirth, symbolize the *sefirah* of *malchut* (kingdom). *Malchut* is personified by King David. In the service of our blessing of the new moon we exclaim: "King David is alive forever." *Malchut* is referred to as the "lower mother," whose "heartbeat" enlivens all of nature.

In *Pirkei Avot* we are taught that "*malchut* is acquired with thirty attributes." The name of the Kingly tribe, Judah (יהודה, the ancestor of David), equals thirty. *Malchut* is the origin of Worlds, as is said: "Your *malchut* is the *malchut* of all worlds."

In general, *malchut* is identified with the woman in Israel. In the specific laws of vows, the "worth" assigned to an adult woman, from the age of twenty to sixty, is thirty *shekel*. The very physiology of woman is linked to the lunar cycle of thirty days. Both *malchut* ("the daughter" or "lower mother," as mentioned above) and its origin, *binah* ("understanding," the "higher mother"), relate to the secret of heart, the basic symbol of the letter *lamed*. The circulatory system is centered in the heart. So, at the level of Worlds, the basic, physically apparent cycle of time is the lunar month, the fundamental unit of the Jewish calendar.

SOULS

In every generation there are a small number of hidden *tzadikim* whose devotion to G-d in learning and good deeds upholds the world. In one place the Sages refer to thirty such *tzadikim* and in another place to thirty-six. The three components of the form of the letter *lamed* (=30), *yud*, *vav*, and *kaf* (10, 6, and 20) total 36. In the quadratic series beginning 6, 10, 20, the following term is 36. Later in the series is the number 608, which equals לב מבין דעת, referred to above. In general, the *tzadik* corresponds to the *sefirah* of *yesod* (foundation), the sixth emotive power of the soul. $6^2=36$. Besides the hidden (underground) "root" of six, thirty revealed "branches" of interinclusion are present. These holy souls, ever involved in revealing G-d's *malchut* to the world (thus affecting the union of *yesod* and *malchut*, as taught in Kabbalah) are truly the "second to the King" as discussed in the name of the letter *beit* (the secret of the ב of לב).

The Midrash correlates the thirty days of the month to the thirty generations of Jewish souls beginning with Abraham and concluding with King Yoshiyahu, who immediately preceded the destruction of the first Temple. From Abraham until Solomon, the builder of the first Temple, there were fifteen generations corresponding to the fifteen days of the waxing of the moon.

Our Sages refer to the generation of Solomon as the "full moon." The reduced value of Solomon's name itself, שלמה, is fifteen. (David, דוד, his father, equals fourteen, as he was the fourteenth generation from Abraham.)

The waning of the moon of Israel begins from Solomon's son, Rechavam, in whose generation the Kingdom of Israel was divided. The waning continued for fifteen generations until King Yoshiyahu, one of the greatest *tzadikim* to stand from the house of David, who was tragically killed in war, and over whom the prophet Jeremiah mourns the whole fourth chapter of Lamentations. There he refers to him as "the *mashiach* of G-d."

Thus, at the level of Souls, the number of the letter *lamed* can be seen to represent Jewish history in general, which ever reflects, until the final coming of *Mashiach*, spiraling cycles of hiddenness and revelation, exile and redemption.

DIVINITY

The "thirty attributes" of *malchut* at the level of *Atzilut*, the world of Divine unity, consist of three dimensions of vessels—inner, middle and outer—each containing ten *sefirot* (3·10=30). The inner vessels are the creative power and lifeforce of the world of *Beriah* (Creation); the middle vessels, of the world of *Yetzirah* (Formation); and the outer vessels, of the world of *Asiyah* (Action). "Your Kingdom is the Kingdom of all worlds," quoted above, is interpreted in *Chassidut* to mean that kingship, as revealed in the world of *Atzilut*, is in truth manifest at all levels of kingship, each in its respective world. Kingship at the level of *Atzilut* is the Divine "I," as in the phrase "I shall reign." The kingship of each lower world is its own sense of ego, "I." In truth, the Divine "I" is present in (and ultimately, responsible for) every created sense of "I." Its revelation depends upon the service of created beings (Worlds) to nullify their own selfconsciousness to that of G-d.

Similar to the thirty *tzadikim* present in every generation at the level of Souls (relatively, the "present" of this world), so, in the World to Come (Divinity), our Sages speak of thirty groups of *tzadikim*. As the *malchut* of *Atzilut* is referred to as the "body" of all Jewish souls, so we can understand these thirty groups of *tzadikim*, to be revealed in the future, as the spiritual power innate in the souls of Israel to rectify (enclothe) the thirty vessels of *malchut* of *Atzilut*, in order to draw down their manifestation into the three lower worlds of *Beriah*, *Yetzirah*, and *Asiyah*.

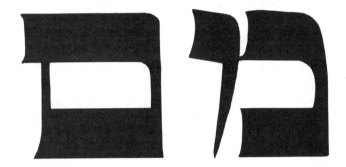

Mem

מַעְיַן הַחָכְמָה

Fountain of Wisdom

Mem: Fountain of Wisdom

The *mem* (מם), the letter of "water" (מים), symbolizes the fountain of the Divine Wisdom of Torah. Just as the waters of a physical fountain (spring) ascend from their unknown subterranean source (the secret of the abyss in the account of Creation) to reveal themselves on earth, so does the fountain of wisdom express the power of flow from the superconscious source. In the terminology of Kabbalah, this flow is from *keter* (crown) to *chochmah* (wisdom). The stream is symbolized in Proverbs as נחל נבע מקור חכמה, "the flowing *stream*, the source of wisdom."

In particular, we are taught that there are thirteen channels of flow from the superconscious source to the beginning of consciousness. These channels correspond to the Thirteen Attributes of Mercy revealed to Moses at Sinai, as well as to the thirteen principles of Torah exegesis, the (superrational) "logic" of Torah.

The *mem* is the thirteenth letter of the *alef-beit*. In Kabbalah we are taught that thirteen *mems*, as it were, appear in the "primordial air," the (outer) "space" into which the letter *lamed* soars. Each attribute of mercy is in fact a contraction of relatively Infinite wisdom, at the level of the superconscious ("waters that have no end"), in order to channel and reveal a flash of wisdom on to the "screen" of consciousness. Conscious wisdom draws its points of insight primarily from that attribute of mercy referred to in Torah as נצר חסד לאלפים, "He retains kindness for thousands of generations," whose initial letters spell the word נחל, "stream," the first word in the previously quoted phrase, נחל נבע מקור חכמה.

In *atbash*, *mem* transforms to *yud*, the point of wisdom or revealed insight, the drop of water emerging from the fountain of the *mem*.

Both אחד, "one," and אהבה, "love," equal thirteen, the secret of the letter *mem*. The "closed" final *mem* (ם), the source of the fountain of wisdom connected and included within its subterranean, superconscious source, corresponds to the secret of אחד, "one." The "open" *mem* (מ), from which emerges the point (*yud*) of conscious insight, is the first manifestation of love (i.e., will to cling to another) in the soul. The connection between the two fountains of the *mem*, the "closed" fountain and the "open" fountain, is by the power of the Thirteen Divine Attributes of Mercy. This is the secret of G-d's Essential Name, *Havayah*—the "Name of Mercy." The Name *Havayah* equals $26 = 2 \cdot 13$, the union of אחד ("one") and אהבה ("love"), the power to draw into consciousness the wisdom of Torah.

MEM

FORM: The open *mem*—a square with a small opening at its lower left corner. The final *mem*—a complete square.

Worlds The open *mem*—a flowing stream.
The closed final *mem*—an underground stream.
The womb.

Souls The soul—the flowing stream, the source of wisdom.
The open *mem*—self-consciousness.
The closed *mem*—unconscious states of being; the power of reproduction.

Divinity The closed *mem*—the arrival of the *Mashiach*.
The waters of *teshuvah*.

NAME: Water; blemish.

Worlds Water's ability to glue substances.
Water's descending nature.
The evil waters of false, external passions.
The plentitude of water and life's dependence on it.
Blemish—the concealment of G-d's Light in the lower worlds—Nature.

Souls The root of the soul is without blemish.
The love of G-d flowing forth like water.

Divinity Water—a parable for Torah.
The closed *mem*—the first saying of Creation.
The open *mem*—the subsequent nine sayings of Creation.
The open *mem*—the exoteric dimension of Torah.
The closed *mem*—the esoteric dimension of Torah.

NUMBER: Forty.

Worlds Forty days of the flood.
Forty *seah*, the minimum quantity of water required for a *kosher mikvah*.
Forty years of wandering in the Desert.

Souls Forty days from conception to the initial "formation" of the fetus.
"Forty less one":
The punishment of stripes;
The categories of work forbidden on the Sabbath;
The weeks of pregnancy.
Forty days of Israel waiting for Moses to descend with the Torah.
The (three) forty-year periods in the lives of Moses, Hillel, Rabban Yohanan ben Zakai, and Rabbi Akiva
Forty generations from Moses to the completion of the Talmud.

Divinity Forty days of "lower *teshuvah*" for the sin of the Golden Calf.
Forty days of "higher *teshuvah*" in which Moses received the second tablets.
Forty cubits—the height of the entrance to the Sanctuary of the Temple.

FORM

The *mem*, a square, is written in one of two ways: an open *mem*—a square with a small opening in its lower left corner, and a "closed" final *mem*—a complete square. The *mem*, whose name's primary meaning is מים, "water," represents in its form as well as its name various bodies of water.

WORLDS

The open *mem* can be visualized as a fountain whose waters run above ground. The closed *mem* can be pictured as an underground fountain, whose waters are sealed below ground.

The form of the *mem* resembles a womb, which for the fetus is a "fountain of life." The fetus "swims" in an all-encompassing environment of water. In Hebrew, the word אם, "mother," also means "womb." Its essential consonant is the letter *mem*. In most languages *mem* is the basic sound of "mother" (mom). In general, the symbol of mother nature, Eve, "the mother of all life," is the womb of all existence at the level of Worlds. This is after she ascends in aspiration—the secret of the letter *lamed*—to receive from Adam the seed of life.

At the level of Worlds, all reproduction, from the womb of nature, obeys the confinement of the "law of conservation of energy/matter." No more leaves the womb than that which enters in the form of nourishment from the mother. This nourishment derives from nature itself, and in turn feeds the embryo and fetus until it reaches its full development culminating in birth. Adam's seed, which impregnates nature, is the secret of the continual recreation of the universe, from nothing to something.

SOULS

The "flowing stream, the source of wisdom" hints at the soul flowing down into the body from its source Above. This takes place primarily at the moments of conception (*Beriah* of the soul), "formation" (*Yetzirah*), birth (*Asiyah*), and other crucial moments of life when one's root, *mazal* (מזל, from נזל, "to flow"), shines with special brilliance. At lower, normal energy levels, this flow continues throughout life. The two different streams, as represented by the open *mem* and the closed *mem*, correspond to two levels of Souls. The open *mem* represents the flow of that level of soul which is conscious of self, whereas the closed *mem* represents the flow of that level of soul which is unconscious of self.

As in the verse: "Who can count the dust of Jacob and the number of 'conceptions' of Israel," the word "conceptions," from the root meaning "square" (literally, "four") implies the act of reproduction. The minimal fulfillment of the *mitzvah* to "be fruitful and multiply," the first, and thereby, in a certain sense, foremost *mitzvah* of Torah, is for two parents to "square" themselves by giving birth to a son and a daughter, as discussed in the number of the letter *dalet*.

Reproduction, at the level of Souls, does not obey the confinement of the "law of conservation of energy/matter," but rather draws truly new energy into the world. For this reason the power of reproduction of Jewish souls is referred to in *Chassidut* as "the power of Infinity."

DIVINITY

In the time of the coming of *Mashiach*, when "the earth will be filled with the knowledge of G-d as the waters cover the sea," even the closed final *mem* will become revealed. Only once in the entire *Tanach*, in reference to *Mashiach*, do we find a closed *mem* in the middle of a word: לסרבה המשרה ולשלום אין קץ, "To increase reign and peace without end."

The power of the final *mem*, when fully revealed by *Mashiach*, will infinitely increase his reign and the peace on earth ensuing therefrom. The waters of *Mashiach*, "waters that have no end," are waters of *teshuvah*, as our Sages interpret the conclusion of the second verse of the Torah: "...and the Spirit of G-d was hovering over the waters." "The spirit of G-d," the soul of the *Mashiach*, hovers over (i.e., is dependent upon) the infinite waters of *teshuvah*.

In particular, *teshuvah* is compared to water when motivated purely by the love of G-d, through which even voluntary transgressions are transformed into actual merits. As noted above, אהבה, "love," equals thirteen, the ordinal value of the letter *mem*. The power of this "*teshuvah* from love" to existentially transform reality is a true manifestation of Divinity in the soul of the *ba'al teshuvah*. For this reason, "in the place that *ba'alei teshuvah* stand, [even] consummate *tzadikim* cannot stand." Although "perfect" in regard to the inner conscious levels of their souls, these *tzadkim* have not yet incorporated in themselves the service of "*teshuvah* from love," love which transcends all bounds of consciousness.

NAME

The word *mem* (מם) with a *yud* between the two forms, open and closed, means מים, "water." When the *yud* is extended, thereby transforming into a *vav*, the result is מום, "blemish."

WORLDS

At all levels of Worlds, Souls and Divinity, water symbolizes lovingkindness and life. One of the unique properties of water in nature is its power of osmosis. Water acts as "glue" ("glue" in Hebrew is from the root "to cling"), as in the clinging of love, "and he shall cling to his wife," especially within organic substances. Furthermore, water is "humble," for it continuously seeks to descend to the lowest plane or energy level. Even when freezing, the liquid (water) descends below the solid (ice), as is also reflected in one of the basic miracles of Creation—"stretching the dry land over the waters."

As for every property on the "side of good" there exists a counterpart on the "side of evil" (as is said: "G-d has made one opposite the other"), so do there exist "evil waters" of this world, which represent false, external loves and passions. These are ultimately responsible for the opposite of life, as in the story of Moses who healed the bitter waters in the desert, and the story of the prophet Elisha who healed the deadly waters of Jericho.

At the level of Worlds, the positive aspects of water include: the womb of "mother nature" at all levels of physical reality, as discussed above; the world's dependence upon rain and drinking water; the fact that the majority of the earth is covered by water; the phenomenon that approximately 90% of the human body actually consists of water. Natural streams of water are referred to as מים חיים, "living waters," in recognition of water's essential role in sustaining life.

Any point of concealment of the Divine Light active in the continuous creative process is referred to as a מום, a "blemish" of nature. In truth, concealment is itself a Divine power, associated with the Name *Elokim* (מום=86=אלקים). The word מום is indeed the final of the seventy-two three-letter Divine Names of Kabbalah, all active in the creative process. As all of nature initially hides the presence of the Creator, the entire dimension of "Worlds" can be seen as a blemish, in relation to the revelations of Souls and Divinity. "Nature" (הטבע)=86=מום=אלקים. In the verse: שמש ומגן ה' אלקים, "A sun and shield are *Havayah Elokim*," the two Names *Havayah* and *Elokim* are compared, respectively, to the sun in all of its brilliance, and the power to shield or filter the light of the sun, so as not to blind the eyes of mortal creatures.

SOULS

The essence of the Jewish soul is without blemish: כלך יפה רעיתי ומום אין בך, "You are all beautiful my beloved one, there is no blemish in you." In accordance with the method of the Ba'al Shem Tov, reading the word אַיִן, "there is no," as אַיִן, "nothingness" (thereby converting the phrase from a negation into an affirmation), a Chassidic interpretation of ומום אין בך is: "only the blemish of nothingness is yours." The "blemish" of the soul is only that it is nothing in face of the true, Absolute, "Something" of G-d, the opposite of the (real) blemish of Worlds, false somethingness. The "blemish" of Souls is not only not a blemish at all, but even a "dimple" of grace in the eyes of G-d.

Because of our innate consciousness of nothingness in the face of G-d, souls of Israel are able to reveal the hidden light of G-d in the world. This light was first revealed by Abraham, who is referred to by G-d as "Abraham, my lover." The innate love of G-d present in every Jewish soul is compared to water. In the prayer for rain, which we say in the *Musaf* prayer of *Shmini Atzeret*, we ask G-d to "remember the father (Abraham) who was drawn after you like water." Loving G-d, as natural to every Jewish soul as downstream flow is to water, is our inheritance from our first father Abraham.

DIVINITY

The comparison of Torah to water—"there is no water except Torah"—
is drawn from the life-giving qualities of water mentioned above. Just as the
material world could not exist without water, so, too, the very existence and
sustenance of all worlds is continuously dependent upon the goodly waters
of Torah. Our Sages teach: "G-d looked into the Torah and created the
world." "The world is built by kindness," the lovingkindness of the waters of
Torah.

Just as water quenches bodily thirst, so do the waters of Torah quench
spiritual thirst. The prophet Isaiah urges: "Oh! all who are thirsty go to
water." The fact that the prophet must exclaim "Oh!..." to human souls indicates that the waters in question are non-obvious to Souls, but rather
belong to a higher level—Divinity.

Our Sages interpret the two *mems* (open and closed) to refer to two "sayings," "the open saying" and "the closed saying," מאמר פתוח and מאמר סתום.
Chassidut explains that the first verse of Creation: "In the beginning..." is the
"closed [concealed] saying" of Creation, for it is not preceded with the explicit
phrase "and G-d said...." The first "open [revealed] saying" is: "And G-d said,
'Let there be light.' "

In relation to Torah in general, the "open saying" corresponds to the
revealed dimension of Torah whereas the "closed saying" corresponds to the
hidden dimension, the secrets of Torah. These two sayings further correspond to the higher and lower waters, the secret of the two *yuds* in the form
of the letter *alef*. As a *vav* connects the two states of water in the *alef*, we can
now "read" the *alef* (from below up) as מום, equalling אלקים (86), the
"shield" of Creation. The essential reading of the three components of the
alef, ייו, is numerically equivalent to the Name *Havayah* (26), the "sun" of
Creation. *Mem* and *yud* themselves transform into one another in *atbash*, as
explained above. The two letters which correspond to the higher waters, the
higher *yud* (י) and final *mem* (ם), spell יﬦ (the י of the Name *Havayah* preceding the ﬦ of the Name *Elokim*), "the sea" or "concealed world"—the hidden waters of the inner dimension of Torah. This is the secret of "The Glory
of G-d is to conceal things." The two letters which correspond to the lower
waters, the lower *mem* (מ) and *yud* (י), spell מי ("who?"), the secret of "the
glory of kings is to investigate things"—the revealed dimension of Torah.

NUMBER

The letter *mem* equals forty.

WORLDS

"And the rain was upon the earth for forty days and forty nights." Except for Noah and his immediate family, the flood annihilated all of mankind, who, throughout their first ten generations of existence, had progressively turned more corrupt and evil. Nonetheless, the very same waters that flooded the earth, G-d's "agent" in the destruction of life, simultaneously cleansed the earth of the evil influences of man. As a result of the flood, new, pure life could replace old, impure life.

This function of water, as the medium of transition and renewal, is the secret of the *mikvah* in Jewish law. In general, transition from a Torah-defined state of impurity (a relative state of death) to a state of purity (life) is through immersion in a *mikvah*. All material vessels, as well as human bodies, pass through stages of purity and impurity. A *kosher mikvah* of gathered rainwater contains at least forty *seah* of water. The rain that descended upon the earth for forty days and forty nights alludes to G-d immersing, as it were, the entire earth in a *mikvah*. The purifying effect of the *mikvah*-waters on the planet allowed for life to be renewed on earth through Noah, who had "found favor in the eyes of G-d."

Ten of the twelve spies that Moses sent to investigate the land of Israel returned to the people with an evil report. The people mistakenly accepted this report and were sentenced to wander in the desert for forty years, corresponding to the forty days the spies had spent investigating the land. During these forty years of wandering, the generation that left Egypt was decreed to die; only a new generation, their children, would enter the land. Thus here, too, the number forty appears as a transition from death to life, a purification from impure to pure.

SOULS

The first forty days of pregnancy culminate with, in the words of our Sages, "the formation of the fetus." In the correspondence of the four worlds to the four basic elements of nature (and their spiritual counterparts), the world of Formation corresponds to the element of water, the secret of the letter *mem* (=40).

In reference to the punishment (rectification of soul) of stripes, the Torah states their number to be: "...in the number forty," which our Sages explain as that number which is "in" forty, i.e. thirty-nine ("forty less one"). So do we find other Torah groupings whose number is "forty less one," such as the number of categories of work forbidden on Shabbat. Our Sages teach that the full number of days of pregnancy (allowing for three days till conception) is 273=7·39, "forty less one" weeks.

Upon the revelation of Sinai, Moses ascended the mountain and remained there for forty days and forty nights. During this period the hearts of the people were filled with great anticipation and longing. Whereas for Moses, the experience of this period was surely one of Divinity (in particular "Worlds in Divinity," relative to the subsequent two periods of forty days that he spent on the mountain), for the people the experience was at the level of Souls. The period from the Exodus, the birth of the collective Soul of Israel, to the giving of the Torah, the relative state of the people, was in particular one of "Worlds in Souls." The spiritual service of the counting of the *Omer* during this period is the soul rectifying its body, Worlds. The first forty-day period from Sinai was, for the people, one of "Souls in Souls." The collective Soul of Israel had received an initial revelation of Divinity, with the giving of the Torah, but had not been able to fully integrate it. All stood in anticipation of Moses's descent from the mountain with the tablets of the covenant. This period ended, tragically, with the sin of the golden calf, the imaginary substitution for the soul of Moses, the leader of the generation.

The one-hundred-twenty-year life span of Moses, as well as those of several of the greatest Sages of Israel (Hillel, Rabban Yochanan ben Zakai, Rabbi Akiva—all of whom were sparks of the soul of Moses), divides into three periods of forty years. Relative to the experience of Souls, they correspond in particular to Worlds, Souls, Divinity in Souls.

Maimonides, in the introduction to his codification of Jewish Law, *Mishneh Torah*, enumerates forty generations from Moses to Rav Ashi, the compiler of the Babylonian Talmud. With the completion of the Talmud, Rav Ashi "sealed" the revelation of the Oral Torah. These forty generations correspond to the initial forty days during which Moses received the Torah from G-d on Sinai. Through our devotion to the study of the Oral Law and the integration, in our daily lives, of its precepts, we preclude the fall that we experienced at the end of that period, the sin of the golden calf.

DIVINITY

After the sin of the golden calf, Moses ascended the mountain once more for a second period of forty days and forty nights. This period was a time of prayer for forgiveness. Prayer is essentially the service of the soul in its "run" to G-d. For Moses, this period was one of most sincere empathy with the souls of Israel, at the level of Souls in Divinity (all of Moses's ascents to the mountain were, for him, at the level of Divinity, as explained above). At the end of this period Moses was instructed by G-d to descend and prepare new tablets of covenant, tablets of *ba'alei teshuvah*, as the first tablets, those of *tzadikim* without sin, had been broken with the sin.

Once more Moses ascended the mountain for a third, final period of forty days, beginning from *Rosh Chodesh Elul* and culminating on *Yom Kippur*, the day of atonement. For Moses, this was the period of highest Divine Revelation, Divinity in Divinity. On *Yom Kippur*, Moses descended with the new tablets engraved, by the hand of G-d, with the Ten Commandments, the crown of the entire Torah. At the beginning of this period G-d revealed to Moses the secret of the Thirteen Attributes of Mercy (*mem*, which equals forty, is the thirteenth letter of the *alef-beit*, as discussed above), for which reason the entire month of *Elul* is called "the month of mercy." The revelation of these Divine Attributes of Mercy reaches its epitome in the *Neilah* prayer, the conclusion and seal of *Yom Kippur*.

Both the second and third periods of forty days are times of *teshuvah* for the Jewish People, yet the second period relative to the third, relates to the "lower *teshuvah*" (that *teshuvah* which is primarily motivated by a sense of bitterness, due to one's existential confrontation with the experience of sin), relative to the "higher *teshuvah*" (that *teshuvah* which is primarily motivated by the joy of the soul having merited to experience the revelation of G-d's Infinite Mercy). The "lower *teshuvah*" is primarily in a state of "running" (away from evil) into G-d. The "higher *teshuvah*" brings the "run" to its peak (in the joy of experiencing G-d's outstretched arm drawing one into Himself) and then begins the process of "return" to fulfill G-d's Will below. Both states entail true *bitul*, selflessness, in the Presence of G-d, and therefore relate to the level of Divinity (whereas the normative service of *tzadikim* is at the general level of Souls). The first state, motivated by the experience of sin, sin before G-d, is in particular at the level of Worlds in Divinity. The service of the "higher *teshuvah*" is at the level of Souls in Divinity, while the actual revelation of G-d's Infinite Mercy, during this third period of forty days, is Divinity in Divinity.

An additional forty, at the level of Divinity, is the forty-cubit height of the opening to the Temple Hall. Of this opening our Sages relate that G-d says to us, as it were: "Open to Me an opening as the point of a needle [in the service of *teshuvah,* Divinity in the service of the soul] and I will open to you an opening as [wide as] the great entrance to the Temple Hall."

TIME	MOSES	ISRAEL
Exodus to Sinai		Worlds in Souls
first forty days	Worlds in Divinity	Souls in Souls
second forty days	Souls in Divinity	Worlds in Divinity
third forty days	Divinity in Divinity	Souls in Divinity
		Divinity in Divinity

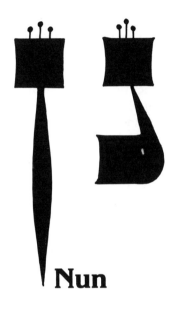

Nun

לִפְנֵי שֶׁמֶשׁ יִנּוֹן שְׁמוֹ

The Messiah: Heir to the Throne

Nun: The Messiah—Heir to the Throne

In Aramaic, *nun* means "fish." The *mem*, the waters of the sea, is the natural medium of the *nun*, fish. The *nun* "swims" in the *mem*, covered by the waters of the "hidden world." Creatures of the "hidden world" lack self-consciousness. Unlike fish, land animals, revealed on the face of the earth, possess self-consciousness.

The souls of Israel divide into two general categories, symbolized by fish and land animals. The two prototypes of these categories are the leviathan and the *behemot*. In the present, these two categories of souls correspond to the two innate tendencies and attractions of the soul, to either the concealed and secret or revealed and legal dimensions of Torah. In the future, the two prototypes, leviathan and *behemot*, will unite in battle, each "killing" the "ego" of the other, thereafter to blend together in true union. Their "meat" will then be served as the feast for the *tzadikim* in the World to Come. The souls of the *tzadikim* will actually consume the very root of consciousness of our present level of soul, in order to integrate ("digest") it into a totally new and higher level of consciousness.

Leviathan (לויתן) equals *malchut* (מלכות, "kingdom," 496). In Kabbalah, *malchut*, in the world of Divine Emanation, is represented by the sea, whose tides are controlled by the power of the moon, the symbol of King David (upon seeing the new moon we say, "David the king of Israel is alive forever"). When *malchut* descends to enliven the lower worlds it is symbolized by the earth. Thus, the leviathan is the symbol of the Divine Source of kingdom. In Hebrew, *nun* means "Kingdom," and in particular, "the heir to the throne."

The *nun* is the fourteenth letter of the *alef-beit*, which equals דוד, David, the progenitor of the eternal Kingdom of Israel. The heir to David is *Mashiach ben* David, of whom is said: לפני שמש ינון שמו, "As long as the duration of the sun his name shall rule." Our Sages teach us that one of the names of *Mashiach* is *Yinon* (ינון, "shall rule"), cognate to *nun* (נון). *Mashiach* is also referred to as בר נפלא, "the miscarriage," or, literally, the "fallen one." As we will learn in the secret of the letter *samech*, the *nun* does not appear in Psalm 145, but is supported by G-d's transcendent mercy, as expressed by the following letter, *samech*. In general, *nun* corresponds in Torah to the image of falling. The soul of *Mashiach* experiences itself as continuously falling and dying; if not for the ever-present Hand of G-d "catching" it, it would crash to the ground and shatter to death. The consciousness of fall is the reflection of the egoless state of the fish, in its natural medium of water, when forced to reveal itself on dry land. This is like the experience of a hidden *tzadik* when forced from Above to reveal himself for the good of Israel and the world. We find this exemplified in the life and teachings of the Ba'al Shem Tov, and so will be epitomized in the life of *Mashiach*. Ultimately, the "destiny" of *Mashiach* and his generation is to assume the level of sea on earth, to experience, paradoxically, selfless-selfconsciousness, as said in the verse of Isaiah with which the Rambam concludes his Code of Jewish Law (whose final section, *The Laws of Kings*, culminates with the description of the coming of *Mashiach*): "for the earth will be filled with the knowledge of G-d, like waters cover the sea."

NUN

FORM: A "bent-over" vessel—the "bent-over servant."
The final nun—an extended vav descending below the line—the "un-bounded servant."

Worlds The receiving vessel.
The faithful one.
Subservience and faithfulness.

Souls Humility—the vessel of true insight into *halachah*.

Divinity The final *nun*—extension of the Infinite.
Light Above and below.
Moses—the faithful servant.

NAME: Fish; kingdom; heir to the throne.

Worlds Fish of the sea—the symbol of reproductivity.
The selflessness inherent in "previous"-world consciousness.
The rectified state of the world.

Souls The souls of Israel are kings and children of kings.
Heir to the throne—*Mashiach*.
The ruling power of the soul.

Divinity The *Shechinah*—origin of the souls of Israel.
The kingdom of G-d on earth.
Moses, "the great fish."

NUMBER: Fifty; the fifty gates of understanding.

Worlds The cycle of fifty years culminating in the Jubilee year.
"Fifty years to counsel."
The fifty queries into the nature of Creation which G-d poses Job.

Souls Fifty references to the Exodus in Torah.
"Her husband is known in the gates."

Divinity Fifty images in Torah "supported" by the Name of G-d.
Fifty days of counting the *Omer* between *Pesach* and *Shavuot*.
Fifty thousand Jubilees of the World to Come.

FORM

The *nun* possesses both a common and final form. The common form is bent over in appearance, whereas the final form is an extended *vav* descending below the lower line-border of the letters.

In the Talmud, the two forms of the *nun* are interpreted to represent two distinct types of servant of G-d, or "faithful one": נאמן כפוף, a "bent-over faithful one," and נאמן פשוט, a "straight, unbounded faithful one." The servant represented by the bent-over *nun* relates to the levels of Worlds and Souls, whereas the servant represented by the straight (unbounded) *nun* relates to the level of Divinity.

נאמן ("faithful") begins and ends with *nun*, just as the full spelling of the letter *nun* itself, נון. When the middle letter of *nun* (נון), *vav*, enters between the two middle letters of נאמן, אמ, the secret Divine Name אום, related to the coming of the *Mashiach*, is formed.

WORLDS

The bent-over form of the *nun*, the "bent-over faithful one," indicates, at the level of Worlds, a sense of poverty and need to receive. This bent-over form is the most fundamental (simple) "vessel" form amongst the letters of the *alef-beit*. In the form of the letter *tet* we envision a vessel filled by (pregnant with) "introverted" light, whereas the *nun* is a vessel alone.

While letters in general are understood to represent spiritual vessels and conveyors of hidden light and energy, the first thirteen letters of the *alef-beit*, in particular (from *alef* to *mem*), correspond to lights, while the remaining nine (ט) letters, from *nun* to *tav*, correspond to vessels. In *atbash*, the pair טנ is the two-letter root of the word for vessel used in Torah in the context of the *mitzvah* of bringing first fruits to the Temple: טנא. The word טנא is numerically equivalent to the more common word for "vessel": כלי (=60). The א of טנא alludes to the "first fruit," the secret of the thousand (אלף) lights which fill the vessel. In Aramaic, טו means body, as used by the Sages in the sense of the experience of woman in marriage. In general, lights are considered male and vessels female. This is reflected in the fact that the middle letter of the first thirteen "light-letters," *zayin*, is the initial letter of זכר, "male," and *nun*, the first of the last nine "vessel-letters," is the initial letter of נקבה, "female." (These two letters, together with the first of the thirteen "light-letters" [א], combine to form the root אזן, "ear." Relating to the inner sense of the ear, אזן means both "scales" and "balance," the secret of perfect marriage, as explained in Kabbalah.)

At the level of Worlds, the vessel or receiver experiences physical need, as mentioned above. This is the state of עני, "poor man," whose secret is "the eye" (ע) focused solely on his "empty vessel" (נ), longing for even a "single point" of sustenance from Above (not yet drawn down into physical manifestation, i.e., the "suspended" י). Unlike a rebellious servant who reacts to his inferior, often impoverished position with frustration or contemptuousness, the trustworthy servant—"the bent-over faithful one"—accepts the service of his master joyously, out of simple faith in his Master's good to all.

SOULS

At the level of Souls, the ‎עני‎ ("poor man") becomes the ‎ענו‎ ("humble man"). Through humility, the yet intangible *yud* of the ‎עני‎ is drawn down and integrated in the vessel, the *nun* of the ‎עני→ענו‎. The fully-integrated light is the secret of the letter *vav* of ‎ענו‎. The more humble and selfless one is (selflessness being the intrinsic property of Souls), so does one's vessel invert concavely into oneself, spontaneously drawing down and internalizing influx from Above, as explained in *Chassidut*.

In particular, humility is the vessel necessary for receiving true insight into G-d's Will, the secret of *halachah*, Jewish Law. When two Sages disagree on a point of *halachah*, the decision accepted as law by the prevailing Rabbinic majority reflects the opinion of the proponent who is more humble, rather than intellectually brilliant. *Halachah*, like water, descends from its source on high to the lowest possible "basin," the soul and mind of the humble Sage. Intellectual brilliance, like fire, is in a state of continual ascent and "climb" to conceive and express new insights and understanding, whereas humility, characterized by the sincere desire to simply receive and faithfully convey the teachings of previous authorities, descends below, like water. For this reason King David was the "master" of *halachah*, as well as Hillel, Rabbi Yosef Karo (the author of the *Shulchan Aruch*), the Chassidic masters and, in the future, *Mashiach* himself.

DIVINITY

Moses was chosen by G-d to be His faithful servant, over Korach (who possessed outstanding intellectual brilliance) and even over his own elder, righteous brother Aaron, because "the man Moses was the most humble of all men on the face of the earth." The Talmud states that "the bent-over faithful one" belongs to this world, whereas "the straight (unbounded) faithful one" refers to his "straightening out" in the World to Come, when released from all of the confining pressures of this world. Moses, in his uniquely great humility, reached a state close to that of the World to Come. Here the *vav* of ענו extends even more so than at the level of Souls, descending below the line of the confines of sanctity in this world in order to draw Divine Light into the otherwise dark realms of existence. The humble one (ענו) becomes the secret of the Divine "cloud [of glory]" (ענן), the power of the Divine to transform darkness into light. The *vav* of ענו מאד, "very humble," thus hints at the secret of the extended-*vav*-become-final-*nun* of the World to Come, when all darkness will vanish from the earth and G-d's Infinite Light—as expressed in the *Zohar*: "Above without end and below without bound"—will become revealed. In the service of the heart, this is the state of loving G-d בכל מאדך, "with all your might," literally "all of your 'veryness,'" dependent upon the same state of "very" as that of Moses, "*very* humble."

Ultimately, the "faithful servant" (עבד נאמן), is one with "G-d, the faithful King" (א״ל מלך נאמן; the average value of the seven letters עבד נאמן equals א״ל, "G-d"), for עבד מלך, "the servant of the king is [as] the king." (The letters עבד נאמן, "faithful servant", permute to spell אדם בענן, "man in the cloud," hinting at the coming of the *Mashiach* of whom is said "Behold, he comes with the clouds of heaven.") Some have the custom of saying א״ל מלך נאמן before reciting "Hear O Israel...G-d is One," the statement of the unity of Souls in Divinity, for the sake of the revelation of G-d's Kingdom (*nun*) on earth.

NAME

The word *nun* (נון) means "fish", and (in Hebrew) "kingdom," particularly, "heir to the throne."

WORLDS

On the fifth day of Creation fish were created from water, just as the letter *nun* (whose reduced value is five)—"fish"—follows (i.e., emerges from) the letter *mem*, "water." The fish were the first creatures whom the Creator blessed: "Be fruitful and multiply and fill the waters in the seas." In nature, fish symbolize reproduction. This is hinted at in the fact that the *nun* is the only letter whose full spelling (נון) is a repetition of itself with a *vav*—meaning "and"—in between, as though to say, "fish and more fish." The previous letter, *mem*, whose meaning is "water," is spelled by repeating itself without a *vav* in between (מם), in the secret of the original state of the creation of water: "water in water." When each of the five final letters מנצפ״ך is given a unique numerical value, the final *nun* (the repeated *nun* in the full spelling נון) equals 700, which is 14—the ordinal value of *nun*—times 50—the normative value of *nun*. This unique phenomenon of the letter *nun* hints that the ideal ratio of reproduction in nature is 1:14 (and 14=2·7; two times דג, "fish").

Just as the English verb "to hunt" is not derived from the word "animal" or "bird," whereas "to fish" comes from the word "fish," so too is the phenomenon in Hebrew (from which derives the phenomenon in English!). Kosher land animals and birds must be slaughtered according to *halachah* in order to become edible for Jews. Kosher fish do not require slaughtering. In Kabbalah we learn that this is because fish reflect the kindness (water) of a "previous" world which does not require rectification by man. The very essence of the fish may be "caught" and directly incorporated into the essence of man. Not so in relation to land animals and birds, who must undergo a spiritual "metamorphosis" before becoming edible. (This is in addition to [and a prerequisite before] the even more spiritual "metamorphosis" of all edible substance: the elevation of its Divine "sparks" through the eating and digestive process of the *tzadik*, which raises Worlds to the level of [Worlds in] Souls, afterwards becoming one with Divinity when, by their energy, the *tzadik* serves G-d.)

SOULS

King David dedicates Psalm 72 to his son and heir, Solomon—"A psalm for Solomon"—and prays: יהי שמו לעולם לפני שמש ינון שמו יתברכו בו כל גוים יאשרהו, "May his name endure forever, as long as the duration of the sun his name shall *rule*, and they will be blessed in him, let all the nations call him happy." This psalm relates not only to Solomon, but to the future "son of David," the *Mashiach*, who will sit, as did King Solomon, "on the throne of G-d." Our Sages read the phrase ינון שמו in the above verse as: "his [*Mashiach's*] name is *Yinon*," as mentioned above.

In the Talmud we find that all Jews are "sons of kings." In the *Zohar* all Jews are referred to as "kings." Thus, from the perspective of the *Zohar*, the hidden wisdom of the Torah which is above the limitations of time, the king-to-be (the heir or "son of a king") is already king. This itself is the secret of the two *nuns*, the bent-over *nun* of this world, the potential king, and the straight, unbounded *nun* of the future, the actual king. Both *nuns* are connected by the *vav* of the full spelling of *nun* (נון). Above, the *nun* was understood to be a "servant" at all levels of Worlds, Souls, Divinity. Here we witness the truth of the saying of our Sages: "The servant of the king is [i.e., becomes one with and assumes the power of] the king."

DIVINITY

" 'The word of G-d' [‎דבר הוי׳‎] is referred to by the name 'Divine Presence' [‎שכינה‎] in the terminology of our Sages and [by the names] 'lower mother' [‎אמא תתאה‎] and 'queen' [‎מטרוניתא‎] in the terminology of the *Zohar*...because it resides and is enclothed in all creations to enliven them. In the terminology of Kabbalah it is referred to by the name 'Kingdom' [‎מלכות‎], as in the verse 'the word of the king is his reign,' for the king controls his kingdom by means of his speech....

"The source of life from which all worlds receive in particular...is called 'the revealed world' [‎עלמא דאתגליא‎] and 'Divine Presence,' from the phrase 'and I shall dwell amongst them'...and therefore it is called 'the mother of children'...and 'congregation of Israel' [‎כנסת ישראל‎], for from this source are emanated the souls of the world of Emanation and created the souls of the world of Creation...."

The *nun*, which means "kingdom" (*malchut*), is the secret of the *Shechinah* (‎שכינה‎), the Divine Presence with Its seven names or images quoted above, from *Tanya*. Its most essential Name, *Shechinah* (‎שכינה‎), equals $385 = 7 \cdot 55$, the latter number being the value of the last two letters (‎נה‎) of *Shechinah* (‎שכינה‎). $55 = \Delta 10$, the sum of all numbers from 1 to 10. $385 = \sum_{n=1}^{n=10} n^2$, the sum of all squares from 1 to 10, as explained in the *Zohar*. These two letters ‎נה‎ are the vessel of the *Shechinah*, the *nun*, and the light of the *Shechinah*, the *hei*, as taught in Kabbalah and *Chassidut*. More than any other letter of the *alef-beit*, the *nun* symbolizes G-d's Kingdom (dwelling) on earth, as is said "and G-d will be King over all the earth, in that day will G-d be One and His Name One." The task of revealing G-d's Kingdom on earth is entrusted to the souls of Israel, "kings" and "sons of kings," to the "congregation of Israel" in general and to the king of Israel in particular. The first king of Israel, Moses, was drawn out of the sea, like a fish, by the daughter of Pharoah, to become revealed on dry land. His greatest disciple and successor, Joshua, is "the son of *Nun* [‎נון‎]." This hints at Joshua's spiritual father, Moses himself, the "great fish" (‎דג גדול‎=50=‎נ‎) of the sea. The ultimate personification of the great fish revealed on dry land is the final king of Israel, the *Mashiach*, as explained above.

NUMBER

The letter *nun* equals fifty. One of the most fundamental concepts of Kabbalah is "the fifty gates of understanding." These fifty gates appear at all levels of Worlds, Souls, and Divinity.

WORLDS

"And you shall sanctify the fiftieth year, and proclaim liberty throughout the land to all its inhabitants; it shall be a Jubilee for you and you shall return every man to his possession, every man to his family shall you return." The fiftieth year, the culmination of seven cycles of seven years, is referred to in Torah as עולם, "a world." This is learned from the law of the "Hebrew slave" who, when not willing to part from his master after seven years of service, must have his ear pierced as he stands next to a door (דלת, the secret of the letter *dalet*) and then continues to serve his master "forever." The word for "forever," לעולם, is interpreted by the Sages, in this context, to mean "until the Jubilee year." The freeing of slaves and the reverting of land to its original owners define the fiftieth year as one of freedom and return to one's true place in the world.

"Who is wise? He who knows his place." "Knows" means not only intellectual recognition but existential identification. For this reason at the age of fifty one becomes able to counsel ("fifty years old to counsel") one's fellow man, for the essence of counsel is helping one find his true place in the world.

At the end of the book of Job, G-d confronts Job with fifty queries into the nature of Creation. Awestruck and unable to respond to these queries, Job is impressed by G-d that he is unable to fathom the mystery of Divine Providence in relation to the fate of man. These fifty queries into the mysteries of nature correspond to the fifty gates of understanding at the level of Worlds.

SOULS

The "Jubilee" freedom of the soul is its daily experience of "the Exodus from Egypt." In particular, the *shofar* blast of freedom (the word "Jubilee," יובל, literally means "the *shofar* of a ram") takes place when we say (and meditate upon) "Hear O Israel, the *G-d* is our G-d, the *G-d* is One," as explained in *Chassidut*. "To hear," in this verse, means "to understand." The *Zohar* interprets the verse (of the hymn "The Woman of Valor") "her husband is known in the gates" to mean that G-d, the "husband" of every Jewish soul, is known (i.e., clung to) by each soul in accordance with its ability of "estimation" (the root שער, "gate," also meaning "to estimate" in the sense of the ability of the mind and heart to "measure" or comprehend). The fifty gates of understanding, fifty "measures" of comprehension at the level of Souls, correspond to the fifty times the Exodus is referred to in Torah. The experience of "Exodus from Egypt" entails transcending one's previous confines (מצרים, "Egypt," means "straights" or "confines"). "Confines" implies not only the confines imposed upon the Divine soul by one's animal soul and physical environment, but also the innate confines and limitations of the initial potential of service of the Divine soul itself. Even the Divine soul, in its day-after-day service of G-d in this world (as well as its initial state of being—service in the higher worlds, before its descent to earth—for each world possesses its own confines), becomes conditioned by habits. Breaking (transcending) habits (spiritual servitude to Pharoah, the king of Egypt, even when appearing to be serving G-d) is the secret of the Exodus from Egypt. At this level the fifty gates of understanding are fifty intellectual, meditative motivations of exodus. One's ability to "know" G-d through one's individual power of "measure" (the secret of returning to one's own individual portion of land in Israel on the Jubilee year), one's "gate" to G-d, is itself the power to break through the spiritual confines imposed by Pharoah, king of Egypt. The "measure" of Divinity (in Souls) breaks (through) the measure (confines) of Worlds (in Souls).

DIVINITY

The ability to abstract (in essence, negate) anthropomorphism, in particular the multitude of anthropomorphic references to G-d that appear throughout the *Tanach*, and thereby to "know G-d through negation," is one of the greatest powers of the Jewish mind, especially as expounded in the writings of Maimonides. In Kabbalah and *Chassidut* every anthropomorphic image in Torah has deep secret significance. "From my flesh I see G-d" implies *positive* "knowledge" of Divinity by means of physical (and, even more significantly, psychological) analogy.

In the Written Torah (the Five Books of Moses) we find fifty basic anthropomorphic idioms: "the eyes of G-d," "the ears of G-d," etc. In each phrase the "image" is "supported" (in the grammatical sense of the word "support," סמיכות, the "construct form") by the Name *Havayah*. The secret of these fifty supported images ("supported" implies that they had previously fallen) corresponds to the fifty gates of understanding at the level of Divinity. For the soul to comprehend their secret one must first "abstract" our initially fallen phenomological image of reality.

"And you shall count for yourselves from the day after the Sabbath [i.e. the first day of Passover], from the day you bring the *Omer* offering, seven complete weeks shall it be. Until the day after the seventh Sabbath you shall count fifty days...." The fifty days of counting the *Omer*, fifty days of spiritual purification in anticipation of receiving the Torah anew on *Shavuot*, are in truth forty-nine days of counting from below (*we* count the *Omer* for only forty-nine days) and one, final, all-inclusive count from Above. This fiftieth count, corresponding to the "fiftieth gate of understanding" (שער הבינן), is the ultimate revelation of Divinity, the giving of the Torah. The entire fifty-day period is an ongoing, step-by-step process of continued Exodus from Egypt. The Exodus reaches its Divine culmination on *Shavuot* with the giving of the Torah to Israel, the Divine directive and power to reach the ultimate freedom of the World to Come (the revelation of the fiftieth gate—Divinity) in this world.

The fifty years of the Jubilee period are the "macrocosm" of the fifty-day period between *Pesach* and *Shavuot*. The Jubilee Year and the worldly freedom it represents correspond to the freedom of the soul that the giving of the Torah on *Shavuot* represents. In reference to the World to Come, the Kabbalah speaks of fifty-thousand Jubilee periods (the Divine "macrocosm" of the fifty-day period between *Pesach* and *Shavuot*, the ascent of the Messianic era, *Pesach*, to the age of resurrection, *Shavuot*) of continuous ascent of all reality into Divinity. In truth, these fifty thousand Jubilees are above time as we know it. With each *shofar* blast (Jubilee), as it were, we transcend our previous sensation of time (and space) altogether, ultimately to unite in G-d.

Samech

נָעוּץ סוֹפָן בִּתְחִלָּתָן וּתְחִילָתָן בְּסוֹפָן

The Endless Cycle

Samech: The Endless Cycle

The circular form of the *samech* symbolizes the fundamental truth reflected at all levels of Torah and reality: "their end is enwedged in their beginning and their beginning in their end." This realization and awareness of inherent unity between beginning and end, which, when comprehended in depth, implies equanimity at all stages of "the endless cycle," is in fact the manifestation of G-d's Transcendent Light (*sovev kol almin*, סובב כל עלמין), which encompasses equally every point of reality. This ever-present Transcendent Light is referred to as השוה ומשוה קטן וגדול, "He is equal and equalizes small and large." In our service of G-d, this implies that in relation to worldly phenomena, all things should be related to and accepted equally. This is the attribute of equanimity (מדת ההשתוות) as taught by the Ba'al Shem Tov, in interpretation of the verse: "I place [שויתי, from the root שוה, "equal"] G-d before me always."

While at outer levels of consciousness one should remain unaffected by the transient events of this world, at deeper inner levels of consciousness, relating to Souls and Divinity, one should continuously be in a state of aspiration to achieve higher and higher levels of clinging to G-d and realizing His Will in Creation through Torah and *mitzvot*.

In *Chassidut* we are taught that the saying of the Sages: "Who is wealthy? He who is happy with his portion" pertains only to worldly possessions, whereas with regard to spiritual matters we should never be satisfied with our present acquisitions but ever strive to obtain more. Nonetheless, as our inner striving takes place within the general context of external equanimity, it also proceeds as a circle, a spiral, in dynamic, ever-ascending motion. Thus an inner, dynamic circle exists within an outer, static circle. This is the secret of the phrase in the vision of Ezekiel: "the wheel within the wheel."

As mentioned in our discussion of the letter *nun*, the *samech*, which means "to support," is the Divine power to support and lift up "the fallen one." One verse reads: "she has fallen and shall not rise, the virgin of Israel." A second verse reads: "as I have fallen, so surely shall I rise." The first verse can be understood as referring to the service of the outer, static circle, the attribute of true equanimity in relation to all worldly phenomena. One can fall to the very "lowest energy level" of physical reality, unable to raise himself, and be totally reliant on the lovingkindness of Divine Providence to sustain him. The second verse, implying inner, active, motivation to rise, though surely dependent upon Divine support and aid, can be understood as referring to the service of the inner, dynamic circle of spiritual aspiration.

As is the case for any two concentric circles, the bottom of the outer circle descends below that of the inner circle, yet its upper portion is higher in origin than that of the inner circle. This in itself is the ultimate manifestation of "the end" being enwedged in "the beginning." "The end" here refers to the service of the outer circle itself. "The beginning" refers to the ultimate objective of the inner circle, the revelation below, in Worlds, of G-d's very Essence, latently present in the simple faith inherent in the "worldy" service of equanimity.

SAMECH

FORM: A circle; a wedding ring.

Worlds The vacuum created by the initial contraction of G-d's Infinite Light.
The lower perspective of reality resulting from the initial contraction.
Circular rings of evolutionary and historical cycles.
The despair inherent in the "philosophy of the void."

Souls The impression of Divine light "left over" in the vacuum.
The *tzadik*—hidden foundation of the world.
The equality of all Jewish souls.
The marriage of two halves of a common soul.

Divinity "Their end is enwedged in their beginning and their beginning in their end."
The Transcendent Surrounding Light.
"The Future to Come" (as opposed to "the Coming World").
The Divine presence in marriage.
The dance of the *tzadikim* in the World to Come.
The dance of the maidens on *Tu b'Av*.

NAME: To support; rely on; ordination; construct form (in grammar).

Worlds Supporting the fallen.
The miraculous continuation of life in the face of entropy.
Welfare: support and encouragement.

Souls The support of one's students.
The secret of ordination.
Signs and summaries.

Divinity Offering oneself to G-d (*semichah*).
The experience of being supported by G-d at all times.

NUMBER: Sixty.

Worlds Numerical symbol of an all inclusive state.
The law of nullification, 1:60.
Sleep is one-sixtieth of death; Dream is one-sixtieth of prophecy.
Fire is one-sixtieth of hell; Honey is one-sixtieth of manna.
Shabbat is one-sixtieth of the World to Come.
The quantum leap from plane to plane.
The nullification of lower dimensional spaces in higher dimensional spaces.

Souls Sixty ten thousands—600,000 souls who left Egypt.
The nullification of the individual Jew in the community of Israel.
Sixty Guards of King Solomon; Sixty students of the Ba'al Shem Tov.
Sixty queens in the Song of Songs; Sixty tractates of the Oral Torah.

Divinity Sixty Letters of the Priestly Blessing.
Sixty bones in the two hands of the *kohen*.
The Transcendent Light of G-d.

FORM

The form of the *samech* is a circle, often symbolizing a wedding ring.

WORLDS

An empty circle represents the vacuum created by the initial *tzimtzum* of G-d's Infinite Light. In our lower perspective of reality (the result of the initial *tzimtzum*), life process and world history appear as ever expanding circles within circles. The relativistic vision of a "finite universe" of space-time is itself a great *samech* whose end is enwedged into its beginning and beginning into end. From the perspective of Worlds, there is no "escape" from this essentially finite endless circle. Wherever you go you ultimately return to your beginning point.

Superficially, this view appears to support "the philosophy of the void." So begins Ecclesiastes: "Vanity of Vanities, says Kohelet, vanity of vanities, all is vanity.... Generation goes and generation comes.... The sun rises and the sun sets and aspires to its place to rise again.... The wind whirls round and round, returning again in accordance with its circles. All the rivers run into the sea...to the place where the rivers run there they return again." The end of Ecclesiastes reads: "The end [סוף] of the matter, all has been heard, fear G-d and keep His commandments, for this is all of man." The word סוף, "end," begins with a large *samech*. This *samech* comes to rectify the existential despair which derives from an adherence to the "philosophy of the void," so prevalent in the world today. The true "end of the matter," commitment to Torah and *mitzvot*, is not a real ending but rather the beginning of fulfilling one's purpose in life. The end of the world and its vanities in the consciousness of man is the beginning of the service of the soul.

SOULS

Whereas at the level of Worlds the form of the *samech* signifies the primordial void, at the level of Souls the *samech* represents the impression (רשימו) of Divine Light "left over" within the vacuum. This impression of Divine Light is the secret of the "Soul of the universe." Just as the foundation of a building, though invisible, upholds it, so too is the world upheld, as it were, by the concealed "underground" impression of Divine Light. This impression, the "foundation of the world," is the secret of the soul of the *tzadik*, as is said: "The *tzadik* is the foundation of the world." As "all of your nation are *tzadikim*, forever they will inherit the earth," the impression is actually the source of the souls of Israel after the initial *tzimtzum*. Unlike a physical foundation which serves only to support the building erected above it, a spiritual foundation (above the building it supports) actually serves to draw light and lifeforce into it. So too, do the souls of Israel serve in relation to the world. From this analogy we learn that even that *tzadik* who is most "revealed" to the eyes of the world must remain "concealed" and "underground" to a much larger extent than being revealed. In the merit of such *tzadikim* the world exists.

In a circle, all points on its circumference are equidistant from its center. In relation to souls this signifies that all souls are in essence equidistant (equally close) to G-d. The whole number approximation of the value of the ratio between the circumference of a circle and its diameter, 3, as frequently used by our Sages, is exactly the ratio between the perimeter of a hexagon inscribed in a circle and its diameter. The six sides of the hexagon correspond, at the level of Souls, to the 600,000 prototype Jewish souls, as will be explained in the secret of the number of the *samech*. Each side of the hexagon exactly equals the radius of the circle, the equidistance (closeness) of the soul to G-d. This geometric phenomenon teaches us that one's distance from G-d is identical with one's distance from one's fellow Jew. The closer we become to each other, the closer we become to G-d.

DIVINITY

All "large letters" in the *Tanach* relate to the level of Divinity, as taught in *Chassidut*. The large *samech* of סוף, "end," which begins the verse with which we conclude the reading of the scroll of Ecclesiastes: "The end (סוף) of the matter...," is the ultimate "beginning enwedged in the end," the primordial "thought" (i.e., desire) of Creation, of which is said סוף מעשה במחשבה תחלה, "the end of deed [arose] in the beginning of thought."

The only completely "closed" letters in the Hebrew alphabet are the *samech* (ס) and the final *mem* (ם) the circle and the square. As the engraved letters of the "tablets of covenant" given to Moses at Sinai penetrated through the tablets "from side to side," the "insides" of these two letters, being entirely closed, were suspended in mid-air, within the stone of the tablets. "Rabbi Chisda said: 'the *mem* and *samech* of the tablets stood miraculously.'" In Kabbalah it is explained that these two letters are the secret of the two levels of the future revelation of Divinity to Souls. The closed *mem* is called עולם הבא, "the Coming World," and the *samech* is called לעתיד לבא, "the Future to Come." The Future to Come is an even higher revelation than that of the Coming World. Grammatically, the phrase עולם הבא—"the coming world"—can be understood in the present tense— or even the past—as well as the future. Thus the Coming World is in truth the revelation of the future comprehensible to the present and past. The Future to Come, the secret of the *samech*, is the absolute revelation of the future, incomprehensible at present: "No eye has seen it, G-d, except Yours." According to one tradition based upon this teaching of Kabbalah, the wedding ring placed by the groom on the "pointing" (index) finger of the right hand of the bride, is in the form of a circle (ס) inside a square (ם). The "pointing" finger of the bride points at the revelation of the future, the Future to Come within the Coming World.

The wedding-ring symbol of the letter *samech* (a simple wedding ring is purely a *samech*, not enclosed within a final *mem*), at the level of Worlds, refers to the union of forces of nature and their inherent state of "marriage" or "symmetry groups." At the level of Souls, the wedding ring symbolizes the marriage of two "halves" (semicircles) of a common soul. At the level of Divinity, the *samech*, the fifteenth letter of the *alef-beit*, hints at the union of the *yud* of איש ("man") and the *hei* of אשה ("woman")—the Divine Name יה (=15), the Divine Presence that resides between man and wife when they merit to realize the secret of the transcendent "circle" of the *samech*. Here the outer rim of the wedding ring represents the constant, super-rational "covenant" of love between groom and bride, while the inner rim represents the ever ascending spiral of Souls into Divinity for the sake of drawing new sparks of Divinity, Jewish souls, into reality—the inner secret of "Generation goes [up, into Divinity] and generation comes [down, into reality], and the earth ['You (Israel) shall be for Me a desired earth'] stands forever [at one with the Eternity of Divinity on earth below]."

"In the future G-d will make a dance for the *tzadikim*." The dance is in the form of a circle, the form of the *samech*. The secret of the equidistance of all points (souls of *tzadikim*) on the circumference from the center is the experience of the awe in the face of the Presence of the Infinite in "the future to come." The souls of the *tzadikim* themselves will cling together in perfect unity. In the time of the Temple this was alluded to by the dance of the maidens of Israel on *Tu b'Av*, the fifteenth day (the ordinal value of the letter *samech*) of *Av* (אב, short for *alef-beit*; i.e. the secret of the fifteenth letter of the *alef-beit*: *samech*).

NAME

The word *samech* (סמך) means "to support." It is often used in the sense of "to rely upon support" (לסמוך על). By "supporting" one's student, the teacher ordains him. In grammar, the "supported form," סמיכות, is the construct form, indicating possession.

WORLDS

At all levels of Worlds, Souls and Divinity, the *samech* supports the fallen *nun*. In the act of support the hands of the supporter descend below and enter under the body of the supported. In Hebrew, "below" and "after" or "following" are often synonymous, especially as used in reference to linguistic phenomena. The very phenomenon that the *samech* follows the *nun* in the order of the *alef-beit* indicates that the *samech* possesses the power to enter under the *nun* to support it. The juxtaposition of the two letters *nun* and *samech* forms the word נס, "miracle" alluding to the miracle of supporting and uplifting (the root נס means "to lift" and "raise") the fallen. The fallen *nun* is actually "surrounded," on both sides, by the final *mem* (before the *nun*) and the *samech*, the two letters which miraculously do not "fall" in the tablets. The *mem* is actually contained within the name of the *samech*: סמך. The two letters מך—the letters "pregnant" in the full spelling of letter סמך—equal (i.e. reflect) the *samech* itself: 60 (ס) = 40 (מ)⊥ 20 (ך).

At the level of Worlds, the very fact that nature continues to exist and function regularly and consistently is in truth a miracle, especially when one takes into account the "falling apart" effect of the power of entropy.

The word for economic or psychological support, "welfare" (סעד) also begins with a *samech*. The remaining two letters of this word (סעד) are the two-letter root of עדוד, "encouragement." Thus welfare (סעד) means support (סמיכה) and encouragement (עדוד).

SOULS

The word *samech*, at the level of Souls, denotes the support given by a teacher to his devoted student. This support or ordination (סמיכה) not only permits the student to judge independently in matters of *halachah*, but, moreover, serves to give the student the ability and insight of the teacher to properly decide the *halachah* (הלכה=60=ס). The teacher, by placing his hands on the head of his student, contracts his "surrounding light," the secret of the letter *samech*, and thereby transmits his wisdom (the secret of his "hand" [יד, from the letter *yud*]) to the inner consciousness of his student.

"And G-d said to Moses, 'Take unto you Joshua the son of *Nun* [נון], a man possessing spirit, and place [וסמכת, 'support'] your hands over him...and you shall give of your majesty on him....' And he [Moses] placed [ויסמך] his hands on him and commanded him as G-d had spoken in the hand of Moses." At the end of the Torah we find: "And Joshua the son of *Nun* was full of the spirit of wisdom, for Moses had placed [סמך] his hands upon him, and the children of Israel listened to him and did as G-d commanded Moses." Thus Joshua can be seen as the archetype of the "supported one," the secret of the *samech*, the son of *nun*. Moses (משה) is here seen to be the secret of the fountain of wisdom, *mem*, who connects to the *samech* to uplift the *nun*. The three words of support or ordination, used in reference to Joshua—סמך, ויסמך, וסמכת—equal two times יהושע, Joshua (526⊥136⊥120=782=2·391). Initially, Joshua's name was Hoshea, הושע, beginning with a *hei*, the secret of the *hei* of אשה, "woman," receiver, or student. Moses gave him a *yud* (י) a drop of his "hand" of wisdom, emanating from his infinite fountain (*mem*), thus transforming him to יהושע. This *yud* is the secret of the *yud* of איש, "man," leader, and teacher. The union of the two letters *yud* and *hei* (=15), the Divine Name *Kah* (י־ה), is the secret of the letter *samech*, the fifteenth letter of the *alef-beit*.

In the Talmud we find that the juxtaposition of the two letters *samech* and *ayin* is read סמנים עשה, "make signs." The *samech* is understood to represent the image of "signs." This means that a student should make signs for himself or concise and condensed statements or "summaries" (סך, "sum" or "summary," is the fundamental two-letter root of the letter *samech*, סמך), in order to remember the lengthy teachings of his teacher. The necessary power of contraction of the student to "make signs" derives from the power of contraction of the teacher, continuously manifest in the process of teaching itself. The teaching process begins with the contraction (*tzimtzum*) of the teacher's relatively "infinite" brilliance of mind in order to "find" a starting point for his student. The student reflects his teacher's power of contraction when, after fully digesting his teachings at length, he "makes signs" for the sake of memory. This indicates the student's total commitment to fully integrate and live by the teachings of his teacher. This "devotion" then rises up into the heart of the teacher to inspire him to "support"—ordain—his student with all of his (the teacher's) power of insight—the ultimate act of contraction. Relatively, the "drop" of teaching is drawn from the external level of wisdom of the teacher, whereas the "drop" of ordination is drawn from his true state of selflessness, his own most internal and essential level of wisdom.

DIVINITY

In the Temple service, before offering a sacrifice, one placed his hands (וסמך ידו), exerting his full weight, on his sacrifice, and confessed. By this *mitzvah* of *semichah* (סמיכה), one became so identified with his sacrifice that he felt he was actually offering himself to G-d. The secret of sacrifice in Torah is the elevation of Worlds (the physical sacrifice) to Souls (who bring the sacrifice) and, ultimately, of Souls to Divinity. "The mystery of the sacrifice ascends to the mystery of the Infinite." In the higher worlds we find that Michael, the archangel of Israel and angelic counterpart to the High Priest, "offers" the souls of the *tzadikim* on the altar of the Temple above. By so doing, the souls are elevated from their previous state of finite experience in the world of Creation to true, infinite experience of Divinity, in the world of Emanation (and even higher).

The inner fulfillment of the *mitzvah* of *semichah*, relevant even in times of exile when we are unable to perform the physical Temple service, is one's placing all of one's weight (effort) on his intended sacrifice, that part of Worlds entrusted to him to uplift into (awareness of) G-d. The more one places his weight on his sacrifice the more one must be conscious of the fact that he would surely fall and drown (טבע, "nature," means "to drown") in the "quicksand" of Worlds, would it not be for the supporting hand of G-d. One must further experience G-d as ever supporting the soul, continuously "falling" due to the weight of its enclothment in a physical body: "Though he falls he shall not be utterly cast down, for G-d supports him [סומך] with His hand"; "G-d supports [סומך] all the fallen and raises up all that are bent over." In the *Ashrei* prayer, recited three times every day, the Name *Havayah* appears ten times, in one-to-one correspondence to the ten *sefirot*, as explained in Kabbalah. The Name of G-d in the verse "G-d supports all the fallen..." is that of *tiferet*, whose inner property is mercy, the most essential attribute related to the name *Havayah*. The verse "You open Your hand..." (as explained in the secret of the letter *yud* at the level of Divinity) extends the power of this Name (i.e. appears after "G-d supports..." before the next appearance of the Name). The supporting Hand of G-d becomes His open Hand of benevolence. The "circle" of the *samech* is thus the dependence of our service of *semichah* on the awareness of the power of G-d's supporting and benevolent Hand and, likewise, the dependence of the revelation of His Hand on giving ourselves over to His service.

NUMBER

The letter *samech* equals sixty.

WORLDS

In *halachah* we find the concept of "nullification in sixty" (בטיל בששים), the quantitative ratio of "disappearance" (from our sense of taste) or nullification (בטיל) of one substance ("fallen") in another. This is hinted at in the very word for "nothing," אין: one (א) to sixty (יון). This ratio appears often in relation to worldly as well as to spiritual phenomena: "sleep is one-sixtieth of death"; "dream is one-sixtieth of prophecy"; "fire is one-sixtieth of hell"; "honey is one-sixtieth of manna"; "Shabbat is one-sixtieth of the World to Come."

At the level of Worlds, the ratio of 1:60 represents the "quantum" leap of physical reality from "plane" to "plane." Phenomena and forces manifest at microcosmic levels become "null" at relatively macrocosmic levels. Ultimately, in a true "unified field theory," microcosmic phenomena "link" to those of the macrocosm. The macrocosm itself is curved and closed, as the form of the *samech*, continuously "falling into itself" and continuously and simultaneously being supported by the Hand of the Creator.

A further example of the experience of "nullification in sixty" in Worlds themselves is the recognition of the nullification of lower dimensional spaces in higher dimensional spaces, as postulated by modern physics.

SOULS

"Sixty ten-thousands" (ששים רבוא) of souls, the particular archetypal roots of the souls of Israel, left Egypt and received the Torah at Sinai. Each of these "sixty ten-thousands" of soul-roots further divides into "sixty ten-thousands" of sparks (the secret of "squaring the circle"), each of which is capable of enlivening a physical body.

"Ones," "tens," "hundreds," "thousands," and "ten-thousands" correspond to the five levels of the soul: *nefesh, ruach, neshamah, chayah, yechidah*. The number sixty, implying the nullification of the individual Jew within the community of Israel ("nullification in sixty"), and thereby the true organic connection between all Souls, appears at the level of "ten-thousands." This is the level of the *yechidah* ("single one") of the soul, whose primary manifestation is in acts of self-sacrifice.

King Solomon possessed sixty heroes who guarded and surrounded his bed. Of the Ba'al Shem Tov it is told that his soul agreed to descend to this world only if accompanied by sixty *tzadikim*, his devoted and "supported" (ordained) students. The great *tzadik* is protected in this world by his own experience of "nullification in sixty" in relation to the souls of the *tzadikim*, be they his own students, around him.

The Oral Torah contains six orders and sixty tractates. Our Sages teach us that the sixty tractates are the secret of the "sixty queens" (souls of Israel) of the Song of Songs. (One of the greatest Chassidic Sages, Rabbi David of Lelov, said that just as today we possess a particular tractate named *Baba Kama*, so, with the coming of *Mashiach*, one of the sixty tractates of the Oral Torah will be named "David of Lelov.") Within the circle of sixty queens: "One is my dove." This is the secret of the great, all-inclusive *tzadik* within his "holy group" (חבריא קדישא) of sixty companions.

DIVINITY

יברכך ה' וישמרך

יאר ה' פניו אליך ויחנך

ישא ה' פניו אליך וישם לך שלום

"May G-d Bless you and guard you.
May G-d shine His Countenance upon you and give you grace.
May G-d turn His Countenance toward you and grant you peace."

In the *Birkat Kohanim* (Priestly Blessing) recited daily in the Temple service, G-d's Ineffable Name *Havayah* was pronounced as it is written. The Divine Transcendent Light aroused by the *Birkat Kohanim* would "rush" down and "flood" the Temple and all souls present with Divine revelation, the source of all blessing.

Birkat Kohanim, perhaps the most manifest "gem" of structure in Torah, consists of three verses. The three verses possess 3, 5, 7 words and 15, 20, 25 letters, respectively. Both series proceed in arithmetic progression. The total number of words, 15 (the number of letters in the opening verse), is the ordinal value of the letter *samech*, while the total number of letters, 60, is the normative value of *samech*.

According to Jewish custom one does not look at the hands of the kohanim while they are blessing the people—even today, when the Name *Havayah* is not pronounced as written. This is due to the great influx of "blinding" Divine light revealed through the means of souls of the *kohanim*. This is similar to the custom of not looking at a rainbow, the revelation of the Divine Covenant as reflected in nature—Worlds.

According to the Mishnah, there are thirty bones in each hand. Thus, when the *kohen* lifts his hands together to bless the people, sixty (*samech*) bones (letters) are used. This relates to the union of the two "face-to-face" *lameds* (ל=30) described above.

In the first account of Creation, the only letter which does not appear in the text is the *samech*. In the second account, it first appears in the word הסובב, "which surrounds" (in reference to the flow of the rivers emerging from the Garden of Eden), the secret of סובב כל עלמין, G-d's Transcendent Light which "surrounds all worlds." This light, not initially revealed in Creation, is that which "rushes forth" in the Temple, when the *kohanim* bless the people. From the Temple it flows to the whole world (in the secret of the full spelling of the *samech*, סמך: from the "surrounding" light—סובב—to the origin or "fountain"—מעין—of the light "filling"—ממלא—"all worlds"—כל עלמין) as is said: "and a fountain from the House of G-d shall flow forth...."

Ayin

הַשְׁגָּחָה פְּרָטִית

Divine Providence

Ayin: Divine Providence

"It [*Eretz Yisrael*, the land of Israel] is the land which G-d your G-d seeks; the *eyes* of G-d your G-d are always [looking] at it, from the beginning of the year to the end of the year."

The yearly cycle, from beginning to end ("end enwedged in beginning"), alludes to "the endless cycle," the secret of the letter *samech*, as explained above. Divine Providence, the "eyes" of G-d in control of the cycle, is the secret of the following letter, *ayin* (עין), which means "eye." Though the primary revelation of supernatural Providence is in *Eretz Yisrael*, the Jew-in-exile is commanded to create something of its sanctity in each of his Diaspora stations by recognizing Divine Providence wherever he is.

Upon entering *Eretz Yisrael*, the second city to be conquered by Joshua was Ai (עי), an abbreviated form of *ayin* (עין), "the Eye" (the *nun* "falls"). Jericho (יריחו), the first city to be conquered, comes from the word ריח, the sense of smell. In *Chassidut* we are taught that the origin of the sense of smell is in *keter*, the superconscious sensitivity directing the motivation of Will. The Hebrew word for "the land," *eretz* (ארץ) derives from the word *ratzon* (רצון), "will," as our Sages teach: "Why is it called *eretz*? It wills to do the Will of its Creator." Sight is the first conscious sense, corresponding to the *sefirah* of *chochmah*, "wisdom."

In the conquest of Jericho, Achan (עכן), related to the word עין: the *kaf* of עכן equals the full spelling of the *yud* [יוד] of עין) coveted forbidden booty. The tragic result was the initial defeat of Israel in the battle of "the Eye." Coveting is the spiritual blemish of the sight of the eye. Only when the sin of coveting was rectified was "the Eye" given to the Jewish people. Upon the initial defeat Joshua fell on his face in despair but was commanded by G-d: "Rise, sanctify the people.... There is an accursed thing in your midst, Israel; you shall not be able to rise before your enemies until you remove it from your midst." Joshua was told to "rise" though the people were unable to "rise." This alludes to the secret of the two concentric circles of the letter *samech*: the outer, static circle supporting the fall of the *nun*, and the inner, dynamic circle directed, ultimately, by the Divine Providence of the *ayin*.

The full spelling of the letter *ayin* (עין) equals 130 or 5·26—26 being the value of the Name *Havayah*. In Kabbalah this phenomenon is understood to mean that the eye possesses five Divine powers. The right eye possesses five states of kindness, whereas the left eye possesses five states of severity or might. In Psalms we find two verses in relation to G-d's Providence over man. One verse states: "The Eye of G-d is on those who fear Him." The other states: "The Eyes of G-d are on the *tzadikim*." The attribute of fear of G-d refers to the consciousness of the *sefirah* of *malchut*, "Kingdom," likened to the woman of valor, "the woman who fears G-d, she shall be praised." *Malchut* is constructed and directed by the five "mights," the secret of the left eye of G-d. For this reason, in the verse "the Eye of G-d is on those who fear Him," "Eye" is in the singular, referring to the left eye alone. In the "male figure," corresponding to the six emotive attributes of the heart, Providence reflects the balance of both the five kindnesses together with the five mights of G-d. So, in the verse "The Eyes of G-d are on the *tzadikim*," "Eyes" appear in the plural form, referring to both the right and left Eyes of G-d.

We are further taught in *Chassidut* that the singular eye of the first verse possesses a hidden reference to the "ever-open eye" of *keter*, the superconscious. Here the singular is the secret of "all right," as "there is no left in the Ancient One, all is right." The fear of G-d which is the vessel in the soul to contain and reveal this most concealed and supernal level of Providence, is the awe in face of the awareness of the Transcendent Light of G-d, permeating each point of reality, as taught in the secret of the letter *samech*.

In the Divine service of the soul these three levels of Providence correspond to the three stages of service: submission, separation, and sweetening, as taught by the Ba'al Shem Tov. All relate to his most fundamental and all inclusive teaching in regard to "particular Divine Providence." The initial experience that even the minutest of one's deeds is observed and recorded Above brings one to a state of submission and fear of the Kingdom of Heaven, Whose Law and Order control the universe. One then experiences the Eyes of G-d lovingly watching over and guarding each one of his children Israel. This brings one to sense the existential separation of the holy from the profane, the righteous from the unrighteous, and to identify with the good. Finally one experiences the Infinite Eye of G-d directing each and every created being to its ultimate fulfillment of purpose in Creation, thereby bringing all of Creation to realize its Divine Purpose. Here, one's awe itself is in the face of the revelation of G-d's Infinite Love for all ("all is right"). This is the secret of sweetening.

AYIN

FORM: An elongated *nun* with an enwedged *vav* or *zayin*.
The vessel of the *nun* receives G-d's blessing, the *vav*.
The two eyes and the optic nerves entering the brain.
The right eye looks up at the *samech*; the left eye looks down at the *pei*.

Worlds   A poor man receiving physical sustenance.
The six (seven) days of Creation and man.
Shammai: the seven together; Hillel: the six separate from the seventh.
The right eye looking up at the sky; the left eye looking down at the earth.

Souls   The humble *nun* draws down joy in the service of G-d and integrates into itself G-d's Will, *halachah*, as revealed in the six orders of Mishnah.
The right eye looks up to G-d; the left eye looks down favorably at the Jew.
The right eye dances; the left eye speaks.

Divinity   Moses, the humble *nun*, draws joy into G-d, as it were, and integrates into consciousness the hidden-most secrets of Torah.
The right eye looks up at G-d's Transcendent Light; the left eye looks down at the Word of G-d.

NAME: Eye; color; fountain; in Aramaic: sheep.

Worlds   Physical vision; Color spectrum; A fountain.
The fountain of wisdom and the ability to perceive wisdom.
The sheep looking toward the shepherd; the shepherd watching his sheep.

Souls   The "eye of Jacob" looking only at blessing, good, and life (בט"ח).
The eye of the soul looking at unification, sanctity, and blessing (יב"ק).
The "searching eye" of the soul looking upwards towards G-d.
Looking favorably on every Jew.

Divinity   "Gazing at the King and no other."
Divine Providence.
Emulating G-d by looking "downwards" to help care for others.
The silent prayer: heart above and eyes below.

NUMBER: Seventy.

Worlds   Seventy archetypal nations and languages; Seventy oxen sacrificed on *Sukot*.
Seventy years of life; Seventy cries of the deer during labor.

Souls   Seventy Jewish souls that descended to Egypt.
Seventy elders chosen by Moses; seventy sages of the Sanhedrin.
Seventy years of King David.
Seventy cries of the soul during "labor."
Seventy years of the Babylonian exile.

Divinity   Seventy Names of G-d; Seventy faces of Torah.
Seventy words of *Kiddush*.
Seventy cries of the birthpangs of *Mashiach*.

FORM

The form of the *ayin*, the "consummated" *nun*—a *vav*, according to the Arizal, enwedged into an elongated *nun*—is the poor man receiving physical sustenance (Worlds); the humble one receiving insight into the Law (Souls); the perfectly humble one (Moses) integrating the secrets of the Law (Divinity).

In addition, the form of the *ayin* (ע) depicts two eyes with connecting "optic nerves" entering the brain. The right eye is looking "up" at the *samech* and the left eye "down" at the *pei*, at all levels of Worlds, Souls, and Divinity.

WORLDS

The *vav* of the *nun*, six (or *zayin*, seven, according to other opinions), corresponds to the days of Creation, each of which receives its particular blessing from the previous Shabbat and draws it down to unite with the *nun*. As explained above, the *nun* represents the vessel or consciousness of the poor man.

Shammai says that each day of the week one must have in mind and prepare for the coming Shabbat. If one finds a delicacy, it should be purchased for Shabbat. Only if he finds an even superior delicacy may one eat the first during the week. Hillel says: "Bless G-d day by day," implying that each day draws down its own blessing and that one needn't be concerned since he will surely find a choice delicacy before Shabbat. These two opinions can be understood to correspond to the two manners of writing the letter *ayin*: with a *zayin*—the seventh (Shabbat)—included together with the six—the opinion of Shammai; or with a *vav*—the six related to independently, with the consciousness of Shabbat hovering above them, appearing spontaneously in its proper time—the opinion of Hillel. (In reduced numbering, the *ayin* itself equals seven, the secret of Shabbat.)

At the level of Worlds, the right eye of the *ayin* looks up at the "surrounding" sky, the "outer space" of the *samech*, reflecting on the greatness of the Creator. The left eye looks down at the open mouth, the *pei*, of the earth, reflecting upon the lowliness of man.

SOULS

In the word ענו, "humble one," the two letters *nun* and *vav* are actually the two individual components of the *ayin*. In the book of Isaiah we find: ויספו ענוים בה' שמחה, "The humble shall increase joy in G-d." The joy of the humble in serving G-d is due to their sense of the infinite, undeserved merit of an insignificant, finite creature to approach the Almighty in His service. Their ever-increasing experience of joy makes them fitting vessels to receive the revelation of the Divine Light inherent in the *mitzvot*.

The six of the *vav* at this level relates to the six orders of the Mishnah. This implies that one receives true insight into G-d's Law, *halachah* (first encoded in the Mishnah), in accordance with his sincere sense of joy in meriting to be His servant.

At this level, the right eye of the *ayin* looks up in its service of G-d and the left eye looks down, favorably, at every Jew in order to continually discover in him previously hidden points of good, as will be explained in the name of the *ayin*. In particular, looking up at the *samech* is seeing the state of union of all souls, the dance of the *tzadikim* in the Future to Come. Looking down at the *pei*, the mouth—the vessel of communication in this world—expresses the will of the "goodly" eye to connect to other souls through "goodly" speech. This is the secret of "the good of eye, he shall be blessed" [the Sages read: "he shall bless"]. Thus, the right eye "dances," in the joy of union, while the left eye "speaks" words of comfort and blessing.

DIVINITY

Here, the elongated *nun* of the *ayin*, whose form is between that of a bent-over *nun* and an extended, final *nun*, connects the two states of consciousness of the humility of this world and that of the World to Come. This is the ultimate, perfect humility of Moses, of whom is said: "And the man Moses was very humble...." The *vav* drawn down into this *nun* is the secret of the subsequent verse: "...in all of My house is he trustworthy [נאמן הוא]." The "trustworthy" *nun* is allowed to perceive all of the treasures of the household of his Master. The hidden treasures of the Torah are the secrets entailed in every particular law of *halachah*.

At this level "joy in G-d" (in the verse "The humble shall increase joy in G-d") is understood to be the addition of joy in G-d Himself, whose greatest joy, as it were, is when His son and faithful servant merits, through his devoted service, to "partake" of His very Essence, the secrets of Torah.

The right eye of the *ayin*, at the level of Divinity, looks up at G-d's Transcendent Light, the "endless cycle" of the *samech*. The left eye looks down at the Word of G-d, the expression of His mouth and His Immanent Light as manifest in the ten sayings of Creation (Divinity in Worlds), the Oral Torah (Divinity in Souls), and the pronouncement of the Ten Commandments (Divinity Itself).

NAME

The word *ayin* (עין) means "eye"; "color"; "fountain"; in Aramaic—"sheep."

WORLDS

The physical eye perceives reality through the kaleidoscope of color. Just as each human eye possesses a unique color, so each particular color is referred to in Hebrew as an "eye." The six primary and secondary colors can be seen as symbolized by the *vav* of the *ayin*, entering into the consciousness of the *nun* of the *ayin*.

Drops of water flow from a fountain (עין or מעין) just as tears flow from the eye. In the word מעין, "fountain"—literally "from (מ) the eye (עין)"—the *mem* (מ) emphasizes the flow of water (מים) of the fountain, whereas the "eye" (עין) is the fountain itself. At higher levels the *mem* is the "fountain of wisdom," as "There is no 'water' but [the wisdom of] Torah," while the *ayin* is the power to perceive (eye) wisdom and "shine" wisdom.

The "Eye" of G-d, as manifest at the level of Worlds, is the Divine Providence and harmony apparent in all the workings of nature.

The relationship between "eye" (עין) in Hebrew, and "sheep" (ען or ענא) in Aramaic, can be understood as the eye of the sheep continuously looking towards its shepherd and the eye of the shepherd always watching over his sheep.

SOULS

At the level of Souls, the eye (fountain) is "the eye of Jacob" referred to in the end of Moses' blessing to Israel: "and Israel shall dwell secure, alone the eye of Jacob...." We find in Torah three positive objects of sight—juxtaposed to their negative counterparts—"seen" by the "eye of Jacob." One verse reads: "Behold [ראה, literally, 'see'] I give before you today blessing [ברכה] and curse." A second verse reads: "Behold [ראה] I have given before you today life [חיים] and good [טוב], and death and evil." The initial letters of the three positive objects of sight: ברכה, טוב, חיים (blessing, good, and life) spell בטח, "secure," as in the above verse: בטח בדד עין יעקב, "*secure, alone the eye of Jacob*." The two words בטח בדד, "secure, alone" can be understood to mean that the eye should only ("alone," בדד, in the sense of לבד) perceive those objects hinted at in the word בטח.

A further hint in the phrase עין יעקב, the "eye of Jacob," is that the letter *ayin* appears in Jacob's name itself (יעקב). The remaining three letters are the initials of יחוד, קדושה, ברכה: "unification," "sanctity," and "blessing," as explained in Kabbalah and *Chassidut*. The eye of the soul looks "forward" at the unification of G-d in every aspect of reality, "upward" in search of His transcendent sanctity, and "downward" to draw down His blessing to all souls of Israel. "The good of eye, he shall be blessed"—"Don't read 'shall be blessed' but 'shall bless.' "

The souls of Israel are the specially chosen flock of G-d. His Providence over Israel is much more apparent than that over the rest of nature. King David says: "G-d is my shepherd, I shall not lack." In the word "my shepherd," רעי, the *ayin*, Eye of G-d, is the middle letter, while the two letters around it, רי, equal three times *ayin* (210=3·70). Thus the one Eye is "enclothed" in three eyes (the three levels of Providence discussed above) which are further "enclothed" in seven eyes of Providence.

DIVINITY

In the Song of Songs, the groom, G-d, praises his bride Israel: עֵינַיִךְ יוֹנִים, "Your eyes are as doves." When the eyes of the bride cling lovingly to the groom, the superconscious root of the soul shines into the consciousness of the soul in the experience of "gazing at the splendor of the King and none else." Doves, unlike other species, are ever faithful to one chosen mate. The ultimate expression of their love is their tireless gazing into each other's eyes. The sublime pleasure inherent in gazing continuously ascends, drawing the soul closer and closer into the Essence of G-d.

Just as the eyes of a fish (the *nun* of the *ayin*, עין) never close (for a fish does not possess eyelids), so "the Guardian of Israel shall never slumber nor sleep." (When eating fish of Shabbat, some have the custom to first eat the eyes of the fish, in meditation upon this level. After the eyes, one eats the mouth, just as the letter *pei* follows the *ayin* in the order of the *alef-beit*, to merit the secret of "the good of eye he shall be blessed—bless.") This is the highest of the three levels of Divine Providence discussed above, the "ever-open eye" of the "Ancient One."

As G-d is always looking "down" at us to care for each and every one of our needs, so are we instructed to emulate Him—"and you shall walk in His ways"—to look "down" in care for one's fellow Jew and that part of the world-at-large entrusted to his soul to rectify.

In the prayer of silent devotion (the *Amidah*), corresponding to the level of the world of Emanation, when one's consciousness links to the source of the soul Above, at one with Divinity, one realizes the state expressed by our Sages: "Heart Above and eyes below." One's heart is linked to the Essence of G-d Above—"He is all." One's eyes are, as His, directed below to see (i.e. reveal) that "all is He."

NUMBER

The letter *ayin* equals seventy.

WORLDS

In the Torah-portion of Noah, Noah's seventy descendants are the original archetypes of the seventy nations of the earth. Each of the seventy nations possesses its own language, from the time of the collapse of the Tower of Babel and the dispersion of the peoples of the earth, as told in the end of this Torah portion.

Spiritual sustenance was drawn down to the seventy nations of the earth by means of our sacrifice of seventy oxen during the festival of *Sukot*. On the first day of the holiday, thirteen oxen were offered. Each successive day the number of oxen was reduced by one, until on the seventh day, seven oxen were offered. This phenomenon indicates that the innate, evil force of the nations is ever being reduced while, simultaneously, their essence is being sustained in order that ultimately will be fulfilled the promise: "then will I transform to peoples a clear tongue [i.e., rectified language] to call all in the Name of G-d and to serve Him together."

The normal, average life span of man on earth is seventy years, as is said in Psalms: "The days of our years are in them seventy years, and if with might eighty years." "Might" alludes to פי הגבורה, the "might of the mouth" from which we received the Torah, the secret of the letter *pei*, eighty.

The seventy words of Psalm 20: "G-d will answer you [יענך, 'will answer you,' is related to the word עין, 'eye'] in the day of distress..." are taken in Kabbalah to correspond to the seventy cries of a deer during labor, whose birthpangs are the greatest of all species in nature, for "her womb is narrow." (צער, "distress," is related to צר, "narrow." From the narrowness [צר] of distress [צער] emerge seventy [ע, the middle letter of צער] cries.)

SOULS

Numerically, עַיִן יַעֲקֹב, the "eye of Jacob," is the secret of the seventy souls of Israel, the descendants of Jacob/Israel who descended to Egypt (מִצְרַיִם, also from the word צַר, "narrow" or "straights"). These seventy archetypal souls of Israel later become manifest in Torah as the seventy elders upon whom descended the spirit of Moses to aid him in the judgement and leadership of the people. In subsequent generations these seventy elders are the seventy Sages of the Sanhedrin, the Supreme Court of Israel.

In general, whenever seventy is found in Torah, the seventy surround one, just as phonetically the "intangible" sound of the *alef*, one, is "enclothed" in the more "tangible" sound of the *ayin*, seventy. The seventy nations of the earth surround Israel as "seventy wolves around a sheep." In the Temple, on *Shmini Atzeret*, the eighth and concluding day of *Sukot*, one ox, symbolizing Israel, was offered after the seventy offerings of *Sukot*. The seventy descendants of Jacob surround their father Jacob who descended together with them to Egypt. The seventy Elders surround Moses and, likewise, the seventy Sages of the Sanhedrin surround the "prince" (or מוּפְלָא, "wondrous one," from פֶּלֶא, "wonder," the inverted spelling of *alef*, אַלֻף, "one") of the Sanhedrin.

King David, the archetypal *nefesh* (that level of soul closest to "nature") of all souls of Israel, lived seventy years. Our Sages teach that these years were given him by Adam, who though destined to live a thousand years after his sin, gave the last seventy years of his life to David, his most essential reincarnation. Adam, אָדָם, is an acronym for אָדָם, דָּוִד, מָשִׁיחַ (Adam, David, *Mashiach*), as explained by the Arizal. On a deeper level, the *Zohar* teaches that David's seventy years were given him by Abraham, who lived five years less than his son Isaac; Jacob, who lived twenty-eight years less than Abraham; and Joseph, who lived thirty-seven years less than Jacob (5⊥28⊥37=70—also the difference between the maximal age of Isaac, 180, and the minimal age of Joseph, 110).

Just as the deer cries out "seventy voices" in labor so too does the soul cry out when giving birth to new levels of spiritual consciousness. In Kabbalah we are taught that when one completes the rectification of one of the levels of his soul, he faces the crisis of either passing away from the world, G-d forbid, or giving birth to an entirely new level of soul, with a newly defined task in life, in need of rectification. Here the soul crying out "seventy voices" corresponds to the seventy years (full lifespan) of the Babylonian exile, between (the service of) the First and Second Temples.

DIVINITY

In Kabbalah we are taught that G-d possesses seventy Names or "faces," i.e. dimensions of revelation. All of these relative "faces" are ultimately at the level of "the back of G-d" that was revealed to Moses, while of His true Face (the inner secret of the Name *Havayah*) is said: "...for no man shall see Me and live...and My Face shall not be seen." The Face is the one, "wondrous One," above, yet enclothed within the seventy. (The Name *Havayah* appears exactly 1820 times in the Torah; 1820=70·26, 26 being the value of the Name *Havayah* Itself). The seventy Names or revealed "faces" of G-d are identical with the seventy faces of Torah. These seventy (7·10) faces are "grasped" by 49 (7²) gates of understanding. This is the secret of the word מעט, "little"—מט (49) around ע (70)—said in reference to Moses: "and You have made him less just a little [מעט] than G-d." This word equals 119, hinting at all but the last day of Moses' life, his 120th birthday. At the moment of his ultimate ascent from the confines of this world he achieved the fiftieth gate and perceived the "wondrous face," as taught in Kabbalah.

"When wine enters in, the secret goes out [is revealed]." Both "wine," יין, and "secret," סוד, equal seventy. The *Kiddush* on Shabbat over wine consists of seventy words (according to the version of the Arizal). The "secret" is the Divine gift of Shabbat to Israel.

At this level the seventy cries of labor are the birth pangs of *Mashiach*, which the world is now experiencing. The birth of *Mashiach* is identical with the birth of the revelation of the Kingdom of G-d on earth, the ultimate purpose of all of Creation.

Pei

דַעַת גְּנִיז בְּפוּמָא

Communication: The Oral Torah

Pei: Communication—The Oral Torah

The mouth, the letter *pei*, follows the eye, the letter *ayin*. The five kindnesses and five mights of the right and left eyes discussed in the letter *ayin* are in fact the dual manifestations of the *sefirah* of *da'at*, knowledge, as taught in Kabbalah. *Da'at* is the power of union and communication. Providence is the power of *da'at* as revealed by the eyes. The power of *da'at* as revealed by the mouth—speech—is the more explicit form of contact and communication between individuals. Just as in the verse: "and Adam knew his wife Eve," "knew," the power of *da'at*, refers to the physical union of man and wife, so is "speech" idiomatically used by our Sages to refer to such union. So are we taught in the *Zohar*: דעת גניז בפומא, "[the power of] *da'at* is concealed in the mouth."

Da'at, contact, at the level of the eyes, is the secret of the written Torah. In reading the written Torah in the synagogue service the reader must see each and every letter of the Torah scroll. Sometimes a "silver finger" is used to point, direct one's sight, to every word. Contact at the level of the mouth is the secret of the Oral Torah.

"There is no good other than Torah." The *pei* is the seventeenth letter of the *alef-beit*, the numerical value of the word טוב, "good," as discussed at length in the letter *tet*. The first words spoken by the "Mouth" of G-d, "Let there be light," upon spontaneously being realized as the actual creation of light, were subsequently seen, by His "Eyes," "to be good." The word "good," טוב, is the thirty-third word of the Torah, the sum of the ordinal values of the two letters *ayin* and *pei* (33=16⊥17), thus alluding to the union of the two levels of *da'at*, contact (that of the eyes, the written Torah, and that of the mouth, the Oral Torah).

Of the people of Israel it is said: "You are my witnesses, says G-d" and "G-d's testimony is within you." With closed eyes we testify twice every day: שמע ישראל ה' אלקינו ה' אחד, "Hear, O Israel, G-d is our G-d; G-d is one." The *ayin* of the first word, שמע, "Hear," and the *dalet* of the last word, אחד, "one," are written large. Together they spell the word עד, "witness." The soul of every Jew is an "eye" witness to the essential unity of G-d. In this world we must close our physical eyes in order to reveal the inner eye of Israel which beholds the Divine Unity. By proclaiming our testimony verbally, we unify the two levels of contact, that of eye and that of mouth.

Expression of wisdom proceeds from the inner eye of the heart to the mouth, as is said: "the heart of the wise informs his mouth." Words of wisdom, when expressed sincerely and humbly by the mouth, find favor and grace in the eyes of G-d and man, as is said: "the words of the mouth of the wise find favor." In *Sefer Yetzirah* we are taught that the "gift" to the holy mouth is grace. In good ("There is no 'good' other than Torah") are inherent two essential properties: truth and grace. Though each dimension of Torah expresses the interinclusion of both of these properties, nonetheless, in particular, truth (the "male figure," primarily defined by the *sefirot* of *tiferet* and *yesod* in Kabbalah) is the primary consciousness of the written Torah, whereas grace (the "female figure," *malchut*) is that of the Oral Torah. The power of the *pei*, the mouth, is thus to express the grace of the Oral Torah.

PEI

FORM: A mouth containing a tooth.
The white space within the *pei* forms a hidden *beit*.

Worlds The mouth of the wicked.
Disease results from the evil mouth.

Souls The power of speech.
The 32 teeth in the mouth correspond to the 32 pathways of wisdom.

Divinity The "mouth" of G-d reveals the Torah through the mouth of Moses.
The "death of the kiss."
The secrets of Torah from G-d's Mouth to be revealed in the future.

NAME: mouth; here (present)

Worlds Here—the awareness of physical time and space.
"Blessed is He who spoke and the world came into being."
Speech—the power to enter the "here and now."
All Creation singing its song.

Souls "The power of the Jew is in his mouth."
"Knowledge is hidden in the mouth."
The power of curse and blessing.

Divinity Immanence. Sitting in the *sukah*.
The Oral Torah.
Traveling the odyssey of life by the Mouth of G-d.
The "Kiss" of G-d.

NUMBER: Eighty; *yesod*—the power of marriage.

Worlds "Eighty years to might."
Eighty-thousand chiselers of rock in the building of the First Temple.
Hewing one's children, the building-blocks of the Temple.
Eighty witches hung by the eighty students of Shimon ben Shetach.
Eighty-thousand Roman horn-blowing soldiers and eighty-thousand Jews killed in the defeat of Betar.
Eight-year periods of quiet in the period of the Judges.
Eight years of *Mashiach* and Temple.

Souls Eighty pairs of kohanite brothers who married eighty pairs of kohanite sisters.
Eighty-thousand young men named Aaron.
Eighty tractates of *baraitot*.
Eighty ten thousands of Jews under the age of 20 left Egypt.

Divinity The age of Moses at the Exodus.
The power of the soul to contact Divinity.
The discovery of the hidden light in Torah through pronouncing it orally.

FORM

The *pei* resembles a mouth with a tooth emerging from its upper jaw and inverting into its cavity. It is similar to a *tet* (ט) turned on its side. In their ordinal value, the *tet*, the ninth letter, is the "middle point" of the *pei*, the seventeenth letter. Both relate to the secret of טוב, "good" (ט=9; טוב=17). In the *pei*, whose meaning is "mouth," the two dimensions of form and name unite more so than in any other letter.

The white space within the *pei* forms a hidden *beit*. Phonetically, the *pei* and the *beit* are interchangeable, both belonging to the phonetic group בומ"פ, the letters of the lips (the labials).

WORLDS

In the name פרעה, "Pharoah," the king of Egypt and subjugator of the Jewish people in exile, the outside letters spell פה, "mouth," while the inside letters spell רע, "evil." Thus Pharoah is the evil mouth. The exile of Egypt is the archetypal exile, as our Sages say: "All exiles are called by the name 'Egypt', for they cause distress to Israel." מצרים, "Egypt," means "distress."

Pharoah spoke to his people: "Behold the people of the Children of Israel are more and mightier than we. Come, let us deal wisely with them, lest they multiply...." The first of the two words "lest they multiply," פן ירבה, begins with a *pei*. Two verses afterwards we find: "But the more they afflicted them, the more they multiplied." In these two verses, the words כן ירבה ("the more they multiplied") are identical with the words פן ירבה ("lest they multiply") except that the *pei* of פן ("lest") is replaced with a *kaf* in the word כן ("the more"). The form of the *kaf* is an empty mouth, a toothless *pei*. The tooth of Pharoah's mouth, the first and primary letter of his name, the strength of his saying פן, "lest..." has been broken, leaving the empty mouth of the *kaf*, as converted for the good of Israel: "the more." The secret of breaking the teeth of the wicked is expressed in Psalms: "You have broken the teeth of the wicked."

Just as Pharoah represents the evil mouth, so do we find that all disease, in particular skin disease, leprosy, results from the evil mouth. Our Sages read מצורע, "leper" as מוציא רע, "[one who] speaks [literally, 'extracts'] evil." "Skin" (עור, whose basic two letters [ער] are רע ["evil"] inverted), is identical, in Hebrew, with "blind" (עור). The good mouth shines "light" (אור, the rectification of עור) which the eye sees to be good (as G-d did at the beginning of Creation). The evil mouth clouds and pollutes the air with darkness which covers and blinds the eyes from perceiving good.

SOULS

The soul is called מדבר, "a speaker," whose essential power is in the mouth, the *pei*. Onkelos translates "and man became a living soul" as "and man became a speaking spirit." Speech is the unique quality which separates man from animal. The tooth, the power of the mouth to chew or clarify its intake and also, symbolically, to express its words of speech forcefully, grows into the cavity of the mouth. It is not present at birth. The upper jaw of the mouth is in fact the lower side of the bone of the skull containing the brain. Initially the cavity of the mouth "reflects" the cavity of the skull, the secret of the form of the *kaf* (כ). The tooth, which subsequently appears in the cavity of the mouth, "reflects" the revelation of wisdom in the brain, first in the immature wisdom of baby teeth and thereafter (after the first set of teeth are "broken" and fall out) in the mature wisdom of adult teeth. The thirty-two teeth of the mouth actually correspond to the thirty-two Pathways of Wisdom, the thirty-two times G-d's Name *Elokim* appears in the account of the six days of Creation.

Around the big *beit* of בראשית (the first word in the account of Creation, the beginning of Torah) is hidden, in the white of the parchment, an even bigger *pei*, "mouth," whose thirty-two teeth are the thirty-two Names *Elokim* of Creation: "All of them You have made with wisdom." The full spelling of the letter *pei* is פא, with an *alef* which splits into יוי, as explained by the Arizal: sixteen (יו) from above and sixteen (יו) from below, in correspondence to the thirty-two teeth, which all derive from the secret of אאלפך חכמה, "I will teach you wisdom."

DIVINITY

G-d Himself "descends" in order to reveal to Aaron and Miriam (after they had spoken in criticism of their younger brother, Moses) the uniqueness of the prophecy of Moses: "...in all of My house he is faithful. Mouth to mouth I speak with him...." "My house" is the secret of the hidden *beit* (whose name means house) in the white of the *pei*, the mouth of G-d which unites with the mouth of Moses. G-d's union with Moses "Mouth-to-mouth" becomes manifest in Moses himself as "the Divine Presence speaks from the throat of Moses."

The giving of the Torah was from the "Mouth of the Almighty," the secret of "eighty years old to might," eighty being the age of Moses at the giving of the Torah.

The "kiss" of the mouth of G-d, first experienced by Moses at Sinai and thereafter in his (unique level of) prophecy in general, was consummated at his moment of expiring, in the secret of "the death of the kiss."

The secret of the "kiss" of G-d's Mouth, as it were, will in the future be experienced by all Souls of Israel. So is said in the opening and all-inclusive verse of the Song of Songs: "He shall kiss me with the kisses of His mouth...." The Sages interpret this verse to refer to the new, inner dimension of Torah that will be revealed to us by *Mashiach* and experienced as the actual "kiss" of G-d, the epitome of the expression of His love and clinging to the souls of His People Israel.

NAME

The word *pei* (פא) means "mouth" (פה), and "here" or "present" (פה).

WORLDS

Awareness of the "here and now" (פה) is, metaphorically, the experience of presence within the "mouth" (פה) or "vacuum" of Creation. The emerging of the tooth within the mouth is the secret of time entering space. "Tooth" (שן, from the letter *shin*, שׁין) relates to "year" (שנה), the general term for time in *Sefer Yetzirah*. Thus the initially "empty" space ("empty" of time), the open *kaf* (כ), is filled with the "tooth" (time) of the letter *pei* (פ, in the secret of the "actual" [פעל] "filling"—i.e., realizing—the "potential" [כח], as explained in the name of the *kaf*), space consummated with time. Through the mouth of space G-d speaks the ten utterances of Creation: "Blessed is He who said...and the world came into being.... Blessed is He who says and [spontaneously] makes."

It is through the power of the mouth, speech, that one enters into full consciousness of the "here and now." Entering the "here and now" is the secret of "communication" at all levels of Worlds, Souls, and Divinity. In the service of Souls (in general, as motivated by the experience of Worlds), this is the experience of sincere prayer to G-d (Divinity).

Korach blemished the power of the mouth by speaking against the true prophet, Moses, the "mouth" of G-d. "Measure for measure," the mouth of the earth (in ordinal numbering, ארץ ["earth"] = 39 = משה [Moses]) swallowed him and his congregation. Nonetheless, *there* his mouth acknowledged, "Moses is true and his Torah is true."

Every created being possesses a "mouth" which speaks and "sings" an individual song, as recorded in *Perek Shirah*. Sometimes the physical, non-human, mouth of a creature is heard to speak, as the mouth of the snake in the garden of Eden or the mouth of the donkey of Balaam. (In ordinal numbering, נחש ["snake"] = 43 = אתון ["donkey"]. 43 is the "middle point" of 85 = פה ["mouth"—"here and now"].) The ability of man to hear the speech of Creation brings all of Creation into his full consciousness of "here and now" and the awareness of the significance and consequences of his present actions in relation to each of its elements.

SOULS

"The power of the Jew is in his mouth." In particular this power refers to the potency of the prayer of Israel to arouse the Will of G-d, as it were, and so to achieve its request.

Knowing he could not defeat them in war, Balak, the king of Moab, feared the approaching camp of Israel. He sent for Balaam to curse them with the power of his mouth. Balaam is the evil counterpart of Moses. His essential power, as that of Moses and Israel, was in his mouth.

Our Sages teach that Balaam's special sensitivity was to know the moment, the "here and now," when G-d daily allows His attribute of anger to express itself. In that moment he would pronounce the curse. But during those days that Balaam attempted to curse Israel, G-d did not allow His anger to express itself at all.

Every negative property has a positive counterpart even greater and stronger than its manifestation on the "other side." The Jewish soul, too, possesses the power to sense moments of good will and love from Above. A Jew "knows" when to bless Israel (one's fellow Jew) and his blessing is potent. This "knowledge" of the spiritual state of the "here and now" is the "knowledge concealed in the mouth," as though the mouth itself instinctively knows when to open with words of blessing.

DIVINITY

"There is no place void of Him." So, in truth, His words never leave His mouth, as explained in *Tanya*.

On the festival of *Sukot* one experiences being "inside" G-d's Mouth, as it were, when fulfilling the commandment of sitting in a *Sukah*. *"Sukah"* (סכה) equals "mouth" (פה, 85). The *halachah* teaches that for the sake of learning Torah one may leave the *sukah*. In speaking the words of Torah one is actually "carrying" the consciousness of the Divine mouth with him. Of one of the greatest of our Sages, Rabbah, is said: "His mouth never ceased from speaking words of Torah." The Oral Torah as a whole is called תורה שבעל פה, which can be read "The Torah of the master of the mouth."

All of the Divinely-directed sojournings of a Jew on earth, which are intended to rectify reality and elevate Divine sparks, are symbolized by the forty-two journeys of the camp of Israel in the desert. Each of these sojourns was an additional step toward the chosen land. Each was על פי ה', "by the Mouth of G-d": "By the Mouth of G-d they camped and by the Mouth of G-d they travelled...by the Mouth of G-d in the hand of Moses."

In the word פי, "Mouth of," the *pei* (mouth) alludes to the "Mouth of G-d" while the *yud* (hand) alludes to the "hand of Moses."

Thus the Mouth (פ) of G-d "takes" us to the promised land where His Eyes (ע) ever shine. The unification of the two letters ע-פ spells עף, "to fly." The bird (עוף) is the union of the power of the eye to see from afar and the power of mouth to sing and commune with Creation. The soul, when inspired by the Divine Eye and taken by the Divine Mouth, "flies" as an angel into the ultimate consciousness of the Divine "here and now."

NUMBER

The letter *pei* equals eighty.

WORLDS

In Kabbalah, eighty is the numerical value of the *sefirah yesod* (יסוד = 80), "foundation," the power which connects or "marries" forces at all levels of Worlds, Souls, and Divinity. *Yesod* can be seen as a *yud* (י, ten) added to סוד, "secret," the secret of seventy, as explained above. This relates to the length of lifespan: "The days of our years are in them seventy years and if in might eighty years." The secret (סוד) of life is the seventy-year lifespan of King David, the "life" of *malchut*, "kingdom." By adding an additional *yud*, ten, one reaches the "mighty" life span of the *sefirah* above *malchut*, *yesod* (the eighty years that Joseph ruled over Egypt). The "mystery" (רז) of the hidden point of the *yud* (Foundation is "underground") joins with the secret (סוד) inherent within revealed reality (*malchut*).

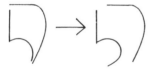

We find this same phenomenon of seventy in relation to eighty with regard to the workers employed by King Solomon in the building of the Temple: "And Solomon had seventy thousand bearers of burdens and eighty thousand hewers in the mountain." Thus the lifespan of seventy years symbolizes the consummation of bearing the burden of one's own task and responsibility in life, whereas the lifespan of eighty years symbolizes the addition of having, with might, hewed out of the raw materials of Creation (the "underground" foundation of reality), building blocks for the Temple. "Hewing" symbolizes the bearing of a child, "hewed" from the "rock" of his father, as is said: "...look unto the rock from which you were hewn and to the hole of the pit from which you were dug. Look to Abraham your father ['Abraham called the Temple site "mountain" '] and unto Sarah that bore you...." David, the secret of seventy, was unable himself to build the Temple. His son Solomon was entrusted with the *mitzvah*. In general, one's "hewn" child becomes the building block of the Temple of G-d. The "might" to hew him is the mystery of eighty.

Pervertly "marrying" the forces of nature is witchcraft, a practice most severely forbidden by Torah. Eighty witches were "caught" by eighty pupils of Shimon ben Shetach, lifted into the air (thereby severing them from their connection to the earth, their source of power), and hung together.

Eighty-thousand Roman soldiers blew horns and eighty-thousand Jews were killed in the defeat of Betar in the rebellion of Bar Kochba, called *Ben Koziba*, "the disappointing one." The teeth of the wicked were not broken due to the blemish of the *yesod*, the covenant of the "marriage" between the Jewish People and G-d. "Covenant" (ברית) is a permutation of "Betar" (ביתר).

In the Book of Judges we find that "the earth was quiet" for a certain period of time after each judge arose for Israel and defeated her enemies. The maximal such period (or lifespan of worldly peace) is eighty years, as we find after the defeat of Moab by the Judge Ehud: "And the earth was quiet for eighty years." As peace is the impression which results from an expression of might—as is said, "G-d will give His people *might*, [and thus] G-d will bless His people with *peace*"—this expresses the secret of "Eighty years to might."

Thus we can understand that when the peace of the Messianic Era will exceed eighty years (forty years of the Kingdom of *Mashiach* and forty years of the third Temple) it will break through the barrier of created nature, Worlds, and enter into a state of eternity—"peace without end."

SOULS

"Eighty pairs of kohanite brothers were married to eighty pairs of kohanite sisters...." Here we find the power of marriage, at the level of Souls, inherent in the number eighty. A further appearance of eighty in relation to marriage and conception ("hewing") at the level of souls: "Eighty-thousand young men all named Aaron went after his bier [in the funeral of Aaron the High Priest], all conceived from men who wanted to divorce their wives and returned [Aaron made peace between—'married'—man and wife] and thereafter bore."

The "sixty queens" of King Solomon in the Song of Songs are followed by "eighty concubines." As explained above in the letter *samech*, the "sixty queens" correspond to the sixty tractates of Mishnah. Similarly, the "eighty concubines" correspond to the eighty tractates of *baraitot*, those parts of Tanaaic Law not codified in the Mishnah. The "one dove" (א) surrounded by the "sixty queens" (ס) and "eighty concubines" (פ) is the secret of the name אסף, Assaf, who speaks in Psalms on behalf of all Israel, especially during exile. The name Assaf (אסף) means "the ingathering" of all souls of Israel (which, as our Sages teach, will be in the merit of the learning of Mishnah) and also is short for אין סוף, "infinity," the infinite powers inherent in the souls of Israel, born anew from generation to generation. The "eighty concubines" themselves are followed by "numberless maidens"—individual laws. As explained above in relation to worldly peace, from eighty one "steps" into "infinity."

Together with the sixty ten-thousands of men older than twenty that left Egypt, were eighty ten-thousands younger than twenty. Moses, whose "weight" equals that of all the sixty ten-thousand adult souls of Israel, is here the secret of the "one dove." As will be explained, he was then eighty years old. The "numberless maidens" are the secret of the infinite potential of Jewish seed-to-be.

DIVINITY

At the time of the Exodus followed by the giving of the Torah, Moses, the "redeemer," was eighty years old. This is the secret of "Eighty years old to might"—"the Mouth [*pei*] of might" of the giving of the Torah. As Moses initially possessed a speech impediment, G-d promised him "I will be with your mouth." "I" is the first word of the Ten Commandments: "I am G-d your G-d...." "I" (אנכי) equals 81, the numerical value of the full spelling of *pei*, פא. This is the "step" of eighty into Infinity at the level of Divinity.

The only two letters filled, "pregnant," with an *alef*, the secret of the Simple Unity of G-d, are the *hei* (הא) and the *pei* (פא), the two letters which compose the word פה "mouth," the meaning of the *pei*. The hidden *alef*, "one," is the secret of "knowledge is hidden in the mouth," as explained above. The "knowledge" of—i.e. contact and communication with—the One is the hidden power of eighty, the ultimate might of the soul, at the level of Divinity.

"Torah and the Holy One Blessed Be He are One." The words of Torah are "[Divine] life for those who find them [למוצאיהם]." Our Sages interpret: "Don't read 'for those who find them [למוצאיהם]' but 'for those who say them with their mouth [למוציאיהם בפה].' " From this we learn that "finding" (as if from "nothing") the hidden, infinite Light concealed in Torah depends on "saying" the words of Torah with one's mouth. Here "saying," למוציאיהם, literally means "extracting"—extracting from the mouth its hidden power, the *alef* of *pei (פא)*, the Infinite One innate in the mouth of every Jew. From this we can understand the tremendous significance of purifying (the words of) one's mouth, in order to be able to reveal, in the oral study of Torah, its innate Divinity, the "I" of the Ten Commandments.

Tzadik

צַדִּיק בֶּאֱמוּנָתוֹ יִחְיֶה

The Faith of the Righteous One

Tzadik: The Faith of the Righteous One

"The tzadik lives by his faith." The form of the letter tzadik (צדיק, or tzadi, צדי) resembles that of the alef more than any other letter. The twenty-two letters of the alef-beit pair into eleven "form mates," the two letters whose forms most closely resemble one another, as taught in Kabbalah. The "mate" of the alef, "the Master of the Universe," is the tzadik, "the righteous one," upon whom the world stands, as is said: "The tzadik is the foundation of the world."

The letter tzadik begins the word צלם, the Divine "image" in which G-d created man. In Kabbalah we are taught that the tzadik of צלם corresponds to the three conscious levels of soul: mind, heart, and action, whereas the two following letters (lamed and mem) of צלם correspond to the two transcendent levels of the soul, "the living one" (chayah) and "the single one" (yechidah), respectively, as discussed in the letter hei (tzadik in atbash). These two levels become conscious as two states of faith in the inner awareness of the tzadik: faith in the Transcendent Light of G-d, the ultimate source of creation, and faith in the very Essence of G-d, the ultimate source of the revelation of Torah and mitzvot. For this reason the word tzadik (צדיק=204) equals two times "faith" (אמונה=102). Also in the verse וצדיק באמונתו יחיה, "The tzadik lives in his faith," the letters of the word "in his faith" (באמונתו) can be read as ב' אמונות, "two levels of faith." "Living in one's faith" means experiencing greatest joy in one's service of G-d, as explained in Tanya.

The word עץ, "tree," created on the third day, equals צלם (=160), the "Divine image" in which man was created on the sixth day. "Man is the tree of the field." In Kabbalah, the third day, tiferet ("beauty"), is the origin of the sixth day, yesod ("foundation"). Tiferet and yesod totally integrate in the secret of the "middle line"—"the body and the brit are considered one." In Sefer Yetzirah we are taught that the twelve simple letters of the twenty-two letters of the alef-beit correspond to the twelve months of the year. Also, each month relates in particular to a specific "sense" in the soul. The letter tzadik is the letter of the month of Shevat, whose "sense" is that of "eating." The fifteenth (middle) day of Shevat, Tu b'Shevat, is the New Year of Trees. (The Rabbinic word for "tree," אילן, equals 91, the union of the two letters alef and tzadik, which is also the union of the two values 26⊥65 [(2·13)⊥(5·13)=7·13=1⊥2⊥...⊥13=Δ13], the value of the name Havayah as it is written [יהו״ה] and read [אדנ״י].)

The "king of trees" is the palm tree, of which is said: "The tzadik like a date palm will flower." The root "to flower" (פרח) equals 288, the secret of the 288 fallen sparks, elevated by the service of the *tzadik* in his Divine consciousness while involved in the act of eating. In all of the seemingly mundane activities of the *tzadik* he "knows" (i.e., contacts, as explained above in the secret of the two previous letters of the *alef-beit*, the *ayin* and the *pei*) G-d, as is said: "In all your [mundane] ways know Him."

The original spelling of the letter *tzadik* is צדי, *tzadi*, which means "to hunt." The holy "sense of eating," the "sense" of the letter *tzadik*, is the ability to "hunt" in order to redeem and elevate the 288 fallen sparks of the breaking of the vessels, as discussed above. "The *tzadik* eats to the satisfaction of his soul" is the verse most relevant to the secret of the service of the month of *Shevat*. The redeemed sparks serve to elevate the consciousness of the soul of the *tzadik* to ever higher levels of Divine perception.

TZADIK

**FORM: A *yud* enwedged in the upper right side of a bent-over *nun*.
The *yud* faces either upwards or downwards, according to two varied
traditions.**

Worlds   Conscious power to actualize potential.
The lifeforce of Creation "running" towards its source Above.
The lifeforce "returning"—downwards.
Form and matter.

Souls   The *nun* represents the "Congregation of Israel"; the *yud* represents the *tzadik* of the generation.
"All your people are *tzadikim*."

Divinity   The thirty-two pathways of wisdom, the *yud*, unites with the fifty gates of understanding, the *nun*.
The higher wisdom (*yud*) and the lower wisdom (*nun*).
The consciousness of *Atzilut* uniting with the source of wisdom and descending to teach Creation.

NAME: A *tzadik*; to hunt; side; in Aramaic: chaos. *Tzadi* becomes *tzadik*.

Worlds   Hunting for the fallen, broken vessels of the world of chaos.

Souls   Hunting for the soul's lost sparks.
The lower *tzadik*—connecting souls.

Divinity   Hunting for G-d and Divine light.
The higher *tzadik*—revealing and drawing down Divinity into the world.

NUMBER: Ninety; "total consciousness."

Worlds   Total consciousness of worlds.
"At the age of ninety one folds over."
Seasons.

Souls   Total consciousness of souls.
The age of Sarah at the birth of Isaac.
Ninety thousand elders danced before the ark when David brought it up to Jerusalem.

Divinity   Total consciousness of Divinity.
Ninety daily "Amens."

FORM

In the form of the *tzadi*, a *yud* is enwedged in the upper right side of a bent-over *nun*. According to the Arizal, the *yud* looks back and up at the *pei*, the preceding letter. According to the other traditions, the *yud* looks forward and down (at the *nun* of the *tzadi*).

WORLDS

At the level of Worlds, the *yud* represents the "point" of creative lifeforce "enwedged" in every created being, the *nun*. In the *tzadi*, the superconscious power of the *kaf* (*keter*), "the power to actualize potential ever present within the actualized," becomes conscious. Whereas the *kaf* is primarily "potential" (כח; the hidden, "pregnant" *pei* of its name כף stands for פועל, "actual"), the form of the *tzadi* is "actualized." The *kaf* and the *tzadi* are the initial letters of the phrase כהן צדק, "the righteous *kohen*," the common Jewish (family) name—Katz. The "righteous *kohen*" is the future companion of *Mashiach*. Through his spiritual aid the *Mashiach* will be able to realize all of his hidden potential.

According to the Arizal, the "point" of creative lifeforce present within every created being looks up and back, running towards its source in the Mouth (*pei*) of G-d (the source of the ten sayings of Creation). According to other traditions the point of lifeforce looks down at Creation, confining itself to the finite limits of its particular objective. In *Chassidut*, this latter level relates to the act of "bringing into being" (התהוות) the level of Divine "energy" present throughout Creation. The previous level relates to the Divine "life pulse" (חיות) present within the act of "bringing into being."

In general, the *yud* and the *nun* represent the two dimensions of form and matter present, simultaneously, in all created reality. The point of the *yud*, pure form, shapes the *nun* of matter into its intended form. The *tzadik*, in "touch" with the inner, pure form of all reality, is able to "shape" reality in accordance with his will, as is said: "The *tzadik* decrees and the Holy One, blessed be He, realizes."

SOULS

At the level of Souls, the *tzadik*, "the foundation of the world," is composed of the *yud*, the point of the all inclusive soul of the generation, enwedged in the *nun*, the "Congregation of Israel," the "body" of all souls of Israel. The great *tzadik* (who sees himself as the "smallest" of the generation) enlivens all of the souls of his generation. In his own prayer he looks upward to G-d for salvation. His prayer is in fact the inner life-pulse of the generation, as all prayers are elevated to G-d by his prayer, as is taught in *Chassidut*. In teaching Torah, he looks downwards, confining himself in accordance with the limited vessels of the souls of his generation, to whom he teaches ("actualizes") the fifty (the numerical value of *nun*) gates of understanding—the potential ability to conceive truth—latent within their hearts. Each soul relates, in particular, to one of the fifty gates. In his teaching of Torah the true *tzadik* brings each soul to his gate of understanding. His Torah actually "brings him into being," inspiring and directing him in life.

The form of the *tzadik* in general is the "female" counterpart of the form of the *alef*, as explained above. The *tzadik* represents the complete stature of the souls of Israel, while the *alef*, "the Master of the universe," chooses the *tzadik* to be His eternal mate. The *alef* gives the power to the *yud* of the *tzadik* to "bring into being" and enliven the *nun* of the *tzadik*, in the secret of אַיִן מַזָּל לְיִשְׂרָאֵל, "the Divine 'Nothing' is the source of life flow [i.e. *mazal*] of Israel." "The Divine Nothing," אַיִן, is the secret of the flow from *alef* (א) to the two components of the *tzadik*, *yud* (י) and *nun* (ן).

DIVINITY

The essence of the world of *Atzilut* is the *sefirah* of *chochmah*, the origin of the Divine wisdom revealed in Torah, as is said in the *Zohar*: *"Aba* [i.e. 'Father,' the fully-developed *partzuf* of *chochmah,* "wisdom"] dwells [literally, 'nests'] in *Atzilut."* The form of the *tzadik—yud* united with *nun*—symbolizes this secret. The *yud* of Divine wisdom "nests," first in continual union with the *nun*, the fifty gates of understanding, in the secret of "the two companions that never part." Thereafter, the *nun* of *Ima* ("mother," the *partzuf* of *binah*, "understanding") reflects itself in the *nun* of *malchut*, in the secret of "like mother, like daughter," and the *yud* of *chochmah* descends to "nest" therein, through the means of the *sefirah* of *yesod*, in the secret of *"Aba* [the 'higher wisdom'] founds [*yesod*] daughter [*malchut*, 'the lower wisdom']." The *nun* of *malchut*, the secret of the Divine Presence, impregnated with the *yud* of Torah (wisdom), descends to shine in the heart of the *tzadik* below. The *tzadik* thereby becomes full with inspired (*yud*) Divine consciousness (*nun*).

In the root of *Atzilut*, אצל, the *tzadik*—the total consciousness of *Atzilut*, is united with the *alef*—its superconscious "form-mate," as explained above, and then descends to teach (*lamed*, which means "to teach") its Divine consciousness to created beings. When the *yud* of the *tzadik* looks upward to the superconscious source of wisdom, the *alef*, the root אצל means "near." When the *yud* of the *tzadi* looks downward at its own *nun* and through the "prism" of the *nun* to the *lamed*, the root אצל means "emanation," as explained in *Chassidut.*

Thus the tradition of the Arizal alludes to the secret of the union of אצ (numerically equivalent to אילן, the inner essence of עץ, the "tree of life," as explained above), while other traditions allude to the secret of the union of צל, the "shadow" of the tree.

NAME

The letter *tzadi*, when spelled צדי, comes from the root "to hunt" (צוד) or the root "side" (צדד). When spelled *tzadik*, צדיק, it refers to the *tzadik*, the personification of "righteousness" (צדק), as inspired by the *yud* of Divine Torah-wisdom, the *yud* of צדיק, as explained above in relation to the *yud* in the form of the *tzadik*.

In Aramaic, צדיא, from צדי (in Hebrew, from the root צדה), is the term used by Onkelos to translate the word תהו, the state of "chaos" in the beginning of the account of Creation.

WORLDS

In Torah, Esau is characterized as "a man who knows [the art of] hunt[ing], a man of the field." Isaac loved his (apparent) first born son for "hunt was in his mouth." The literal reading of "hunt was in his mouth" is that Isaac ate the physical animal hunted by Esau. However, our Sages interpret that Esau would "hunt" (deceive) his father Isaac with the words of his mouth. The Arizal teaches that Isaac himself would hunt for fallen Divine sparks trapped in the mouth (the inner spiritual domain) of Esau. These sparks were actually great souls, deriving from Esau, to be born in the far future, as that of Rabbi Akiva, whose name (עקיבא) is a permutation of יעקב, Jacob, Esau's twin brother, with an additional א, in the secret of "his hand was holding the heel of Esau," said of Jacob at birth. The literal interpretation as well as that of the Sages are at the level of Worlds while the interpretation of the Arizal is at the level of Souls.

Esau is a "great artist" (said of the evil inclination) that hunts for the fulfillment of his physical desires and egocentric ambitions in life. The positive counterpart of Esau's art of hunt, at the level of Worlds, is hunting for lost or misplaced parts of the broken vessels of the world of chaos, in order to elevate their concealed sparks and thereby reveal new creative power, to restore harmony in nature.

SOULS

Hunting for lost souls, fallen sparks trapped in the world of chaos (צדי-תהו), is the work of the *tzadik*, the rectified soul of Israel. In particular, this is the work of the "lower *tzadik*," Benjamin, as taught in Kabbalah and *Chassidut*. Benjamin was the only son of Jacob to be born in the land of Israel, to the right (south) side of the land of Haran where the first eleven tribes were born. Jacob called his youngest son "Benjamin" (בנימין), literally "the son of the right [side]." The right side, *chesed* (lovingkindness), is the power that finds and connects souls. *Tzadik* (צדיק) is numerically equivalent to צד ימין, the "right side." The *kuf* (the next letter of the *alef-beit*, which equals the three letters מין of ימין, "right") of the *tzadik* represents the fallen spark itself to which the *tzadik* links. In Jacob's blessing of Benjamin he likened him to "a preying wolf." Rashi comments that this refers prophetically to Benjamin's hunting after and catching soul-mates in the account of "the concubine of Givah," related at the end of the Book of Judges.

When "the end" (ק) of the *tzadik*, his uplifted and "returned" fallen spark, becomes "enwedged in the beginning" (צ) of the *tzadik*, the "*tzadik* is the foundation [i.e., beginning] of the world," the word קץ, the final "end," is formed. This alludes to the concluding verse of the book of Daniel:

ואתה לך לקץ ותנוח, ותעמד לגרלך לקץ הימין.

"And you go to the end [meaning: 'and you shall go your way until the end be'] and rest, and stand to your fate at the end of days."

Here, "days" appears (i.e., is written) as ימין, "right." This teaches that the end of days and ultimate fate of the *tzadik* is the "extreme [קץ, 'end,' means also 'extreme'] right [side]." The "right side" or "end of days" (קץ הימין) is the secret (numerical equivalent) of כפרה (=305), "atonement," the cleansing of the soul from all impurity and "foreign matter" by the merit of one's devoted service of finding and connecting fallen sparks (souls), the extreme good (right) of G-d, the destiny of every soul of Israel.

DIVINITY

The task of the "higher *tzadik*," personified in Torah by Joseph, is to draw down Divine Revelation to those souls found and connected by the "lower *tzadik*." From the Congregation of Israel—Souls—the revelation passes to Worlds. The task of drawing down Divine Revelation is that of the "higher *tzadik*," who first runs upward towards the Infinite Light and source of all souls in G-d, absorbs this experience, and then returns to the level(s) of Souls (and Worlds) with great strength and light, to infuse all reality with the revelation of G-d's Presence. This "run and return" is the secret of the two traditions in regard to the form of the letter *tzadi*, as described above. The "higher *tzadik*" "hunts" for Divine lights. His "passion"—"the passion of *tzadikim* is exclusively good"—is to reveal these lights in Souls and Worlds.

"A mighty tower is the Name of G-d, the *tzadik* runs into it and is exalted." The "mighty tower," the "Name of G-d," is the secret of *malchut*, the Congregation of Israel, as explained in Kabbalah. The *tzadik*, *yesod*, infused with the strength and light of *chochmah*, runs down to enter and unite with *malchut*. The "passion" of the run into the tower is the "life[force]" of the *tzadik*, the eighteenth (=יח, "life") letter of the *alef-beit*. When the union becomes consummated, the *tzadik* is "exalted" to stand to his fate in eternal life.

NUMBER

The letter *tzadi* equals ninety.

WORLDS

At all levels of Worlds, Souls, and Divinity, the number ninety, *tzadi*, represents "total consciousness," relative to that level. In Kabbalah and *Chassidut* the powers of consciousness divide into three groups of three: The three powers of intellect (מושכל, the *sefirot* of *chochmah, binah,* and *da'at*); the three powers of feeling (מורגש, the *sefirot* of *chesed, gevurah,* and *tiferet*); and the three powers of innate behavior (מוטבע, the *sefirot* of *netzach, hod,* and *yesod*). As each one of these nine powers of consciousness manifests itself in the full spectrum of ten dimensions, the resulting number, ninety, becomes representative of "total consciousness."

At the level of Worlds all of these ninety states of consciousness are "folded over" (the powers of intellect and feeling folded into those of innate behavior) in the womb of nature, in a state of "pregnancy" (עבור). Pregnancy (עבור) implies the liability to עברה, "anger." This is due to the innate "severity" of worldly consciousness, as yet unconscious of the higher levels of Souls and Divinity.

"At the age of ninety one bends over" hints at returning to the womb, in the state described in Kabbalah as "folded over." Afterwards, at the age of 100, the *kuf* connected to the end of the name *tzadik*, one "disappears from the world," as though returning to the state of preconception in the womb.

"There are ninety-one days and seven-and-a-half hours from season to season." Here the number ninety, total consciousness, together with the *alef*, its "form-mate," the secret of the union of the two Names *Havayah* as written and read, appears at the level of Worlds. The significance of the additional seven-and-a-half hours is a quarter of a day (six hours, a quarter of the twenty-four hours of a day) and the quarter of the quarter (one-and-a-half hours, a quarter of six hours). A "quarter" is the secret of *chochmah*, the *yud* of the name *Havayah*, the first quarter of its four letters, as explained in *Chassidut*. *Chochmah* corresponds to *Atzilut* in general, and *chochmah* of *chochmah* (quarter of the quarter) corresponds to *Atzilut* of *Atzilut*. *Atzilut* is the secret of the *yud* of the form of the *tzadik* looking down at the *nun*—*Atzilut* in the sense of "emanation." *Atzilut* of *Atzilut* is the *yud* looking upward at the concealed *alef*, its "form-mate"—*Atzilut* in the sense of "near" its Source, as explained above. Each of the four seasons of the year itself is a quarter. The period of ninety-one days and seven-and-a-half hours implies, here at the level of Worlds, that total consciousness (90=ע) depends upon contact with the superconscious (1=א) which connects to and appears in consciousness by the power of *Atzilut*.

SOULS

The Arizal instructs one to say before prayer: "I hereby accept upon myself the positive commandment of 'you shall love your fellow Jew as yourself.'" Through the sincere arousal of the soul to connect to all other souls of Israel in love, one reaches total consciousness, at the level of Souls, the prerequisite for potent prayer to G-d.

Sarah, the first mother of Israel, was ninety years old at Isaac's birth. In the womb of her total soul-consciousness Isaac was nurtured. Her consciousness expressed itself as laughter: ותצחק שרה בקרבה, "and Sarah laughed inside herself." "Inside herself" hints at the womb. The two words "around" the name Sarah in the phrase ותצחק שרה בקרבה allude to the union of the roots of her son Isaac and his soul-mate Rebecca: Isaac (יצחק), from "and she laughed" (ותצחק); Rebecca (רבקה), a permutation of "inside herself" (בקרבה)—the womb. Upon Isaac's birth Sarah said: "G-d has made laughter of me; all who hear shall laugh with me." צחק, "laughter," the root of יצחק, "Isaac," begins with a *tzadik*, ninety, the age of Sarah, and ends with a *kuf*, one hundred, the age of Abraham at Isaac's birth. Abraham also laughed when told by G-d of Isaac's coming birth. Here the two ages, combined in laughter, total soul-consciousness and its ultimate end, correspond to the return to the womb (the age of ninety) and the further return to the seed of preconception (the age of one hundred), as explained above.

When King David brought the ark with its contained Tablets of Covenant to Jerusalem, he appointed ninety thousand elders to dance joyously before the ark. The *kohanim* carried the ark, the Levites sang and played musical instruments and all Israel "played" in joy. All the souls of Israel were here united in total consciousness of one another before the Holy Ark. The consciousness of the Elders dancing before the ark actually bridged total consciousness at the levels of Souls to that at the level of Divinity.

DIVINITY

The four letters of the word צדיק (*tzadik*) allude to the *tzadik*'s daily fulfillment of one's requirement to say ninety (צ) "amens," four (ד) *kedushot*, ten (י) *kadishim*, and one hundred (ק) blessings. As "all goes after the beginning," the full service of the *tzadik* is concentrated in the secret of his daily saying of ninety "amens." Paradoxically, "amen" is said at the end of a blessing. Not only does the pronouncement of the blessing precede the "seal" of amen, but the very essence of the power of the blessing relates to the secret of beginning, the secret of the big *beit* of בראשית, the *beit* of ברכה, "blessing." In the hint of the four letters of the word *tzadik* (צדיק), the letter *tzadik*, corresponding to ninety amens, begins the word, while the letter *kuf*, corresponding to one hundred blessings, ends the word. Sarah (ninety years old at Isaac's birth) appears at the beginning, while Abraham (one hundred years old at Isaac's birth) appears at the end. This is the secret of "all that Sarah tells you, listen to her voice"—"Sarah is greater than Abraham in prophecy." The simple faith and deep awareness of truth as expressed in the statement of "amen" is ultimately higher than (in truth, the source of) the power of blessing.

Amen (אמן=91) is the secret of the union of 26 (the Name *Havayah* as written) and 65 (the Name *Havayah* as read, אדנ־י): *tzadik* at one with *alef*, as explained above. "Amen" (אמן) is the root of both אמונה, "faith," and אמת, "truth." (In אמת, the *nun* of אמן "falls" from the root as does the *nun* of בן, "son," in בת, "daughter").

"The people who are a *tzadik* shall come, those who guard their faith." "Those who guard their faith," שומר אמונים, is read by the Sages: "those who guard the saying of ninety 'amens' daily." By our pronouncement of "amen" we affirm in oath, as it were, our faith, "stamped" with the seal of truth, total consciousness at the level of Divinity, in the Absolute Unity of G-d.

Kuf

אֵין קָדוֹשׁ כַּהוי׳

**Omnipresence:
Redemption of Fallen Sparks**

Kuf: Omnipresence—Redemption
of Fallen Sparks

Two letters, a *reish* and a *zayin*, combine to form the letter *kuf*. The *zayin*, to the left, descends below the line, while the *reish*, to the right, hovers above it. The paradoxical union symbolized by the two components of the *kuf* is the secret of "There is none holy as G-d." In general, the *kuf* stands for קדושה, "holiness." The unique level of holiness inherent to G-d is expressed, in the words of the *Zohar*, as: "He is grasped within all worlds, yet none grasps Him." The descending *zayin* of the *kuf* symbolizes His being grasped in all worlds, permeating even realms of reality "below the line," i.e., worlds antithetical to those in whom G-d's Presence is revealed. The *reish*, G-d's ever-present transcendence, remains "separate" and holy (in Hebrew, "holy" means "separate") in relation to His descending immanence.

In the name of the letter *tzadik*, its initial reading, *tzadi*, "hunts" for fallen sparks. The holy spark, encaptured "below the line" in physical matter ("anti-matter," relative to that of spiritual realms) is the secret of the following letter, the *kuf* (ק), to which the *tzadi* (צדי) connects to form the full, rectified name—*tzadik* (צדיק).

The *tzadik* is the eighteenth letter of the *alef-beit*, חי, "life," thus symbolizing the power to enliven the fallen sparks, as represented by the *kuf*. The *kuf*, the nineteenth letter, is the secret of Eve (חוה=19; in ordinal numbering, Adam, אדם=1⊥4⊥13=18=חי), whose name also derives from the root meaning "life," as is said: "...and Adam called the name of his wife Eve [Chavah, חוה], for she was the mother of all life." Nonetheless, of her is said: "her feet descend into death," for in the primordial sin of eating (the "sense" of the letter *tzadik*, as explained above) from the Tree of Knowledge, she was ultimately responsible for bringing death to the world. Even within the "broken" (dead) corpse, a spark of life remains hidden, awaiting the power of the *tzadik* (חי, "life") to reinforce its dormant potential of life and to resurrect the body to whom it belongs.

As well as the hidden inner spark of life, a hovering, relatively transcendent "vapor" is present above every corpse or fallen, "dead," physical object. (The word for "vapor," הבל, is also the name Abel, the second son of Adam and Eve, who was killed by his older brother Cain. הבל=37=18⊥19.) These two components of life present within the seeming state of death, correspond to the two letters, the *reish* (the hovering vapor) and the *zayin* (the hidden spark), which compose the letter *kuf*. For this reason the *kuf* symbolizes in particular the reality of fallen sparks, as well as the paradox of the simultaneous omnipresence of G-d's transcendence and immanence. The innate holiness of each spark insures its ultimate redemption and elevation by the *tzadik* (i.e., souls of Israel).

The most fundamental significance in Torah of the number nineteen, the ordinal value of the *kuf*, is the nineteen-year cycle of the moon in relation to the sun, the basis of our Jewish calendar. The moon represents the female figure, the secret of the *sefirah* of *malchut* ("kingdom"), personified by Eve (חוה=19, as above). The sun represents the male figure (the bestower of light, whereas the moon is the receiver of light), and in particular the *sefirah* of *yesod* ("foundation"; יסוד=80=8·10, חי=י·ח), as personified by Adam. Just as explained in the secret of the form of the letter *zayin*, the "woman of valor" who is "the crown of her husband," when the letter *kuf* (ק) precedes the letter *tzadik* (צ), the word קץ, the "end" of time, is formed. This hints at the verse: "...He has set an end [קץ] to darkness." The "end," the coming of *Mashiach* and the subsequent era of resurrection, is the ultimate revelation of the great light and energy latently present within the secret of the letter *kuf*.

KUF

FORM: A *reish* above with a *zayin* descending below the line on the left.

Worlds   "Shells" of impurity "suck" lifeforce in this world.
The *zayin* and *reish* spell *zar*, "foreign."

Souls   The mission of the soul—its descent to clarify sparks of holiness.
The *zayin* and *reish* spell *zeir*, "crown."
The "boomerang" property of the soul.

Divinity   "He is grasped in all worlds [the *zayin*], yet no one grasps Him [the *reish*]."
The *reish* and *zayin* spell *raz*, "mystery."

NAME: Monkey; to surround or touch; strength; in Aramaic: the eye of a needle.

Worlds   Monkey—vanity, the false imitations of this world.
The eye of the needle—the empty point of *tzimtzum*.

Souls   The touching and connection between souls.
The soul opening to G-d.

Divinity   Great strength as revealed in miracles.

NUMBER: One hundred.

Worlds   The one-hundred year life span of the eagle.
"The youth will die at the age of 100."
"At the age of 100 one is as though dead, passed away and 'null' from the world."

Souls   The age of Abraham at the birth of Isaac.
"Go to you": to the source of your soul or to enter your body.

Divinity   Perfect beauty.
The perfection of the square, 10·10.
The ten *sefirot* interincluded.
The one hundred daily blessings.

FORM

Two letters combine to form the *kuf*, a *reish* above and a *zayin* descending below the line on the left. The *reish* hovers, as an aura, above the descending *zayin*. Just as the *yud* is the only letter of the *alef-beit* suspended in mid-air and only the *lamed* rises above the "ceiling" of the letters, so the *kuf* is the only letter whose normative, "inner" form of this world (in contrast to the four *final* letters דזנצ of the World to Come, whose "descending below" is purely the filling of all reality with Divine revelation) descends below the "floor" of the letters.

WORLDS

The descending "foot" of the *kuf* below the "ground level," into the grave, as it were, hints at the verse: "Her feet descend into [the realms of] death." "Her" refers to *malchut*, as personified by Eve, the first woman, responsible for impairing the initially created barrier of immunity between the realms of life (the *kuf* of קדושה, *kedushah*, "holiness") and death (קליפה, *kelipah*, literally, "the shell," the *kuf* descending into "profanity" and allowing it to "suck" from it). Before the final rectification of this world, when "death will be swallowed up forever," the realms of death (the three impure *kelipot* enumerated in Kabbalah) "suck" lifeforce from the "excess products" of *kedushah*, just as Eve, who added to G-d's command not to eat of the tree of knowledge the prohibition of even touching it (*kuf* means "touch") and was thereby seduced by the snake to not only touch but eat of it, as explained by the Sages.

The two letters, *zayin* and *reish*, the components of the *kuf*, spell זר, "foreign" or "strange," as in the phrases מחשבה זרה, "evil [literally, 'foreign'] thought," and עבודה זרה, "idolatry" (literally, "foreign service"). (Today, "strangeness" is a "property" of quantum physics.) In Torah, even an Israelite is considered "foreign" and thereby unworthy and forbidden to perform the service of the *kohanim* in the Temple. Thus "foreign" or "strange" is a relative term. G-d Himself, the Creator, appears to our lower perspective of consciousness to be totally incomprehensible, and so is existentially foreign and strange to our natural, as yet unrectified, senses.

Though now the *zayin* of the *kuf* gives "suck" to the *kelipah*, nonetheless the *reish* of the *kuf* hovers above and envelops the *zayin* as an aura of "untouched" protective lifeforce, ensuring the eventual "passing away" of death, "...and the impure spirit [death] I will make pass away from the earth," forever.

SOULS

The Will of G-d hovers above the soul in its source, and decrees upon it to descend, against its own initial will, into a physical body. The soul's mission below requires it to become totally involved in the process of the rectification, clarification, of its body and "portion" in the world. By means of the inner power of the Divine decree, the soul's initial state of unwillingness and fear to descend below is transformed into a state of willingness and readiness, as explained in *Chassidut*. The hovering aura of Divine Will is symbolized by the *reish* of the *kuf* (the initial letter of רצון, "will") while the readiness of the soul and its actual descent into this world is symbolized by the *zayin* of the *kuf* (whose "crown" is its own, newly-aroused will and whose descending "foot" is its manifestation in the unconsciousness of the body below, together with the impressions it retains from having first passed through seven [ז] spiritual heavens in its journey to earth). The *zayin* also represents the "scepter" of the Divine Will, the power and expression of the King, which, subsequent to the descent of the soul, extends itself below to bestow to the soul its "magic touch," the power of the soul to ascend and "return" to G-d, together with its "booty" of holy sparks.

Here, the *zayin* and *reish* of the *kuf* spell זר, "crown," the term used in Torah to refer to the three "crowning borders" of the ark, table, and inner altar in the Temple. They symbolize "the crown of Torah," "the crown of Kingdom," and "the crown of *kehunah* (Priesthood)," respectively. These three crowns are all given to the souls of Israel to help them realize their mission below, the clarification and elevation of holy sparks.

The two components of the *kuf*, the *zayin* and the *reish*, together with the letter *kuf* itself, spell זרק, "to throw" (the name of the first "cantillation" of Torah: זרקא), whose secret is the "throwing" of the soul below in order that it redeem and "throw" holy sparks upward to their source, as explained in Kabbalah. "Throw a stick, and it will [eventually] fall to its source." This "boomerang" property of the soul is the secret of the form of the letter *kuf*.

DIVINITY

Both זָר, "foreign," and זֵר, "crown," "spell" the two component letters of the *kuf ascending* (from ז to ר), in the secret of "returning light." At the level of Divinity, the *descending* union of the *reish* and the *zayin*—the secret of "straight light"—spells רז, "mystery." רז ("mystery") = אור ("light") = אין סוף ("infinite") = אדון עולם ("the Master of the universe"). Though זֵר ("crown") and זָר ("foreign") belong to the same "gematria-class" (i.e., the set of all words or phrases which equal 207), nonetheless, in particular, זר ("crown") corresponds to גדר, "fence" or "confinement of consciousness" (as in הגדרה, "definition"), making that which is outside one's "fence" of consciousness זר, "foreign" and "strange." גדר ("fence") permutes to דרג ("level," "step," and "finite order") alluding to the three different levels assumed by the souls of Israel: "the crown of Torah," "the crown of Kingdom," "the crown of *kehunah*," as explained above.

The Divine mystery symbolized by the two components of the *kuf* is the secret of "He is grasped within all worlds [the *zayin*], yet none grasps Him [the *reish*]." The *zayin* is immanent while the *reish* remains transcendent.

In script form, the two letters רז, "mystery," form the border of the *yud*, ק→ק , the initial point of creation and consciousness. The *yud*, uniquely, is suspended in mid-air, neither "touching" nor "not touching," yet simultaneously "touching" and "not touching"—"the mystery of mysteries." The *yud* also resembles a "microcosmic" *lamed* (and is therefore its "form-mate"), as expounded in the *halachah*.

The three letters of the *alef-beit* each unique in its form, the suspended *yud* (י) , the ascending *lamed* (ל), and the descending *kuf* (ק), spell a Divine Name in Kabbalah, לקי. This name derives from the initial letters of the three words of the verse which epitomizes the forcefulness of our father Jacob's blessing to his sons (the concluding verse of the blessing of Dan, the "end" of the tribes; only in this verse does the Name *Havayah* appear in Jacob's blessings): לישועתך קויתי יהו־ה, "For Your salvation do I hope, G-d." The three letters of the Name לקי hint at a sequence of spiritual motions of the soul. In the *lamed*, the soul runs up to learn. In the *kuf*, the soul is thrust down to realize its mission on earth. The *yud* is the ultimate universal point of Divine revelation to the soul. Together they spell the mysterious Name לקי (ascent to the unknown, descent into the unknown, the point of the unknown—known) of salvation.

NAME

The word *kuf* means קוֹף, "monkey"; הקפה, "to surround" or "touch"; and תקף, "great strength." In Aramaic it means קופא, "the eye of a needle."

WORLDS

The Arizal explains that the monkey is the intermediate state between animal and man. (So do there exist intermediate states between the inanimate and vegetable, and between vegetable and animal. The concept of the "intermediate," more fully expounded in *Chassidut*, is one of the basic secrets of Creation, the power of "continuum" hidden within the "quantum leaps" of nature). The Midrash states that the descendents of Cain (who murdered his "human" brother, Abel) "degenerated" into monkeys.

A monkey is a false imitation or "copy" (from the Hebrew קוֹף) of man. The book of Ecclesiastes (Kohelet, קהלת, which begins with a *kuf*; the two subsequent letters, הל, allude to הבל, "vanity") begins: "Vanity of vanities said Kohelet, vanity of vanities, all is vanity." This alludes to the seven vanities of this world (according to the principle: "the plural indicates at least two," "vanity of vanities" implies three vanities; "vanity of vanities" implies another three vanities; "all is vanity" brings the total number of vanities to seven).

According to one interpretation of the Sages, these seven vanities refer to seven periods, or seven "worlds," through which one passes in life. In each world one is likened to a different creature. First, when born and placed in a crib, one is like a king, to whom all come to bow down and give homage. At the age of two, one crawls the floor sticking his fingers into filth like a pig. Later, at the age of ten, one jumps and plays like a goat. At eighteen one combs his hair and runs after a mate like a horse. After marriage one bears the burden of earning a livelihood as a donkey. Later, with a large family to support, one barks after livelihood with insolence, like a dog. Finally comes the difference: if, through one's first six worlds of vanity, one remained close and devoted to Torah, one ends his life on earth as a king, this time a real king (though, the Torah of this world, before the coming of *Mashiach*, is itself considered "vanity" relative to the inner truth of the Torah, the inner essence of *malchut* [kingdom] inherent in Torah to be revealed by *Mashiach*). If, however, one strayed from Torah, one ends his life like a monkey. Thus, the monkey symbolizes the epitome of the vanity of this world.

Ultimately, vanity reflects the existential state of emptiness. All of nature evolves in the empty space, actually no more than an empty point (of zero-dimension), "created" (as it were, for in truth, from G-d's perspective, the *tzimtzum* is not real) by the *tzimtzum* or "contraction" of the infinite light. This is symbolized by the "empty eye of a needle," קופא דמחטא, to be discussed at the levels of Souls and Divinity.

SOULS

The soul of Israel, the true "man," knows that "there is no place vacant of Him." Though, when enclothed in the physical consciousness of this world the soul experiences apparent emptiness, it ever strives to touch the omnipresent surrounding light. Though this world, as experienced by our physical senses, is "the world of deceit," the truth of Torah is "very close," as Moses assures us at the end of his life: "For the thing [Torah and *teshuvah*] is very close to you, in your mouth and in your heart to do it."

Awareness of the omnipresent surrounding light depends upon individual souls touching one another and connecting consciously. The individual Jew is called "man" (in contact with truth, unlike the vanity of the monkey) only when part of the collective stature of the Man of Israel, the organic union of all souls. This experience reaches its height during the *hakafot* (הקפה from קוף) of *Simchat Torah*.

"Open to me [an opening] as the eye of a needle and I will open to you [an opening] as the great entrance to the Temple Hall." The opening of the soul as the eye of a needle is not an experience of emptiness and vanity, but rather becoming an "empty vessel," fitting to receive light and life, in greatest anticipation and yearning to be filled. The empty point is the contraction (*tzimtzum*) of one's ego, making a point empty of "me," in order for Him to enter and dwell; for "I [G-d] and he [the arrogant man] cannot dwell together."

DIVINITY

"Then Esther the queen, the daughter of Avichail, and Mordechai the Jew, wrote with 'all strength' [את כל תקף, from קוף] to confirm this second letter of Purim." Rashi interprets "all strength" as "the strength of the miracle." "Great strength" (תקף) refers in particular to strength of conviction and determination to overcome obstacles (in "victory" over one's enemies, Amalek, the ancestor of Haman, being the "arch-enemy" of Israel) and to fulfill one's decisions. Miracles in general, and that of Purim, overcoming nature while enclothed in nature, in particular, are the expression of G-d's greatest strength (תקף).

Purim occurs in the month of Adar. In *Sefer Yetzirah*, the letter of *Adar* is the *kuf* (ק), and its sense is that of laughter, צחק. In Adar, "the strength of the miracle" makes all "turn over," even until the "world of deceit" turns into the "world of truth." The miracle of Purim is the secret of the "elephant entering the eye of a needle," which even in the vivid, often wild imagination of a dream is "impossible," unless explicitly thought of by day. The word "elephant" (פיל) relates to the word אלף (פלא turned over), "wonder" (as it is said, "One who sees an elephant in his dream, wonders of wonders shall happen to him"). The "song" of the elephant in *Perek Shirah* is "How great are Your deeds, G-d; Your thoughts are very deep." The unique strength of the miracle of Purim is that G-d's greatness (symbolized by the elephant) actually entered into the vanity of the world (monkey) of the empty point of the eye of a needle. The Divine miracle enclothed itself in the "strange" vanity and folly of King Ahashuerus, whose love for his first wife, Vashti, turned into hatred and determination to do away with her, and then fell in love with Esther, as elucidated by the Sages and in *Chassidut*. The effect of the miracle of Purim on Israel was our acceptance of the yoke of Torah with infinitely firmer conviction and determination to realize its truth than when first accepted at Sinai.

NUMBER

The letter *kuf* equals one hundred.

WORLDS

The life span of an eagle is said to be one hundred years. Every ten years the eagle soars upward, aspiring to reach the sun, faints from the heat of the sun, falls into the ocean and is thereafter rejuvenated, only to repeat this process ten years later. The tenth time he soars with greater strength and higher than ever before, is totally burnt and dies. The rejuvenation of the eagle is referred to several times in the Bible, as in Psalms: "May my youth be renewed like an eagle." In the future, "a youth will die at the age of a hundred," as before the flood man became liable to punishment only at the age of one hundred.

In Kabbalah, the eagle, the third of the four faces of the "chariot," corresponds to the *sefirah* of *tiferet*, "beauty" (its synonym is יפי, the secret of 100, 10 times 10, as will be explained), the secret of the "youth of Israel." Worldly beauty is the origin of vanity and deceit, whereas the beauty of Torah and the soul of Israel is the ultimate manifestation of truth.

"Remaining young" in nature is the result of repeated trauma of frustrated episodes of love. Death is the actual achievement and consummation of one's love. This deep parable of life and death has its parallels at the higher levels of Souls and Divinity as well.

The passing away of the eagle at the age of one hundred relates to the previously quoted saying of the Sages in Pirkei Avot: "...at the age of one hundred one is as though dead, passed away and is 'null' from the world." The three expressions "dead," "passed away," and "null" mean "dead" in relation to action, "passed away" in relation to emotion, and "null" in relation to mind and perception of the vanities of this world (עולם, "world," from העלם, "concealment" of Divine Light, the secret of *tzimtzum* and the consciousness of the "eye of the needle" at the level of Worlds, as explained in *Chassidut*).

SOULS

Isaac was miraculously born to Abraham at the age of one hundred, the age when Abraham totally "passed out" of worldly consciousness and became one ("Abraham was one") with the source of the soul of Israel, to "pass on" the soul to his descendents forever. In Isaac's name (יצחק), the final letter, *kuf*, stands for the one hundred years of his father Abraham, as taught by the Sages and mentioned above, while the first letter, *yud*, 10, the "root" of 100 (10^2), stands for the ten trials Abraham withstood by the power of superrational faith. At the time of the giving of Isaac's name, when Abraham had reached the age of one hundred, eight trials had passed in his life and become actual while two were still potential. Though potential in relation to their manifestation at the level of Worlds, they were already present at the level of Souls (of Abraham and Isaac), as the secret of the *yud* of Isaac's name indicates.

The first words G-d spoke to Abraham, commanding him to leave his land, birthplace, and father's house and go to "the land which I will show you," were לך לך, "Go to you" (the name of the third Torah-portion). In the *Zohar*, "go to you" is interpreted as upward travel to reach the source of the soul above, the spiritual "promised land" (the secret of the upward soaring *lamed*, the initial letter of לך לך, as explained above). The Arizal interprets its secret as the downward journey of the soul to earth to enter a body (the secret of the downward thrust of the *kuf*, the full value of לך לך, 100) with the sense of purpose and mission to spread to the knowledge of G-d on earth (the revelation of the "suspended" yud, all in the secret of the Name לקי, as explained above). The two words (לך לך, "go to you"), spelled identically, equal 50⊥50=100. When these two words are written fully, (למד כף למד כף), their "pregnant" letters equal 248, the numerical value of אברהם, Abraham. This hints that the true fulfillment of Abraham's journey shall come at the age of one hundred with the birth of his son Isaac (the existential projection of his essential "you"—"Go to *you*").

The two words לך לך ("go to you") are "encoded" in the text of the first paragraph of the *Shema*, recited twice daily, in the two verses:

ושננתם לבניך ודברת בם בשבתך בביתך ובלכתך בדרך ובשכבך
ובקומך. וקשרתם לאות על ידך והיו לטטפת בין עיניך.

"And you shall teach them to your children, and you shall speak of them when you sit at home and when you go on the way, and when you lie down and when you stand up. And you shall bind them for a sign on your hand, and they shall be as frontlets between your eyes."

From the *lamed* of לבניך ("to your children") one "skips" 25 letters to the *kaf* of ובלכתך ("and when you go," just as לך לך, "go to you"). Once more one skips 25 letters to the *lamed* of לאות ("for a sign") and then to the *kaf* of עיניך ("your eyes"). Three skips of 25 equal 75, the age of Abraham when told "go to you." The fulfillment of "go to *you*" came with the birth of Isaac after an additional 25 years (the secret of the 25 letters of the opening verse of the *Shema*, the first letter of which is "returned" to after an additional skip of 25 letters "over" the last verse of the first paragraph of the *Shema*—which itself contains 24 letters) at the age of one hundred.

DIVINITY

At all levels of Worlds, Souls, and Divinity, the number 100 represents perfection and completion, the "interinclusion" (התכללות) of ten *sefirot*, each reflecting all the others. Physically, perfect "interinclusion" is represented by a square, *n* by *n*. In particular, in regard to the fundamental structure of ten *sefirot*, $n=10$. Ten is the full number of dimensions of any manifestation, as in the secret of the first letter, *yud*, of the Name *Havayah*, whose secret is "the beginning of revelation." *N* in the second dimension is the interinclusion of all of the initial properties in each unit (individual property) of *n* in the first dimension. The ultimate beauty of interinclusion finds its full expression in Divinity, in the secret of the ten *sefirot* of *Atzilut* perfectly reflected in one another. The true beauty of *Atzilut* is the consummate, paradoxical (to our mind) union of the many and the one ("the elephant in the eye of the needle," who himself is "great" in the sense of incorporating a multitude—"many"—of parts, yet wondrously "small," to enter the needle's eye, in the sense of "one").

The word "beauty," יפי, itself equals 100. It can be read as an acrostic for י פעמים י, "*yud* [ten] times *yud*." In *Sefer Yetzirah*, the *yud* is the letter of the month of *Elul*, which "faces" the month of *Adar*, whose letter is *kuf*.

In the reduced numbering system, the sum of all the 22 letters of the *alef-beit* is 100, 10^2. This is one of the secrets of the "ten intangible *sefirot* and 22 letters of foundation," the "32 pathways of wisdom" of *Sefer Yetzirah*. The sum of the first 10 letters from *alef* to *yud* is 46, the normative numerical value of the word מאה, "one hundred." (46 equals לוי, Levi, the "highest" of the tribes of Israel, while the remaining 54 equals דן, Dan, the "lowest" of the tribes.) The "triangle" of 46 (the sum of all numbers from 1 to 46) is 1081, the *gematria* of *tiferet* (תפארת, consummate "beauty" and splendor).

In our service of G-d, one hundred is the number of blessings to be said daily. The consciousness of truly blessing G-d is the awareness that all one receives from His open Hand (the secret of the *yud* at the level of Divinity) is, in truth, a Divine miracle enclothed in nature, as was the miracle of Purim.

Reish

עֲבוֹדַת הַבֵּרוּרִים

Process: The Art of Clarification

Reish: Process—the Art of Clarification

Although the letter *reish* is situated close to the end of the *alef-beit*, its primary meaning is "head" or "beginning." There are four "beginnings" in the *alef-beit* (comparable to the four New Years enumerated in the beginning of the tractate *Rosh Hashanah*) relative to four different categories of phenomena. The ordinal beginning of the *alef-beit* is the letter *alef*. Phonetically, the vapor, the amorphic "matter" from which the pronunciation of every letter is formed, is the secret of the letter *hei*. In script, every letter begins from a point, the secret of the letter *yud*. In relation to meaning, cognizant intelligence or wisdom, *reish* means "beginning." These four letters combine to spell אריה, "the lion," the first of the four "holy animals" of the Divine chariot of Ezekiel. They further combine to spell יראה, "fear" or "awe."

"The beginning of wisdom is the fear of G-d." In *Chassidut* we are taught that the inner experience of the soul which serves as the vessel to arouse and contain ever new flashes of insight, wisdom, is *bitul*, "selflessness." Fear, the beginning of wisdom, corresponds to the source of this state in the soul. Fear "shocks" ego, breaking the innate coarseness of the heart, that coarseness or egocentricity that prevents one from being truly receptive and perceptive to reality outside oneself in general, and the Divine Essence of all reality in particular.

The two letters that fill the letter *reish* (ריש) are יש, meaning "something," in general identified in *Chassidut* with the consciousness of ego or being a separate, independent entity—a "something." *Reish* is the only letter "pregnant" with this "filling." In *Chassidut* we are taught that though the lower "something," the "created something" (יש הנברא), appears to be totally separate from the consciousness of its Creator and the creative force which continuously brings it into existence, nonetheless its seeming separate "somethingness" serves, in truth, to reflect the Absolute and "True Something" (יש האמיתי) who is truly and uniquely independent, "the Cause of all causes."

The insight of Divine wisdom is the "nothing" (אין) between the two states of "something," whose ultimate purpose is to serve to draw the consciousness of the "True Something" (יש האמיתי) into the experience of the lower "something." In the power of the process of rectification, the ego must first be "shaken" by the fear of G-d, the beginning of wisdom. Thereafter one's "matter" can be purified and clarified in order to become a fitting "mirror" to reflect the True Something. This process of clarification, dependent upon wisdom and its beginning, fear, is expressed in the verse: "You have made all in wisdom." "Made" (עשׂית) refers throughout the Torah to the process of rectification and clarification. The *Zohar* paraphrases this verse: "You have clarified them all with wisdom." The "art of clarification" is the "beginning of the end"; the three final letters of the *alef-beit*, ר־שׁ־ת, are the beginning, middle, and end of the end, respectively. Just as the *tzadik* connects to the *kuf* in its full spelling (צדיק), so the *reish* "leads in" to the *shin* (ריש), all of the clarifications of wisdom ascending upward to their Divine Source in the flame of the love of G-d and His people Israel.

REISH

FORM: The profile of a head; a bent over head.

Worlds   A man bent over in poverty and servitude.
Conformity to social norms.

Souls   The mind "bending over" in order to express itself in speech.
Devoted service to G-d.

Divinity   The revelation of G-d's thoughts through speech.
The union of Kabbalah and *halachah*.
The presence of Shabbat in the weekdays.

NAME: Head or beginning; poor man.

Worlds   The state of poverty of this world.
The experience of poverty prior to it leading to selflessness.

Souls   The conscious state of mind.
The second day of *Rosh Hashanah*—conscious beginning.
The power to procreate.

Divinity   The superconscious state of mind.
"My thoughts are not your thoughts."
The first day of *Rosh Hashanah*—unconscious beginning.

NUMBER: Two hundred.

Worlds   The upper limit of poverty—two hundred *zuz*.
The two hundred lights that shine out of the self.
"The sun is charity."

Souls   Two hundred heads of the Sanhedrin from the tribe of Issachar.
Time.

Divinity   The numerical half way point of the *alef-beit*.
Creation begins from the "middle point" of G-d's Infinite Light.
The evolving of the "Kingdom of the Infinite."
The King and His people.

FORM

The *reish*, whose meaning is "head," profiles, in its form, the head of man. Its horizontal top depicts the head facing left (the next letter of the *alef-beit*, the *shin*), bent over. Its downward extension to its right depicts the beginning of the spinal column, the "backbone," the support of the head.

WORLDS

As one of the meanings of the *reish* is רש, "a poor man," so, at the level of Worlds, its form represents the bent-over head of a poor man experiencing and acknowledging his state of poverty and servitude to the worldly source of his sustenance. At a deeper level, this poverty and servitude is expressed by the bowing of the head to accept the yoke of conforming to the "laws" of society with its secular culture and standards. This is the opposite of the strength of conviction and determination of the previous letter, *kuf*. It is actually a lower manifestation of the *reish* included in the form of the letter *kuf*, without the ability to penetrate and "fight" reality, the secret of the *zayin* ("weapon") of the *kuf*. Physical poverty weakens one's conviction and "backbone," as is said: "poverty causes man to lose possession of his own *da'at* [his power to make descisions and forcefulness to implement them against the obstacles of nature] and the *da'at* of his Creator [the conviction necessary to implement the decisions of G-d, the *mitzvot* of His Torah]."

No rectification in the world can take place without the power of "mind over matter." The "poor head" has lost this power. The Ba'al Shem Tov teaches that, although being "clever" in the worldly sense may lead to negative ramifications when unconnected to the yoke of Torah, nonetheless the first *mitzvah* of a Jew is to be "smart," even in relation to the level of Worlds, when committed to Torah. Otherwise he remains a "poor head" incapable of dealing forcefully with the world.

SOULS

In order to speak, the thought of the mind must "bend over" and contract its own inner brilliance for the sake of communication to others. Speech is the most essential characteristic of man. When G-d created man "He blew into his nostrils the breath of life and man became a living creature"—"a speaking spirit," as discussed above in the letter *pei*. The bending over of the head in order to speak is thus the beginning of man's assuming his true role.

We are told of two of the greatest Chassidim who would assume different postures while deeply immersed in meditation. While Rabbi Yitzchak Isaac of Homil, the great "intellect" of *Chassidut*, would throw back his head with open eyes gazing up, Rabbi Hillel of Poritch, the great "servant" of *Chassidut*, would place his thumb in his mouth and bend his head over between his knees. The ultimate purpose of meditation is devoted service, which requires the bending over of the head.

The *reish* included in the form of the letter *kuf*, at the level of Souls, is the Divine Will bending over to "force" the soul into a state of willingness to descend below. So, the letter *reish* itself is the inner bending over of the mind to force the heart to respond in accord with the mind's perception, to speak from the heart, thereby giving one's words the power to penetrate the hearts of others. First the mind speaks to the heart and then the heart speaks to others. The two basic words for speech in Hebrew are אמר, "to say," and דבר, "to speak." In particular, אמר signifies the inner speaking of mind to heart, while דבר refers to the outward speaking of the mouth. Both roots end with a common letter, the *reish*.

DIVINITY

"The concealed things are to *G-d* our G-d, while the revealed things are to us and our children...." In Kabbalah, "the concealed things" refers to the secret of the first two letters of the Name *Havayah*, י־ה, corresponding to the continual union of the two *sefirot* of *chochmah* and *binah* which transcend (and are thereby concealed from) the lower *sefirot* of Creation. "The revealed things" refers to the last two letters of the Name *Havayah*, ו־ה, which correspond to the emotions of the heart (the six *sefirot* from *chesed* to *yesod*) and speech (the *sefirah* of *malchut*). G-d Himself "bends over" His "concealed things" (His power of intellect, as it were) in order to reveal "the revealed things" and permeate them with light from the realm of the concealed.

Amalek, the arch-enemy of Israel and, as it were, of G-d, wishes to disassociate "the concealed things," the letters י־ה, from the "revealed things," the letters ו־ה, to separate mind from heart and speech and thus make knowledge impotent, i.e., incapable of effecting rectification of one's emotive attributes and instinct of communication.

At a deeper, more refined level, this is like one who wishes to disassociate the study of the hidden dimensions of Torah—Kabbalah and *Chassidut*—from the revealed body of the Law. Would the head not bend over, there would be no contact between them. The bending over of the head, in devotion to Divine service, the essence of *Chassidut*, as above, draws Kabbalah into *halachah*. This is the secret of drawing Shabbat into the six days of the week, as explained by the Arizal and in *Chassidut*.

NAME

The word *reish* (ריש) means both "head" or "beginning" (ראש) and "a poor man" (רש).

WORLDS

After the episode of David and Bat Sheva, Nathan the prophet came to David and said:

> " 'There were two men in one city, one rich and the one poor [ראש,
> i.e. רש written with an additional *alef*, as ראש, "head"]. The rich man
> had exceedingly many flocks and herds. But the poor man had
> nothing [ולרש אין כל], save one little lamb, which he had bought and
> nurtured, and it grew up together with him and his children, it ate
> of his own meat and drank of his own cup and lay in his bosom and
> was to him a daughter. And there came a traveler to the rich man
> and he spared to take of his own flock and of his own herd...but took
> the poor man's lamb....' And David's anger was greatly kindled
> against the man...and Nathan said to David, 'you are the man.' "

As long as the poor man is in a state of *"one* poor," אחד ראש, he keeps
his "head," even in his state of poverty, connected to the *one*, the *alef*, just as
the *"one* rich" ("There is none rich but in knowledge [of G-d] and there is
none poor except in knowledge [of G-d]"). When his poverty causes him to
lose "head," the *alef* disappears, replaced by the words אין כל (=111=אלף),
"had nothing," literally "had not *all*." The only thing that remains to him is
the physical comfort of this world, the lamb of the poor man. David's "sin"
was that he temporarily lost "head," especially severe as he was the "head"
(i.e. king) of Israel. He identifies emotionally with the poor man while in
truth he behaved as the rich man.

King David is the secret of *malchut*, initially poor, as explained in the
secret of the *dalet*. *Chassidut* explains the difference between the forms of
the *dalet* and the *reish*, and their respective states of poverty, based upon
the verse "the poor man had not *all*." The *dalet* (ד), in its upper right,
possesses a point of *bitul*, selflessness, in recognition and connection to the
source of its sustenance, whereas the *reish* (ר) lacks this point of "all." The
task of the *reish* is to internalize the *alef* into its very being, thus overcoming
the negative implications of the state of poverty of this world and becoming
a ראש, "head," a leader rather than just a receiver.

SOULS

The two days of *Rosh Hashanah*, the head of the year, correspond, in Kabbalah, to the "depth" of *keter*—the unknowable (superconscious) head—and the "depth" of *chochmah*—the knowable (conscious) head. The ten days of *teshuvah* between *Rosh Hashanah* and *Yom Kippur* are the secret of the ten "depths" of the ten *sefirot*. Each one of these days we add to our morning prayers Psalm 130, "from the depths I call unto You, G-d." Though initially only one day, *Rosh Hashanah* is now observed for two days and will remain so even with the coming of the *Mashiach*, just as now even in the land of Israel two days of *Rosh Hashanah* are observed, in contrast to the other holidays which are observed for two days only in the Diaspora.

The second day of *Rosh Hashanah* is the head, the *reish*, at the level of Souls. It was first revealed by the souls of the Sages of the Oral Torah, though eternal in essence, as explained above. "Everything primordial [קדמון] is eternal [נצחי], but not everything eternal is [necessarily] primordial." The first day of *Rosh Hashanah* is the secret of the primordial eternal, at the level of Divinity. The second day of *Rosh Hashanah* is the secret of the eternal alone, at the level of Souls.

The soul of Israel comes from the wisdom of G-d, just as the drop of seed of the son is drawn from the brain of the father, as explained in *Tanya*. On the first day of *Rosh Hashanah*, the sixth day of Creation, Adam and Eve were created and given the commandment not to eat of the Tree of Knowledge (which they transgressed). Though commanded "be fruitful and multiply" on this very day, G-d intended the fulfillment of this positive command to take place the next day, the first Shabbat of Creation, the second day of *Rosh Hashanah* (primordial in the secret of Shabbat, and eternal in the secret of *Rosh Hashanah*). Thus the secret of the second day of *Rosh Hashanah* is the power to reproduce souls on earth imbued with the mission "...fill the earth, conquer it and rule...."

DIVINITY

The unknowable, superconscious head of the first day of *Rosh Hash-anah* is the secret of " 'for My thoughts are not your thoughts, neither are your ways My ways,' says G-d; 'for as the heavens are higher than the earth, so are My ways higher than your ways, and My thoughts than your thoughts.' " These two verses precede the verse: "Seek G-d while He may be found, call upon Him while He is near. The wicked shall forsake his way, and the unrighteous man his thoughts, and he shall return to G-d, and He will have mercy upon him, and to our G-d for He will abundantly pardon," which our Sages understand to refer to the ten days of *teshuvah* in general and to the first day of *Rosh Hashanah* and *Yom Kippur* in particular.

The spiritual service of the first day of *Rosh Hashanah* is to coronate the King by our total subdual and bowing of head to accept the yoke of heaven. Thereby our own head is actually elevated to a level absolutely higher than our previous state of consciousness. The knowable head of Souls is lifted into the unknowable head of Divinity. "Your thoughts," when totally subdued to the Will of G-d, are lifted into "My thoughts" and "your ways" into "My ways" (the *mitzvot* of Torah, the ways of G-d).

This is the secret of "lift up the head of the Children of Israel." The root "to lift up" in Hebrew, נשא, means the power to bear opposites, the Divine paradox of the unknowable head. When the letters ראש, "head," are "lifted" to the next letters of the *alef-beit*, they become שבת, Shabbat, the secret of the Primordial One, as explained above. One of the great *tzadikim* of *Chassidut*, Rabbi Chaim of Tchernovitch, is said to have actually become a head taller on Shabbat.

NUMBER

The letter *reish* equals two hundred.

WORLDS

So long as a man possesses up to 199 *zuz*, he is halachically considered a poor man, worthy of receiving charity. Upon obtaining the 200th *zuz* he leaves the category of a poor man and is no longer eligible to receive charity. The word "charity" (צדקה) equals 199.

The upper limit of charity, 200, is thus the secret of ראש, "poor man" (רש) with an *alef* (א), i.e. no longer poor but a ראש, "head," in control of his worldly affairs. This is hinted at in the verse: "the thousand is to you, Solomon, and two hundred to the keepers of its fruit." The "thousand" (האלף) is the secret of the letter *alef*; in its source—one, which completes (Solomon, שלמה, means "completion") the 200 to become a "head" worthy of keeping the fruit of the garden—i.e., responsibly attending for the nature of Worlds.

When the *alef* of Solomon is joined to the *reish* of the "keepers" by the connecting force of the letter *vav*, the word אור ("light") is spelled. Initially the thousand are the secret of the "thousand lights" which shine inwardly to the "completed" self. The two hundred, the "fifth" of the thousand, are those lights which shine outwardly to the other. In the word אור, "light," the two, opposite "vector" forces of light combine, the inner drawn down to augment the outer.

At the level of Worlds, "lights," אורות, means fruit (and vegetables) in Hebrew. This is an obvious allusion to the phenomenon of photosynthesis, where physical sunlight is transformed into the lifeforce of vegetation. This relates to the phrase שמש צדקה, "the sun is charity." The essence of the sun first consumates the 199 (=צדקה) to become 200 (ר), and then joins the 1,000 (its own inwardly shining light) to the 200 (outwardly shining lights), in the full secret of the word אור, "[sun]light."

SOULS

"And from the children of Issachar were those that knew the under-standing of times, to know what Israel aught to do, their heads were two hundred and all their brethren were by [the word of] their mouth." Our mother Leah, in her strong desire to keep (bear) the fruit (seed) of Jacob, merited to give birth to Issachar, as told in Genesis and elucidated by the Sages. The tribe of Issachar, the wisest of the tribes in knowledge of Torah in general, and especially in knowledge of "the secret of impregnation," possessed 200 heads (*reish* at both levels of Number and Name) of the San-hedrin.

Issachar was the ninth tribe to be born to Jacob, alluding to the secret of the nine months of pregnancy. *Reish* (ריש) is the only letter of the *alef-beit* pregnant with "something" (יש), as explained above. In general, preg-nancy is the secret of process in time. Issachar יודעי בינה לעתים, "knows the understanding of times," in the secret of "if there is no *da'at* [knowledge] there is no *binah* [understanding] and if there is no *binah* there is no *da'at*." The two *sefirot* of *binah* (בינה=67) and *da'at* (דעת=474) unite numerically to equal Israel (ישראל=541)—"to know what Israel ought to do." This union takes place in the womb of *binah* (the mother), oriented to experience process and time as happiness: "The mother of children is happy," as ex-plained in *Chassidut*. The "times" of the Jewish calendar are times of joy. Even on days of mourning one is conscious that in the future they will be transformed into days of greatest joy. This is the experience of time at the level of Souls.

DIVINITY

Though the *reish*—the 20th of the 22 letters of the *alef-beit*—is the "beginning of the end," nonetheless, numerically, its value is the halfway point between that of the *alef*, one, and that of the *tav*, four hundred. As a circle can be seen to begin from its center, the "circle" of the *alef-beit* (whose diameter equals 400=ת) "begins" (ראש—ריש) from its middle-point, the *reish*, 200. (In addition, since the *reish* is the 20th letter, the circle of the *alef-beit* can be seen to be a square of its center, 20^2=400.)

In Kabbalah we are taught that the *tzimtzum* of the Infinite Light took place in its "middle point," leaving over an "impression" of "dark" light within the vacuum-point of the *tzimtzum*. ("Impression," *reshimu* (רשימו), begins with the syllable *reish*; the *mem* of the root רשם is one of the "non-essential" letters האמנתיו, and thus not an essential part of the root.) To speak of a "middle point" within infinite expanse is itself a paradox, as explained in Kabbalah. The secret of the middle point is the "Kingdom of the Infinite" (מלכות דאין סוף), the point through which the Creator "emerges" into His Creation as King ("head") of the universe. This "emerging" of the King is represented by the word "King," מלך, evolving in three stages beginning from its first letter: מלך→מל→מ, which together equal 200, *reish*. The two letters of the second stage of "emergence," מל, combine numerically to become the letter *ayin* (=70), which then links, backwards, to the *mem* of the first stage to spell עם, "people," in the secret of אין מלך בלא עם, "there is no king without a people." First the people are potential in the root of the Being of the King. Thereafter they become an external reality which bows down, on the first day of *Rosh Hashanah*, to coronate the King and ultimately to become one with Him, in the secret of עם (people) ⊥ מלך (King) = מ⊥מלך⊥מ = ר, *reish*.

Shin

שַׁלְהֶבֶת קְשׁוּרָה בְּגַחֶלֶת

The Eternal Flame

Shin: The Eternal Flame

The letter *shin* appears engraved on both sides of the head-*tefilin*. On the right side, the *shin* possesses three heads, while on the left side it possesses four heads. In Kabbalah we are taught that the three-headed *shin* is the *shin* of this world while the four-headed *shin* is the *shin* of the World to Come.

The secret of the *shin* is "the flame [Divine Revelation] bound to the coal [Divine Essence]." A simmering coal actually possesses an invisible flame within it, which emerges and ascends from the surface of the coal when the coal is blown upon. The three levels: coal, inner flame, and outer flame, correspond to the secret of *chash-mal-mal*, as will be explained in the next letter, the *tav*.

One of the meanings of the word *shin* (שׁין) is שׁנוי, "change." The coal symbolizes changeless essence, the secret of the verse: אני ה' לא שניתי, "I am G-d, I have not changed," meaning that relative to G-d's Essence absolutely no change has occured from before Creation to after Creation. The inner flame is the paradoxical latent presence of the power of change within the changeless. The outer flame of the *shin* is continuously in a state of motion and change.

As in the above-quoted verse, the changeless Essence is the secret of the Name *Havayah*, אני יהו־ה לא שניתי. The power of change, as latently present within G-d's Essence before Creation and thereafter revealed in the infinite intricacy and beauty of an ever-dancing flame, is the secret of the explicit Name of Creation, *Elokim* (אלקים), the only Name of G-d which appears in the plural. The number of the letter *shin*, 300, unites these two Divine Names as the "flame bound to the coal." In *atbash*, the Name *Havayah* transforms to the letters מצפצ, which total 300. The five letters of *Elokim* (אלקים) when written in full (אלף־למד־הי־יוד־מם) also equal 300.

The three heads of the *shin* of this world correspond to the three levels of the changeless, potential, and actual change as discussed above. In this world, the changeless is symbolized only by a black, dark coal, not as the revealed light of the flame. Nonetheless the endurance of the flame depends upon the changeless essence of the coal. In the World to Come, the changeless essence will reveal itself within the flame. This revelation of the future is the secret of the fourth head of the *shin*.

In the flame of a candle one sees three levels of light: the "dark light" around the wick of the candle, the white flame encompassing it, and an amorphous aura around the white flame itself. Each of these three levels of revealed light manifests a dimension contained within the invisible flame present in the coal. In general the flame symbolizes love, as is said: "as mighty as death is love...the flame of G-d." The dark light corresponds to the love of Israel, souls enclothed within physical bodies. The white light corresponds to the love of Torah. The aura corresponds to the love of G-d. These are the three essential manifestations of love as taught by the Ba'al Shem Tov. The fourth head of the *shin* of the future—the revelation of the essence of the coal itself—corresponds to the love of the Land of Israel and, as our Sages teach: "the Land of Israel will in the future spread to incorporate all of the lands of the earth."

SHIN

FORM: Three *vavs*, each with a *yud* on top, rise from a common base-point. Symbol of symmetry; Form of a flame.

Worlds   Stability and harmony in nature.
Positive and negative grace; Symmetry groups.

Souls   Finding grace in the eyes of G-d.
The grace of the Jewish people in each other's eyes.
The 3 *vavs* represent the three Patriarchs; the 4 *vavs*, the Matriarchs.
The 3 *vavs* represent *Kohanim*, Levites, Israelites; the 4th, righteous converts.
"No lie can endure if not based on truth."

Divinity   Divine Perfection and Grace; The three lines, or pillars, of the *sefirot*.
The "army of G-d"; The *shin* of the *tefilin*.

NAME: A year; change; a tooth; scarlet; serenity; to sleep; to teach; two; sharp; old; viceroy.

Worlds   Natural changes in the yearly cycle.
Tooth—power of decomposition and entropy.
The firey scarlet of the priestly garments.
"I am asleep..."—"in exile"; Aging.

Souls   The fire of Torah; Sharpness in learning.
The second to the King; The double Shabbat loaves.
The Mishnah; "...yet my heart is awake."

Divinity   The "immovable power" that causes all motion.
"I am G-d, I have not changed."
Peace and serenity; The *shin* of the *mezuzah*.
The accelerated change of the future toward the changeless.

NUMBER: Three hundred.

Worlds   Three hundred foxes sent to burn down the fields of the Philistines.
Three hundred arrows pierced King Yoshiyahu.
Three hundred years Israel worshipped idolatry in the days of the Judges.

Souls   Three hundred fox-parables of Rabbi Meir.
Three thousand parables of King Solomon.
Three hundred first-born Levites; Three hundred soldiers of Gideon.

Divinity   Three hundred *halachot* concerning "a mighty bright spot."
Three hundred *halachot* concerning "you shall not let a sorceress live."
Three hundred *halachot* concerning "the tower soaring in air."
Three hundred *halachot* concerning "and the name of his wife was Meheitavel."
"Is not my word like fire and like a hammer that breaks rock into pieces?"
"The spirit of G-d hovered over the face of the waters."
The full spelling of the Name *Elokim* (and the Name *Havayah* in *atbash*).

FORM

The *shin* is composed of three *vavs*, each with a *yud* on its top, rising from a common base-point. The form of the *shin* symbolizes symmetry at all levels of Worlds, Souls, and Divinity. Its shape resembles flames of fire, as does its phonetic sound. In *Sefer Yetzirah*, the *shin* is the letter of fire.

WORLDS

Of the eight synonyms for beauty in Hebrew, חן, "grace," the beauty of *malchut*, relates to the property of symmetry. This is alluded to in the verse: ונח מצא חן בעיני ה', "and Noah found grace in the eyes of G-d." The word "grace" (חן) is the symmetric invert of the name "Noah" (נח). In the eye, the image of sight inverts, for which reason the pupil of the eye is called אישון, "a little [upside down] man," as explained by Rabbi David Kimchi in *Sefer Ha-Shorashim*. The letter whose form possesses the most revealed state of grace (that letter whose form is most visibly, "linearly," symmetric) is the *shin*, the "middle" of the end of the *alef-beit*. The form of the *alef*, the beginning of the *alef-beit*, possesses the most "subtle" state of grace ("angular" symmetry). It represents the grace (symmetry) of soul. Together, these two most graceful letters of soul and body spell אש, "fire." At the general level of Worlds, the *shin* of אש represents the physical flame of the fire itself (bound to the coal or wick), while the *alef* represents the surrounding medium of air (in *Sefer Yetzirah* the א stands for אויר, "air"; air is "soul" or "spirit"—רוח, a synonym for אויר—at the level of Worlds) necessary for the fire to burn, as explained in *Chassidut*.

The word חן ("grace") equals fifty-eight, the sum of the seven components of the form of the *shin*: three *yuds* above three *vavs* on the *yud* of the base. The sum of the components of the *shin* (58) and its *gematria* (300) is 358, which equals משיח, *Mashiach*, whose anti-being, the snake (נחש) also equals 358. The snake symbolizes the false, deceiving grace of this world, whereas *Mashiach* is the true grace (the secret of "And Noah found grace in the eyes of G-d") of the coming world. Noah, the tenth, consummate generation from Adam and the central personality of the end of the first portion of Torah, the portion of Creation, hints at the future perfection of Creation by *Mashiach*.

The mathematics of modern physics is based on "symmetry groups," where the property of symmetry serves to "cancel out" undesirable phenomena and thereby establish stability and harmony in nature. In a rectified world true grace and symmetry eliminates ("cancels out") evil, thereby "proving" that, in truth, evil never really existed.

SOULS

The soul of the *tzadik*—"Noah was a *tzadik*"—who serves G-d in humility and truth, finds favor in the eyes of G-d, as explained above. This favor saves him from the "destruction" (entropy) of Worlds.

In the *Zohar*, the *shin* is referred to as "the letter of the fathers." The three ascending *vavs* of the *shin* correspond to the three patriarchs, Abraham to the right (*chesed*), Isaac to the left (*gevurah*), and Jacob in the middle (*tiferet*). The four-headed *shin* of the future (the secret of mother, *binah*, "the depth of the future") corresponds, at this level, to the four matriarchs, the middle *vav* (of Jacob) splitting into two, his two wives Rachel and Leah.

The three *vavs* also correspond to the three divisions of the Jewish people, *kohanim* to the right, Levites to the left, and Israelites in the middle. In the future, the fourth *vav*, corresponding to the righteous converts of Israel, will become independently revealed, in recognition of their special role and unique merit in the bringing of *Mashiach*.

The three *vavs* come to a point in the secret of the union of *yesod* and *malchut*, personified by Joseph and David. Joseph, the *tzadik* of the generation—"*tzadik*, the foundation of the world"—ignites the holy fire in the hearts of the Congregation of Israel, *malchut*, personified by King David. The essential origin-point of King David, Ruth the Moabite, the archetypal righteous convert, will in the future "rise" from the "dark" base-point of the *shin* to become fully manifest as the fourth *vav* of the *shin*, as explained above. Our Sages teach that *shin*, the letter of truth, begins the word שׁקר, "lie," as "no lie can endure if not based on truth," in the secret of the Exile of the *Shechinah*. "False is grace" (שׁקר החן) sucks its lifeforce from the *shin*. When the souls of Israel ignite in the mighty flame of the love of G-d, this very *shin* "consumes" the lie it began, and ascends into its source of truth.

DIVINITY

Symmetry at the level of Worlds manifests itself as the balance and har-mony apparent throughout nature. At the level of Souls, symmetry is the grace one soul finds in the eyes of another, binding them together in love, and the grace the soul finds in the eyes of G-d. At the level of Divinity, the grace of the *shin* is the secret of "the grace of place [חן מקום] is on one who inhabits it," for "He is the Place of the world yet the world is not His place." This is the grace that G-d, the all-encompassing "Place of the world," finds, so to speak, in the eyes of Israel.

The Divine Place is G-d's Transcendent Light which "surrounds all worlds." The three vavs of the *shin* are here the origin of the three lines, or columns, in the Divinely emanated space of *Atzilut.* They meet below at a point, the *yesod* and *malchut* of *Atzilut.* From this base-point the *shin* reflects its Divine symmetry into the three lower worlds of Creation, Formation, and Action, in the secret of the Name *Tzevakot* (צבאות, "Hosts"). *Tzevakot* is one of the seven Divine Names, explicitly mentioned in *Tanach,* which we are forbidden to erase. The Sages interpret the meaning of *Tzevakot:* "He is a sign [אות] is His hosts [צבא]." This Divine Sign, present in all worlds as an axis around which the hosts of heavens and earth revolve, is the inner pillar of Immanent Light which "fills all [lower] worlds."

In recognition and identity with this inner Divine symmetry the Jewish people becomes צבאות ה', "the hosts [army] of G-d," as stated in Torah at the time of the Exodus: "And it was in that very day that all of the Hosts of G-d left Egypt." Leaving Egypt symbolizes leaving all states of physical (Worlds) and spiritual (Souls) confinement. This is only possible for a sol-dier in the "army of G-d," one totally committed to fulfill G-d's Will and thereby become a fitting vessel to receive G-d's strength and inspiration, by His grace.

On the right side of the head-*tefilin* is engraved a three-headed *shin,* the *shin* of *chochmah,* the secret of the root of the souls of the three patriarchs. On its left side is engraved a four-headed *shin,* the *shin* of *binah,* the secret of the root of the souls of the four matriarchs. This is the *shin* of the World to Come: when the symmetry-axis of this world will itself split into two, and reveal that the "intermediate," the middle line, entails the roots of the two extremes which it serves to unite.

NAME

The word *shin* (שׁין) means "a tooth" (שׁן), "change" (שׁנוי), "year" (שׁנה), "two" (שׁנים), "the viceroy" or "second [to the king]" (משׁנה), "sharp" (שׁנון)—especially in the sense of "to teach [diligently, לשׁנן]" (as in ושׁננתם לבניך, "and you shall teach them diligently to your children"), "sleep" (שׁנה), "old" (ישׁן), "scarlet" (שׁני), "rest" or "serene peace" (שׁאנן). The spectrum of meanings associated with the name of the *shin* is the richest and most splendrous of all of the letters of the *alef-beit*.

WORLDS

The word שׁנה, "year," derives from the root which means "change," שׁנוי. In *Sefer Yetzirah*, "year" is the term used for (the changes of) time in general.

In physical nature, the "teeth of the wicked," discussed above in the form of the *pei*, represent the power of decomposition and deterioration, or the law of entropy. This natural "breaking down" of all matter in pursuit of the "lowest energy level" is the continuation, in the present, of the primordial stage of Creation referred to in Kabbalah as the "breaking of the vessels." The fire of the *shin* is the power that breaks matter apart, in contrast to water that acts as glue to cause matter to stick together. In *atbash*, the *shin* reflects the *beit*, the secret of splitting into "two," שׁנים, as in the phenomenon of cellular division. The fire of the *shin* is reflected in the scarlet hue of שׁני, one of the materials used in the clothing of the *kohanim*.

The *Zohar* explains that in the time of exile "I [the Divine soul] am asleep...." The present Lubavitcher Rebbe *shlita* states that even when returning to the קoly Land of Israel, if one is unconscious of the significance of its deep essence, one may be carried on clouds to Israel "asleep in bed," as it were, and in this same state of spiritual slumber enter Jerusalem, and so on until, with the rebuilding of the Temple, he will suddenly awaken in shock, to find himself in the Temple itself.

Some things (such as wine) become better with age (ישׁן) while others deteriorate. In general, the secret of life is "staying young." Asleep (ישׁן), one grows old (and "outmoded," ישׁן); awake (ער), one stays young and "modern," צעיר). So do we find that when Choni HaMa'agel slept for seventy years, he awoke to find himself old and "out-of-place," and so preferred to die rather than be "friendless." Had he, for the same period, remained awake, he would have "stayed young" with the time, naturally "readjusting" to the changes of generations. Old wine is superior because its vital ("youth") process continues without wearing. So by the power of ever-new insight ("awakeness") into the depths of Torah does the true Torah Sage remain young while continually maturing. Of the Guardian of Israel it is said: "He does not slumber nor sleep."

SOULS

In the first paragraph of the *Shema* we read וְשִׁנַּנְתָּם לְבָנֶיךָ, "...and you shall teach them [diligently] to your children." Diligent teaching ignites the holy flame of the *shin* in the hearts of one's students ("your children" means "your students," as taught by the Sages). Literally, וְשִׁנַּנְתָּם means "to sharpen," as in חֵץ שָׁנוּן, "a sharpened arrow." "A sharp sword shines flashes of lightning." So a "sharp" student, though innately "sharp," further sharpened ("initiated" into the pure and authentic "sharpness" of Torah tradition) by the diligent teaching of his mentor, begins to experience in himself lightning-flashes of new insight in Torah. (These flashes actually come from the Torah he was taught in the womb when a candle shone over his head, the secret of the *shin* of Shabbat [שבת] above the *reish* of ראש ["head"], as explained above.) These in turn ignite his heart to strive to fulfill G-d's Will as expounded in Torah.

The word "soul" itself, נשמה, is a permutation of the word משנה, the "viceroy" (or "second" to the King, משנה למלך), from the root שנה, "two." The king is the secret of "one," as in the phrase אחד העם, "the one of the nation," while the ministers and officers under the viceroy are called שלישים, "thirds [in command]", from שלש, "three." Both Joseph and Mordechai served as viceroys (משנה למלך). The name of Joseph's first born son, Menasheh (מנשה), is a permutation of נשמה ("soul") and משנה ("viceroy"). The soul of Israel is the "second" to the "King of kings," blessed be He, and the counselor to the king, as it were, as in the Midrashic account of G-d as (the King) taking counsel with the souls of Israel before He decided to create the world. The word "second" also appears in the phrase לחם משנה ("double loaves"), the two *challah*-loaves over which are recited the blessing over bread at the Shabbat meal. They commemorate the double portion of manna that fell for Israel on Friday, one portion for Friday and the other for Shabbat.

In addition, the Mishnah (משנה, from the root וְשִׁנַּנְתָּם, "and you shall [diligently] teach"), is the fundamental compilation of the laws of the Oral Torah, that "half" (in חֵץ שָׁנוּן, "sharp arrow," חֵץ ["arrow"] means "half"; from שָׁנוּן, "sharp," derives משנה, "Mishnah") of Torah entrusted to the souls of Israel.

DIVINITY

אני הוי' לא שניתי, "I am G-d, I have not changed." Paradoxically, the property of absolute "unchangeability" is actually the source of all change in created reality. "The power that moves is unmovable." This is the secret of "rest" or "serene peace" (שאנן) associated with the name *shin* at the level of Divinity. שלום, the common word for "peace," and a name of G-d, begins with the letter *shin*.

The "unmovable mover" is the secret of the *mitzvah* of *mezuzah* (מזוזה, which derives from the root זוז, "to move"). One interpretation of מזזות (*mezuzot*, as written in the chapter of *Shema*) is זז מות, "death is made to move away." The only "fixed" *mitzvah* (as indicated by its blessing: "...to *fix* a *mezuzah*") is that of the *mezuzah*, and yet it channels the Divine power of Providence that "moves" and simultaneously guards one in all of his activities: "G-d shall guard your going out and your coming in," for which reason the *mezuzah* is fixed on the doorpost of exit and entrance.

On the outside of the scroll of the *mezuzah* is written the name *Shakai* (ש־די), beginning with a *shin*. Often the letter *shin* appears alone on the *mezuzah*-container, as short for ש־די (the initial letters of the phrase שומר דלתות ישראל, "The guardian of the doors of Israel").

In the form of the *shin*, the three *vavs* indicate three general "vectors" of change. Their common base-point symbolizes the changeless origin. The four-headed *shin* of the future indicates that in the future, change itself will increase, for all reality (especially the souls of Israel) will ascend in ever accelerating motion, while simultaneously, in direct proportion to the acceleration of change, the changeless Source will become manifest.

Just as light represents maximal motion and—as motion produces heat—alludes to heat, so darkness represents motionlessness and cold (whose extreme is absolute zero—"external" motionlessness, in the sense of inability to move, frozen and without any manifestation of true changelessness). The verse אני הוי' לא שניתי, "I am G-d, I have not changed," equals the verse קץ שם לחשך, "He has set an end to darkness" (=888), for the property of maximal change inherent in light reflects and reveals the truly "unchangable."

NUMBER

The letter *shin* equals three hundred.

WORLDS

After the Philistines had deceived him and stolen his wife, Samson took three hundred foxes, turned them tail to tail, tied a torch to each pair, and thereby burned down the fields of the Philistines. The fox (שועל, beginning with a *shin*) symbolizes worldly cunning. Here Samson used two "sharp" forces of nature, the fox together with the element of fire (the *shin*), to burn down the "hold" of evil on nature itself. Samson, שמשון, means "small sun." The secret of שמש, sun, is water (*mem*, hydrogen) transforming into the fire of solar energy and radiation (a *shin* on both sides).

King Yoshiyahu, יאשיהו, one of the most righteous kings to arise from the house of David and referred to as "the *Mashiach* of G-d", was killed—due to the great transgressions of Israel—in battle with Pharoah Necoh by three hundred Egyptian arrows. Three hundred arrows is the secret of חץ שנון, the "sharpened arrow," mentioned above. (The fact that חץ, "arrow," also means "half" alludes to the splitting of Samson's three hundred foxes into two halves of a hundred and fifty each and then tying their "tails" together by the power of the flame.) The death of Yoshiyahu, the thirtieth generation from Abraham, marks the temporary disappearance of the "moon" of Israel. After having risen to "full moon" in the generation of Solomon (שלמה, who, in reduced numbering, equals fifteen), the fifteenth generation from Abraham, it then descended gradually until the days of Yoshiyahu, the end of the "month."

In the days of the Judges, the Jewish people worshipped idolatry for a period of three hundred years. For three hundred years the people were "asleep" in the land of Israel itself, as mentioned above. Physical nature, even in Israel, can hide consciousness of Souls and Divinity, to the extent of seducing one to bow down to nature. Nonetheless, the inner "nature" of Israel (both the People of Israel and the land of Israel) is not to stand for such concealment indefinitely, and ultimately G-d will "work salvations in the midst of the land," just as Samson used the very forces of nature against its own evil manifestations. He thereby brought the three hundred idolatrous and relatively anarchous years of the days of the Judges to an end—he was the last Judge of Israel—and paved the way for the revelation of true Kingdom (Souls in Divine control of Worlds) in Israel.

SOULS

Rabbi Meir taught three hundred parables of foxes, of which only three were handed down to us. The fox, the wisdom and cunning of this world, serves as a parable for the wisdom of the Divine soul and its "good inclination" in "outsmarting" the wolf, the "evil inclination" of the animal soul. As explained in the form of the *reish* at the level of Souls, the power of speech is deeper and more essential in the soul of man than that of conscious thought, for speech reflects the wisdom of the soul's superconscious. In *Chassidut* we are taught that the ability to relate a precise parable derives from the deepest levels of the superconscious mind, as apparent from the fact that only rarely is one able to "find" a true parable in which to "enclothe" the knowledge of his conscious mind. King Solomon spoke three thousand parables (300 *times* 10, related to the three hundred *and* ten worlds of the *tzadikim* in the World to Come: להנחיל אהבי יש, "to give inheritance to those that love Me," יש being the experience of true "something," as above.)

The three lines of the form of the *shin* correspond to the division of Jewish souls into three categories: *kohanim*, Levites, and Israelites, as mentioned above; in particular, however, the element of fire—the fundamental power of *shin*—corresponds to the left line of the *sefirot*, the line of ascent-as-fire, the service of the Levites. Thus, we find three hundred first-born Levites in the desert.

By a Divinely instructed test, Gideon, one of the great and righteous Judges of Israel, chose three hundred men to fight with him against the multitudes of Midian and other nations. The test served to indicate those who had not bowed down to the Ba'al (idolatry). The souls of these three hundred men of Israel are the secret of the rectification of the three hundred years that Israel worshipped idolatry during the days of the Judges.

DIVINITY

Often we find in Torah "three hundred *halachot*": "Three hundred *halachot* concerning 'a mighty bright spot' [area of skin, in the laws concerning leprosy]"; "three hundred *halachot* concerning 'you shall not let a sorceress live' "; "three hundred *halachot* concerning 'the tower soaring in air' [the letter *lamed*, as discussed above]," and so on. Three hundred is thus seen to represent a maximal revelation of "differentiated" Divine Will in Torah, in relation to the particular rectification of worldly phenomena.

Though three hundred here appears to represent a quantitative maximum, we are taught in *Chassidut* that every quantitative property of Torah implies, and actually derives from, a corresponding qualitative property. Thus it is said: " 'Is not My word like fire?' says G-d, 'and like a hammer that breaks rock into pieces?' "—three hundred pieces. The "rock" of Torah itself, when broken into sufficient (300) pieces—in the merit of those devoted to the study of Torah with a "broken heart" (the *only* perfect vessel to perceive the Divine, as explained in *Chassidut*)—repairs and elevates the broken pieces of *Tohu*, the primordial world of chaos (resulting in physical reality as we know it).

The *Zohar* relates an additional instance of "three hundred *halachot*": "Three hundred *halachot* concerning 'and the name of his wife was Meheitavel.' " These hidden *halachot* are the secret of the rectification of the world of *Tohu* and the breaking of the vessels symbolized by the death of the first seven kings of Edom, as expounded by the Arizal. None of the first seven Kings was "married," i.e. in a state of rectification. The eighth king, Hadar, the "key" of rectification, was the first to marry. "The name of his wife was Meheitavel." Of each of the first seven kings it is said: "and he ruled...and he died." Of Hadar (and Meheitavel) is said: "and he ruled..." but not that he died.

"The spirit of G-d" (רוח אלקים) in the second verse of the Torah, "And the earth was *tohu* and *vohu* [chaos and void] and darkness was on the face of the abyss, and the spirit of G-d hovered over the face of the waters"—which, according to our Sages refers to the spirit or soul of *Mashiach*—equals three hundred. As stated above, the full spelling of *Elokim* (אלף למד הי יוד מם) equals three hundred, as does the Name *Havayah* in *atbash* (מצפצ). Thus the "spiritual," "pregnant" letters of the full spelling of *Elokim* equal רוח, "spirit." "The spirit of G-d," Divinity, is the "spirit of grace," רוח חן, the secret of the letter *shin*. When the *shin* (ש), "the spirit of G-d," hovers over the waters (מים), the word "heaven" (שמים) is formed. The "waters" are the "waters of Torah" and the "waters of *teshuvah*." שמים ("heaven") is often used as a connotation for G-d Himself, whose spirit (the soul of *Mashiach*) hovers over the "waters" of Israel, our devoted study of Torah and service of *teshuvah*.

Tav

תָּיו רָשִׁים רְשִׁימוּ לְעַתִּיק יוֹמִין

Impression: The Seal of Creation

Tav: Impression—the Seal of Creation

The *Zohar* states: תיו רשים רשימו לעתיק יומין, "the *tav* makes an impression on the Ancient of Days." "The Ancient of Days" refers to the sublime pleasure innate within the "crown" (Will) of Divine Emanation. The letter *tav* (here referring to the "Kingdom of the Infinite One, Blessed be He") leaves its impression on "the Ancient of Days." The impression is the secret of simple faith in G-d's ultimate omnipresence, the Infinite present in the finite, for "there is none like unto Him" (the conclusion of the above quotation from the *Zohar*).

This faith passes in inheritance from generation to generation, from world to world, the *malchut* (kingdom) of the higher world linked to the *keter* (crown) of the lower world. The *tav*, the final letter of the *alef-beit*, corresponds to *malchut* (kingdom), the final Divine power, in the secret of "Your Kingdom is the Kingdom of all worlds." The impression of the *tav* is the secret of the power that links worlds—generations—together.

The initial impression of true faith was that which was stamped upon the soul of our first father, Abraham, "the first of all believers." This is the secret of Abraham's purchase of the Cave of Machpelah, the original Jewish cemetery, for four hundred (the numerical value of *tav*) *shekel*, the secret of our eternal inheritance of "four hundred worlds of pleasure," sealed with the stamp of simple faith.

G-d's seal (in Creation) is truth (אמת, the final letters of the three last words in the account of Creation: ברא אלקים לעשות, "...G-d created 'to do' "). The last letter or seal of the word truth (אמת) itself—the seal of G-d's seal—is the letter *tav*, simple faith, the conclusion and culmination of all twenty-two forces—letters—active in Creation.

The three letters which spell truth (אמת) are the beginning, middle and ending letters of the *alef-beit*. The *alef* (א) corresponds to one's initial awareness of Divine paradox in the infinite source (where the higher and lower waters, joy and bitterness, are absolutely one). From this awareness issues *mem* (מ), the fountain of Divine wisdom, ever-increasing power of insight into the mysteries of Torah. "The final end of knowledge is not to know." The culmination of the flow of Divine wisdom in the soul (after all is "said and done") is the "majestic" revelation of the infinite "treasure-house" of simple faith in G-d's absolute omnipresence below innate in the soul of Israel. The culmination of truth (אמת), simple faith (אמונה), is the secret of the *tav* (ת).

"All follows the seal," in the secret of "returning light" from the *tav* to the *alef*, thereby forming the word תא, "cell." Around the inner Sanctuary of the Temple were constructed many תאים, "cells" or "small chambers." These "cells" were without windows, thus being completely dark inside. *Chassidut* teaches that these "cells" reveal the level of "He places His concealed place in darkness," the awareness of simple faith reaching into the absolutely "dark" Essence of G-d.

So we are taught: "Torah is the impression [the *tav*] of Divinity; Israel is the impression [the *tav*] of Torah." Divinity is perceived first through the service of deepest meditation in complete silence (submission), the secret of חש ("silence") of *chashmal* (חשמל). Then, through the means of an intermediate stage of "circumcision," comes a first expression of מל, from ברית מילה, "circumcision." Torah is the secret of separation between good and evil—circumcision—the cutting off of the foreskin (evil).

Israel, the ultimate manifestation of G-d's Word in Torah (ישראל, "Israel" is an acronym for יש ששים רבוא אותיות לתורה, "There are six hundred thousand letters in the Torah") corresponds to the final level of "speech," מל of חשמל. Speech, communication of G-d's oneness between souls, is the ultimate level of Divine service, "sweetening" all reality, as taught by the Ba'al Shem Tov. The *tav*, simple faith, is here seen to be the power of impression and linkage uniting the apparently paradoxical extremities of Divine service, from the utter silence of meditation to the loving communication between souls.

TAV

FORM: A *dalet* joined to a *nun*.
A stamp or seal.

Worlds   Physical "stamps" on reality—fossils, footprints.
Judgement and Law.
Primordial matter.

Souls   The tribe of Dan—humility and selflessness.
Returning the lost sense of purpose and direction.
Salvation
Reincarnation; The "stamp" of previous lifetimes.

Divinity   The reading of the Name *Havayah*.
G-d as Judge.
G-d's seal on all of reality: the source of *teshuvah* and the potential of individuality.

NAME: Sign; impression; code; in Aramaic: more.

Worlds   The sign on the forehead of Cain.
Natural law and codes of life.
The music of Creation.

Souls   The sign of righteousness.
The *tzadik* is alive even in death.
Teshuvah, prayer, Torah.

Divinity   The Divine power of continuation present in the end.
The advantage of light which shines from darkness.
The last letter of the account of Creation: rectification, the seal of truth.
The last letter of the first word of Creation: the ultimate origin.

NUMBER: Four hundred.

Worlds   Four hundred men of Esau.
Four hundred men of David.
Four hundred years of exile in Egypt.

Souls   The four hundred pieces of silver with which Abraham purchased the cave of Machpelah to bury Sarah.
The four hundred gates of mutual knowledge amongst the four couples buried in the Machpelah.
Efron—evil eye; Abraham—pure eyes.
The dimensions of the Land of Israel—four hundred *parsah* by four hundred *parsah*.

Divinity   The four hundred worlds of Divine pleasure in the World to Come.
The G-d of Israel, the people of Israel, the Torah of Israel, and the Land of Israel.

FORM

The *tav*, formed by joining a *dalet* to a *nun*, resembles a stamp or a seal.

WORLDS

Previous states of being leave their impression or stamp on present reality. In nature, fossils are stamps of creatures who lived in previous "worlds." Our Sages teach that these "worlds" were created and subsequently destroyed, for they did not find favor in the eyes of the Creator (the entire process being designed from Above for the sake of the creation of this world). These worlds were spiritual, not physical, as taught by the Arizal, though from the impression they make in the physical world they appear to have been physical. This total integration of the impression of higher reality on lower reality is symbolized by the union of the two components of the *tav*, the *dalet* (impression of higher reality) and the *nun* (so totally integrated in lower reality that it appears to have been a part of it). The two component letters, *dalet* (ד) and *nun* (נ), read דן, "to judge." Just law on earth is actually the reflection and impression of higher spiritual law, as explained in *Chassidut*.

Of course, there are also "footprints" of past physical events upon the present. In addition to actual human and animal footprints, nature is full of footprints, as the "paths" left by the elementary particles of quantum physics.

The letter *tav* itself, the last of all the letters of the *alef-beit*, is actually the stamp and seal of all the previous letters. It possess nothing of its own (*dalet*) and completes the nine "vessel" letters beginning with *nun*.

SOULS

In the spiritual service of the soul, the two components of the *tav*, the *dalet* and the *nun*, represent selflessness and humility, as discussed above. Together, they spell the name of one of the Tribes of Israel—דן, Dan. Dan also denotes a camp of three tribes (Dan, Asher, Naphtali), the last of the four camps of Israel in our sojourn through the desert. When camping around the Tabernacle the camp of Dan was situated to the north (see the letter *beit*). The Sages teach that Dan assumed the responsibility of returning losses to all of the other (previous) camps. In *Chassidut* we are taught that not only did Dan have an eye to find and return lost items but, on a deeper level, he found and returned lost souls (i.e., returned the sense of purpose and awareness of their task in life to souls who had lost this). His devotion to "finding" others derived from his own state of existential lowliness, always regarding others greater and more worthy than himself.

Jacob blesses Dan: "Dan shall judge [דן ידין] his people as one of the tribes of Israel." The phrase "one of the tribes of Israel" refers to the tribe of Judah, the king ("one" in the sense of "special" and "outstanding") whose camp was first. Thus "the end is enwedged in the beginning": the *tav* (whose form is דן) in the *alef* ("one"). In the construction of the Tabernacle, the two chief craftsmen were from the tribes of Judah (Bezalel) and Dan (Oholiav). The conclusion of the blessing of Dan is "To Your salvation I hope, G-d." This is the only time the Name *Havayah* appears in Jacob's blessing of the tribes. The power of both salvation from all of the evil powers of the north and their ultimate annihilation (with the coming of the *Mashiach*—the closing of the "open north side") is the secret of the *tav* at the level of Souls.

In addition, *tav* ("impression") is, at the level of Souls, the secret of re-incarnation, the impression of previous lifetimes on one's present lifetime. Occurences and situations of this lifetime serve to rectify blemishes ("return" lost items) of previous lifetimes (in addition to one's conscious service of Torah and *mitzvot*). The "blemish" (מום, *mum*, related to מ, *mem*) inherent in the "impression" (ת, *tav*), the secret of "death" (מת), comes to life (becomes rectified) by Divine Providence (symbolized by the *alef*, א), and the soul's experience of G-d's Presence in one's present lifetime. One need not know of (and certainly not dwell upon) one's past lifetimes, for the essence of rectification depends solely on one's Divine consciousness in the present. One must experience the existential "freedom" of the present from the past (by the Infinite power of the Omnipotent One) in order to rectify the blemish inherent in the impression of the past. When "resurrected," the blemish itself, the *mum*, opens its "scar" to issue *mem*, living waters of Torah insight ("no one is wise [in Torah] but the master of [traumatic] experience," and "one cannot understand the law unless one has stumbled over it [failed to perform it]"). The *tav*, the general impression of past lives, becomes the source of simple faith ("not to know," after "all is known"). The resurrection itself depends on the *alef*, consciousness of G-dliness in the present, in the full secret of the "seal" of G-d, אמת, "truth" (*alef*, א, resurrects the "dead," א' מחיה מת—מת), as explained in Kabbalah and *Chassidut*.

DIVINITY

The two letters *dalet* and *nun* are the two middle letters of G-d's Name of Kingdom, the "reading" of the Name *Havayah*—אדנ"י. These are the strong consonant letters of the Name, whose meaning is "L-rd" or "Master [of the universe]" Who controls all of reality by Divine law and judgement—דן. At the level of Divinity, the "one" in the verse "Dan shall judge his people as *one*, the tribes of Israel" refers to the One Above, blessed be He, as revealed through His attribute of *malchut*, of which is said דינא דמלכותא דינא, "the law of *malchut* is law." *Malchut* is the end and seal of the *sefirot*, just as the camp of Dan is the end ("collector") of the souls, the secret of *tav*, the end and seal of the letters.

Self-consciousness and ego are the expression of the *malchut* ("kingdom") of every world and creature. "Your Kingdom is the kingdom of all worlds" means that the Divine *malchut* stamps its impression and seal upon every subsequent created *malchut*. The power of this impression of Divine *malchut* in every creation gives it the power to choose to transcend its own finite ego and subdue itself, and thereby to ultimately identify and unite with the true *malchut* of G-d.

The consciousness of this impression produces an awareness that there exists something "beyond," something much more essential than anything we can comprehend. The feeling of "beyond" entails the sense of individual as well as universal purpose—the true source, desire, and motivation of *teshuvah*. Even one moment's experience of this sincere feeling of "beyond" stamps its mark on the soul forever. Imbued with this power, one shall eventually come to stamp the eternal mark of his Divine soul on Creation.

NAME

The word *tav* (תו, variant spellings: תאו, תיו) means a "sign," "impression," or "mark." It also signifies "encoded lettering" or "notes." In Aramaic, תו means "more" or "moreover."

WORLDS

After Cain killed his brother Abel and was punished to ever wander and be "lost" on earth, "G-d set a mark upon Cain, lest any finding him should kill him." The word "mark" (אות), literally "letter" or "sign" (in the sense of "wonder"), is a permutation of תאו (*tav*), which also means "mark." Thus the final letter of the *alef-beit* is the "letter" or sign of all the letters. It is the "collector" (as the tribe of Dan) of all "lost" fallen sparks, one's loss of sense of purpose and meaning in life, the result of sin. Though the "letter of the law" should have demanded immediate capital punishment for Cain's sin, the wondrous "mark" of G-d saved him from being killed.

When David "played mad" before Achish, the King of Gat, "he scribbled [ויתו, from the word תו] on the doors of the gate...." "The doors [*dalet*] of the gate" (*nun*, the fiftieth "unintelligible" gate of understanding) are the two components of the form of the letter *tav*. The seemingly unintelligible scribbling on the doors is in truth the secret of hidden "codes" in nature, which derive from the *sefirah* of *malchut*, the source of the soul of King David.

These secret codes of nature—DNA and the like—are similar to musical notation (תוי נגינה), for each and every part of Creation sings, by the very essence of its nature, to the Creator.

SOULS

Job said: "verily, in accordance with my impression [תֻּוִי] shall the Almighty answer me." Rashi explains that "in accordance with my impression" means the words (inscription) with which G-d Himself had described Job at the beginning of the book: "and that man was perfect and upright, and one that feared G-d and eschewed evil." This is the mark of the *tzadik* at the level of Souls.

Of this mark we find in the prophecy of Ezekiel: "And G-d said to him, 'Go through the midst of the city, through the the midst of Jerusalem, and set a mark [וְהִתְוִיתָ תָּו] upon the foreheads of the men that sigh and that cry for all the abominations done therein.... Slay the old, young men and maidens, children and women; but come not near any man upon whom is the mark [הַתָּו]....' " The "mark of life" stamped upon the forehead of the *tzadik* remains impressed upon him even in his apparent physical death: "*Tzadikim* in their death are called alive; the evil in their life are called dead."

In the above text, the root *tav* (תו) appears three times: הַתָּו, תָּו, וְהִתְוִית. These correspond to the secret of the three essential services of the soul which begin with the letter *tav*: *teshuvah* (תשובה), prayer (תפלה, and Torah (תורה) (in correspondence with the three patriarchs Abraham, Isaac, and Jacob, respectively).

The first two words—וְהִתְוִית and תָּו—equal numerically three times the third word, הַתָּו (3·411=1233). That the three together equal four times the third (תָּו⊥הִתְוִית⊥הַתָּו=1644=4·411 [=הַתָּו]) hints at the hidden fourth "foot of the chariot," King David, *malchut*. King David comprises each of the three services of תקון, "rectification." In particular, his rectification derives from the תשובה (*teshuvah*) of Abraham, the first man to fully "return" and "find" himself in G-d. The word הַתָּו itself (the common denominator) is a permutation of תהו, "chaos," the opposite of תקון, "rectification." The "proper" permutation of the initially "chaotic" elements (letters) of תהו (התו→תהו) is the secret of its rectification. The "code" of rectification is inscribed in the elementary particles of chaos. The average value of the three letters of תהו—התו ([5⊥400⊥6=411]÷3) is 137, now known to be the most basic "code" number of quantum physics (the reciprocal of the fine structure constant), the numerical value of the word קבלה, "Kabbalah."

DIVINITY

The word תו, "more" or "moreover" in Aramaic, commonly appears in the Talmud in the phrase: ותו לא מידי, "and *no* more" (or, "*nothing* else"). This phrase ends a discussion of listing of categories, just as the letter *tav* ends the *alef-beit*. Paradoxically, the end (תו) implies more, and must be negated (תו לא) in order to state "no more." This reflects the power of Divinity present in the end. This experience of "more" at the "end" can be imagined as the experience of an enthused and inspired concert audience applauding for an encore.

The "more" revealed at the end is the secret of "the advantage of light which shines from darkness." The "dark" end (the *tav* of מות, "death") becomes the beginning of eternal תקון, "rectification," the secret of resurrection, the absolute "once more" of life. Thus (according to one spelling) the *tav* is full and "pregnant" with the beginning of light: אור—תאו, the *reish* of אור (200) being half of the *tav* of תאו (400). This alludes to the infinite potential of darkness to shoot arrows (חץ, "arrow," means "half") of light (flashes of lightning, the "arrows" of G-d).

So, the final letter of the account of Creation is the *tav* of לעשות, "to do" (as interpreted by the Sages: "to rectify"). The final letters of the last three words, ברא אלקים לעשות, "...G-d created 'to do,' " spell the "seal" of G-d, אמת, "truth." In the final three letters of the beginning of the Creation account, בראשית ברא אלקים, "In the beginning G-d created...," the *tav* appears *before* the *alef-mem* of אמת. (The final letter of the next word, את, reverts the permutation to אמת.) This teaches us that all light and truth shines, ultimately, from the hidden Essence of G-d, the Absolute Darkness and End (of the beginning, בראשית, "In the beginning") before the beginning (of the end of ברא אלקים, "G-d created").

NUMBER

The letter *tav* equals four hundred.

WORLDS

After residing twenty years in Haran, Jacob returned to Israel and sent angels as messengers to his brother Esau. They returned saying: "We came to your brother Esau and he also is coming to meet you with four hundred men [for war]." In Kabbalah we are taught that Esau is a reincarnation of Cain, while Jacob is a reincarnation of Abel. Thus, Esau seeks to kill Jacob as his predecessor Cain killed his brother Abel. His four hundred men represent four hundred fallen sparks that permeate nature, the domain ("field"— Esau is called "a man of the field") of Esau. Four hundred, the value of *tav*, the culmination of the *alef-beit*—and, in a certain sense, the consummation of the consciousness of number, as taught in *Chassidut*—is 20 (*kaf*) squared. *Kaf* ends the first half of the *alef-beit*, the first eleven letters from *alef* to *kaf*, just as *tav* ends the second half and entire *alef-beit*. Through the merit of Jacob's twenty-year service of elevating the Divine sparks enclothed in the "trial" of exile, he possessed the power to subdue Esau and his four hundred men. These subsequently dispersed, and later appear in the *Tanach*, reincarnated, now at the true level of Souls, in the four hundred men of David (David himself, is the rectification of the "red one," [the kingdom of] Esau).

The number four hundred first appears in Torah in the Covenant Between the Pieces, G-d's first covenant with Abraham, in which He promised him the land of Israel. There he is told that his descendants shall be in exile for a period of four hundred years. The four hundred years actually began from the birth of Isaac and only one hundred ninety years later did Jacob and his family descend to Egypt, to remain there for two hundred ten years (according to the rule: $n^2=\Delta(n-1)\perp\Delta n$; for $n=20$: $20^2=\Delta19\perp\Delta20$, or $400=190\perp210$). It was only for the last eighty-six (the value of G-d's name of Judgement, *Elokim* [אלהים]) of these two hundred ten years that the Jews were subjected to their most oppressive enslavement. The suffering, both spiritual and physical, inherent in exile and slavery itself, elevates and rectifies fallen sparks in nature, though we may be unconscious of the process of rectification at the time.

SOULS

Abraham purchased the Cave of Machpelah from Efron the Hittite for four hundred *shekel*. Four pairs of "living" souls ("*tzadikim* in death are considered living") are buried in the Machpelah: Adam and Eve, Abraham and Sarah, Isaac and Rebecca, Jacob and Leah. Each pair has perfect knowledge of one another, in the secret of "her husband is known in the gates," the fifty gates of understanding, of which is said: "If there is no knowledge there is no understanding." The fifty gates of husband-knowing-wife and the fifty gates of wife-knowing-husband total the "one hundred gates" of Isaac (יצחק, from צחק, "laughter," the holy laughter and joy inherent in the union of husband and wife). Four times one hundred are the four hundred *shekel* of the Cave of Machpelah. Eight times fifty (ח times נ) is the secret of חן, the grace and favor that one finds in the eyes of the other.

Efron (עפרן) equals four hundred. "He said much but did not even a little" (he offered the Machpelah as a gift but actually took for it the highest price). He is the secret of עין רע, "the evil eye," which also equals four hundred. Abraham is the secret of טהור עינים, "pure eyes" (also four hundred), the rectification of the four hundred of "the evil eye."

The land of Israel (whose microcosm is the Cave of Machpelah, the first purchase of land in Israel by the first Jew, Abraham) is four hundred *parsah* by four hundred *parsah*. Every *parsah* is four *mil* (a *mil* being approximately a kilometer). This is the full measure of the land promised to Abraham at the Covenant Between the Pieces, the land of ten nations to be inherited only in the future with the coming of *Mashiach*. The land of Israel in relation to the other lands of the earth is identical with the soul of Israel in relation to other created souls. Just as the task of the soul is to reveal Divinity in Worlds, so the place most conducive to such revelation is the Holy land, over which the "pure eyes" of G-d continuously look.

DIVINITY

In the *Zohar*, the four hundred silver shekels of Abraham symbolize "four hundred worlds of Divine pleasure" ("pleasure," כסופין, from כסף, "silver"), the soul's Divine inheritance of the World to Come. Of the seven metals of the Torah (silver, gold, copper, tin, lead, mercury, iron), silver is the metal of love, corresponding to the *sefirah* of *chesed*, the attribute of Abraham, the first Jew, who knew G-d in perfect love. In this world the soul's full potential of love can never be actualized. The soul can never realize its infinite Divine resources of love. In the World to Come one's love becomes consummate. Abraham truly achieves the desire of his life, the union with Sarah to bear infinite Divine images in the "land of the living," "trees of life" (עץ ["tree"] = צלם ["Divine image"] = כסף ["silver"] = 160, a thousandth part of 400 by 400, the area of the land of Israel).

The *tav*, when spelled in full (תיו), equals 416, which in turn equals 13 (אחד ["one"] or אהבה ["love"]) times 32 (לב ["heart"]), the "one heart" or "loving heart." Two times *tav* (תיו by תיו) equals ארץ ישראל, "the land of Israel," of which (in particular) is said: מלא כל הארץ כבודו, "the whole earth [or: the land of 'wholeness'] is full of His glory." The product of the two words כבוד ה', "the glory of G-d" (as in ברוך כבוד ה' ממקומו, "Blessed be the glory of G-d from His place"—"His place" being the land of Israel), 32·26, is 832, the value of ארץ ישראל, "the land of Israel."

"The G-d of Israel," "the people of Israel," "the Torah of Israel," and the "land of Israel" (all "supported"—the grammatical "construct" form—by their common essence, Israel), correspond to the four letters of the Name *Havayah*, and are, in essence, one and the same. Moreover, these four correspond to the four pairs of the Machpelah, the Patriarchs and Matriarchs and Adam and Eve. Abraham and Sarah, in their love of G-d and life's work to bring all peoples to recognize the unity of G-d, were the first to reveal "the G-d of Israel." Isaac and Rebecca in their deepest, spiritual love for one another, in which merit they bore Jacob, "the choice of the fathers" and "general soul" of Israel, revealed the secret of the "people [souls] of Israel." Jacob and Leah, whose love for one another was primarily at the level of mind, the wisdom of Torah, revealed "the Torah of Israel" (as in the secret of the birth of Issachar, the master of Torah). Adam and Eve—the origins of the souls of David and Bat Sheva—"the keepers of the garden," first revealed the secret of "the land of Israel" (though with the sin its secret became hidden, only to be fully revealed by the *Mashiach*, who will complete the rectification of Adam and Eve's sin). The land is the beginning and the land is the end, in the secret of "all was from the earth and all returns to the earth" and "I am first and I am last...." The four "one hundred gates" of each level total four hundred, as above.

The soul of "the people of Israel" connects upward to "the G-d of Israel" through the means of "the Torah of Israel," the "three links" of the upward flame of the *shin*. In the downward flow from G-d to the land, the ultimate purpose of Creation (the holy land being the physical context of the "dwelling place for G-d below"), the Divine Light and influx of "the G-d of Israel" pass through the souls of "the people of Israel" to their "soul-mate," "the land of Israel," through the means of (the souls' devotion to) "the Torah of Israel." This is the secret of the truly consummated love of G-d, His seal which stamps its impression, its power of "actualization" (the ultimate secret of the *tav* of אמת), from Divinity to Souls to Worlds. His seal is truth and "there is no truth but Torah."

Appendix

Appendix

Gematria, "Filling," Substitution Systems

GEMATRIA

In Hebrew, each letter possesses a numerical value. *Gematria* (גימטריא) is the calculation of the numerical equivalence of letters, words, or phrases, and, on that basis, gaining insight into the interrelation of different concepts.

The assumption behind this technique is that numerical equivalence is not coincidental. Since the world was created through G-d's "speech," each letter represents a different creative force. Thus, the numerical equivalence of two words reveals an internal connection between the creative potentials of each one. (See *Tanya, Sha'ar HaYichud VeHaEmunah*, chapters 1 and 12.)

There are three ways to calculate the equivalence of individual letters:

1. **Absolute value** (מספר הכרחי), also known as **Normative value**. Each letter is given the value of its accepted numerical equivalent. *Alef* (א, the first letter) equals 1, *beit* (ב, the second) equals 2, and so on. The tenth letter, *yud* (י), is numerically equivalent to 10, and successive letters equal 20, 30, 40, and so on. The letter *kuf* (ק), near the end of the alphabet, equals 100; and the last letter, *tav* (ת), equals 400.

In this reckoning, the letters ך, ם, ן, ף, ץ, which are the "final forms" of the letters *chaf, mem, nun, pei,* and *tzadi,* used when these letters conclude a word, generally are given the same numerical equivalent of the standard form of the letter. However, sometimes the final *chaf* is considered equivalent to 500, the final *mem* to 600, etc.

Following that alternate form of reckoning, the Hebrew alphabet is a complete cycle. The final *tzadi* equals 900 and thus, the *alef* equals both one and one thousand. Indeed, the same spelling is used for *alef* (אלף), the name of the letter, and *elef* (אלף), meaning "one thousand."

Noting this phenomenon, Rabbi Avraham Abulafia interprets the verse (Deuteronomy 32:30) איכה ירדוף אחד אלף, "How can one pursue one thousand!" to mean: One, the first number, follows after one thousand in a complete and perfect cycle.

2. **Ordinal value** (מספר סדורי). Each of the 22 letters is given an equivalent from one to twenty-two.

3. **Reduced value** (מספר קטן, *modulus 9* in mathematical terminology).

Each letter is reduced to a figure of one digit. For example, in this reckoning, א (=1), י (=10), and ק (=100) would all have a numerical value of 1; ב (=2), כ (=20), and ר (=200) would all have a numerical value of 2, and so on. Thus, the letters have only nine equivalents, rather than twenty-two.

Letter	Absolute value מספר הכרחי	Ordinal value מספר סדורי	Reduced value מספר קטן
א	1 or 1000	1	1
ב	2	2	2
ג	3	3	3
ד	4	4	4
ה	5	5	5
ו	6	6	6
ז	7	7	7
ח	8	8	8
ט	9	9	9
י	10	10	1
כ,ך	20	11	2
ל	30	12	3
מ,ם	40	13	4
נ,ן	50	14	5
ס	60	15	6
ע	70	16	7
פ,ף	80	17	8
צ,ץ	90	18	9
ק	100	19	1
ר	200	20	2
ש	300	21	3
ת	400	22	4

In both the Ordinal and Reduced reckonings, the five letters whose form changes when they conclude a word are generally equivalent to their value when they appear within a word. However, they are sometimes given an independent value. For example, the ordinal value of the final *nun* is at times considered 14 and, at times, 25. Similarly, its reduced value is at times 5, and at other times, 7.

Letter	Absolute value מספר הכרחי	Ordinal value מספר סדורי	Reduced value מספר קטן
ך	500	23	5
ם	600	24	6
ן	700	25	7
ף	800	26	8
ץ	900	27	9

In addition, there is a fourth manner of reckoning, **Integral Reduced value** (מספר קטן מספרי). Here, the total numerical value of a *word* is reduced to one digit. Should the sum of these numbers exceed 9, the integer values of the total are repeatedly added to each other to produce a single-digit figure. The same value will be arrived at regardless of whether it is the absolute values, the ordinal values, or the reduced values that are being counted.

For example, the word חסד, "lovingkindness," has three letters. The *absolute* or *normative* value of ח is 8, that of ס is 60, and that of ד is 4. The sum of these three figures is 72. Thus, the integral reduced value is nine.

Similarly, the *ordinal* value of ח is 8, that of ס is 15, and that of ד is 4. The sum of these three figures is 27. Thus, the integral reduced value is again nine.

Finally, the *reduced* value of ח is 8, that of ס is 6 and that of ד is 4. The sum of these three figures is 18. Again, the integral reduced value is nine.

Another example: the word חן, "grace", is often used as an appellation for the Kabbalah. (It can be taken as an acrostic for the words חכמה נסתרה, "hidden knowledge".) Its absolute value is 58 (ח=8, ן=50), or 708 when ן is given an independent value of 700.

Its ordinal value is 22 (ח=8, ן=14) according to the normal reckoning, or 33 when the ן is assigned a value of 25.

Its reduced value is 13 (ח=8, ן=5), or 15 if the ן is assigned an independent value.

Its integral reduced value is 4 or 6.

The *Tikunei Zohar* explains that the concept of reduced value is related to the spiritual world of *Yetzirah*. On that basis, a relationship can be established between these four forms of calculation, the four spiritual realms, and the four letters of G-d's name:

Letter	Calculation Form	World
י *yud*	מספר הכרחי Absolute value	*Atzilut*
ה *hei*	מספר סדורי Ordinal value	*Beriah*
ו *vav*	מספר קטן Reduced value	*Yetzirah*
ה *hei*	מספר קטן מספרי Integral reduced value	*Asiyah*

FILLING

At times, words are given a further numerical value, *milui* (מלוי, "filling"; pl. מלויים, *miluim*). Here, not only are the letters given numerical equivalents, they are considered complete words. In such cases, the letters used to spell out the main letter are considered to be "pregnant" within it.

For example, the word חן is made up of a חית (=418) and a נון (=106). Thus, the value of חן with its *milui* is 524.

In this context, we must add that certain letters have more than one possible *milui*. For example, the letter ה can be spelled הא, הה or הי, arriving at equivalents of 6, 10, or 15 respectively. Similarly, the letter ו can be spelled וו, ואו or ויו, with equivalents of 12, 13, and 22 respectively.

It must be emphasized that these different calculations are not mere mathematical exercises. Rather each different numerical equivalent represents a different aspect of Divine influence.

The most classic use of these alternate *miluim* is with regard to the Divine Name *Havayah* (יהו־ה). The *gematria* of the letters themselves is 26. However, with the *milui*, different figures are reached dependent on how the *vav* and *heis* are spelled.

Following are the principle *miluim* of the Name *Havayah* discussed in Kabalah:

יוד = 20	יוד = 20	יוד = 20	יוד = 20
הי = 15	הי = 15	הא = 6	הה = 10
ויו = 22	ואו = 13	ואו = 13	וו = 12
הי = 15	הי = 15	הא = 6	הה = 10
72	63	45	52

These four sums, 72, 63, 45, and 52, correspond themselves to the four letters of G-d's name (and the ten *sefirot*) as follows:

yud	י	72	Chochmah	Insight, wisdom
hei	ה	63	Binah	Understanding
vav	ו	45	Chesed to Yesod	The Emotional Attributes
hei	ה	52	Malchut	Kingship

Each of the letters ה־ו־ה of the Name *Havayah* possesses three variant spellings. Thus, there are 27 (3^3) possible *miluim* of the holy Name. There are thirteen possible numerical equivalents ranging from 44 to 72, with a midpoint of 58 (=חן). When added together, the total of all the *miluim* is 1521, which equals 39^2. Thirty-nine is the numerical equivalent of יהו־ה אחד, "G-d is One."

The four forms of the Name *Havayah* cited above are considered to be the most essential forms and each correspond to a different letter of G-d's name, as above. When their sum, 232, is divided by four, the number 58 (=חן) is again reached. Similarly, 232 is numerically equivalent to יהי אור, "Let there be light," the first of the utterances of Creation.

SUBSTITUTION SYSTEMS

An additional technique in letter manipulation is the systematic substitution of one letter for another. Although there are several such systems, only two are referred to in this book.

1. **Atbash**. In *atbash*, the last letter of the *alef-beit* is substituted for the first, the second-to-the-last for the second, and so on. The name *atbash* is simply formed by the first two pairs: א״ת ב״ש.

2. **Atbach**. Here, a similar substitution is performed, but on the *alef-beit* as it is split into three groups (which numerically correspond to the integers, tens, and hundreds). Again, the name *atbach* is simply formed by the first two pairs: א״ט ב״ח.

Letter	Atbash substitution	Letter	Atbach substitution
א	ת	א	ט
ב	ש	ב	ח
ג	ר	ג	ז
ד	ק	ד	ו
ה	צ	ה	ה
ו	פ	ו	ד
ז	ע	ז	ג
ח	ס	ח	ב
ט	נ	ט	א
י	מ	י	צ
כ	ל	כ	פ
ל	כ	ל	ע
מ	י	מ	ס
נ	ט	נ	נ
ס	ח	ס	מ
ע	ז	ע	ל
פ	ו	פ	כ
צ	ה	צ	י
ק	ד	ק	ת
ר	ג	ר	ש
ש	ב	ש	ר
ת	א	ת	ק

Since, as noted above, it is possible to consider the final forms of the letters as completing the hundreds-series, the last group can alternatively be augmented to:

Letter	Atbach substitution
ק	צ
ר	ף
שׁ	ו
ת	ם
ד	ד
ם	ת
ו	שׁ
ף	ר
צ	ק

Glossary

Glossary

Note: For further elucidation of the Kabbalistic concepts referred to here, the reader is referred to the sources listed in the "Suggestions for Further and Background Reading," particularly to Rabbi J. I. Schochet's *Mystical Concepts in Chassidism* and Rabbi Adin Steinsaltz's *The Thirteen Petalled Rose*.

Action, world of: see *Asiyah*.

Adar (אדר): the twelfth month of the Jewish calendar.

Alef-beit (אלף־בית): the Hebrew alphabet.

Amidah (עמידה, "Standing"): the central core of the prayer service, recited silently while standing feet together and facing Jerusalem.

Arich Anpin (אריך אנפין, "The Long Face" or "The Patient One"): the external *partzuf* of *Keter*.

Arizal (אריז״ל): acronym for האלקי רבינו יצחק זכרונו לברכה, "the Divine Rabbi Isaac [Luria] of blessed memory" (1534-1572), who received and revealed new insights into the ancient wisdom of Kabbalah.

Ashrei (אשרי, "Happy"): a prayer consisting of Psalm 145 preceded and followed by other verses, of central importance in two of the three daily prayers.

Ashuritic script: the standard way of writing the Hebrew letters in Torah, *tefilin*, and *mezuzah* scrolls.

Asiyah (עשיה, "Action"): lowest of the four Worlds.

Atbach: see appendix.

Atbash: see appendix.

Atik Yomin (עתיק יומין, "the Ancient of Days"): the internal *partzuf* of *keter*.

Atzilut (אצילות, "Emanation"): the highest of the four Worlds.

Ba'al Shem Tov (בעל שם טוב, "Master of the Good Name [of G-d]"): title given to Rabbi Yisrael ben Eliezer (1698-1760), the founder of *Chassidut*.

Ba'al Teshuvah (בעל תשובה, "returnee"; pl. *Ba'alei Teshuvah*, בעלי תשובה): one who returns to the way of Judaism after a period of estrangement. *Cf.* Teshuvah.

Baba Kama (בבא קמא, "The First Gate"): one of the tractates of the Talmud.

Baraita (ברייתא, "external [material]"; pl. *baraitot*, ברייתות): Tannaic traditions and teachings not included in the Mishnah.

Behemot (בהמות, "beasts" or "animals"): name of the archetypal land animal.

Beinoni (בינוני, "intermediate"): a Jew who does not sin but still possesses an evil urge. *Cf. tzadik* and *rasha.*

Beriah (בריאה, "Creation"): second of the four Worlds.

Bimah (בימה, "platform"): the table in the synagogue on which the Torah-scroll is placed when read publicly.

Binah (בינה, "understanding"): one of the ten *sefirot.*

Birkat HaMazon (ברכת המזון): "The Blessing over Food," recited after eating a meal containing bread.

Birkat Kohanim (ברכת כהנים, "The Priest's Blessing"): Numbers 6:24-26, recited by the *kohanim* as part of the morning liturgy in the Temple and later incorporated in the daily prayers.

Bitul (בטול): "self-nullification".

Bitul Bimtziut (בטול במציאות, "nullification of existence"): a level of *bitul.*

Bitul Bimtziut Mamash (בטול במציאות ממש, "absolute nullification of existence"): a level of *bitul.*

Bitul HaYeish (בטול היש, "nullification of [one's] somethingness"): a level of *bitul.*

Brit (ברית, "covenant"): the covenant of circumcision; euphemism for the organ on which circumcision is performed.

Cantillation: the tunes to which the Torah is traditionally sung, indicated by a set of diacritical marks around the words in printed texts. They serve also to punctuate the text.

Chabad (חב"ד): acronym for *Chochmah-Binah-Da'at* (חכמה בינה דעת, "Wisdom Understanding Knowledge," the names of three of the *sefirot*); the "intellect"; the name of the branch of *Chassidut* that emphasizes the role of the intellect in the service of G-d, founded by Rabbi Shneur Zalman of Liadi (*cf. Tanya*).

Challah (חלה, "dough"): braided loaves traditionally eaten at Shabbat and Festival meals.

Chanukah (חנוכה, "Dedication"): the 8-day holiday celebrating the victory over Hellenism and the restoration of the Temple after its defilement by the Greeks.

Chashmal (חשמל, "glow," "fire"): a key, mystical word in the vision of Ezekiel interpreted to mean "silent speech" or "silence-circumcision-speech."

Chassidut (חסידות, "lovingkindness"): the movement within Judaism (also sometimes known as "Chassidism") founded by Rabbi Yisrael Ba'al Shem Tov, the purpose of which is to awaken the Jewish people to its own inner self and connection to G-d through the inner dimension of the Torah and thus to prepare the way for the advent of the *Mashiach*; the oral and written teachings of this movement.

Chatoteret (חטוטרת, "hunchback"): the arch connecting the *vav* and the *zayin* which together form the *chet*.

Chayah (חיה, "the living one"): the fourth of the five levels of the soul.

Chayot (חיות, "living beings"): a type of angel referred to in the first chapter of Ezekiel.

Chayut (חיות): "lifeforce".

Chesed (חסד, "lovingkindness"): one of the ten *sefirot*.

Chochmah (חכמה, "wisdom"): one of the ten *sefirot*.

Chupah (חפה, "canopy"): the canopy under which the Jewish wedding ceremony takes place.

Creation, world of: see *Beriah*.

Crown: see *keter*.

Cubit: unit of linear measure. Various opinions fix it at 48 or 60 centimeters.

Da'at (דעת, "knowledge"): one of the ten *sefirot*.

Echad (אחד): "one."

Elokim (אלקים): G-d's holy Name אלהי־ם spelled with a *kuf* instead of a *hei*. The real spelling is used only in liturgical texts and is pronounced only when reciting a complete Scriptural verse or in liturgy.

Elul (אלול): the sixth month of the Jewish calendar.

Emanation, world of: see *Atzilut*.

Eretz Yisrael (ארץ ישראל): "the land of Israel."

Etrog: see *Lulav*.

Formation, world of: see *Yetzirah*.

Full spelling: see appendix, "Filling."

Gaon (גאון, "genius" or "excellency"): title of sages during post-Talmudic period (roughly 7th to 11th centuries). This period is thus known as the "Gaonic" period.

Gematria: see appendix.

Gerah (גרה): a type of coin, equivalent to approximately 0.64 gram of silver.

Gevurah (גבורה, "strength"): one of the ten *sefirot*.

Haftorah (הפטרה, "desert"): the reading from the Prophets accompanying the weekly or holiday Torah-portion.

Haggadah (הגדה, "Telling"): the text used for the ritual of retelling the story of the Exodus from Egypt on the first (and in the Diaspora: second) night(s) of Pesach.

Hakafot (הקפות, "Encirclings"): processions with the Torah-scroll and/or *lulav* and *etrog* in the synagogue around the *bimah* on *Sukot*, *Shemini Atzeret*, and *Simchat Torah*.

Halachah (הלכה, "Way" or "Walking"; pl. *halachot*, הלכות): prescribed Jewish behavior; Jewish Law; a specific Jewish law.

HaNeirot Halalu (הנרות הללו, "These Lamps"): a liturgy recited after the kindling of the *Chanukah* lamps.

Havayah (הויה): An altered spelling of the ineffable Holy Four-letter Name of G-d (יהו־ה). The real spelling is used only in liturgical texts and is nowadays never pronounced. When reciting a complete Scriptural verse or liturgy the word *Adonai* (another Name of G-d) is used; otherwise one says *HaShem* ("the Name") or *Havayah*.

Hod (הוד, "splendor", "thanksgiving"): one of the ten *sefirot*.

Hoshanah Rabbah (הושענא רבה, "The Great [Prayer of] 'Please Save!' "): the seventh day of *Sukot* on which the world is judged with regard to water and many prayers and ceremonies are added to the liturgy.

Israel (ישראל): a name of the patriarch Jacob, and by extension, the entire Jewish people.

Israelite (ישראל): a Jew who is neither *kohen* nor *levi*.

Kabbalah (קבלה, "tradition"): the esoteric dimension of the Torah.

Kadish (קדיש, "Holy"; pl. *Kadishim*, קדישים): a transition-prayer used to signal passage from one stage of prayer to another.

Kedushah (קדושה, "Holiness"; pl. *Kedushot*, קדושות): holiness; a declaration of G-d's holiness incorporated into the daily prayers.

Kehunah (כהונה): "priesthood." See *kohen*.

Kelipah (קליפה, "shell"; pl. *kelipot*, קליפות): a name for a realm of evil or of evil itself.

Keter (כתר, "crown"): one of the ten *sefirot*.

Kiddush (קדוש, "Sanctification"): the ritual by which the Sabbath is announced in the home, consisting of a liturgical text recited over a full goblet of wine.

Kipah (כפה): "skullcap".

Kohen (כהן, "priest"; pl. *kohanim,* כהנים): a descendant of Aaron (the brother of Moses), who, when the Temple is standing, officiates at the various rites performed in the Temple. Someone who is not a *kohen* is not allowed to perform these rites.

Kosher (כשר): "fit," "proper."

Levi (לוי, "levite"; pl. *leviim,* לויים): a descendant of Levi (the son of Jacob); specifically, one of the descendants of Levi who is not also a descendant of Aaron (which would make him a *kohen, q.v.*). When the Temple is standing, the Levite performs assistive functions in the Temple rites.

Leviathan (לויתן): name of an archetypal sea-animal.

Light: commonly used metaphor for the influx of Divine "energy" constantly creating and sustaining the universe. In this context it of course does not refer to physical light.

Lubavitch(er): having to do with the Chassidic group (i.e. *Chabad*) formerly based in the Russian town of Lubavitch.

Lulav and *Etrog* (לולב ואתרוג, "palm stalk" and "citron"): two of the four plants held and moved in various directions during the holiday of *Sukot*. The other two are the *hadas* (הדס, "myrtle") and *aravah* (ערבה, "willow"). Since these latter two are tied to the *lulav* for the purposes of this practice, the phrase "*Lulav* and *Etrog*" is colloquially used to refer to all four.

Maggid of Mezeritch (המגיד ממעזריטש, "The Preacher of Mezeritch"): Rabbi Dov Ber (?-1770), the successor to the Ba'al Shem Tov in leadership of *Chassidut*.

Maimonides: see Rambam.

Malchut (מלכות, "kingdom"): one of the ten *sefirot*.

Mashiach (משיח, "messiah"): a descendant of King David who will redeem the Jewish people, rebuild the Temple, usher in the era of eternal peace and reveal the inner dimensions of the Torah.

Masorah (מסורה, "tradition"): the transmitted rules regarding the precise writing of the Written Torah.

Mazal (מזל, "sign" or "spiritual channel"): one's soul-root in spiritual realms.

Mazal Tov (מזל טוב, "[May it be in] a good sign"): an expression of congratulations.

Menorah (מנורה, "candelabrum"): the seven-branched candelabrum in the Tabernacle/Temple. Not to be confused with the *eight*-branched candelabrum used on *Chanukah*.

Menorah (מנורה, "candelabrum"): the seven-branched candelabrum in the Tabernacle/Temple. Not to be confused with the *eight*-branched candelabrum used on *Chanukah*.

Mezuzah (מזוזה, "doorpost"): a parchment placed on the doorposts on which is written the first two paragraphs of the *Shema*.

Midrash (מדרש, "seeking"; pl. Midrashim, מדרשים): the homiletic or hermeneutic material of the Oral Torah (see "Torah"); or the name of a number of works of this genre, the chief being *Midrash Rabbah* ("The Great Midrash").

Mikvah (מקוה, "gathering [of water]"): either a natural body of water or a specially-constructed pool of water used for ritual purification rites.

Mil (מיל): a unit of measure equivalent to approximately 1.087 kilometers.

Minyan (מנין, "number"): the quorum of ten men required for Jewish communal prayer.

Mishnah (משנה, "repetition"): the basic Tannaic core of the Talmud, written down in the second century.

Mishnah (משנה, "repetition"): a passage from the Mishnah.

Mishneh Torah (משנה תורה, "Repetition of the Torah"): the Rambam's codification of the Oral Torah.

Mitzvah (מצוה, "commandment"; pl. *mitzvot*, מצות): one of the six-hundred thirteen commandments communicated by G-d to the Jewish people at Mt. Sinai.

Modeh Ani (מודה אני, "I Acknowledge"): name of the prayer recited upon awakening in the morning.

Mum (מום): "blemish."

Musaf (מוסף, "Additional [Prayer]"): the additional prayer recited on Shabbat, *Rosh Chodesh*, and *Yom Tov*.

Nachmanides: see Ramban.

Nefesh (נפש, "soul"): the lowest of the five levels of the soul.

Neilah (נעילה, "closing", "locking"): the final of the five prayer services recited on *Yom Kippur*.

Nekudah (נקודה): "point."

Neshamah (נשמה, "soul"): the third of the five levels of the soul.

Netzach (נצח, "victory"): one of the ten *sefirot*.

Nisan (ניסן): the first of the twelve months of the Jewish calendar.

Normative numbering: see appendix.

Omer (עומר): a dry measure mentioned in the Torah; a sacrifice brought in the Temple on the second day of Pesach consisting of this amount of barley; the period of counting the days from the time of this offering until *Shavuot*.

Or Chozer (אור חוזר, "returning light"): Creational responses to *or yashar*.

Or Yashar (אור ישר, "straight light"): Divine emanations reaching the universe from G-d.

Ordinal numbering: see appendix.

Pardes (פרדס, "Orchard"): Acronym for the four levels of Torah-study: פשט (*peshat*), the plain, literal meaning of the text, רמז (*remez*), hints and allusions in the text, דרוש (*derush*), additional levels of meaning derived by verbal analogy, and סוד (*sod*), the esoteric, mystical dimension of the text.

Parsah: (פרסה): a measure of distance equivalent to approximately 4.35 kilometers.

Partzuf (פרצוף, "face"; pl. *partzufim*, פרצופים): a *sefirah* metamorphosed into a human-like arrangement of sub-*sefirot*. As such it can productively interact with other *sefirot*.

Perek Shirah (פרק שירה, "The Chapter of Song"): a Midrash describing the specific Scriptural verse sung by each element of Creation.

Pesach (פסח, "Passover"): the holiday of liberation from Egypt.

Pirkei Avot (פרקי אבות, "Chapters of the Fathers"): popular name for the tractate of the Mishnah called *Avot* (אבות, "Fathers"), containing ethical wisdom transmitted in the name of various Sages of the Oral Torah.

Pregnant (regarding a letter): see appendix.

Priestly Blessing: see *Birkat Kohanim*.

Rambam (רמב"ם): acronym for רבי משה בן מימון "Rabbi Moses ben Maimon"; Maimonides (1135-1204), famous medieval scholar and philosopher.

Ramban (רמב"ן): acronym for רבי משה בן נחמן, "Rabbi Moses ben Nachman"; Nachmanides (1194-1270), famous medieval scholar and philosopher.

Rasha (רשע, "wicked person"): a Jew who commits a sin and has not yet done *teshuvah*. *Cf. beinoni* and *tzadik*.

Rebbe (רבי, "teacher"): a leader of a Chassidic group, often identified by the city in which he taught or the branch of *Chassidut* he heads originated.

Reshimu (רשימו, "impression"): the residual impression of the original infinite light of G-d that remains after the *tzimtzum*.

Rosh Chodesh (ראש חדש, "Head of the Month"): the first day of the Jewish month, a day of celebration.

Rosh HaShanah (ראש השנה, "Head of the Year"): the Jewish New Year.

Ruach (רוח, "spirit"): the second of the five levels of the soul.

Safra d'Tzniuta (ספרא דצניעותא, "The Book of Modesty"): a section of the *Zohar*.

Sages: The rabbis of the Talmudic period. Their teachings, recorded in the Talmuds, the Midrashim, and *Zohar* constitute the "Oral Torah."

Seah (סאה): a unit of measure, equivalent to approximately 6 liters.

Seder (סדר, "order"): the festive meal and ceremony of the first night of *Pesach*. The liturgical text for this meal is the "Haggadah".

Sefer Yetzirah (ספר יצירה, "The Book of Formation"): a fundamental text of Kabbalah, containing teachings that date back to Abraham and that was redacted by Rabbi Akiva.

Sefirah (ספירה; pl. *sefirot*, ספירות): channel of Divine energy or lifeforce. The ten *sefirot* are the stages in the Creative process imprinted on all aspects of reality. In order, they are:

Keter	כתר	Crown
Chochmah	חכמה	Wisdom
Binah	בינה	Understanding
Da'at	דעת	Knowledge
Chesed	חסד	Lovingkindness
Gevurah	גבורה	Strength
Tiferet	תפארת	Beauty
Netzach	נצח	Victory
Hod	הוד	Splendor
Yesod	יסוד	Foundation
Malchut	מלכות	Kingdom

Keter and *Da'at* are superconscious and conscious aspects of the same phenomenon, and therefore although there are eleven listed here the *sefirot* are considered only ten.

Semichah (סמיכה, "support"): the act of leaning on an animal (in order to confess) prerequisite to its being offered as a sacrifice; rabbinic ordination.

Service of G-d: the religious life of the Jew.

Shabbat (שבת, "Sabbath"): the Friday-sunset to Saturday-dusk period of rest and spirituality.

Shavuot (שבועות, "Weeks"): the holiday celebrating the wheat harvest and the giving of the Torah. Cf. Omer.

Shechinah (שכינה, "Indwelling"): the Presence of G-d in the universe, as opposed to transcendent aspects of G-d's revelations.

Shekel (שקל, "weight"): a unit of weight of silver (and therefore of money), equivalent to approximately 12.3 gram.

Shema (שמע, "Hear"): the fundamental statement of Judaism, consisting of three paragraphs (Deuteronomy 6:4-9, Deuteronomy 11:13-21, and Numbers 15:37-41) and an additional sentence added after the first verse, recited twice daily.

Shemoneh Esrei (שמונה עשרה, "eighteen"): the central portion of the liturgy when the Jew directly addresses G-d. Originally composed of eighteen blessings, the weekday version now has nineteen; the Sabbath and holiday versions have seven, and the version used for the Musaf of Rosh HaShanah has nine.

Shevat (שבט): the eleventh month of the Jewish calendar.

Shiflut (שפלות): "lowliness."

Shlita (שליט"א): acronym for שיחיה לאורך ימים טובים אמן ("May he live for long and good days, Amen"), a phrase used when mentioning a living rabbi or sage.

Shmini Atzeret (שמיני עצרת, "The Eighth [-day] Gathering"): the festival occurring on the day immediately following the last day of Sukot. Cf. Simchat Torah.

Shmitah (שמיטה, "Release"): the sabbatical year, in which the Holy land is not worked.

Shofar (שופר, "ram's horn"): blown on Rosh HaShanah, and to be blown when the Mashiach arrives.

Shulchan Aruch (שלחן ערוך, "Set Table"): the Code of Jewish Law, written by Rabbi Yosef Karo (1488-1575).

Simchat Torah (שמחת תורה, "The Rejoicing of the Torah"): the holiday celebrating the giving of the Torah anew after the sin of the Golden Calf. In the Diaspora, where most major Jewish holidays are celebrated for an extra day, Simchat Torah is celebrated on the second day of Shmini Atzeret; in the land of Israel, Simchat Torah coincides with the one day of Shmini Atzeret.

Sovev Kol Almin (סובב כל עלמין, "Encompassing all Worlds"): the transcendent Divine emanations.

Sukah (סוכה, "hut"): hut resided in on the holiday of *Sukot*.

Sukot (סוכות, "Huts"): the 8-day holiday celebrating the gathering of the harvest and the Clouds of Glory with which G-d surrounded the Jewish people during their trek in the desert subsequent to the Exodus from Egypt.

Ta'avah (תאוה): "lust," "desire," "passion."

Tabernacle: the temporary, portable version of the Temple used by the Jews during their journey in the desert from Egypt to the land of Israel, and for some time thereafter in Israel until the Temple was built.

Talmud (תלמוד, "learning"): the recension of the greater part of the Oral Torah (see "Torah"), comprised mostly of legal but also of much homiletic and even some explicitly mystical material. There are two Talmuds: the one composed in the Holy Land, known as *Talmud Yerushalmi* ("The Jerusalem Talmud"), completed in the third century and the one composed in Babylonia, called *Talmud Bavli* ("The Babylonian Talmud"), completed in the sixth century. The Talmud is divided into tractates.

Tana (תנא, "teacher"; pl. *tanaim*, תנאים): a sage of the period of the Mishnah.

Tanach (תנ"ך): Acroynm for *Torah* (תורה, "The Teaching"), *Nevi'im* (נביאים, "The Prophets"), and *Ketuvim* (כתובים, "The Writings"); the 24 books of the Bible. *Cf.* Torah.

Tanya (תניא, "It has been taught"): first word and title of the fundamental work of *Chabad Chassidut*, written by Rabbi Shneur Zalman of Liadi (1745-1812).

Tefilin (תפילין): leather boxes containing parchments, worn on the head and left arm by adult men during weekday morning prayer.

Temple: The structure in Jerusalem where the sacrificial service takes place. Physically, the focal-point of Divine service.

Teruah (תרועה, "broken blast"): the name of one of the three types of *shofar* blasts.

Terumah (תרומה, "Offering"): a Torah-portion.

Teshuvah (תשובה, "returning"): the return of the individual (or community) to a heightened state of favor with G-d after a period of estrangement or simply as an outgrowth of the existential limitations of Creation. *Cf.* Ba'al Teshuvah.

The Letters of Rabbi Akiva (אותיות דרבי עקיבא): a Midrash dealing with the Hebrew letters, written by the 2nd century sage Rabbi Akiva.

Tiferet (תפארת, "beauty"): one of the ten *sefirot*.

Tishrei (תשרי): the seventh month of the Jewish calendar.

Tohu (תהו, "Chaos"): a premature state of Creation.

Torah (תורה, "Teaching"): the five books of Moses; the entirety of authentic teaching that comprises the Jewish religion. Also divided into the "Written Torah," synonymous with *Tanach*, and the "Oral Torah," those teachings given orally together with the Written Torah and originally also transmitted orally but eventually committed to writing in the form of the Talmuds, the Midrash, the *Zohar*, and so forth.

Torah-portion: one of the fifty-four sections into which the five books of Moses is divided for the purpose of the weekly reading in the synagogue.

Triangle: the sum of all the whole-numbers from 1 to a specific number (*n*). E.g.: $\triangle 5 = 1 \perp 2 \perp 3 \perp 4 \perp 5$.

Tu b'Shevat (ט"ו בשבט, "The Fifteenth Day of *Shevat*"): the day each year on which the trees begin to receive nutrients from the ground; the *New Year* of the Trees.

Tzadik (צדיק, "righteous one"; pl. *tzadikim* צדיקים): as defined in *Tanya*, a Jew who has succeeded in eliminating his evil inclination.

Tzevakot (צבקות, "Hosts"): G-d's holy Name צבאות spelled with a *kuf* instead of an *alef*. The real spelling is used only in liturgical texts and is pronounced only when reciting a complete Scriptural verse or in liturgy.

Tzimtzum (צמצום, "contraction"): the primordial contraction of G-d's infinite light. One of the initial stages in the creation process.

Worlds: the four general, spiritual levels of Creation between the Creator and the final creation, our physical universe. The ten *sefirot* are manifest in each of the four worlds. Since the highest world, *Atzilut*, is in a class by itself, reference is sometimes made to "the three lower worlds" as a unit.

Vav HaChibur (ו' החבור, "the *vav* of connection"): the letter *vav* used as the conjunction "and."

Vav HaHipuch (ו' ההפוך, "the *vav* of conversion"): the letter *vav* used in Biblical Narrative Hebrew to reverse the tense of a verb from future to past or vice versa.

VaYahkel (ויקהל, "And He Gathered Together"): a Torah-portion.

Yarmulke (יארמלקע [Yiddish]): "skullcap."

Yechidah (יחידה, "the single one"): the highest of the five levels of the soul.

Yesod (יסוד): "foundation"; one of the ten *sefirot*.

Yetzirah (יצירה, "Formation"): third of the four Worlds.

Yom Kippur (יום כפור, "Day of Atonement"): the tenth day of Tishrei, the holiest day of the Jewish year.

Yom Tov (יום טוב, "a good day"): the festive holidays (*Pesach*, *Shavuot* and *Sukot*) and high holidays (*Rosh HaShanah* and *Yom Kippur*), on which weekday work is prohibited, like Shabbat, with certain exceptions.

Zohar (זהר, "Splendor"): the major seminal work of the Kabbalah, composed by Rabbi Shimon bar Yochai (2nd century) and his students.

Zot Chanukah (זאת חנוכה, "This is the Dedication"): the eighth and last day of Chanukah.

Suggestions for Further Reading

Suggestions for Further Reading on Kabbalah and *Chassidut* in English (Partial Listing)

1. General Introductions

Mystical Concepts in Chassidism. R. Jacob Immanuel Shochet. New York: Kehot, 1979, 169 pp. Definitive exposition of major Kabbalistic concepts and terminology, extensively footnoted and cross-referenced. (Also printed in the back of the English edition of the *Tanya* [see below].)

The Thirteen Petalled Rose. R. Adin Steinsaltz. New York: Basic Books, 1980, 181 pp. A thematic treatment of the main concepts of Kabbalah and *Chassidut*.

Yedid Nefesh: Introduction to Kabbalah. R. Yechiel Barlev. Petach Tikvah: Author, 1988, 351 pp. Exposition of major concepts in Kabbalah based on *Kelach Pitchei Chochmah* by R. Moshe Chaim Luzatto.

2. Translations of Classic Source Texts

The Bahir. R. Nehuniah ben HaKanah (1st century CE). Translated with notes, introduction, etc., by R. Aryeh Kaplan. New York: Weiser, 1979, 244 pp. Discusses the Hebrew alphabet, the verse "In the beginning G-d created...," the *sefirot*, and the soul.

Derech HaShem: The Way of G-d. R. Moshe Chayim Luzzatto (1707-1746). Translated with notes, introduction, etc., by R. Aryeh Kaplan. New York: Feldheim, 1983, 407 (bilingual) pp. Synopsis of Jewish Theology based on Kabbalah. Pre-Chassidic.

Likutei Amarim—Tanya. R. Shneur Zalman of Liadi (1745-1812). Bilingual edition. New York: Kehot, 1973 (first published in Hebrew in 1796), 888 pp. Translated with notes, introduction, and glossaries by Rabbis Nissan Mindel, Nisen Mangel, Zalman I. Posner, Jacob Immanuel Schochet. The *Chabad* classic, the first systematic presentation of the Ba'al Shem Tov's teachings. Book I deals with the service of G-d, book II with philosophical foundations of Chassidism, book III with *teshuvah*, books IV and V are collections of letters and notes by the author, the most mystical being No. 20 of book IV. English translators' introductions are found in the back.

Likutei Moharan. R. Nachman of Breslov (1773-1810). Jerusalem/NY: Breslov Research Institute. Vol. 1: Translated by R. Simcha Bergman, 1986, 213 pp.; Vol. 1B: Translated by Moshe Mykoff, 1989, 380 pp. Basic text of *Breslov Chassidut.*

Rabbi Nachman's Wisdom. R. Nathan of Nemirov. Translation of *Shivchei HaRan* and *Sichot HaRan* by R. Aryeh Kaplan. Jerusalem/NY: Breslov Resarch Institute, 1980, 458 pp. Teachings of R. Nachman of Breslov.

Rabbi Nachman's Stories. R. Nachman of Breslov (1773-1810). Jerusalem: Breslov Research Institute, 1983, 552 pp. The stories contain deep teachings, many of which are discussed in the extensive footnotes by R. Aryeh Kaplan.

Beggars and Prayers: Adin Steinsaltz Retells the Tales of Rabbi Nachman of Breslov. New York: Basic Books, 1979, 186 pp. A selection of the stories, each followed by an insightful essay.

Tefilin: A Chassidic Discourse. R. Nathan of Nemirov (1780-1844). Translated by Avraham Greenbaum. Jerusalem/NY: Breslov Research Institute, 1989, 121 pp. Translation of an excerpt from the author's *Likutei Halachot.* R. Nathan was the chief disciple of R. Nachman of Breslov.

Heichaltzu—On Ahavas Yisrael: A Chassidic Discourse. R. Sholom Dov Ber Schneersohn (1860-1920). New York: Kehot, 1988, 148 pp. Mystical dimensions of the commandment to love all Jews.

Kuntres Uma'ayon. R. Shalom Dov Ber Schneersohn. Translated by R. Zalman I. Posner. New York: Kehot, 1978, 142 pp. Chassidic ethics.

Chassidic Discourses. R. Yosef Yitzchak Schnersohn (1880-1950). Translated by R. Shalom B. Wineberg. New York, Kehot, 1986, Volume I, 223 pp., Volume II, 229 pp. Wide range of topics.

Likutei Dibburim. R. Yosef Yitzchak Schnersohn. Translated with notes by Uri Kaploun. New York: Kehot, Volume I, 1987, 339 pp., Volume II, 1988, 319 pp. Talks of the 6th *Chabad* Rebbe, rich with insights into the applications of Chassidic teachings to daily life.

HaYom Yom: "From Day to Day." R. Menachem M. Schneerson (b. 1902). Based on the teachings of R. Yosef Yitzchak Schneersohn. Translated by R. Zalman I. Posner, Yitzchak M. Kagan, and Shalom B. Wineberg. New York: Kehot, 1988, 173 (bi-lingual) pp. Short excerpts of Chassidic Wisdom.

Basi LeGani. R. Yosef Yitzchak Schneersohn. Translated by R. Eliayhu Touger & Shalom B. Wineberg. NY: Kehot, 1990, 103 pp. Last Chassidic discourse by the previous Lubavitcher Rebbe, in which he details the specific nature of this generation's spirituality. Includes also the first Chassidic discourse of his successor, the present Lubavitcher Rebbe *shlita.*

Likutei Sichot: An Anthology of Talks. R. Menachem M. Schneerson. New York: Kehot, Volume I (Genesis): 1980. 230 pp., Volume II (Exodus): 1983, 223 pp., Volume III (Leviticus): 1987. 248 pp. Translated by R. Jacob Immanuel Schochet. Chassidic teachings from the Lubavitcher Rebbe on the Torah-portion of the week.

On the Essence of Chassidus. R. Menachem M. Schneerson. Translated with extensive notes by Y. H. Greenberg and Sheina Sarah Handelman. New York: Kehot, 1978, 130 pp. Scholarly discourse on the nature, function, and role of the teachings of Chassidut for the individual person and in the world-at-large.

3. Commentaries on the *Tanya*

The Philosophy of Chabad. R. Nissan Mindel. New York: Kehot, 1973, 255 pp. A synopsis and rephrasing of the first book of *Tanya*.

Lessons in Tanya. R. Yosef Wineberg, translated by R. Shalom B. Wineberg. New York: Kehot, Volume 1 (Book I, ch. 1-34), 1987, 449 pp., Volume 2 (Book I, ch. 35-end), 1988, 365 pp., Volume 3 (Books II-III), 1989, 308 pp. Includes synopses and introductions.

The Long Shorter Way: Discourses on Chasidic Thought. R. Adin Steinsaltz. Edited and translated by Yehuda Hanegbi. Northvale, NJ-London: Jason Aronson Inc., 1988, 353 pp. On the first book of *Tanya*.

The Sustaining Utterance: Discourses on Chasidic Thought. R. Adin Steinsaltz. Edited and translated by Yehuda Hanegbi. Northvale, NJ-London: Jason Aronson Inc., 1989, 129 pp. On the second book of *Tanya*.

4. Anthologies

The Light Beyond: Adventures in Hassidic Thought. R. Aryeh Kaplan. New York: Maznaim, 1981, 372 pp. Excerpts from Chassidic words, organized under topics, including Meditation and Prayer. Includes short bibliographies.

Chasidic Masters: History, Biography and Thought. R. Aryeh Kaplan. New York: Maznaim, 1984, 192 pp. More excerpts and biographies, this time grouped historically under each master. Some repetition of material from *The Light Beyond*.

Garden of the Souls: Rabbi Nachman on Suffering. Avraham Greenbaum. Jerusalem/NY: 1990, 96 pp. Collection of teachings of R. Nachman of Breslov on suffering and hope.

The Strife of the Spirit. R. Adin Steinsaltz. Selected and foreword by Arthur Kurzweil. Northvale, NJ-London: Jason Aronson, Inc., 1988, 259 pp. Articles and essays.

5. Specific Topics

I am asleep yet my heart is awake. R. Yitzchak Ginsburgh. Jerusalem: Gal Einai, 1984, 51 pp. A discourse on the existential relationship between the soul and G-d.

Chassidic Insights: A guide for the Entangled. R. Mattis Kantor. New York: Ktav, 1978, 117 pp. A prose setting of several topics in Chassidic philosophy.

Outpouring of the Soul. R. Alter of Teplik (based on the teachings of R. Nachman of Breslov and R. Nathan of Nemerov.) Translated by R. Aryeh Kaplan. Jerusalem: Breslov Research Institute, 1980, 72 pp. Techniques of meditation and prayer.

6. Tapes

The Hebrew Letters: Their Secrets and Teachings in the Way of the Ba'al Shem Tov. R. Yitzchak Ginsburgh. Jerusalem: Gal Einai, (POB 14132 Jerusalem) 1988, 6 cassettes. Mystical exposition on the hidden dimensions of the letters of the Hebrew alphabet. The present book is an outgrowth of these tapes.

Basic Principles of Chabad Chassidic Philosophy. R. Shlomo Majeski. New York: Sichos in English. Several sets of tapes.

Notes

Notes

Note: In the following notes, we have attempted to trace the concepts, whenever possible, to their earliest source. It should be noted, however, that ideas—especially concepts in *Chassidut*—are often most fully developed only in later sources. To this end we have occasionally cited later sources as well.

In either case, these notes should in no way be considered exhaustive. Limitations of time and space proclude detailed citation from the abundance of source material in the vast Talmudic, Midrashic, Kabbalistic and Chassidic literatures. The serious student is encouraged to avail himself of the various published indices and compendia that open up this treasure house.

Introduction

Rosh HaShanah of the year 5507: This was 12 years and 12 days after the Ba'al Shem Tov had begun teaching publicly (18 Elul, 5494 [1734 C.E.]). Since the Ba'al Shem Tov taught publicly until his passing in 1760, the events described in this letter occurred at the mid-point of this period.

The Ba'al Shem Tov: Rabbi Yisrael Ba'al Shem Tov (1698-1760), founder of the Chassidic movement.

An elevation of soul: to the higher realms of spirituality.

The chamber of the *Mashiach*: Referred to in the *Zohar* as קן צפור, "the bird's nest," described in detail at the end of *Etz Chaim*. Cf. also *Zohar* 2:8a, 3:196b; *Kehilat Yaakov*, s.v. קן צפור; *Or HaTorah, Ki Tetzei* p. תתקט"ז.

The seven Shepherds: As listed in *Sukah* 52b: Adam, Seth, Methuselah, Abraham, Jacob, Moses and David. In later rabbinic literature this term is also used to refer to the "seven guests" of the *Zohar* (3:103b): Abraham, Isaac, Jacob, Moses, Aaron, Joseph, and David. (See *Likutei Sichot*, vol. 20, p. 643 and sources cited there.) See the discussion of the Souls-dimension of the number of the letter *zayin*.

"When will the Master come?": This question had already been posed to the *Mashiach* in Talmudic times by Rabbi Yehoshua ben Levi (*Sanhedrin* 98a). Then, the answer was: "Today," which was interpreted by the prophet Elijah as meaning: "Today—if you would only listen to G-d's voice" (Psalm 95:7). According to Rabbi Yosef Yitzchak of Lubavitch (*Likutei Diburim, Simchat Torah* 5690, section 30 [p. 618 ff]), the Ba'al Shem Tov was in effect saying to the *Mashiach*: "We have already listened to His voice, even to the extent of giving up our lives in order to do so. Why, then, have you not come?" To this the *Mashiach* replied that it is dependent on the dissemination of the Ba'al Shem Tov's teachings.

Your wellsprings will burst forth to the farthest extremes: Proverbs 5:16

Shells: קליפות, the realms of evil. See *Mystical Concepts*, ch. 10.

I was not given permission all the days of my life to reveal this: Nonetheless, according to Rabbi Mordechai of Neshchiz (1748-1800, in *Imrei Kodesh* 40; *Sefer Ba'al Shem Tov* p. 122, end of note 13), the Ba'al Shem Tov alluded to these practices in the continuation of his letter.

Your way shall ever be in the presence of G-d: *Cf.* Judges 18:6.

And never leave your consciousness: par. Proverbs 4:21

Worlds and Souls and Divinity: See section 8, below.

"Give to the wise and he will become ever wiser": Proverbs 9:9

A letter by Rabbi Yisrael Ba'al Shem Tov: This letter never reached its destination. It was first published as an appendix to *Ben Porat Yosef* (128a) by Rabbi Yaakov Yosef of Polnoye. A comparison between this letter and a different "version" may be found in *Shivchei HaBa'al Shem Tov—A Facsimile of a Unique Manuscript*, by Rabbi Yehoshua Mundshein, p. 229 ff. The letter has been translated into English in Rabbi Aryeh Kaplan's *Chasidic Masters*, p. 12, and *Meditation and Kabbalah*, p. 272. See also *Ascent Quarterly* #16, p. 11 ff.

Rabbi Gershon of Kitov: (?-1760) A noted scholar, he emigrated from Europe to Israel in 1747, settling first in Hebron, then Jerusalem.

Distinct creative powers: G-d used the Hebrew alphabet to create the world. *Bereishit Rabbah* 18:4, 31:8; Rashi to Genesis 2:23; *Sha'ar HaYichud Ve-HaEmunah*, ch. 1

Energy, life, light: *Sha'ar HaYichud VeHaEmunah*, ch. 12 in gloss

The inner life-pulse permeating the universe as a whole...: *Sha'ar HaYichud VeHaEmunah*, ch. 1

"Pulsing" every created being...in and out of existence: This is called in Kabbalah מטי ולא מטי, "reaching and not reaching." See *Etz Chaim* 7.

"And man became a living soul": Genesis 2:7

"A speaking spirit": *Onkelos ad. loc.* Hence the connection between "life" and "speaking."

"Think" with meditative power: מחשבה מועלת; *cf. Likutei Diburim* 1:1. *Cf.* also the Chassidic exhortation טראכט גוט עס וועט זיין גוט ["Think positively and things will go well"] (*Igrot Kodesh Admur HaRayatz*, vol. 2, p. 537, vol. 7, p. 197; *Ma'amar Marg'la BePumei d'Rava 5746*, beginning).

"G-d looked into the Torah and created the universe": *Zohar* 2:161b

The Divine act of creation is referred to by the metaphor of speech: As throughout the entire Creation account: "And G-d *said*: 'Let there be...' and there was...."

אמר...is an acronym for light...water...firmament: *Zohar* 2:136b, 167a; *Pardes Rimonim* 8:20

The first three primary creations, light, water, firmament: Light: Genesis 1:3; water: Genesis 1:2; firmament: Genesis 1:6

The three stages in the materialization of the creative seed: *Mevo Shearim* 5:1:9

The spiritual origin of the seed in the mind: See *Etz Chaim* 39:1; *Derech Mitzvotecha, Mitzvat Peru uRevu.*

"Living waters": spring water. Genesis 26:19 is the first instance in the Torah of this common expression.

After each individual act of creation...: Genesis 1:4,10,12,18,21,25

"G-d observed all that He had made, and, behold, it was very good": Genesis 1:31

"There is no good other than Torah": *Avot* 6:3; *Berachot* 5a; *Kalah* 8, etc.

"Clarification": ברור, *birur*, also meaning "elevation."

The positive critique of one's deeds: חשבון הנפש or חשבון צדק, a necessary component of spiritual life and a prerequisite for spiritual growth. See *Likutei Torah* 3:64d ff.

"Before" creation is the secret of the right eye...: In the imagery of Kabbalah, the right and left eyes respectively allude to the *sefirot* of *chochmah* and *binah*. These two *sefirot* are referred to in *Sefer Yetzirah* as עומק ראשית and עומק אחרית, "the primordial depth" and "the last depth," respectively, and thus are the "secret" of "before creation" and "after creation."

They are the ultimate origins of light and life, respectively: *Chochmah* is associated with light and the sense of sight; *binah* with life. Relative to each other, *chochmah* and light are מקיף, "encompassing" or "transcendent," and *binah* and life are פנימי, "internal" or "immanent."

"'Good,' refers to the angel of life; 'very [good]' refers to the angel of death": *Bereishit Rabbah* 9:10; *Zohar* 2:149b, 163a

The final, "resurrected," state of eternal life...: One of the principles of Judaism. Rambam, *Commentary to the Mishnah, Sanhedrin,* ch. 10

The mouth, the secret of creation in the "present" moment: *Etz Chaim* 4:4

"A memory between your eyes, so that the Torah of G-d shall be in your mouth": Exodus 13:9

"In that place that I will allow you to *speak* My Name...": Exodus 20:24

The Torah commands to emulate G-d: Deuteronomy 11:22, 28:9, etc.; Mechilta to Exodus 15:2; *Shabbat* 133b; *Y. Peah* 1:1; *Sotah* 14a; *Tana d'vei Eliahu Rabbah* 26 (end); *Sifrei* to Deuteronomy 11:22; *Mishneh Torah, Deiot* 1:6

"Two stones build two houses; three stones build six houses...": *Sefer Yetzirah* 4:12

Jacob rested (his head) on stones: Genesis 28:11

And...referred to the Temple site to be as "house": Genesis 28:17,19,22

Not as Abraham, who called it "mountain," nor as Isaac, who called it "field": *Pesachim* 88a

Abraham...called it "mountain": Genesis 22:14

Isaac...called it "field": Genesis 24:63

Meaning "rests" (hovers above) individual letters, yet "resides" (lives) within words: *Sha'ar HaYichud VeHaEmunah*, ch. 12; *BeSha'ah SheHikdimu 5672*, p. 41 ff

Only their energy level..is known: When looking at the letter as only a letter, we are focusing on its "energy" aspect, its power as a quantum building-block of Creation. At this point the letter conveys an explicitly conscious message. Of course, each letter contains many levels of meaning to its form, name, and number in their dimensions of Worlds, Souls, and Divinity. But these are latent within the letter, not immediately, consciously evident.

Meaning, in general, lives within the completed permutation of a word: When letters are used to form a word, there occurs a quantum leap with regard to meaning. The combination of letters produces a meaningful word, which is much more than the sum of the individual meanings of each letter. When we see the letter as part of this greater whole, we are focusing on its "life" aspect; it becomes a cell of a living organism, and takes on significance as a vehicle for conveying an idea.

The unique essence of meaning...shines above the word: As is readily observed, the same idea can be expressed in various choices of words. Yet each subtle variation on the choice of words or arrangement of words produces a corresponding subtle change in meaning. Just as in the leap from letter to word the whole is greater than the sum of the parts, so in the leap from word to style or rhetoric, more is conveyed than the aggregate meanings of each individual word. (In English this is referred to as the meaning "between the lines.") Here, the letter reveals its "light" aspect.

The stones, previously beneath his head, come to life and merge to become one: *Chulin* 91b; Rashi to Genesis 28:11

Upon awakening he experiences, in awe, the light...: Genesis 28:16-17. Jacob's awakening from his dream symbolizes his becoming conscious of his own unique mission on earth, continuing from yet distinct from that of his father and grandfather. He takes his "dream," his contact with the subconscious origin of his unique soul/personality, and "wakes," integrates it into his conscious mind. This is "awesome": he realizes he must forge his own path in life and the service of G-d. Thus he serves G-d at the same place where his fathers did, but he calls it a different name; he does what they did but in his own, unique style, expressing his unique soul-origin. This symbolizes the unique sense of meaning conveyed by the choice of word.

As will be explained in the secret of the letter *alef*: introduction and discussion of the form of the letter *alef*

Adam...was...gifted with the insight...to...call every being by its proper name: *Bereishit Rabbah* 17:4

"And from the ground, G-d formed every animal of the field...": Genesis 2:19

After Adam named all creatures, G-d asked him to call Him by Name: *Bereishit Rabbah* 17:4

The Hebrew name of every being is the Divine power...active in its continual recreation "something from nothing": *Sha'ar HaYichud Ve-HaEmunah*, ch. 1

One's name contains the secret of one's mission on earth: *Pelach HaRimon* 7a

Every living creature possesses a spark of *Mashiach*: Cf. *Maor Enaim, Pinchas*, in the name of the Ba'al Shem Tov; *Likutei Sichot* vol. 2, p. 599, 692, a.e.

His name...stands for...Adam, David, *Mashiach*: *Sefer HaGilgulim*, ch. 62; *Torah Or* 46d

In the act of calling names, Adam actually "mated" with...every living creature: *Yevamot* 63a, Rashi to Genesis 2:23; *Gur Aryeh* and *Levush Orah ad loc.*

"Knew"—"fertilized": "Knowledge" is a euphemism for intercourse, as in Genesis 4:1: "And Adam knew his wife Eve, and she became pregnant...."

Bezalel, the artisan of the Tabernacle: Exodus 31:2

"Knew how to permute letters through which were created heavens and earth": *Berachot* 55a

"To shadow" means "to emulate": *Keter Shem Tov* (ed. Kehot) addendum 60; *Kedushat Levi, Naso*

All of creation become a "house" for G-d: *Midrash Tanchuma, Naso* 16

"I will be like the One on High": Isaiah 14:14

"The image of G-d": Genesis 1:27

"And they shall make for Me a Sanctuary...: Exodus 25:8

The Temple...is considered to be a greater "creation" than that of heavens and earth: Ketubot 5a

Interinclusion: One of the properties of the realm of holiness is that everything in it exists in a state of interinclusion, i.e. there is a reflection of all other elements of the realm of holiness in it. See Mystical Concepts, ch. 3, section 9.

"Holy sign of the covenant": The phrase "sign of the covenant" occurs in Genesis 17:11 referring to circumcision.

A Jewish female is "born circumcised": Avodah Zarah 27a

The twenty-two letters are called "twenty-two letters of foundation": Sefer Yetzirah 1:2

The power of Foundation, יסוד: See Mystical Concepts ch. 3, section 6.

The brit, which...serves...to open the secret teachings of the letters of Torah to one's inner mind and heart: As indicated by the relation between the words יסוד, "foundation," the sefirah which corresponds to the organ of the convenant, and סוד, "secret" or "mystery," the name of the esoteric dimension of the Torah. (Zohar 1:186b, 236b; Zohar Chadash, Likutim 73b; Tikunei Zohar 19 [38a])

When guarded in sanctity: i.e. from illicit sexual relationships, voluntary emission of semen (or even involuntary, when caused by lewd thoughts) and the like, prohibited by the Torah. See Shulchan Aruch, Even HaEzer 23; Kitzur Shulchan Aruch 151.

The letters of the Torah and the souls of Israel are one: "Three are bound together: G-d, Torah and Israel" (Zohar 3:73a). "Israel (ישראל) stands for יש ששים רבוא אותיות לתורה, 'there are 600,000 letters in the Torah' " (Megaleh Amukot 186). There are also 600,000 general souls of the Jewish people (Tanya 37 [48a]). On the number 600,000 letters of Torah, see sources cited in Handbook of Jewish Thought, p. 135 (7:49:n108)

"The tzadik decrees and G-d fulfills": Midrash Tanchuma, VaYeira 19; Sotah 12a; Shabbat 59b; Ketubot 103b. Cf. "G-d decrees and the tzadik nullifies": Moed Katan 16b; Shabbat 63a; Midrash Tanchuma, Tavo 1; Zohar 1:10a.

The splitting of the Red Sea: Exodus 14:1-15:21

Form: The forms of the letters were revealed to Moses on Mount Sinai, and were handed down from generation to generation. See Piskei Maharai #45; Likutei Torah 4:94a; cf. Sefer HaTemunah 1, Alef. The forms of the letters were one of the things created on the first Friday at sundown. See Avot 5:6 and the other sources cited below under "מכתב, 'script.' "

Name: "So have we received from our forefathers" (*Avot d'Rabbi Natan* 15). This includes the variant spellings of the letters' names, such as צדי and צדיק for the letter צ.

Number: That every letter represents a specific number follows from the fact that the letters of the *alef-beit* have a specific order, and from the Torah's assumption of the decimal system. Use of the letters as numbers is found throughout the Oral Torah.

מכתב, **"script":** This is the term used in *Avot* 5:6 (etc.), as understood by the Rambam (*Commentary to the Mishnah ad loc.*).

The lower of the three general classes of created worlds: See Glossary: "Worlds"; *Mystical Concepts*, ch. 4, section 2.

חשבון הנפש, **the "reckoning" or "assessment" of the soul:** See note above under "Firmament, Water, Light."

The "vessels" of the world of Emanation: See *Mystical Concepts*, ch. 5.

"Brilliance"..."tale"..."number": See sources cited in *Mystical Concepts*, ch. 3, note 5

The three "books" with which G-d created the world: "G-d...created His world with three books: with ספר וספר וספור" (*Sefer Yetzirah* 1:1). These three "books" are:

    —the first three letters of the Name *Havayah* (R. Avraham ben David and Nachmanides, *ad loc.*);

    —form, number and meaning (R. Eliezer of Worms and R. Moshe Botaril, *ad loc.*, R. Eliahu the elder, quoted in remarks of R. Moshe Botaril);

    —the letters אמש, בגדכפרת, and הוזחטילנסעצק (R. Shabtai Donolo, *Sefer Chachmoni* [also quoted in remarks of R. Eliezer of Worms], R. Aharon, quoted in remarks of R. Moshe Botaril);

    —number, form, and meaning (commentary attributed to R. Saadia *Gaon*, R. Moshe ben Yaakov [*Otzar HaShem*] *ad loc.*);

    —chochmah, binah, and da'at (The Arizal in *Likutei HaShas* to *Rosh HaShanah* 16b; R. Eliahu of Vilna to *Sefer Yetzirah*, *ad loc.*; *Likutei Torah* 5:46c; *Or HaTorah*, *Ekev*, p. תקפ"ו);

    —chochmah, the Written Torah and the Oral Torah (*Torah Or* 52c; *Torat Chaim* 17a ff);

    —chochmah, binah, and malchut (*Or HaTorah*, *Balak*, p. תתק"ח);

    —the Infinite Light, *Adam Kadmon*, and the rest of Creation (*Or HaTorah*, *Bereshit*, p. תק"צ-1180; see there for variant interpretations).

    These various interpretations of course complement, rather than contradict each other. The first four are from the period before the Arizal, known as that of the "early Kabbalah." The Arizal identified these concepts with the sefirotic structure of reality, and in *Chassidut* this structure is given application in the life of the soul.

The three "books" opened on the Day of Judgment: *Rosh HaShanah* 16b

The experience of the world of Emanation is one of selflessness (בטול): See *Sefer HaLikutim, Alef*, p. 1450 and sources cited there.

As will be explained in the secret of the letter *alef*: in the discussion of the Worlds-dimension of its Number

Number is "counted" by *chochmah*: As explained in *Chassidut*, the experience of *chochmah* by the conscious mind is likened to that of a flash of lightning (ברק המבריק), a quantum pulse of seminal insight. Therefore it corresponds to the first book, סופר, "the counter" of quantum phenomena.

Form "sculptured" by *binah*: Again, as explained in *Chassidut*, *binah* is the function of the mind that develops and forms the seminal insight of *chochmah* into a complete mental structure, integrated with one's already existing mental vision of reality. As such, it corresponds to the second "book," ספר ("book"), a complete idea.

Name "called" by *da'at*: *Da'at* is the mental function that relates the fully-developed mental structure of *binah* to one's subjective life; through *da'at* the new idea goes beyond the realm of the abstract and actually makes one into a new person, as subsequently evinced by his more mature emotional responses. (Thus the *Zohar* calls *da'at* "the key to the six [emotions].") Hence, *da'at* makes the lifeless "academic" idea come alive as a new means of relating to reality. This is why it corresponds to the third book, ספור (the "story"): here the idea becomes a way of life. (Note that even in English, the verb "to relate" contains both these ideas: relation and story.)

The "crown" possesses three "heads": *Zohar* 3:288a

The three superconscious states of faith, serene pleasure and will: *Sod HaShem Lireiav*, p. 33 ff

"Counting" is an act of faith: Faith in someone or something is belief in their reality, and by that we mean not simply that they exist but that they are relevant and important in one's life. (To say that something exists but that it has no relevance in one's life is tantamount to saying that for him it really doesn't "exist.") In the Torah we find that G-d expresses His consideration of something's importance by counting it: "He counts the stars by number" (Psalms 147:4; *cf.* Exodus 1:1 and Rashi *ad loc.*; *Pelach HaRimon* 1:18bc; *Likutei Sichot*, vol. 6, p. 1 ff). Even in English, one can say he believes in someone else by saying to him "you count." This relation is also reflected in the fact that the word for "faith," אמונה, can be read א' מונה, "the number one counts." אמונה is also cognate to ממון, "money," the entity through which value is counted.

Form, an experience of pleasure: Form is seen, and sight is the sense of delight, as the Talmud says: "the eyes and the heart are the two agents of sin:

the eye sees and the heart desires..." (*Y. Berachot* 1:5; *Bamidbar Rabbah* 10:2; *Midrash Tanchuma, Shelach* 15; *Midrash Tanchuma* [ed. Buber] 31).

Name, a statement of will: By naming or defining something one is expressing what he wants out of it. *Cf.* the expression רוצה לומר, "He/it means to say."

The plenitude of "triangles", "squares" etc. apparent in the mathematical structure of Torah: See *Introduction to Mathematical Structure in Torah* (publication pending).

"To hear" means "to understand": See *Sotah* 30b; R. Hillel of Poritch, commentary to *Sha'ar HaYichud* of R. Dov Ber of Lubavitch, ch. 1. The Yiddish term used for "deep understanding" is דערהער, "deep hearing."

"And all the people saw the voices...": Exodus 20:15

"Hearing sight" nonetheless transcended "seeing sound": "Hearing sight" is referred to in *Sefer Yetzirah* as הבן בחכמה, "understand in wisdom"; "seeing sound" as חכם בבינה, "be wise in understanding" (see *Likutei Sichot*, vol. 6, p. 119 ff).

While sight may "attract": Upon seeing something deeply one becomes "glued" to it. Sight corresponds to *chochmah*, which attracts, as is said, משך חכמה, "the draw of wisdom" (Job 28:18).

Hearing "moves": Hearing corresponds to *binah*, the source of the *midot*, the emotions. The latter are the experience of movement (as seen in the usage "deeply moved" to mean "emotionally affected" and in the relation between the words "emotion" and "motion").

The "ten intangible *sefirot*": *Sefer Yetzirah* 1:2 etc.

The "ordinal numbering system": See appendix.

"Ten intangible *sefirot* and twenty-two letters of Foundation": *Sefer Yetzirah* 1:2

Thirty-two pathways of wisdom: *Sefer Yetzirah* 1:1

Numerical analysis of letter form: *Cf. Sefer HaTemunah.*

Intangibility is the general state of the world of Creation: Commentary of Rabbi Moshe Nachmanides to beginning of Genesis

"Interinclusion"...is fundamental to all truth: See note on interinclusion above.

The Souls of Israel are one with G-d: *Tanya*, ch. 2, quoting Job 31:2 with the addition of the word ממש; also Deuteronomy 32:9: "For His people is a part of G-d..."; *Igeret HaTeshuvah* ch. 3-6

And "partners" with Him in the act of creation: *Bereishit Rabbah* 8:7; *Ruth Rabbah* 2

"A dwelling place for the Holy One Blessed be He below": *Midrash Tanchuma, Naso* 16 (ed. Buber 24)

A "son," whose very essence derives from that of his father: *Tanya*, ch. 2

When not performing G-d's Will, one is actually lower...than all other creatures: *Tanya*, ch. 24

"A gnat precedes you": *Sanhedrin* 38a

"Last in creation...First in creation": *Cf. Bereishit Rabbah* 8:1: "after the deeds of the last day, and before the deeds of the first day."

"The thought of Israel preceded everything": *Bereishit Rabbah* 1:4

"In whom did He take counsel, with the Souls of the tzadikim": *Bereishit Rabbah* 8:7; *Ruth Rabbah* 2

A "measuring rod": קו המדה

The soul continues to descend...until...it enters a physical body below: This process is reflected in the morning blessing אלקי נשמה, "G-d, the soul which You have placed in me is pure...."

"Filling of the earth with the knowledge of G-d as waters cover the sea": Isaiah 11:9

In Hebrew, "future" means "ready": as in Esther 3:14, 8:13: עתידים ליום הזה.

Faith, pleasure and will correspond to the three "heads" of keter: *Sod HaShem Lireiav*, p. 33 ff

The Throne of G-d on earth: "The face of Jacob is engraved upon My Throne" (*Bereishit Rabbah* 82), and "all the souls of Israel are hewn from underneath the Throne of Glory" (*Zohar* 3:29), i.e., derived from the soul of Jacob.

All souls are essentially equal: *Tanya*, ch. 32

Light above All: See above, section 3

"Submission, separation, sweetening": *Keter Shem Tov* (ed. Kehot) 28, 160, 302

As received by him from the prophet Achiah: *Toldot Yaakov Yosef, Balak*. *Cf. Likutei Sichot* vol. 2, p. 512 in note.

"Give to the wise and he will become ever wiser": Proverbs 9:9

"Open an opening": See below, end of the Introduction.

"From the general to the particular": In Rabbi Yishmael's thirteen principles of Torah exegesis (*Sifra*, beginning), both deduction (כלל ופרט) and induction (פרט וכלל) are listed. Deduction is the methodology of the Jerusalem Talmud (and the prevalent consciousness of the land of Israel), and corresponds in Kabbalah to *mochin d'Abba*, the mind-state of *chochmah*. Induction is the methodology of the Babylonian Talmud (and the prevalent consciousness of the rest of the world) and corresponds in Kabbalah to *mochin d'Ima*, the mind-state of *binah*.

Point, line, area: *Ma'amarei Admur HaZaken 5567*, pp. 26, 166, 236-9; *cf. Torat Chaim* 1:65d, etc.

Point, sefirah, partzuf: *Cf. Mevo Shearim* 2:2:1; *Etz Chaim* 31:6; *Likutei Torah* 2:37d, 3:74b, 5:19d, *Imrei Binah* 74b ff; *Sha'ar HaYichud* 20, etc.

Chashmal...the "mystery" word of Ezekiel's vision: Ezekiel 1:27

Potent speech is one of the secrets of the *Mashiach*: The *Mashiach's* power is in his mouth: "He shall smite the earth with the rod of his mouth, and with the breath of his lips shall he slay the wicked" (Isaiah 11:4). The other word for "speech," דבר, also means "to rule"; דבר as a noun means "ruler." And any king is seen to rule with speech: "For the word of a king has authority..." (Ecclesiastes 8:4).

Every Jew possesses an active "spark of *Mashiach*," as described above: See note under section 4, "The Wisdom of Adam and Bezalel."

"Open to Me as the opening of the eye of a needle...": Introduction to *Sefer Chareidim*; *Likutei Torah* 2:40a; 3:55a, 4:4a, 5:24b; *Ma'amarei Admur HaZaken 5668*, pp. 19, 20, 23, 24. *Cf. Shir HaShirim Rabbah* 5:2:2; *Yalkut Shimoni ad loc.*; *Midrash Tanchuma* (ed. Buber), *Toldot* 18; *Zohar* 3:95a; *Pesikta Rabati* 15:6; *Pesikta d'Rav Kahana, Parshat HaChodesh.*

"Give to the wise and he will become ever wiser": Proverbs 9:9

Alef

The *alef* is formed by...: See *Pardes Rimonim* 1:6; *Or HaTorah, Ki Tisa*, p. 1915; *ibid, Breishit* 524b; *Sefer HaMa'amarim 5680*, p. 268-9

Two yuds: In *tefilin* the lower *yud* is written as a small inverted *dalet* (*Shulchan Aruch HaRav, Orach Chaim* 36:2, according to Kabbalah of the Arizal). Nevertheless the concept is the same.

Higher and lower waters and the firmament between them: *Pardes Rimonim* 1:6, 23:13 (*s.v. mayim*); *Meorei Or* 1:4; *Likutei HaShas* to *Chagigah* 14b

"And the spirit of G-d hovered...": Genesis 1:2

Water in water: Y. *Chagigah* 2; *Bereishit Rabbah* 5:2

On the second day: Genesis 1:6

"Stretching": See Isaiah 40:22, and the commentary R. Saadia *Gaon ad loc.*

The higher water is water of joy: *Torat Shmuel 5626,* p. 23, *Torat Shmuel 5630,* p. 153; *Sefer HaMa'amarim 5680,* p. 268; *cf. Tanya* ch. 1: המים מצמיחים כל מיני תענוג.

The lower water is water of bitterness: *Ma'amarei Admur HaZaken 5572,* *Vaeira; Imrei Binah* p. 16d; *Yahel Or,* p. 340-1; *Sefer HaMa'amarim 5666,* p. 108; *cf.* Rashi on Leviticus 2:13.

The two intrinsic properties of water: All material reality is seen to be composed of four "elements" (see the discussion of Worlds of Number of the *dalet*): fire, air, water, and earth. Fire is hot and dry, air is hot and wet, water is cold and wet, and earth is cold and dry. *Cf. Mishneh Torah, Yesodei HaTorah* 4:2.

Separation..."lowliness of man": *Imrei Binah* p. 16d; *Yahel Or,* p. 340-1; *Sefer HaMa'amrim 5666,* p. 108.

The "exaltation of G-d"...oneness of all in His Absolute Being: called שעשועים עצמיים . See *Sefer HaMa'amarim 5666,* p. 100-4.

The Talmud tells of four sages: *Chagigah* 14b; see also *Zohar* 1:26b; *Tikunei Zohar, Tikun* 40.

Pardes: פרדס, literally "orchard," but seen also as an acronym for the four levels of Torah-study: פשט *(peshat)*, the plain, literal meaning of the text, רמז *(remez)*, hints and allusions in the text, דרוש *(derush)*, additional levels of meaning derived by verbal analogy, and סוד *(sod)*, the esoteric, mystical dimension of the text. The garden of Eden was also an apple orchard.

Kabbalistic intentions: i.e. meditative techniques.

'Water-water': "Slabs of marble look like water": *Bava Batra* 4a; Rashi on *Chagigah* 14b.

For it is said: Psalms 101:7

The Arizal explains: *Likutei HaShas* to *Chagigah* 14b; *cf. Sha'ar Ma'amarei Razal ad loc.; Pardes Rimonim, Sha'ar Ha-Kinuyim, s.v. mayim.*

"Pure marble stone": "pure" in the sense of "as the essence of heavens is purity" (Exodus 24:1), i.e., homogeneous and non-compound.

The higher and lower waters unite: *Ma'amarei Admur HaZaken 5564,* pp. 96-7; *Or HaTorah, Beshalach,* p. 480; *ibid, Va'eira,* p. 153; *Sefer HaMa'amarim 5672,* p. 964, 972; see *Pardes Rimonim, loc. cit.*

Truth...power to bear two opposites simultaneously: *Sefer HaMa'amarim 5677,* pp. 28-9; *ibid, 5678,* pp. 419-21; *ibid, 5672* p. 1191; *Ma'amar Mayim Rabim 5717* sec. 9-11; *Likutei Sichot,* vol. 12, p. 74-5, notes 25,30; vol. 10, p. 178; *Likutei Torah* 3:68a

In the words of Rabbi Shalom ben Adret: *Responsa* 1:418, cited in *Sefer Ha-Chakirah*, p. 34b; *Sefer HaMa'amarim 5677*, pp. 28-9; *ibid. 5678*, pp. 419-21

"In the beginning G-d created": Genesis 1:1

"I am G-d your G-d who has taken you...": Exodus 20:2-14; Deuteronomy 5:6-18.

The Midrash states: *Midrash Tanchuma, VaEira* 15; *Shimusha Rabbah* 12:3.

"And G-d came down on Mount Sinai": Exodus 19:20

"And Moses approached the cloud": Exodus 24:1

"And G-d came down...And Moses approached...": See *Likutei Torah* 4:28b; *Ma'amarei Admur HaZaken 5562*, p. 12; *Sefer HaMa'amarim 5654*, p. 48 ff; *ibid. 5672*, p. 930 ff; *Likutei Sichot* vol. 21, p.150-3; *ibid.* vol. 8, p. 23 ff.

The connecting *vav* of Torah: *Sefer HaTemunah* 3, *Vav*; *Or HaTorah, Ki Teitzei*, p. 591

In the *Zohar*: *Zohar* 3:104b, and commentary of Rabbi Moshe Zacuto *ad loc.*; *cf. Zohar* 1:34b; see also *Besha'ah Shehikdimu 5672*, ch. 391; *Sefer HaMa'amarim 5680*, p. 52.

"Let us make man in our image": Genesis 1:26

The name אָדָם, man, itself, is a compound: *Shnei Luchot HaBrit* in introduction to *Beit Yisrael—Beit David*—p. 21a; *Yahel Or*, p. 357; *cf. Or HaTorah, Bo*, p. 313, 325.

א, corresponding to "our image": The *alef* is the "form-mate" of the *tzadik*, the initial letter of צֶלֶם, "image," as will be explained in the letter *tzadik*. Furthermore, the form of the *alef* depicts the form of a man.

The two-letter root: Although Hebrew is based on three-letter roots (שְׁרָשִׁים), these further reduce to more general two-letter roots (שָׁעֳרִים).

דְּ..."as our likeness": *Or HaTorah, Beshalach*, p. 401-9; *Sefer HaMa'amarim 5663*, p. 12 ff; *Sefer HaMa'amarim 5664* p. 265 ff; *Sefer HaMa'amarim 5668*, p. 186 ff. etc.

"The man of G-d": Deuteronomy 33:1; Joshua 14:6; Judges 13:8, etc.

"Run and return": Ezekiel 1:14

Unifying Torah with G-d: *Zohar* 3:222b; *Or HaTorah, Beshalach*, p. 438

The inherent "moisture"...serves to "lubricate"...: *Likutei Moharan* 1:60:3

The innate "moisture" of the intellect: known as the אֲוִירָא (*avira*, "the air"). See *Mevo Shearim* 3:2:5 (קְרוּמָא דְאַוִירָא), 3:2:8 (same); *Likutei Torah* 4:87c, 5:30b, 33a; *Ma'amarei Admur HaZaken 5565*, p. 446, etc.

"We want to be close to G-d": *Tikunei Zohar, Tikun* 5

This will come to be only in the time of universal redemption: Nonetheless, the lower water does ascend in the form of the salt (derived from the ocean) offered on the altar in the Temple, and as the salt eaten at the Jew's table (which substitutes for the altar when the Temple is not functioning) at the beginning of every bread-meal.

"I shall make the impure spirit pass away...": Zechariah 13:2

Vav represents the force of Torah and mitzvot: See note above, end of introduction to *alef*.

"Crying is enwedged in my heart...": *Zohar* 3:75a; *cf. Tanya*, end of ch. 34, *Igeret HaTeshuvah*, ch. 11.

The power to enwedge is the power of da'at: as is stated, "with *da'at* the rooms (חדרים) are filled" (Proverbs 24:4), חדר taken as an acronym for חסד (*chesed*), דין (*din*, a synonym for *gevurah*), and רחמים (*rachamim*, a synonym for *tiferet*), the three primary emotions (*Zohar* 3:291a; *Sefer HaMa'amarim 5686*, p. 56). Furthermore, the word יתד ("stick" or "wedge") is taken as an acronym for יסוד (*yesod*), תפארת (*tiferet*), and דעת (*da'at*) (references cited in *Kehilat Yaakov, s.v.* יתד).

The secret of the letter vav: The first three letters of the Name *Havayah* correspond respectively to *chochmah*, *binah*, and *da'at* (See *Sod HaShem Lireiav*, p. 102-3). In the *Zohar* (*cf.* 3:120b), *da'at* is called the "key that contains the six," six being the numerical equivalent of the *vav*.

G-d's light: "Light" in this context is a metaphor for all Divine emanations. See *Mystical Concepts*, ch. 1, section 3.

"Transcendent Light" and "Immanent Light": *Zohar* 3:225a; *Or HaTorah, Bereishit* 525b; *ibid., Yitro* 987-8

The...contraction...the impression: *Torah Or, Yitro* 69c; *Sefer HaMa'amarim 5464*, p. 215; see also *Pelach HaRimon, Chanukah*, 104a.

Having been taught Torah in the womb: *Nidah* 30b

To be "drawn" entirely into the Essence of G-d: *Zohar* 1:217b; *Torah Or* 71a; *Likutei Torah* 5:34b, etc.

Name: See *Sefer HaShorashim, Alef*.

Cattle: Deuteronomy 7:13; Isaiah 30:24

Thousand: Numbers 31:4

Teaching: Job 15:5; *ibid.*, 35:11; *ibid.*, 33:33

Master: Psalms 55:14; Jeremiah 3:4; Micah 7:5

Basic animal image: אלף in the sense of אלוף, as in Jeremiah 11:19

The "animal soul": The Jew possesses two souls: an animal soul and a Divine soul. See *Tanya*, ch. 1 & 2.

"The animal spirit descends to the earth": Ecclesiastes 3:21

As manifest in every aspect of reality: i.e., 10^3 implies the complete set of ten manifest in all three dimensions.

"A thousand to you Solomon": Song of Songs 8:12

Its return to unity: the letter *alef* has the numerical value of both one and a thousand. See appendix.

"A thousand mountains": Psalm 50:10

Devouring their grass daily: *Targum Yonatan* to Psalms 50:10; *cf. Midrash Tanchuma*, *Pinchas* 12; *Zohar* 1:18b; *Torah Or* 47d.

The initial rectification of reality: Eating and digestion are archetypal acts of rectification of reality, because through them the impurities of "raw material" are separated and rejected in order that the assimilable elements can be internalized and utilized.

Lower *teshuvah*: See *Igeret HaTeshuvah*, ch. 4 ff.

By accepting the yoke: i.e., when the Jew harnesses his animal drives by accepting the "yoke of the Kingdom of Heaven."

"Many are the yields of the power of the ox": Proverbs 14:4. This is referred in *Chassidut* to the power of the harnessed animal soul to boost the drive towards holiness.

Is drawn directly from the inner wisdom of G-d: *Tanya*, ch. 2

Just as the seed is drawn from the brain: This does not, of course, imply that the seminal drop originates *physically* in the brain, but rather that it exists within the brain as a "spiritual" entity which sequentially "materializes" as it descends via the spinal cord, etc. The steps in this successive materialization can be seen to correspond to the archetypal souls of Israel, as follows:

1. the "air"	(אוירא)	Abraham
2. the brain	(מח)	Isaac
3. the spinal cord	(שדרה)	Jacob
4. the kidneys	(כליות)	Moses
5. the testicles	(בעין)	Aaron
6. the male reproductive organ	(ברית)	Joseph
7. the female reproductive organ	(יסוד דנוקבא)	David

The explanation of these terms and correspondences are beyond the scope of the present work, but we have listed them in order to give the reader a basis for further research. See also sources cited in the note on the section "Firmament, Water, Light" in the Introduction.

Torah refers to the Jewish people as G-d's children: Exodus 4:22; Deuteronomy 14:1, etc.; *Tanya*, ch. 2

The wisdom-point: Wisdom is seen as a seminal point of insight that is only developed into a complete mental structure when "processed" in the next intellect-power, *binah* ("understanding"). See *Tanya*, ch. 3.

Whose innermost property is the sense of selflessness: See *Tanya*, ch. 35 in gloss.

"The soul of man teaches him": *Keter Shem Tov*, addendum 127

"I am young of days...": Job 32:6-8

"In the beginning": Genesis 1:1

"Be still and I will teach you wisdom": Job 33:33

"Hear O Israel...G-d is One": Deuteronomy 6:4

Is interpreted as: See *Sefer Mitzvot Katan* 2, 104, cited in *Beit Yosef, Orach Chaim* 61; *Shulchan Aruch, Orach Chaim* 61:6; *Likutei Torah* 2:23c.

The seven firmaments: *Chagigah* 12b, etc.

"Not like the ways of men are the ways of G-d": Rashi on Deuteronomy 32:41

"How does one pursue a thousand": Deuteronomy 32:30

Is interpreted in Kabbalah: in the writings of Rabbi Avraham Abulafia

The countable one: *Cf. Keter Malchut* of Rabbi Shlomo ibn Gabirol; *Sefer HaEchad* of Rabbi Avraham ibn Ezra, beginning.

"In the beginning": Genesis 1:1

The silence...within...the audible...: "Silence" (חש) and "audible" (מל) spell חשמל, *chashmal*, the secret word in Ezekiel's vision of the chariot (Ezekiel 1:4). See the section "Silence, Circumcision, Speech" in the Introduction.

The two which begins the process of rational deduction: Two axioms are necessary to begin a process of deduction.

Faith...the first power of the soul: from which all the other powers issue

One counts "something from something": *Cf.* the *Avodah*-section of the *Musaf*-prayer of *Yom Kippur:* וכך היה מונה: אחת, אחת ואחת, אחת ושתים, i.e., one is simply the beginning of the series, followed by two, etc.

"Something from something": *Cf. Sha'ar HaYichud VeHaEmunah,* ch. 2.

Causation and evolution: Faith at this level is thus faith in G-d as the one who "forms" the world out of the primordial elements rather than yet the one who "creates" all *ex nihilo.*

Organic unity of all Jewish souls: *Cf.* Rashi on Exodus 19:2; *Tanya,* ch. 32; *Ma'amar Atah Echad* (R. Dov Ber of Lubavitch); *Derech Mitzvotecha, Ahavat Yisrael,* etc.

"And they camped there": Exodus 19:2

Rashi comments: *ad loc.*

"One nation in the land": 1 Chronicles 17:21; Liturgy, *Minchah*-prayer of Shabbat

Unity is reflected in the function of the liver: Of the three major organs of the body (the brain, the heart, and the liver), the liver is seen to control the involuntary, natural processes of life. It is through these that the body functions as a unified aggregate of diverse organs.

Unity is experienced in the inner eye of the mind: The unity meant here is the unity of G-d, i.e., the ascription of all world phenomena ultimately to Him.

"Something from nothing": *Cf. Sha'ar HaYichud VeHaEmunah, loc. cit.*; *Tanya,* ch. 2, 18.

"Nothing is the *mazal* of Israel": This is a re-reading of the phrase, "Israel has no *mazal*" (*Shabbat* 156a), meaning that the Jewish people are not under the influences of astrology and other natural determinisms.

As taught by the Ba'al Shem Tov: *Maor Einaim, Likutim s.v.* כשרצה אברהם (Jerusalem 1976 ed.: p. 277a); *Likutei Amarim* (the *Maggid*) 137, 172; *Or Torah* 147, 191

Begins from His contemplation of the Land of Israel: Deuteronomy 11:12

"Hear O Israel, G-d is our G-d, G-d is One": Deuteronomy 6:4

"You have been shown to know that G-d is G-d": Deuteronomy 4:35

The Midrash interprets: quoted in *Ma'amar Mayim Rabim 5717,* sec. 3

This...refers to the very deepest level of G-d's Essence...: *Ma'amar Mayim Rabim 5717,* sec. 3, and sources cited there.

"A land flowing with milk and honey": Deuteronomy 6:3

"Nothing from something": *Torat Chaim, Shemot* 266a; *Torat Shmuel 5631,* p. 34; *Torat Shmuel 5637,* p. 191; *Sefer HaMa'amarim 5653,* p. 167; *Sefer HaMa'amarim 5661,* p. 191 ff

"The perspective from Above"…"the perspective from below": *Or Ha-Torah, Sukot*, p. 1433 ff, *VeEtchanan*, p. 423 ff, a.f.

Beit

"My house will be called…": Isaiah 56:7

The Holy One Blessed Be He desired a dwelling place in lower reality: *Midrash Tanchuma, Naso* 16 (ed. Buber 24)

To "conquer" the whole world: As is stated: "Replenish the earth and conquer it" (Genesis 1:28).

"You shall build me a Temple and I will dwell in them": Exodus 25:8

Not "in it," but "in them": *Reishit Chochmah, Sha'ar HaAhavah* 6 (beginning); *Shnei Luchot HaBrit* 69a, 201a, 325b, 326b

The "sanctuary of G-d": Exodus 15:17; *cf.* Rashi to Leviticus 20:3.

"The land of Israel will in the future spread out…": *Sifrei* to Deuteronomy 1:1: "…spread out on all sides like a fig." *Cf. Pesikta Rabati, Shabbat veRosh Chodesh* 2: "Jerusalem in the future will be like the land of Israel and the land of Israel will be like the whole world."

"The passion of the *tzadik* He will fulfill": Proverbs 10:24

"The passions of *tzadikim* are only good": Proverbs 11:23

The "*Tzadik* of the world": G-d is called a *tzadik* in Deuteronomy 32:4 a.e.

As expressed by the Alter Rebbe: as cited in *Sefer HaMa'amarim 5666*, beginning; *Sefer HaMa'amarim 5702*, p. 34; *Likutei Sichot*, vol. 6, p. 21, vol. 20, p. 284

"With whom did the Holy One Blessed Be He…: *Bereishit Rabbah* 8:7

"All of your people are *tzadikim*": Isaiah 60:21

"The final deed arose first in thought": Shabbat night Liturgy, *Lecha Dodi* hymn

The natural permutation of בראשית: *Tikunei Zohar*

"And you shall be [the bestower of] blessing": Genesis 12:2; Rashi *ad loc.*

He was given the small *hei* of creation: when his name was changed from Abram (אברם) to Abraham (אברהם), Genesis 17:5. See explanation in letter *hei*.

The Priestly Blessing: Numbers 6:24-26

"And full with the blessing of G-d": Deuteronomy 33:23

From the perspective of Torah: The Torah calls east "forwards" (קדמה, Genesis 28:14), south "towards the right" (תימנה, Exodus 26:18, 35, 27:9, 36:23, 38:9; Numbers 2:10, 3:29, 10:6; Deuteronomy 3:27), west "towards the [Mediterranean] sea (ימה, Genesis 28:14), which is also called "the sea behind" (ים האחרון, Deuteronomy 34:2), since it is behind one standing in the land of Israel facing east. Thus, if one imagines the *beit* lying on the ground, it assumes the orientation mentioned in the text.

The natural, animal, soul of the Jew is itself a mixture...: *Tanya*, ch. 1

Modesty, mercy, and kindness: *Yevamot* 79a; *Tanya*, ch. 1

"Evil begins from the north": Jeremiah 1:14

North corresponds to the property of *gevurah*: *Zohar* 1:26b

"Who is courageous? He who conquers his evil inclination": *Avot* 4:1

"Be a *tzadik* and don't be a *rasha*": *Nidah* 30b

On one's (Hebrew) birthday this power "shines": *Y. Rosh HaShanah* 3:8; *Korban HaEdah ad loc.*

The birthday of the Jewish people is...: See Ezekiel 16, and basic commentaries *ad loc.*; *Torah Or* 55a, a.e.

The conventions and restrictions of society: In Hebrew, "Egypt" (מצרים) is cognate to "restrictions" or "confinements" (מצרים).

"All is in the hands of heaven except for the fear of heaven": *Berachot* 33b

Fear is understood...to be the ultimate motivation of acts of might: since fear is the inner dimension of might. See *Sod HaShem Lireiav*, p. 39 ff.

The *Mashiach*...will be the one to close the fourth side of the letter *beit*: that the *beit* will be closed in the future is indicated in *Megaleh Amukot* (*VeEtchanan*) 166 (quoted at the beginning of *Yalkut Reuveni*). Cf. *Zohar Chadash* (to *Shir HaShirim*) 74a.

The Divine soul of Israel, an actual part of G-d: *Tanya*, ch. 2

***Mashiach* will reveal the inner dimension of the Torah:** Rashi on Song of Songs 1:2; *Torah Or* 49a; *Likutei Torah* 2:17a; *Sha'ar HaEmunah* 56; see *Kohelet Rabbah* 11, 2: תורת עולם הזה הבל הוא לפני תורתו של משיח.

"In the beginning": Genesis 1:1

"In peace": *Uktzin* 3:12; Psalms 29:11

"And you shall speak in them": Deuteronomy 6:7

His innate "spark of the *Mashiach*": *Maor Einaim, Pinchas*, in the name of the Ba'al Shem Tov; *Likutei Sichot* vol. 2, p. 599, 692, a.f.

"The beginning of wisdom is the fear of G-d": Psalm 111:10

"To increase reign and peace without end": Isaiah 9:6

The secret of the left, in Kabbalah: *Zohar* 1:143b, 2:11a, 3:151b, 176a, etc.

"The Levi serves [the level of] He": Numbers 18:23; *Zohar* 3:171a

So darkness exists above light: *Likutei Torah* 5:5a, etc.

"A man without a house is not a man": *Yevamot* 63a: "A man without land is not a man"; *Tosefot ad loc., s.v.* שאין: "to build on in order to live there"; *cf.* *Avot d'Rabbi Natan* 25: "There are three whose lives are not life: one who dwells in an attic...."

"Whoever is without a wife is without blessing": *Yevamot* 62a

"For himself and for his house": Leviticus 16:6

"'His house' is his wife": *Yoma* 2b

An unmarried High Priest: *Yoma* 1:1

Blessing the people "in love": *Sotah* 39a

The daughter of the priest: Leviticus 21:9, 22:12, 13; *Zohar* 2:95a f, 101a, 3:7a; *Igeret HaKodesh* 12 (p. 118a)

בינה represents the mother: See *Mystical Concepts*, ch. 8.

"My daughter": *Shemot Rabbah* 52:5; *Zohar* 3:262a

The Divine Presence, symbolized by the letter *yud*: The four letters of the Name *Havayah* correspond to the sources of the four levels of Jewish souls: kohen, levite, Israelite, and convert. Thus the kohen is the secret of the *yud* of G-d's Name.

To become a dwelling place below: *Midrash Tanchuma, Naso* 16 (ed. Buber 24)

"Not as Abraham who called it...": *Pesachim* 88a

Abraham...called it...'a mountain': Genesis 22:14

Isaac...called it 'a field': Genesis 24:63

Jacob...called it 'a house': Genesis 28:19

"How awesome is this place...": Genesis 28:17

"Verily the heavens and the heavens of the heavens...": 1 Kings 8:27

In other verses: 2 Samuel 12:20, a.f.

"And it shall be the place that G-d shall choose...": Deuteronomy 12:11

"And they shall make for Me a sanctuary...": Exodus 25:8

Sanctity and holiness imply separation and transcendence: *Tanya*, ch. 46

The 36 *tzadikim* of every generation: *Sukah* 45a

"*Havayah* is our G-d, *Havayah*": Deuteronomy 6:4

The minimal level of plurality is two: *Cf. Yoma* 62b.

Initially one on the first day of creation: literally, in the Torah text, *"one* day" (Genesis 1:5)

Were separated by the firmament into two: Genesis 1:6

The higher waters and the lower waters: In the *alef*, all three components— higher water, firmament and lower water—are essentially one, as explained above.

The crying of the lower waters: *Tikunei Zohar, Tikun* 5

Until the time of the giving of the Torah, G-d decreed...: *Midrash Tanchuma, VaEira* 15; *Shimusha Rabbah* 12:3

The second to the King: Esther 10:3; *cf.* 2 Chronicles 28:7.

"In whom did G-d take counsel...": *Bereishit Rabbah* 8:7; *Ruth Rabbah* 2

"Your people are all *tzadikim*": Isaiah 60:21

Joseph was second to Pharoah: Genesis 41:39-44

Mordechai was second to Ahashuerus: Esther 10:3

Even a non-Jewish king is connected Above to the Kingdom of Heaven: *Bad Kodesh* 2 ff

"The kingdom of earth is like the kingdom of heaven": *Berachot* 58a

"In him all of the higher lights become revealed": *Zohar* 1:210a

The Arizal, in the name of the Sages: *Meorei Or, s.v. Achashverosh*

Malchut is often symbolized as a "prism": in Aramaic: אספקלריא. *Zohar* 2:186b; *Pelach HaRimon*, vol. 1, p. 105d

Malchut is also the origin of time: *Sha'ar HaYichud VeHaEmunah*, ch. 7; *Torah Or* 37a; *Or HaTorah, Bereishit*, p. 1112, p. 848; *Derech Mitzvotecha, Ha'amanat Elokut*, ch. 12; *Sefer HaMa'amarim 5666* p. 41 ff

"G-d is King, G-d was King, G-d will be King...": Liturgy, Daily Morning Service

"G-d will be King for ever and ever": Exodus 15:18

"The commemoration of Purim will never cease...": *Midrash Mishlei* 9:2

G-d contains two antithetical states: as already referred to in the paradox of the letter *alef*.

The revelation of light to higher states of consciousness and the concealment of light to lower states of consciousness: as explained in regard to the form of the letter *beit*.

In the first account of creation: Genesis 1:1-2:3

In the second account of creation: Genesis 2:4-3:24

The vessels of Havayah: Isaiah 52:11

"The two companions that never separate": Zohar 3:4a

"All that Sarah says to you, listen to her voice": Genesis 21:12

The rectification of...Adam and Eve: Zohar 1:102b, 2:245a; Zohar Chadash, Yitro 42a

Gimel

The gimel symbolizes a rich man running after a poor man...: Shabbat 104a

The Rambam (Maimonides), in particular, places great stress...: Mishneh Torah, Teshuvah 5:3

The world to come...is a totally spiritual world: Mishneh Torah, Teshuvah 8:2; Commentary to the Mishnah, Sanhedrin, ch. 10; Treatise on Resurrection

The Ramban (Nachmanides) disagrees...: Sha'ar HaGemul (end), p. 309 (ed. Chavel)

Kabbalah and Chassidut support the opinion of the Ramban: Likutei Torah 2:15c, 4:65d; Teshuvot uViruim (5734), p. 57 n23

"Today to do them": Deuteronomy 7:10

"Tomorrow to receive their reward": Eruvin 22a; Avodah Zarah 3a

"Better one hour of teshuvah and good deeds in this world...": Avot 4:17

"Better one hour of serenity in the world to come...": Avot 4:17

Water (the masculine power of chesed): Zohar 3:255a; Tikunei Zohar 19 (38a)

Runs down to fill the lowest...: Tikunei Zohar 69 (105a), 25 (70b); Igeret HaKodesh 8, 12; Torah Or 14c

"Run and return": Ezekiel 1:14

"And He blew into his nostrils the breath of life...": Genesis 2:7

Jacob (yud-heel): Kehilat Ya'akov s.v. ישראל; Torah Or 21a

Whose hand at birth took hold of Esau's heel: Genesis 25:26

As taught in Kabbalah and Chassidut: Torah Or 29a

The "run" of the soul of Israel is to its truly Divine Source...: *Likutei Torah* 5:11c, a.f.

"And I shall give you 'walkers' amongst those 'standers' ": Zechariah 3:7

"And Abraham travelled walking...": Genesis 12:9; see *Torat Shmuel 5627*, p. 28.

The south symbolizes G-d's Infinite Transcendent light: *Sefer HaMa'amarim 5699*, p. 86

The south symbolizes *chochmah*: *Bava Batra* 25b: הרוצה להחכים ידרים; *Zohar* 1:2b, a.e.

The south symbolizes *chesed*: *Zohar* 1:259a

"Greatness," the attribute of Abraham: *Zohar* 3:277a, 2:276b

"Greatness," the ultimate motivation of all true acts of kindness: *Or Ha-Torah, Tehillim,* p. תקמ"ז, *VaYeira,* p. 186-צ"ג

"Might," the attribute of Isaac: *Zohar* 3:31a

The waters of kindness: See note on the discussion of the Worlds-level of Form, above.

The camel...symbolizes...the angel of death: *Zohar* 2:236a

Rebecca fell off the camel when she first saw Isaac: Genesis 24:64

"All of them You have made with wisdom": Psalms 104:24

The word *chochmah* is read as כח מה: *Zohar* 3:28a, 34a

Chochmah corresponds to the yud of G-d's Name *Havayah*: *Tikunei Zohar,* Introduction (5a), 18 (32a); *Zohar* 2:123b, 1:31a

In Psalm 131: verse 2, according to Rashi and Onkelos

Some commentaries interpret: *Metzudat David ad loc.*

In Psalm 119: verse 17, the first of the eight verses that begin with the letter *gimel*. Psalm 119 is arranged alphabetically—each letter begins eight verses.

"And you shall walk in His ways": Deuteronomy 8:6, 19:9, 26:17, 30:16 (*cf.* 28:9)

We further find in the Talmud: *Sotah* 14a

"After G-d your G-d you shall walk": Deuteronomy 13:5

"G-d your G-d is a consuming fire": Deuteronomy 4:24

"And G-d made for Adam and his wife garments...": Genesis 3:21

"And G-d appeared to him in the plane of Mamre": Genesis 18:1

"And it was after the death of Abraham...": Genesis 25:11

"And He buried him in the valley": Deuteronomy 34:6

G-d continuously...by recreating, from nothing...: *Sha'ar HaYichud Ve-HaEmunah* 1

He is all: See Deuteronomy 4:35, 4:39; letter of Rabbi Yitzchak Isaac of Homil at the end of *Chanah Ariel, Chelek HaMa'amarot* and in *Toldot Yitzchak Isaac* (5747), p. 173; *Likutei Diburim* 36 (p. 1322).

We become "partners" with Him in the process...: See *Avot* 1:2; *Bereishit Rabbah* 8:5; *Otiot d'Rabbi Akiva.*

The world stands on three things: *Avot* 1:2

Returning light: *Etz Chaim* 39:14

The three pillars correspond to the three Patriarchs in reverse order: *Zohar* 1:146b

The three primary elements of Creation: See the discussion of the Souls-dimension of the Number of *dalet.*

Air derives from the root of "Torah," the middle line: for the study of Torah must be done audibly. Sources cited in *Sefer HaArachim,* vol. 2, col. 229, n188.

Air derives...Fire derives...Water derives: sources cited in *Sefer HaArachim,* vol. 2, col. 229, n189

The Temple sacrifices which are called "fires": Exodus 29:18, a.f. thereafter

Water descends and gives of itself to those below it: See note on discussion of Worlds-dimension of Form.

These elements correspond to the three Hebrew letters א...מ...ש: *Sefer Yetzirah* 3:3-5

The three divisions...derive from...the three patriarchs: *Or HaTorah, Baha'alotcha,* pp. שנ"ז-ד

Chosen people: Exodus 19:5

Segol: *Zohar* 3:119b; *Or HaTorah, Yitro,* p. תת"ד-ר

The triple Torah: *Shabbat* 88a

"Have I not written to you excellent things...": Proverbs 22:20

"A string braided from three strands will not...": Ecclesiastes 4:12

"Torah and G-d are one": *Zohar* 1:24a

"Three bonds are bonded together": *Zohar* 3:73a. See *Sefer HaMa'amarim 5657,* p. 28 in note, *Sefer HaMa'amarim 5700,* p. 61 in note.

The direct bond of the Divine Essence of the souls of Israel to G-d: *Likutei Sichot,* vol. 18, p. 408, vol. 26, p. 181

Dalet

"That has nothing of her own": See *Zohar* 3:180b; *Pardes Rimonim, Sha'ar HaOtiot* 3.

Malchut...has no light of its own...: *Zohar* 2:218b

"He gives you the power to achieve success": Deuteronomy 8:18

"My power and the strength of my hand": Deuteronomy 8:17

If not for G-d's help he would not have been able...: *Kidushin* 30b; *Tanya*, ch. 13

The Talmud describes...: *Shabbat* 93a

Explains the Ba'al Shem Tov: *Keter Shem Tov* (ed. Kehot) 193; *cf. ibid*, 354.

"For to You G-d is kindness, for You pay man...": Psalms 62:13

The Ba'al Shem Tov asks: *Keter Shem Tov* (ed. Kehot) 191; *Likutim Yekarim* 5d; *Or Torah* (ed. Kehot) 273; but in these sources different answers are given. The answer given in the text is found in *Keter Shem Tov* (ed. Kehot) 193, cited above, and in fact, the editor in this edition indicates that sections 191-193 can be considered one passage.

The *Zohar* reads חסדו as חס ד': *Tikunei Zohar* 22 (67b)

"I and he cannot dwell together": *Sotah* 5a

[G-d's] dwelling place below: *Midrash Tanchuma, Naso* 16 (ed. Buber 24)

One's feeling of indebtedness to G-d: On this subject at length, see the author's essay "A Chapter in the Service of G-d" or its Hebrew original, *Perek BeAvodat HaShem*.

"Give Him that which is His, for you and yours are His": *Avot* 3:7

"For all is from You, and from Your hand...": 1 Chronicles 29:14

Bitul hayeish: *Likutei Torah* 2:42b, 3:20a, a.f.

Every aspect of Creation possesses...a "spark" of bitul hayeish: *Tanya*, ch. 21; *Sha'ar HaYichud VeHaEmunah*, ch. 3, a.f.

Bitul bimtziut: *Ma'amarei Admur HaZaken 5668*, p. 230, p. 479, a.f.

The ten miracles that were witnessed in the Temple: *Avot* 5:5

The two states...correspond to the two states of bitul...: See *Sefer HaMa'amarim—Kuntresim*, vol. 1, p. כב

All Jews are considered by halachah pure: *Beitzah* 11b

"Hear O Israel, G-d is our G-d, G-d is One": Deuteronomy 6:4

Each letter corresponds to a Jewish soul: "Israel (ישראל) stands for יש
ששים רבוא אותיות לתורה, 'there are 600,000 letters in the Torah' " (*Megaleh
Amukot* 186). There are also 600,000 general souls of the Jewish people (*Tanya*
37 [48a]).

The *halachah* requires that each letter be surrounded...: *Shulchan Aruch,*
Yoreh Deah 274:4. According to Rabbi Yoel Sirkes (*Bach, ad.loc*) this law dates
back to Moses.

Bitul alone is the "doorway" to truth: *Zohar* 1:8a; *Likutei Sichot,* vol. 3, p.
991

A Hebrew servant goes free after six years: Exodus 21:2-6

"They are my servants": Leviticus 25:42, 55

And not servants to servants: *Kidushin* 22b; Rashi to Exodus 21:6

The Jubilee year corresponds, in Kabbalah...: *Zohar* 3:108ab, 2:115b;
Tikunei Zohar 32 (76b)

On the Jubilee year all ears hear the great *shofar*-blast: Leviticus 25:9

דלית ליה מגרמיה כלום: References cited in the note on the top of the previous page.

Nonetheless continuously felt himself as a "miscarriage": *Yalkut Shimoni*
to Genesis, par. 41; *Zohar* 1:168a; Psalm 22:7; *Chidushei Agadot* of R. Shlomo
Idels to *Chulin* 89a

King David is symbolized by the moon: *Zohar* 3:287a; Commentary of Rabbi
Moshe Zacuto to *Zohar* 1:168a

Which possesses no light of its own: *Zohar* 1:249b

A symbol of the Jewish soul: *Bereishit Rabbah* 6:3

"David, the King of Israel, is alive forever": *Rosh HaShanah* 25a; *Zohar*
1:192b

"I will exalt you G-d for you have lifted me up": Psalms 30:2

Wherever transcendent light is revealed...: *Zohar* 2:128b; *Tanya,* ch. 27

The understanding of the physical world: E.g., in *Mishneh Torah* and *Sefer*
Yetzirah

In Kabbalah we are taught: See *Mystical Concepts,* ch. 4.

The Torah speaks of four (types of) sons: *Y. Pesachim* 10:4, *Haggadah.* The
four sons are derived from Exodus 12:26, 13:8, 13:14, and Deuteronomy 6:20.

"Educate the youth in accordance with his way": Proverbs 22:6

Four cups of wine in commemoration of the four expressions: *Y. Pesachim*
10:1; *Zohar* 3:95b

The four expressions of redemption from Egypt: in Exodus 6:6-7

Constitute the four feet of the Divine Throne: *Zohar* 1:248b, 1:154b, 3:262b

"Be fruitful and multiply": Genesis 1:28

Two children, a son and a daughter: *Mishneh Torah, Ishut* 9:4; *Shulchan Aruch, Even HaEzer* 1:5

"The Name of four letters": *Kidushin* 71a

Before the creation of the world He and His Name were alone: *Pirkei d'Rabbi Eliezar* 3

The *yud* represents...: *Likutei Torah* 4:2c, a.f.

The Torah text possesses four components: See *Etz Chaim* 5.

"The concealed things are to G-d our G-d...": Deuteronomy 29:28

As taught in the *Zohar*: *Tikunei Zohar* 10 (25b), 70 (129a), p. 158a citing the *Zohar Chadash* (101b); see *Etz Chaim* 42:1.

Four basic levels of Torah interpretation: See note on *Pardes* in introduction to *alef*.

Hei

"Take for yourselves seed": Genesis 47:23

"Take" expresses revelation of self: since the word הא is also the Aramaic demonstrative pronoun, "this." מאי ה"א, כמאן דאמר הא אנא: *Zohar Chadash, Bereishit* 6b

The highest form of charity: *Mishneh Torah, Matnot Ani'im* 10:8; *Shulchan Aruch, Yoreh Deah* 249:6-13. Actually, this is the second highest form, the highest being to help the poor man support himself.

"The concealed gift subdues anger": Proverbs 21:14

Joseph...corresponds to the *sefirah* of *yesod*: *Zohar* 3:236a

Yesod, whose function is to express self in the form of giving seed: "Yesod is the culmination of the body, the sign of the holy covenant": *Tikunei Zohar*, introduction.

They were unable to recognize him: Genesis 42:8

Similar to the *dalet* in relation to the *gimel*: that is, similar to the highest form of charity mentioned above, when the giver is completely concealed from the receiver.

Instead of grain (בר) he now gave seed (זרע): The Hebrew for "grain" (בר) means "external" in Aramaic.

The soul possesses three..."garments": *Tanya*, ch. 4

The three lines...correspond to these three garments: *Torah Or* 95b, a.f.

One must realize that each of us possesses...: *Tanya*, ch. 32

"There is one leader in a generation...": *Sanhedrin* 8a

"By the word of the King is His sovereignty": Ecclesiastes 8:4

"Many are the thoughts in the heart of man...": Proverbs 19:21

"We will do and understand": Exodus 24:7

The three powers of intellect and the seven powers of emotion: See *Tanya*, ch. 3; *Mystical Concepts*, ch. 3.

"This world was created with the letter *hei*": *Menachot* 29b

Our service of G-d...takes place at the "servant" level of our souls: *Tanya*, ch. 14

The true *tzadik*...: *Tanya*, ch. 14

The world to come was created with the letter *yud*: *Menachot* 29b

The two levels of thought: *Sha'ar HaYichud*, ch. 2; Commentary of R. Hillel of Poritch, *ad loc.*

As will be explained in the letter *yud*: discussion of Worlds-dimension of Number

"He fills all worlds, He surrounds all worlds...": *Zohar* 3:225a

Though uniformly present...appears to "surround": *Tanya*, ch. 48 (67b)

All...is equally naught in the presence of...the Essence of G-d: *Likutei Torah* 5:4b ff, a.f.

"And I, Daniel, was broken and became sick for many days": Daniel 8:27

The breaking of the vessels: sources cited in *Mystical Concepts*, ch. 7, notes 1 & 2

"And the earth was chaos...": Genesis 1:2

"Chaos"...refers to...where "the breaking of the vessels" occurred: See *Mystical Concepts*, ch. 9

"And G-d said 'Let there be light,' and there was light": Genesis 1:3

"And G-d saw the light as good, and G-d separated...": Genesis 1:4

"And G-d called the light day....one day": Genesis 1:5

Not 'first,' as noted by the Sages: *Bereishit Rabbah* 3:8; Rashi on Genesis 1:5

"Take for yourselves seed, and sow the earth": Genesis 47:23

Joseph forced the Egyptians to circumcise themselves...: *Bereishit Rabbah* 91:4

Thereby intending...: See *Sha'ar HaPesukim* to Genesis 41:55.

"Force the end": לדחוק את הקץ, i.e. try to cause the Redemption to occur. *Ketubot* 111a

Through "merit" in Torah we are able to achieve the "speeding up" of the end: *Sanhedrin* 99a

The form of the letter *hei* symbolizes the stable state of pregnancy: *Zohar Chadash, Shir HaShirim*, p. 88b

As in the case of the birth of Moses: *Sotah* 12a

Moses took Joseph's bones: Exodus 13:19

One's seed is...an indivisible part of one's very being: *Kuntres Acharon* 4 (157a); *Likutei Torah* 5:39d; *Sefer HaMa'amarim 5659*, p. 10 ff

"Behold this is our G-d that we have been waiting for": Isaiah 25:9

"Upon their being created": Genesis 2:4

The letters בהבראם when rearranged spell באברהם: *Bereishit Rabbah* 12:9

The Divine attribute represented by Abraham is lovingkindness: *Zohar* 1:47b

"The world is built with lovingkindness": Psalms 89:3

When, at the age of ninety-nine, G-d commanded Abraham to circumcise himself: Genesis 17:5

The premature attempt of Joseph...: See above, under the discussion of Souls of Name.

Five represents the power of division: *Sod HaShem Lireiav*, p. 86

"Vanity of vanities, says Ecclesiastes...": Ecclesiastes 1:1

"There is no *mazal* for Israel": *Shabbat* 156a

The inclination of the heart of man is evil from birth: Genesis 8:21; Rashi *ad loc.*; *Sanhedrin* 91b

Begins to shine...from the moment of circumcision: *Seder HaYom*; *Menorat HaMaor* (Al Nakawa); *Shulchan Aruch, Yoreh Deah* 263:5; *Shulchan Aruch HaRav* (2nd. ed.) 4:2; *cf. Likutei Sichot*, vol. 3, p. 763.

The Jewish woman is "born circumcised": *Avodah Zarah* 27a

The five different levels of the soul: *Bereishit Rabbah* 14:9; *Devarim Rabbah* 2:37; *Zohar* 1:81a, 206a; *Etz Chaim* 6; *Sefer HaMa'amarim 5701*, p. 82 ff

King David repeats the phrase...five times: 103:1, 2, 22, 104:1, 35

In Jeremiah: 33:11

The Torah...was given with five voices: The word "voice" is mentioned five times in Exodus 19:16-19.

The giving of the Torah...is referred to as G-d's marriage to Israel: *Ta'anit* 4:8, referring to Song of Songs 3:11

Whoever gives joy to groom and bride...: *Berachot* 6b; *cf. Likutei Sichot*, vol. 6, p. 107.

In the first day of creation the word "light" appears five times: Genesis 1:3-5

"The Torah is light": Proverbs 6:23

Five "ends," or redemptions: *Kedushat Levi, Likutim, s.v.* מכנף הארץ, quoting *Pirkei d'Rabbi Eliezar*

"And your People are all *tzadikim*": Isaiah 60:21

The *Tzadik* of the world: See note on the introduction to *beit*.

"From the end of the earth we have heard songs...": Isaiah 24:16

"Light is implanted in the *tzadik*": Psalms 97:11

Vav

In the beginning of creation...: beginning of *Etz Chaim*, etc.

"In the beginning G-d created the heavens and the earth": Genesis 1:1

The word את is generally taken to represent...: *Recanati*, p. 3, quoted in *Yalkut Reuveni* 5a; *Or HaTorah* 147, etc.

Our Sages interpret the word את, in this verse...: *Bereishit Rabbah* 1:14: "את השמים is to include the sun, moon and planets; ואת הארץ is to include the trees, plants, and the garden of Eden."

"And G-d said, 'Let there be light,' and there was light": Genesis 1:3

Through *teshuvah* from fear...when a Jew returns in love...: *Yoma* 86b

Every Jew has a portion in the World to Come: *Sanhedrin* 10:1 (90a)

"And all your nation are *tzadikim*; forever they will inherit the land": Isaiah 60:21

"May he kiss me with the kisses of his mouth, for your love is better than wine": Song of Songs 1:2

"The world stands on pillars": *Chagigah* 12b

In the Talmud we find three opinions: *ibid.*

In *Sefer Yetzirah*: 5:1

They...correspond to the twelve tribes of Israel: *Sefer Yetzirah, ibid.*

In the Tabernacle...there were long rods...: Exodus 26:26-28

The seven "shepherds" of Israel: See note to Introduction, excerpt from the Ba'al Shem Tov's letter.

The structure and components of the Tabernacle directly correspond to the secrets of creation: *Zohar* 2:149a, 231b; *Tikunei Zohar*, introduction (13a)

Knew how to permute letters through which heavens and earth were created: *Berachot* 55a; *Zohar* 2:234b

Standing crowded together: *Avot* 5:5

The Rambam...speaks of the "middle path"...: *Mishneh Torah, Deiot* 1:4 ff

"That G-d has made man upright but they have sought out many schemes": Ecclesiastes 7:29

"Which is the straight way that a man should choose?...": *Avot* 2:1

This is the secret of the letter *vav*: 'ו את דא קו: *Tikunei Zohar* 19 (38b); קו המדה איהו ו': *Tikunei Zohar* 5 (19b)

The *vav*...represents...the "pillar of truth": *Zohar* 1:241b, 3:2a (אות אמת)

The pillar of truth: *Cf. Avot* 1:18.

Truth is one and only one: *Likutei Moharan* 1:51, 66

The structure of the *sefirot*...is made up of three lines or channels: See *Mystical Concepts*, ch. 3, section 8, and sources cited there in note 157.

"The hooks of the pillars": Exodus 27:10

This phrase...is repeated six times in the account of the Tabernacle: Exodus 27:10, 11, 38:10, 11, 12, 17

The curtains...represent the power of concealment...: since they in fact conceal

The pillars stand for manifest revelations of light...: as in the phrase תר"ך עמודי אור (*Pardes Rimonim* 8:3)

Concealment is merely a means towards an end—revelation: *Keter Shem Tov* (ed. Kehot) 292; *Tanya*, ch. 49

All Jewish souls are connected and one: *Tanya*, ch. 32

"Even the wicked amongst you are as full of *mitzvot* **as a pomegranate...":** *Berachot* 57a

" 'And you shall be for Me a desired land,' says G-d": *Cf.* Malachi 3:12.

Rabbi Shalom Dov Ber of Lubavitch would frequently recite...: *Likutei Diburim* 33:4,5 (p. 1202)

"Blessed are You G-d, teach me Your Laws": Psalms 119:12

We then perceived G-d's command from every direction: Rashi to Exodus 20:2; *Pesikta d'Rav Kahana* 12: "from every direction."

"I am the L-rd your G-d...": Exodus 20:2

The Ten Commandments...were first pronounced as one Word: *Mechilta* to Exodus 20:1

The first word of creation...is read in the *Zohar***...:** *Tikunei Zohar, Tikun* 11

"Six days did G-d make the heavens and the earth": Exodus 20:10, 31:17

"Each day performed its action": *Zohar* 3:94b

The six millennia of the endurance of our present state of reality: *Sanhedrin* 97a; *Avodah Zarah* 9a; *Rosh HaShanah* 31a

"A thousand years in Your eyes are as a day of yesterday": Psalms 90:4

According to the basic orientation of Torah...: See Rashi to Exodus 27:13 and Numbers 34:15

The six days of Creation relate to south...: *Sefer Yetzirah* 4

The traditional shaking of the *lulav* **and** *etrog* **on** *Sukot***:** *Sha'ar HaKavanot, Sukot* 5 (105d); *Pri Etz Chaim, Sha'ar HaLulav* 3; *Siddur Im Dach*, p. 214b; *cf. Sefer HaMa'amarim 5704*, p. 59; a different tradition regarding the order of the shaking is cited in the *Shulchan Aruch, Orach Chaim* 651:9-10 and *Mishnah Berurah, ad. loc.*

"*Serafim*** stood above Him, each one had six wings...":** Isaiah 6:2-3

In general, wings symbolize...love and fear: *Tanya*, ch. 40

Mitzvot **performed without love and fear...:** *Tikunei Zohar* 15

"Walking humbly with your G-d": Michah 6:8

"Give truth to Jacob": Micah 7:20

"Stamp of truth": Joshua 2:12 (אות אמת); *Zohar* 1:241a, 3:2a: אות אמת דא 'ו; *Shabbat* 55a; *Sanhedrin* 1:1 (חותמו של הקב"ה אמת)

"I shall be that which I shall be": Exodus 3:14

The letter of truth: *Zohar* 1:241a, 3:2a

"The Torah of G-d is perfect, restoring the soul...": Psalms 19:8-10

These six phrases...hint at the basic structure of the Oral Torah: *Midrash Tehilim* 19:14

The Oral Torah...links the essence of the Jewish soul to the Will of G-d....: *Gitin* 60b

The second finger...whose function is to "point" at Divine revelation: *Ta'anit* 31a.

The finger upon which the bride accepts her betrothal ring: *Shulchan HaEzer* 8:2:2

They were cubes measuring six hand breadths in each direction: *Bava Batra* 14a; according to *Nedarim* 38a: 6 x 6 x 3 handbreaths

"Inscribe them on the tablet of your heart": Proverbs 3:3, 7:3

"The heart of the wise teaches his mouth": Proverbs 16:23

Zayin

"A woman of valor is the crown of her husband": Proverbs 12:4

Or yashar...or chozer: *Etz Chaim* 39:14

"There is no left in that Ancient One, for all is right": *Zohar* 3:129a

"Who is a good woman? She who does her husband's will": *Tana d'vei Eliahu Rabbah* 9

The word "does" also means "rectifies": *Likutei Sichot*, vol. 4, p. 1069

"...that which G-d created to do": Genesis 2:3

"To do" in the sense of "to rectify": "Rashi" to *Bereishit Rabbah* 11:7

"All the king's servants and the people....": Esther 4:11, 5:2-3

"How great are your workings G-d, infinitely deep are your thoughts": Psalms 92:6

"For My thoughts are not your thoughts, nor My ways your ways": Isaiah 55:8

The opening verse...refers...to...Sarah: *Cf. Midrash Tanchuma, Chayei Sarah* 4.

"Everything that Sarah says to you—listen to her voice": Genesis 21:12

Sarah was greater than Abraham in prophecy: *Shemot Rabbah* 1:1

The six weekdays are the secret of halachah...: *Likutei Torah (Arizal)* on Psalms 100; *Sha'ar HaPesukim* on Psalms 100; *Siddur Im Dach* 44a ff; *Pirush HaMilot* 2:141; *Likutei Sichot*, vol. 1, p. 53, etc.

"And Abram traveled, going and traveling southward": Genesis 21:9 ff

"Chesed to Abraham": Micah 7:20

Her ability to distinguish between Jewish and non-Jewish souls: See also *Bava Batra* 58a; *Or HaTorah, Bereishit*, p. תמ״ב ff.

She distinguished between her son, Isaac....: Genesis 21:9 ff

A non-Jew that keeps Shabbat is liable to death: *Sanhedrin* 58b

"And G-d blessed the seventh day and sanctified it....": Genesis 2:3

"Selflessness"...the state of the soul's Divine service on Shabbat: *Likutei Torah* 3:42c ff; see *Kuntres Acharon* 9.

"Bow down to G-d in sacred splendour": Psalms 96:9; see references cited above under "The six weekdays are the secret of *halachah*..."

A sword is considered an ornament in certain halachic contexts: *Shabbat* 6:4

Jacob's wrestling with the archangel of Esau: Genesis 32:25 and Rashi *ad loc.*; *Bereshit Rabbah* 77:3

The first iron sword was produced during the seventh generation of mankind: Genesis 4:22 and Rashi *ad loc.*; *Bereishit Rabbah* 23:3

Lemech himself, mistakenly, first killed his ancestor Cain...: *Midrash Tanchuma, Bereishit* 11

The descendants of Cain actually degenerated...: *Bereishit Rabbah* 23:6,7; *Targum Yonatan* to Genesis 4:26; *Sanhedrin* 109a

Naamah...according to the Sages...was Noah's wife: *Bereishit Rabbah* 23:3

When man and wife do not merit to assume their proper roles...: *Sotah* 17a: "When husband and wife are worthy, the *shechinah* dwells with them; when they are not worthy, fire consumes them." *Yevamot* 63a: "If he merits, she aids him; if not, she opposes him."

Each day when we say "Holy Holy Holy is the G-d of Hosts...": *VaYikra Rabbah* 24:8, etc.

"Holy Holy Holy is the G-d of Hosts...": Isaiah 6:2-3

"We will do and we will hear": Exodus 24:7

The hundred blessings a Jew is required by the Sages to say every day: *Menachot* 43b

"When you have eaten and are satiated, then you shall bless the L-rd your G-d....": Deuteronomy 8:10

The hundred daily blessings express...: *Pelach HaRimon* 86b

The first blessing, originally composed by Moses himself: *Berachot* 48b

"You open up Your Hand and satisfy the desire of every living thing": Psalms 145:16

In Kabbalah we are taught...: See *Sidurei HaArizal* on Grace after Meals.

"The working of the hands of the craftsman": Song of Songs 7:2

"All sevens are beloved": *VaYikra Rabbah* 29:10

On Shabbat one's mental attitude should be as though "all your work is done": *Mechilta* to Exodus 20:8

"And you shall count for yourselves from the day after the Shabbat....": Leviticus 23:15

"Six years you shall sow your field....": Leviticus 25:3-5

All produce becomes "ownerless": Leviticus 25:6 and Rashi *ad loc.*

Land returns to its original owner on the fiftieth or Jubilee year: Leviticus 25:8-13

The consummation of the six thousand years of this world: *Sanhedrin* 97a; *Rosh HaShanah* 30a; *Avodah Zarah* 9a

"All Shabbat and rest for eternal life": *Tamid* 7:4

The seven fruits of Israel: Deuteronomy 8:8

The seven seas: *Bava Batra* 74b

The seven heavens: *Chagigah* 12b

The seven chambers of Paradise: *Beit HaMidrash* (Jellinek) 2:49, 53; *Zohar* 1:23b, 41a

"The candle of G-d is the soul of man": Proverbs 20:27

The seven candles of the *menorah*...correspond to the seven archetypal levels of Souls of Israel: *Torah Or* 32b; *Likutei Torah* 3:29c, etc.

"Love as water"..."love as fire": *Imrei Binah, Keriat Shema* 74; *Or HaTorah, VeEtchanan,* p. שע״ח; sources cited in *Sefer HaArachim,* vol. 1, col. 467 ff

"All Israel are princes": *Shabbat* 67a *et al.*

On...*Sukot* we invite...seven spiritual guests: *Zohar* 3:103b

The bride circles the groom seven times: Jeremiah 31:21; *Tikunei Zohar* 6 (23a)

Seven blessings are recited: *Ketubot* 7b-8a; *Shulchan Aruch, Even HaEzer* 62:1

The celebration of the wedding is continued...seven days: *Ketubot* 8a; *Shulchan Aruch, Even HaEzer* 62:6

The seven Rabbinic *mitzvot*: Sabbath candles, Chanukah candles, Blessings (before eating, smelling spices, etc.), washing hands, reading the *Megillah*, reciting the *Hallel*, and *Eruv*

The Sages are the "woman of valor"...: *Sefer HaMa'amarim 5666*, pp. 404-5

"The crown of her husband": Proverbs 12:4

"There are seven eyes of G-d that traverse the entire earth": Zechariah 4:10

As in the verse: Song of Songs 4:8

"See from the head of faith": This is the translation according to Rashi *ad loc.*

The seven clouds of glory: *Midrash Tanchuma, Beshalach* 3

The *sukah*, **symbolic of the seven clouds of glory:** *Sukah* 11b

On the seventh day of *Sukot*...**seven** *hakafot*...**are made...:** *Shulchan Aruch, Orach Chaim* 664:1

On *Simchat Torah*...**seven...***hakafot*: *Shulchan Aruch, Orach Chaim* 669:1 in the *Mapah*; *cf. Mishnah Berurah, ad loc.*, 10.

Chet

Whose most important letter is *chet*: in that it is the first letter (see *Sha'ar HaYichud VeHaEmunah*, chapter 1) and the only consonant-letter in the word.

There are two levels of life: *Sefer HaMa'amarim 5663*, p. 1 ff, etc.

"Run and return": Ezekiel 1:14

According to the Arizal...: *Matzat Shemurim* 31a; *Mishnat Chassidim, Tikun Tefilin* 1:9; *Shulchan Aruch HaRav, Orach Chaim* 36:2

"Touching yet not touching": *Y. Chagigah* 2:1

"And the spirit of G-d was hovering over the waters": Genesis 1:2

This word is...the secret of the Divine power to resurrect the 288 fallen sparks...: *Etz Chaim* 18:1; *Torah Or* 27d

The "Spirit of G-d" here referred to is...the soul of *Mashiach*: *Bereishit Rabbah* 2:8

"As an eagle arouses her nest and hovers over her young": Deuteronomy 32:11

As taught by the Maggid of Mezeritch: *Likutei Amarim* 99, 137, 162, 184, 225; *Or Torah* 57, 83, etc.

The eagle...is a metaphor for G-d in relation to His children: *Cf.* Rashi and *Sifrei* to Deuteronomy 32:11.

"Touching yet not touching"...reflects itself as "run and return": *Sefer HaMa'amarim 5679*, p. 237 ff

"And the living creatures run and return like the appearance of lightning": Ezekiel 1:14

"Do not read *chayot* but *chayut*": See *Keter Shem Tov* 34, 37, 90, 121, 139, 188, 356; *Or Torah* 184; *Or HaTorah, Shavuot*, p. קל"ט ff, a.f.

Before Shabbat all of the worlds begin to ascend...: *Pri Etz Chaim*, introduction to *Sha'ar HaShabbat*; *Torah Or* 53a, a.f.

The ability to exit is greater than that to enter: See *Zohar* 3:292a, 2:213b.

"There are three partners in man....": *Kidushin* 30b

"Face to face": Deuteronomy 34:10; Exodus 33:11

"Grace unto her": Zechariah 4:7

The holy balance, whose manifestation is the state of "looking face to face": *Zohar* 2:176b

As taught by the Ba'al Shem Tov...: *Or HaTorah, Eikev*, p. תקכ"ב; sources cited in *Keter Shem Tov*, addendum 40

"Then shall the maiden be joyous in dance": Jeremiah 31:12

The "*mitzvah*-dance": *Shulchan HaEzer* 9:8:5

"He who lives at the summit of the world": Isaiah 33:5 (שׁוֹכֵן מָרוֹם)

Though at every point of reality...: *Tanya*, ch. 48

"G-d, You are my G-d, I will exalt you...": Isaiah 25:1

The "far encompassing Light": *Torah Or* 54c, a.f.

"The fear of G-d": Genesis 35:5

"Fear of G-d to life": Proverbs 14:27

"See, I have placed before you today life and good...": Deuteronomy 30:15

"For He is your life": Deuteronomy 30:20

"All my bones say 'G-d, who is like unto you....' ": Psalms 35:10

"Every soul shall praise G-d, Hallelujah": Psalms 150:6

י״ה...the Name of Divine Wisdom: Zohar 3:10b; Tikunei Zohar 19 (41b), regarding any two-letter name

The physical experience of loving G-d...: HaYom Yom, 20 Menachem Av (without specific reference to breath)

The true, unselfish experience of another soul...: Tanya, chapter 32

As expounded by the present Lubavitcher Rebbe, Shlita: See Likutei Biurim to Tanya, ch. 32

"Run and return": Ezekiel 1:14

All Jewish souls constitute one organic whole....: Tanya, ch. 2

The "key of resurrection": Ta'anit 2a

"Even the smallest of you is able to resurrect the dead": Avodah Zarah 10b; VaYikra Rabbah 10:4

The "living Torah": Liturgy, Amidah

"Now I know that the word of G-d is true in your mouth": 1 Kings 17:24

The word echad is interpreted to read....: Sefer Mitzvot Katan 104; Shulchan Aruch, Orach Chaim 61:6

"A plurality after a plurality comes to diminish": Pesachim 23a; Bava Kama 45b

The Torah prescribes....: Genesis 17:12; Leviticus 12:3

These eight days must always include at least one Shabbat: Pesikta d'Rav Kahana, Shor o Chesev; Zohar 3:44a, 91a

The thirty-six tzadikim: Sukah 45b

The tzadik is the secret of the power inherent in circumcision: Zohar 1:260a

The foreskin of the flesh: Genesis 17:14-25; Leviticus 12:3

The foreskin of the lips: Exodus 6:12, 30

The foreskin of the ears: Jeremiah 6:10

The foreskin of the heart: Deuteronomy 10:16; Jeremiah 4:4

"He who lives at the summit of the world": Isaiah 33:5 (שוכן מרום)

Seven heavens: See note to the Worlds-dimension of the Number of the zayin.

"Abraham was one": Ezekiel 33:24

"The deeds of the fathers are signposts for the children": Or HaTorah, Lech Lecha, beginning; Torat Chaim 1:83c; cf. Ramban to Genesis 12:6, 10; Midrash Tanchuma, Lech Lecha 9; Bereishit Rabbah 40:6.

At the moment of birth, it is "sworn in" to be a *tzadik*: *Nidah* 30b; *cf. Chidushei Agadot ad loc.*; *cf. Midrash Tanchuma, Pekudei* 3.

The function of this oath is to "satiate" it: *Sefer HaSichot 5704*, p. 50 and other sources cited in *Tanya beTziruf Ma'arei Mekomot etc.*, ch. 1, #3-13

Tet

"Its good is hidden within it": *Cf. Zohar* 2:230a.

The letter *chet* symbolizes the union of groom and bride: *Sha'arei Gan Eden, Sha'ar HaOtiot, Tet* 1:1

The eight synonyms for "beauty" in Hebrew: שפר, יפי, טוב, פאר, נוי, הוד, הדר, חן.

Personified in Torah by Rebecca...: Genesis 24:16

And Bat Sheva: 2 Samuel 11:2

"And G-d saw the light was good": Genesis 1:4

"Good, to be hidden for the *tzadikim* in the future to come": *Chagigah* 12a; *Y. Berachot* 8:6; *Bereishit Rabbah* 3:6; Rashi on Genesis 1:4

"And where did He hide it?—In the Torah...": See *Keter Shem Tov* 84; *Shemot Rabbah* 35:1: "in the garden of Eden."

"There is no good other than Torah": *Avot* 6:3

The "Time to Come": not only the "World to Come"—see their secrets in the letter *samech*.

The "Time to Come" refers...to each and every generation: *Cf. Keter Shem Tov* 84.

"And your people are all *tzadikim*": Isaiah 60:21

"In the beginning G-d created the heavens and the earth": Genesis 1:1

G-d's "hidden Name" in Creation: *Zohar Chadash* 8a; sources cited in *Sefer HaArachim*, vol. 1, col. 644

***Tzadikim*, who are called "good":** as in the verse, "Say of the *tzadik*—how good!" (Isaiah 3:10)

"In the world yet out of the world" simultaneously: *Cf. Tzava'at HaRibash* 84.

"There is none other besides Him": Deuteronomy 4:35

"And she saw him that he was good": Exodus 2:2

Rashi quotes: *ad loc.*

The words of the Midrash: *Sotah* 12a

The early *Masorah***:** *Minchat Shai ad loc.*

Yesod...symbolizing peace: *Zohar* 3:115b

"The Holy One, Blessed be He, found no vessel that could hold blessing for Israel other than peace": *Uktzin* 3:12

"...and He shall grant you peace": Numbers 6:26

An ever more potent "vessel" to receive "additional" blessing: as the sages have said, "The addition of G-d is greater than the original" (*Bereishit Rabbah* 61:4).

"And they shall place My Name...": Numbers 6:27

"Peace," the Name of G-d: *Shabbat* 10b; *BaMidbar Rabbah* 11:7

Our Sages interpret this word to be composed of two elements: *Chagigah* 12a

"Days of the heavens on earth": Deuteronomy 11:21

"He makes peace in the heavens": Job 25:2

"Michael, the angel of water and Gabriel, the angel of fire do not extinguish one another": *Midrash Tanchuma, VaYigash* 6

Within this aspiration...the new world...nurtures: This new world is alluded to in the verse, "New heavens and new earth" (Isaiah 66:22).

"Who can give pure from impure, only One": Job 4:4

Becomes manifest as ever present: that is, when one sees all the diverse phenomena of the world as necessary means to its ultimate fulfillment, and relates to each phenomenon in that light.

The root of the word עולם, "world," means "concealment": *Likutei Torah* 3:37d, a.f.

"This is My Name forever": Exodus 3:15. The original sense of "world" in Hebrew is "forever."

"This is My Name to conceal": *Kidushin* 71a; Rashi *ad loc.*; *v.* also *Pesachim* 50a; Rashi to Exodus 3:15

"...and He shall grant you peace. And they shall place My Name...": Numbers 6:26-27

The word שלום, "peace," itself is a Name of G-d: Cf. *Shabbat* 10b; *VaYikra Rabbah* 9:9; *BaMidbar Rabbah* 11:7; *Zohar* 3:10b, 176b; *Tikunei Zohar*, introduction (3a).

The essential property of the Name is mercy: *Zohar* 1:251b, 3:11b, 65a

"Behold the maiden is pregnant and will bear a son...": Isaiah 7:14.
הנה העלמה ("Behold the maiden") numerically equals הרה ("is pregnant"), thus indicating that the state of pregnancy is innate and essential throughout seemingly virgin nature.

Whose account in (the beginning of) Torah contains 52 words...: Genesis 1:1-4

As in the story of the Divine sign: Exodus 7:10

In the story of the Garden of Eden: Genesis 3

When rectified: i.e., when properly channeled and utilized for holy purposes.

The snake...was intended to be the "great servant of man": *Cf. Sanhedrin* 59b.

The snake is pregnant for seven years: *Bechorot* 8a

"You shall not guess": Leviticus 19:26

"For there is no guessing in Jacob": Numbers 23:23

"Give truth to Jacob": Michah 7:20

Joseph, the most essential "extension" of Jacob's property of simple truth: One's children are considered "extensions" or "manifestations" of one's attributes. Joseph was the most essential extension of Jacob, as indicated in the verse (Genesis 37:2): "These are the progeny of Jacob: Joseph...," and Jacob's most essential property was truth, as stated in the text.

"For a man like me is surely able to guess": Genesis 44:15

We are taught that "Mashiach" equals "snake": *Cf. Erkei HaKinuim, s.v.* משיח.

He will kill the evil snake and thereupon be given the "princess": *Tikunei Zohar* 21 (43a), 13 (29b); see *Likutei Moharan* 1:1.

The consciousness of "Divine Inspiration" in prayer: *Likutei Torah* 4:35c

The twelve tribes of Israel are referred to as staffs: Numbers 30:2

Each tribe represents a unique "sense": *Sefer Yetzirah* 5:3 ff

The breastplate worn by the High Priest: Exodus 28:15

A secret Name of G-d, concealed within the breastplate: Rashi to Exodus 28:30; *cf. Yoma* 73b.

Its purpose was to rectify the property of judgement: *Zevachim* 88b; *Erachin* 16a

The Shechinah...the third partner in the act of conception: *Nidah* 31a

As the Sages say in reference to the bed of our father Jacob: *Shabbat* 55b; Rashi *ad loc.*; *cf.* Rashi to Genesis 49:4.

In the reading of the Torah this is the secret of traditional Torah cantillation: See *Likutei Torah* 5:1c

The forms of the signs...resemble different positions and motions of a...snake: *Sefer HaMalchut*

The wisdom concealed in the trope is superconscious: *Likutei Torah* 2:37b; *Or HaTorah, VaEira,* p. 2558, *Nach,* p. 943, a.e.; *cf. Sanhedrin* 21b: "Why were the reasons of the Torah not revealed?...."

The first eight of these nine categories are from the Written Law: *Kelim* 2; *Ma'aseh Torah* 9; *Mishneh Torah, Kelim* 1:1; *Kelalei HaTuma'ah* (Vilna *Gaon*); *Yevakesh Da'at* (R. Yom Tov Lippman Heller) 44

The ninth, glass, is an addition of the Oral Law: *Mishneh Torah, Kelim* 1:5

Job speaks of a form of glass more precious than gold: Job 28:17

"Pure olive oil": Exodus 27:20; *cf.* Rashi *ad loc.*.

The Ba'al Shem Tov's "intention for immersion in a *mikvah*": *Siddur Im Dach,* p. 315a; *Keter Shem Tov* (ed. Kehot) p. 66a; *Peri HaAretz* 3b. If one adds up all the Names used in this meditation, the total is 463.

Prophecy...is referred to as a glass pane: *Sukah* 45b, etc.

"The coarse skin": משכא דחויא: *Tikunei Zohar,* introduction (10b), 58 (92b); *Etz Chaim* 49:4; sources cited in index to *Tanya, s.v.* עור

Moses's prophecy was through the "transparent pane"...: *Yevamot* 49b

Malchut...the "lower mother": *Zohar* 3:78a

The "five kindnesses": *Zohar* 3:142a

A total number of 248 limbs: *Ohalot* 1:8

Originally Abraham was named Abram...Subsequently he was given an additional *hei*...: Genesis 11:26, 17:3-5

"Kindness to Abraham": Micah 7:20

These 248 limbs each contain a corresponding power of soul: *Ma'amarei Admur HaZaken 5562,* p. 15, a.e.

The text of the complete recitation of the *Shema*: *Tikunei Zohar* 18; *Shulchan Aruch, Orach Chaim* 61:3; *Mishnah Berurah (ad loc.)* 6,7,14

To the initial 239 words an additional nine words...are added: *Shulchan Aruch, Orach Chaim* 61

Each considered by the Sages sufficient to support the entire Torah: Faith-knowledge of G-d: *Makot* 24a; Love of Israel: *Shabbat* 31a (*cf. Chidushei Agadot ad loc.*), *Y. Nedarim* 9:14.

These first nine positive commandments: Until this point the Rambam enumerates four negative commandments, completing the nine (in the secret of the two letters את of אחד) to "one," אחד, which equals 13.

The nine months of spiritual pregnancy: *Likutei Torah* 4:85c, etc.

Certain...souls...only require six months of pregnancy: *Rosh HaShanah* 11a

Such as Moses': *Targum Yonatan* and Rashi to Exodus 2:3

Nine, in Kabbalah, represents the qualities of truth and eternity: *Sod HaShem Lireiav*, p. 88

The *teruah*...itself consists of nine short staccato sounds: *Shulchan Aruch, Orach Chaim* 590:3

The Torah-reading of the first day of *Rosh HaShanah*: Genesis 21:1-34

The *Haftorah* of the first day of *Rosh HaShanah*: 1 Samuel 1:1-2:10

Three great women were "remembered" (for pregnancy) on *Rosh HaShanah*: *Rosh HaShanah* 11a; *Berachot* 29a; *Yevamot* 64b

Serach, the daughter of Asher: *Sotah* 13a; Ramban on Numbers 26:46 says she was his step-daughter.

The level of mother: *Likutei Torah* 4:79d ff, a.f.

"There are three crowns...the crown of the goodly name ascends above them all": *Avot* 4:13

The "woman of valor": Proverbs 12:4

The "crown of her husband": Proverbs 12:4

Serach was the one to bring to her grandfather, Jacob...: *Targum Yonatan* to Genesis 46:17; Rashi to 2 Samuel 20:19; *MeAm Loez* to Genesis 45:23

"And the spirit of Jacob came to life": Genesis 45:28

For this she was blessed with eternal life: *Targum Yonatan* to Genesis 46:17; *cf. Perush Yonatan ad loc.*; *MeAm Loez* to Genesis 45:28.

Yud

Subsequent to the initial *tzimtzum*...there remains...an "impression": רשימו. *Etz Chaim*, beginning

The secret of this point...: See *BeSha'ah SheHikdimu 5672*, p. 15 ff

Point, line, surface: נקודה קו שטח: *Ma'amarei Admur HaZaken 5567*, pp. 26, 166, 236-9; cf. *Torat Chaim*, part 1, p. 65d, etc.

Point, spectrum, figure: נקודה ספירה פרצוף: Cf. *Mevo Shearim* 2:2:1; *Etz Chaim* 31:6; *Likutei Torah* 2:37d, 3:74b, 5:19d, *Imrei Binah* 74b ff; *Sha'ar HaYichud* 20, etc. See above, Introduction, section "Point, Line, Area."

"Little that holds much": *Bereishit Rabbah* 9:7; *VaYikra Rabbah* 10:9

Before the *tzimtzum*, the power of limitation was hidden: *BeSha'ah SheHikdimu 5672*, p. 20, a.e.

The ten *sefirot*: "Ten not nine, ten not eleven" (*Sefer Yetzirah* 1:4)

Ten...the number of commandments revealed by G-d to His People Israel at Sinai: Exodus 20:1-14

"Formed point": *Sefer HaMa'amarim 5659*, p. 73

A "pathway" below: All of the 32 pathways of Wisdom of *Sefer Yetzirah* are concentrated in this one lower pathway; these pathways have their counterparts in the higher dimensions of Souls and Divinity.

The 32 pathways of Wisdom of *Sefer Yetzirah*: 1:1

"The wisdom of Solomon": 1 Kings 5:10, 14, 10:4; 2 Chronicles 9:3

"...and he spoke of trees, from the cedar tree that is in Lebanon...": 1 Kings 5:13-14

This level of wisdom..."attracts" all of the "sparks" of Worlds...: as reflected in the fact that in the days of Solomon the sparks were drawn to Israel to be elevated (as in the case of the Queen of Sheba, and as is stated [2 Chronicles 9:23-24], "and all the kings of the earth sought to see Solomon...and each one brought his gift"), whereas when the Jewish people are in a state of exile, they must go to the sparks in order to elevate them. (*Ma'amarei Admur HaZaken 5563*, p. 73)

Even inanimate beings possess lifeforce: *Etz Chaim* 39:3; *Sha'ar HaYichud VeHaEmunah*, ch. 1

"The wisdom of G-d" possessed by Solomon: 1 Kings 3:28

King Solomon's...judging truly between souls: 1 Kings 3:16-28

The phrase "the wisdom of Solomon" appears three times: 1 Kings 5:10, 14, 10:4

"He who is small is big and he who is big is small": *Zohar* 3:168a; see *Likutei Diburim* 28 (p. תק"ה-1010)

זעירא...strived, and succeeded, to come to the land of Israel...: *Bava Metzia* 85a

"He suspends the earth on nothingness": Job 26:7

"In the beginning": Genesis 1:1

Three levels of Divine influx: light, life, and energy: *Sha'ar HaYichud Ve-HaEmunah,* ch. 12 in gloss; see above, Introduction, first section.

The script of every letter begins and ends with a *yud*: *Zohar* 3:290b

"There is no place empty of His Presence": *Tikunei Zohar* 91b (*Tikun* 57)

"And a place shall be for you outside of the camp...": Deuteronomy 23:13

The waste product of a higher being becomes...: *Likutei Torah* 5:5b

"And they have cast a stone at me": Lamentations 3:53

"The left hand pushes away and the right hand draws near": *Sotah* 47a

In Hebrew, "to thank" implies...: See *Siddur im Dach,* p. רדש

Malchut (kingdom) as personified by King David: *Zohar* 1:72a, 87a, 3:21a, 45b

דוד, which is related to the root of ידיד: See Isaiah 5:1

"Giving one's hand" to another is interpreted...to mean promising to follow his advice: Ezra 10:19

King David empathized and related...to every Jewish soul: *Midrash Tehilim* 18:1

King David possessed a close friend, Chushai: 2 Samuel 15:32 ff

"You open Your hand and satisfy every living being with favor": Psalms 145:16

ידך, "Your Hand," is interpreted as יודך, "Your [power of] *yud*": *Tikunei Zohar,* introduction (7b)

"The 'companion,' son of the 'companion' shall come...": *Menachot* 53a

G-d created the world with one Hand, whereas the Temple is built with two hands: *Ketubot* 5a

According to one supposition...: *Yoma* 19a, *Kidushin* 23b; cf. *Nedarim* 35b.

"These and these are the words of the Living G-d": *Eruvin* 13b; *Gitin* 6b

The...significance of the *yud*...the power of Divine Thought...: *Sha'ar HaYichud VehaEmunah,* ch. 4

Rashi states: on Job 1:5

"Israel ascended in thought": See *Bereishit Rabbah* 1:4; *Tikunei Zohar* 6 (and other sources cited in note to *Likutei Torah* 2:16c).

"The smallest of peoples": Deuteronomy 7:7

"The tenth shall be Holy for G-d": Leviticus 27:32

"Through ten utterances was the world created": *Avot* 5:1

The ten utterances of creation are considered to be "mundane words": *Zohar* 3:149b; *Likutei Torah* 2:25d; *Or HaTorah, Chayei Sarah* p. 129a ff

On the very first day of creation, ten things were created: *Chagigah* 12a

At...twilight of the sixth day...ten things were created: *Avot* 5:6

The ten generations from Adam to Noah...from Noah...Abraham: *Avot* 5:2-3

His great knowledge of the workings of nature: astrology: *Shabbat* 156a; author of *Sefer Yetzirah*: *Zohar* 2:37b

"And He took him outside": Genesis 15:5

"Outside the universe": *Bereishit Rabbah* 44:12

When given the additional *hei* to his Name at circumcision: Genesis 17:5

"Ten Kings ruled over the whole world": *Pirkei d'Rabbi Eliezar* 11

"Ten nations were given to Abraham": Genesis 18:31; v. *Bereishit Rabbah* 44:23

"Ten pure animals are explicitly mentioned in Torah": *Bamidbar Rabbah* 21:16; 20:5

"Ten categories of forbidden magical practice in Torah": *Zohar* 2:30b

"The ten battles of Joshua": *Ma'aseh Torah* 244 in the name of Rabeinu Bachya

"Ten essential limbs of the body": *Ma'aseh Torah* 142

Ten general categories: Deuteronomy 23:10-11; *Kidushin* 4:1; *Tikunei Zohar*, introduction (beginning) (this is the source for the listing given here); *Likutei Torah* 4:44a; *Likutei Sichot*, vol. 20, p. 385 n40

"With ten trials was our father Abraham tried...": *Avot* 5:3

A *minyan* is the quorum of ten men required for Jewish communal prayer: *Megilah* 23b

Jews upon gathering together express as many spiritual powers as their number of permutations: *Likutei Moharan* 2:8:6

"Ten synonyms for prayer": *Devarim Rabbah* 2:1

"Ten synonyms for song": *Pesachim* 117a; *Zohar* 1:23b (synonyms for praise in the book of Psalms)

"Ten cardinal songs sung through history": *Yalkut Shimoni, Yehoshua* 20; *Mechilta, Beshalach* 15:1; *Shir HaShirim Rabbah* 6:10; *Midrash Tanchuma, Beshalach* 10

"Ten martyrs of Israel": *Eichah Rabbah* 2:5

"Ten spiritual functions of the heart": *Yalkut Shimoni* 2:174

Ten miracles were performed for our fathers in the Temple: *Avot* 5:5

"Ten Days of Repentance": *Abudraham, Seder Tefilat Rosh HaShanah*

The High Priest...would pronounce the Ineffable Name...ten times: *Yoma* 39b

Miraculously, open space would appear around each prostrating individual: *Avot* 5:5

"Ten names of *Ruach HaKodesh*": *Avot d'Rabi Natan* 34:8

"Ten are called 'the man of G-d'": *Yalkut Shimoni*, Samuel 91

"Ten verses of the Kingdom of G-d...": *Rosh HaShanah* 32a

"Ten synonyms for *teshuvah* corresponding to the ten days of *teshuvah*": Rashi on Isaiah 1:16

Kaf

The Divine potential must remain as an ever-present cause...: *Sha'ar HaYichud VeHaEmunah*, ch. 1

The power to actualize potential ever present within the actualized: See *Etz Chaim* 47:2 (end); *Shever Yosef* 14; *Likutei Torah* 3:47a, a.e.

This should be one's initial awareness upon awakening: *Benei Yissachar*

To place palm on palm upon awakening, before the recitation of *Modeh Ani*: See *Sefer HaMa'amarim 5710*, p. 244

"I thank You....": Morning Liturgy

In bowing one totally nullifies one's consciousness in the presence of the King: "bowing" here means השתחואה, prostration.

"You have placed Your Palm over me": Psalms 139:5

"The formation of the Palms of the Holy One Blessed Be He": *Pesikta Rabati* 47

"He suspended the mountain over them as a barrel": *Shabbat* 88a

The Divine motivation...was actually one of greatest love for Israel: *Likutei Torah* 4:22a, a.e.

Forming the image of a crown lying on its side: R. Yitzchak Isaac of Homil, *Ma'amar HaShiflut VeHaSimchah*

The natural perspective of man...is perfectly tenable: *Likutei Sichot*, vol. 10, p. 181

The highest of the spheres...: *Mishneh Torah, Yesodei HaTorah* 3:1 ff

This continuous heavenly motion symbolizes prostration to the Divine Presence...revealed in the west: *Sanhedrin* 91b; *Bava Batra* 25a; *cf. Tanya*, ch. 42 in gloss

"When I see Your heavens, the work of Your fingers...": Psalms 8:4-5

The three properties of the superconscious: See above, Introduction, sections "Form, Name, Number" and "Past, Present, Future."

"The three heads of the crown": See above, Introduction, sections "Form, Name, Number" and "Past, Present, Future."

"Wait for me a little": Job 36:2

Every Jewish soul possesses the...power to decree its will upon reality: *Likutei Sichot*, vol. 4, p. 1188 ff, a.f.

"Make His Will as your will...": *Avot* 2:4

The three levels present within G-d's Infinite Light: See *Sefer HaArachim*, vol. 3, col. 158 ff, 170 ff

Each individual soul...linked...to a specific letter of the primordial Torah: "Israel (ישראל) stands for יש ששים רבוא אותיות לתורה, 'there are 600,000 letters in the Torah' " (*Megaleh Amukot* 186).

G-d learns Torah, as it were, "for its own sake": See R. Hillel of Poritch, end of *Hakdamah LeDerech Chaim*.

"I will exalt You": Psalms 145:1

"The toil of your palms you shall eat, happy are you...": Psalms 128:2

Mashiach will..."force" all people to abide by the Divine statutes of Torah: *Mishneh Torah, Melachim* 10:4

When light is reduced, expression of power increases: See *Ma'amar Ner Chanukah 5713*. The basic idea is that שם ס"ג is identified with כח העצם and שם מ"ה with כח האור. These two are not revealed together; when one decreases, the other increases.

"Who is the mighty one? He who suppresses his evil inclination": *Avot* 4:1

Itkafia: *Zohar* 2:128b; *Tanya*, ch. 27, ch. 39; *Likutei Torah* 1:3a, 3:65c; *Sefer HaMa'amarim 5710*, p. 111 ff

"And Moses entered into the cloud and ascended to the mountain": Exodus 24:18

Which becomes ever stronger and pronounced in times of: *Menachot* 53b

"Who will ascend to the mountain of G-d...": Psalms 24:3-4

"A full palm of satisfaction": Ecclesiastes 4:6

"Israel sustains her Father in Heaven": *Shir HaShirim Rabbah* 1; *Yalkut Shimoni, Pekudei* 418; *Zohar* 3:7b

"Great satisfaction is before Me, for I have spoken and My Will has been done": *Sifrei* to Numbers 28:8

"Behold on Palms I have engraved you": Isaiah 49:16

"We shall lift up our hearts to the clouds to G-d in heaven": Lamentations 3:41

Joseph was sold by his brothers for twenty pieces of silver: Genesis 37:28

With which they purchased shoes: *Targum Yonatan* to Genesis 37:28

Shoes...represent enclothement in lower physical desires and passions: *Zohar* 3:180a; *Likutei Torah* 5:43d

"For the place that you are standing on is Holy earth": Exodus 3:5

Is interpreted as referring to...stripping off physicality: *Zohar* 3:180a

The maximal permissible height of a *sukah* is twenty cubits: *Sukah* 1:1

The maximal vertical range of eyesight...is twenty cubits: *Sukah* 2a

The *sukah*...symbolizes the clouds of glory: *Shulchan Aruch, Orach Chaim* 625; see *Likutei Sichot, Emor 5749*

The value of a *shekel*...is twenty *gerah*: Exodus 30:13; Leviticus 27:25; Numbers 3:47, 18:16

The first time: Exodus 30:13

The inner secret...of this donation is to atone for both the sale of Joseph and the sin of the golden calf: *Bereishit Rabbah* 84:17; *Y. Shekalim* 2:3; *Midrash Tanchuma, Ki Tisa* 10

Ten *gerah*...corresponding to the ten levels of his soul: *Likutei Sichot*, vol. 3, p. 927-8

The second time: Leviticus 27:25

The third time: Numbers 3:47

The fourth time: Numbers 18:16

Abraham...who corresponds to love: *Tikunei Zohar*, introduction (10b); *Zohar* 1:47a

Jacob...who corresponds to mercy: *Zohar* 1:157b; 3:137b

Isaac...who corresponds to...fear and awe of G-d: *Tikunei Zohar*, introduction (10b); *Zohar* 3:302a

Twenty is the age when a Jewish male is enlisted to serve in the army: Numbers 1:3

Twenty is the time to begin to "pursue" a livelihood: *Avot* 5:22

"The toil of your palms you shall eat...": Psalms 128:2

The period of twenty years that Jacob worked for Laban: Genesis 31:38

The *sefirah* of *keter*..."develops" into two "twin" *partzufim*: See *Mystical Concepts*, ch. 8.

The 613 commandments of the Torah together with the seven Rabbinic injunctions...total 620: *Tanya*, ch. 53; *Igeret HaKodesh* 29

The seven Rabbinic injunctions: These are initially contained within the secret of the 613, but thereafter revealed explicitly by the Sages, each one in its pre-ordained time, relative to the Divine Providence revealed in the events of Jewish history.

Each letter corresponds to the ultimate root of one...mitzvah: As explicated in the book *Otzar HaChaim*

"Which are to your companion": Exodus 20:14

The Sages of Israel are referred to as the "companions" of G-d: *Menachot* 53a

Lamed

In Kabbalah and *Chassidut* these...are developed and explained in depth: *Zohar* 1:338a, 2:153a, 3:161b; *Likutei Torah* 3:22c, 5:33d, etc.

"And Adam knew his wife Eve": Genesis 4:1

Adam and Eve...represent teacher and pupil: *Cf. Likutei Moharan* 2:91

"A tower soaring in air": *Chagigah* 15b; *Sanhedrin* 106b and Rashi *ad loc.*; *Zohar* 2:91a; *Zohar Chadash, Shir HaShirim* (81a); *Emek HaMelech* 1:40; sources cited in *Sefer HaArachim, Lamed*, col. 135 ff

Three hundred...laws relate to the secret of this "flying tower": *Chagigah* 15b; *Sanhedrin* 106b

The Ba'al Shem Tov would place the palm of his hand...: told in relation to the Shpoler Zeide (*HaYom Yom*, 14 *Tevet*)

The only letter...that ascends above the "upper bound": *Zohar* 3:246b

"A tower soaring in air": See note above, Introduction to *Lamed*.

Lamed...is the secret of the rectification of the...imagination: See below, in the discussion of the Souls-dimension of Name.

"The mother of all life": Genesis 3:20

The lamed is referred to as the "biggest" of letters: as is seen in the fact that it is referred to as a "flying *tower*."

Rabbi Avraham Abulafia explains: *Imrei Shefer*

"One who learns in order to teach...One who learns in order to do": *Avot* 4:5

"Touching yet not touching": See above, the introduction to the *chet*

The "higher Shechinah": See *Zohar* 3:296a; *Tikunei Zohar* 55 (89a).

"In every place that you find the greatness of G-d, there you will find His humility": *Megilah* 31a

"Private domain": *Shabbat* 1:1; this term in Hebrew (רשות היחיד) can also be translated: "the domain of uniqueness."

"And after him was Shamgar son of Anat...": Judges 3:31

The Philistines, the animal desire to cast off yoke: *Torah Or* 61cd

Directing...the...animal soul...implies: *Likutei Sichot*, vol. 16, pp. 556-7, quoting Rabbi Shneur Zalman of Liadi

Learning Torah...is the most all-inclusive of mitzvot: *Mishneh Torah*, *Talmud Torah* 3:3; *Hilchot Talmud Torah* (R. Shneur Zalman of Liadi) 4:2

"Learning Torah is equal to them all": *Shabbat* 127a

Learning Torah...rectifies one's...imagination: *Likutei Moharan* 1:54

"Submission, separation, sweetening": See above, Introduction, section "Submission, Separation, Sweetening" and notes thereon.

"He who learns in order to teach is granted the ability to learn and teach...": *Avot* 4:6

Teaching a beginner...is the greatest of all "deeds": *Hilchot Talmud Torah* (R. Shneur Zalman of Liadi) 4:4

"And all of your children are 'students of G-d'...": Isaiah 54:13

"Don't read 'your children' rather 'your builders' ": *Berachot* 64a

Ever conscious of G-d's continual giving of the Torah: *Sefer HaMa'amarim—Kuntresim*, vol. 1, p. 36-38

"New heavens and new earth": Isaiah 65:17

A "full month" possesses thirty days: as opposed to a "defective" month, which possesses only twenty-nine.

The moon...symbolizes the *sefirah* of *malchut*: *Zohar Chadash* 40a

"King David is alive forever": *Rosh HaShanah* 25b

***Malchut* is referred to as the "lower mother":** *Zohar* 3:78a

"*Malchut* is acquired with thirty attributes": *Avot* 6:6

Judah, the ancestor of David: Genesis 38:29 and Ruth 4:18-22

"Your *malchut* is the *malchut* of all worlds": Psalms 145:13

***Malchut* is identified with the woman in Israel:** *Tikunei Zohar* 22 (68a)

The "worth" assigned to an adult woman: Leviticus 21:4

Thirty such *tzadikim*: *Chulin* 92a

Thirty-six: *Sanhedrin* 97b

The *tzadik* corresponds to the *sefirah* of *yesod*: *Zohar* 3:11b

Thus affecting the union of *yesod* and *malchut*: *Zohar* 3:46a

The Midrash correlates the thirty days of the month...: *Shemot Rabbah* 15:26

Our Sages refer to the generation of Solomon as the "full moon": *Shemot Rabbah* 15:26; *Zohar* 1:225b

Rechavam, in whose generation the Kingdom of Israel was severed: 1 Kings 12

King Yoshiyahu...was tragically killed in war: 2 Kings 23:29

"...the spirit of our nostrils, the *mashiach* of G-d": Lamentations 4:20

The "thirty attributes" of *malchut*...: *Etz Chaim* 30:2, 44:2; *Likutei Torah* 4:69a; *Igeret HaKodesh* 20; note 30 in English translation *ad loc.*

Kingship...is in truth manifest at all levels of kingship...: *Tanya*, ch. 52

Kingship at the level of *Atzilut* is the Divine "I": *Zohar* 3:276a; *Tikunei Zohar* 26 (71b)

"I shall reign": 1 Kings 1:5

Thirty groups of *tzadikim*: *Sifrei* to Deuteronomy 11:21

Malchut of *Atzilut* is referred to as the "body" of all Jewish souls: *Zohar Chadash* 56b; *Tikunei Zohar* 47 (84b)

Mem

The abyss in the account of creation: Genesis 1:2

This flow is from *keter*...to *chochmah*: *Sha'ar HaYichud* 1; commentary of R. Hillel of Poritch *ad loc.*

"The flowing stream, the source of wisdom": Proverbs 18:4

There are thirteen channels of flow from the superconscious source to the beginning of consciousness: known as the א תקוני דיקנא ג״י, the "thirteen rectifications of the beard"; see *Zohar* 3:131a ff, 2:176b ff.

The Thirteen Attributes of Mercy revealed to Moses at Sinai: Exodus 34:6-7

The thirteen principles of Torah exegesis: *Sifra*, beginnning

Thirteen *mems*...appear in the "primordial air": *Emek HaMelech, Sha'ar Avir HaKadmon* 5

"Waters that have no end": *Yevamot* 121a

"He retains kindness for thousands of generations": Exodus 34:7

Havayah—the "Name of Mercy": *Zohar* 3:11a, a.f.

"Fountain of life": Psalms 36:10; Proverbs 10:11, 13:14, 14:27, 16:22

"The mother of all life": Genesis 3:20

The continual recreation of the universe, from nothing to something: *Sha'ar HaYichud VeHaEmunah* 1

"Formation": which occurs 40 days after conception.

Crucial moments of life when one's root...shines with special brilliance: as on one's birthday (*Y. Rosh HaShanah* 3:8)

That level of soul which is conscious of self: the *nefesh-ruach-neshamah-chayah* levels

That level of soul which is unconscious of self: the *yechidah* level

"Who can count the dust of Jacob and the number of 'conceptions' of Israel": Numbers 23:10

"Be fruitful and multiply": Genesis 1:28

Giving birth to a son and a daughter: *Mishneh Torah, Ishut* 9:4; *Shulchan Aruch, Even HaEzer* 1:5

The power of reproduction of Jewish souls is referred...as "the power of Infinity": *Derech Mitzvotecha*, p. 4

"The earth will be filled with the knowledge of G-d...": Isaiah 11:9

Even the closed final *mem* will become revealed: *Derech Chaim*, end

"To increase reign and peace without end": Isaiah 9:6

"Waters that have no end": *Shulchan Aruch, Even HaEzer* 17:32

"And the Spirit of G-d was hovering over the waters": Genesis 1:2

"The spirit of G-d," the soul of the *Mashiach*: *Bereishit Rabbah* 2:5; *VaYikra Rabbah* 14:1

Even voluntary transgressions are transformed into actual merits: *Yoma* 86b

"In the place that *ba'alei teshuvah* stand, consummate *tzadikim* cannot stand": *Berachot* 34b; *Sanhedrin* 99a; *Zohar* 1:39a, 129b, 2:106b, 3:16b

"And he shall cling to his wife": Genesis 2:24

Water...continuously seeks to descend to the lowest plane: *Tanya*, ch. 4

"Stretching the dry land over the waters": Psalms 136:6; Liturgy, morning blessings

For every property on the "side of good" there exists a counterpart on the "side of evil": *Zohar* 3:47b; *Tanya*, ch. 6, a.f.

"One opposite the other has G-d made": Ecclesiastes 7:14

"Evil waters": 2 Kings 2:19

The story of Moses who healed the bitter waters in the desert: Exodus 15:22-26

The Prophet Elisha who healed the deadly waters of Jericho: 2 Kings 2:19-22

"Living waters": Genesis 26:19; Leviticus 14:5, a.f.

The seventy-two three-letter Divine Names of Kabbalah: These are derived from the juxtaposition of three consecutive verses in Exodus (14:19-21) that contain 72 letters each. See *Pesikta Zutrata* on Exodus 14:21; Rashi to *Sukah* 45a (*s.v.* אני); Ibn Ezra to Exodus 33:21; *Sefer HaBahir* (ed. Kaplan) 110; *Zohar* 2:270, 3:151b; *Pardes Rimonim* 21:5; *Raziel HaMalach* (ed. Margolies) p. 54 ff; *Chayei Olam HaBah*; *Sefer HaCheshek*; *Sha'arei Kedushah*, part 4.

All of nature initially hides the presence of the Creator: as indicated in the fact that the word "nature" (טבע) is cognate to "submerge" or "drown" (לטבוע) and the word "world" (עולם) is cognate to "conceal" or "hide" (העלם).

"A sun and shield are *Havayah Elokim*": Psalms 84:12; see *Sha'ar HaYichud VeHaEmunah,* ch. 4

"You are all beautiful my beloved one, there is no blemish in you": Song of Songs 4:7

"Abraham, my lover": Isaiah 41:8

The innate love of G-d...is compared to water: *Kuntres HaAvodah,* ch. 4

"There is no water except Torah": *Bava Kama* 17a

"G-d looked into the Torah and created the world": *Zohar* 1:134a

"The world is built by kindness": Psalms 89:3

"Oh! all who are thirsty go to water": Isaiah 55:1

The two *mems*...refer to..."the open saying" and "the closed saying": *Shabbat* 104a

The first verse of Creation...is the "closed saying"...: *Derech Chaim,* end

"And G-d said, 'Let there be light' ": Genesis 1:3

The "open saying" corresponds to the revealed dimension of Torah...: *Likutei Sichot,* vol. 2, p. 611; sources cited in *Sefer HaArachim, Mem,* col. 194 n46

"The Glory of G-d is to conceal things": Proverbs 25:2

"The glory of kings is to investigate things": Proverbs 25:2

"And the rain was upon the earth for forty days and forty nights": Genesis 7:12

Throughout their first ten generations of existence...: *Avot* 5:2

The very same waters that flooded the earth...simultaneously cleansed the earth of the evil influences of man: *Torah Or* 8c; *Torat Shmuel 5627,* p. 7

Transition from a...state of impurity...to a state of purity...is through the means of immersion in a *mikvah*: Leviticus 11:32, 36, ch. 14-16, etc.

A minimum of forty seah of water: *Mikvaot* 1:7

"Found favor in the eyes of G-d": Genesis 6:8

Ten of the twelve spies that Moses...: Numbers 14:33-34

The first forty days of pregnancy culminate with "the formation of the fetus": *Bechorot* 21a

"...in the number—forty": Deuteronomy 25:2-3

That number which is "in" forty, i.e. thirty-nine: *Makot* 22a

The number of categories of work forbidden on Shabbat: *Shabbat* 7:2

Moses ascended the mountain and remained there for forty days and forty nights: Exodus 24:18

The subsequent two periods of forty days that he spent on the mountain: Rashi to Deuteronomy 9:18

The Exodus, the birth of the collective Soul of Israel: Ezekiel 16 with standard commentaries; *Torah Or* 55a, a.e.

The counting of the *Omer* during this period: See *Likutei Torah* 2:35a, etc.

The sin of the golden calf: Exodus 31:18ff

Maimonides...enumerates forty generations from Moses to Rav Ashi: *Mishneh Torah*, Introduction

Moses ascended the mountain...for a second period of forty days: Exodus 32:30

Prayer is...the service of the soul in its "run" to G-d: *Torah Or* 1d, a.e.

At the end of this period...: Exodus 34:1-2

Tablets of *ba'alei teshuvah*...: *HaYom Yom*, 17 *Tamuz*

Moses ascended the mountain for a third, final, period of forty days: Exodus 34:2-9

The entire month of Elul is called "the month of mercy": *Sefer HaMa'amarim 5700*, p. 155, a.e.

The forty-cubit height of the opening to the Temple Hall: *Midot* 3:7

"Open to Me an opening as the point of a needle and I will open to you an opening as [wide as] the great entrance to the Temple Hall": See note to "Conclusion" of Introduction.

Nun

The "hidden world": "All that exists on dry land exists also in the sea" (*Chulin* 127a, etc.). Based on this statement, the sea and the dry land are taken to allude to "the hidden world" (עלמא דאיתכסיא) and "the revealed world" (עלמא דאיתגליא), respectively. These are not absolutely-defined levels of the spiritual realm, but rather relative terms that can be used to describe the relationship of various levels of spirituality to each other. In general, the "higher" realm of spirituality is "concealed" to the "lower," "revealed" realm.

Creatures of the "hidden world" lack self-consciousness: *Likutei Torah* 2:14b

The souls of Israel divide into two general categories, symbolized by fish and land animal: *Likutei Torah* 2:18b, 2:7a; *Biurei HaZohar* (Mittler Rebbe) 41c; *Sha'ar HaEmunah* 53

The leviathan and the behemot: *Likutei Torah* 2:18a ff

In the future, the...leviathan and behemot will unite in battle: *VaYikra Rabbah* 13:3

Their meat will be served as the feast for the tzadikim in the world to come: See *Bava Batra* 74b, 75a; *Midrash Tanchuma, Shemini* 7; *Targum Yonatan* on Psalms 50:10, etc.

Malchut...is represented by the sea: *Zohar* 3:58a, a.f.; *Likutei Torah* 2:14b

The moon, the symbol of King David: *Zohar* 3:287a

Upon seeing the new moon we say "David the king of Israel is alive forever": Liturgy, the Blessing over the New Moon; see *Rosh HaShanah* 25a; *Zohar* 192b

When malchut descends...it is symbolized by the earth: *Zohar* 3:243b; *Likutei Torah* 2:14b

Nun means "kingdom," and in particular, "the heir to the throne": Rashi to Psalms 72:17; cf. *Likutei Moharan* 1:1.

"As long as the duration of the sun his name shall rule": Psalms 72:17

One of the names of Mashiach is Yinon: *Sanhedrin* 98b

Mashiach is also referred to as..."the miscarriage": *Sanhedrin* 96b

The life and teachings of the Ba'al Shem Tov: See *HaTamim*, p. 14 ff; *Likutei Diburim* 5:27-30 (pp. 272-278)

The verse...with which the Rambam concludes his Code of Jewish Law: *Mishneh Torah, Melachim* 12:5

"For the earth will be filled with the knowledge of G-d...": Isaiah 11:9

Two distinct types of servant of G-d: *Shabbat* 104a

The secret Divine Name, אום: See note to the Worlds-dimension of the Name of the letter *mem*, above.

אום, related to the coming of the Mashiach: See the *piut* for *hakafot*, אום אני חומה.

The first thirteen letters of the alef-beit...correspond to lights...: As explained in the writings of the Arizal, the first thirteen letters correspond to the "thirteen rectifications of the *dikna* of *Arich Anpin*," whereas the last nine letters correspond to the "nine rectifications of the *dikna* of *Z'eir Anpin*." And relative to each other, *Arich Anpin* is light and *Z'eir Anpin* is vessel.

The *mitzvah* of bringing first fruits to the Temple: Deuteronomy 26:2

The thousand lights which fill the vessel: referring to the thousand lights that Moses received at Mt. Sinai

The experience of woman...in marriage: *Kidushin* 7a

The secret of perfect marriage: *Zohar* 2:176a ff

The more humble and selfless one is...so does one's vessel invert concavely into oneself...: *Likutei Torah* 5:45a ff

Humility is the vessel necessary for receiving true insight into G-d's Will: *Pelach HaRimon* 1:19a

King David was the "master" of *halachah*: *Sanhedrin* 93b; On King David's humility, see *Sotah* 10b, etc.

Hillel: *Eruvin* 13b

Rabbi Yosef Karo: *Shem HaGedolim, Sefarim, s.v. Beit Yosef*

Moses was chosen by G-d to be His faithful servant: as he is called in the liturgy of the Shabbat-morning *Amidah*: "Moses shall rejoice with the gift of his portion, for You have called him 'faithful servant.' "

Moses was chosen...over Korach: Numbers 16

"And the man Moses was the most humble of all men...": Numbers 12:3

"The bent over faithful one" belongs to this world...: Rashi to *Shabbat* 104a

The Divine "cloud" (of glory): See Exodus 16:10

"Above without end and below without bound": *Tikunei Zohar* 57; *Zohar Chadash, Yitro* (34c); *Sefer HaMa'amarim 5666*, p. 165 ff; *Sefer HaMa'marim 5710*, p. 132 ff

"With all of your might": Deuteronomy 6:5

"Moses shall rejoice with the gift of his portion...": Liturgy, Shabbat morning *Amidah*

"G-d, the faithful King": *Shabbat* 119b; *Zohar* 3:185b

"The servant of the king is (as) the king": *Shavuot* 47b; *Bereishit Rabbah* 16:5; *Midrash Tanchuma, Tzav* 13

"Behold, he comes with the clouds of heaven": Daniel 7:13

Some have the custom of saying נאמן מלך ל־א before reciting...: when reciting *Shema* alone. *Shulchan Aruch* 61:3, in *Mapah*; *Shuchan Aruch HaRav* 61:4

"Hear O Israel...G-d is One": Deuteronomy 6:4

On the fifth day of creation fish were created: Genesis 1:20

"Be fruitful and multiply and fill the waters in the seas": Genesis 1:20-22

Kosher land animals and birds must be slaughtered according to *hala-chah*: *Chulin* 28a (based on Deuteronomy 12:21)

Kosher fish do not require slaughtering: *Chulin* 27b (based on Numbers 11:22)

Fish reflect the kindness...of a "previous" world...: *cf. Sha'arei Gan Eden*, introduction.

The..."metamorphosis" of their...Divine "sparks"...elevated through the eating and digestive process of the *tzadik*: *Tanya*, ch. 7

"May his name endure forever...": Psalms 72:17

This Psalm relates...to...the *Mashiach*: Ibn Ezra to Psalms 72:1

Solomon sat on the throne of G-d: 1 Chronicles 29:23

All Jews are "sons of kings": *Shabbat* 67a; *Bava Metzia* 113b; *Zohar* 3:28a, a.e.

All Jews are "kings": *Zohar* 2:26b; *Tikunei Zohar*, Introduction

The wisdom of the land of Israel above the limitations of time: "The atmosphere of the land of Israel makes one wise (מחכים)" (*Bava Batra* 158b), and "wisdom" (חכמה) is above time. A further allusion: "The eyes of G-d are upon it [the land of Israel] from the beginning to the end of the year" (Deuteronomy 11:12), i.e., unaffected by time; the eyes allude to *chochmah*.

"The servant of the king is the king": *Shavuot* 47b; *Bereishit Rabbah* 16:5; *Midrash Tanchuma, Tzav* 13

"For 'the word of G-d' is referred to by the name 'Divine Presence'...": *Igeret HaKodesh* 25

"The word of G-d": *Zohar* 1:31a, 2:230b, 3:228a

"Lower mother": *Zohar* 3:78a

"Queen": *Zohar* 1:27b, 3:20a, 3:146a

"The word of the king is his reign": Ecclesiastes 8:4

"...The source of life from which all worlds receive...": *Tanya*, ch. 52

"The revealed world": See note above, beginning of introduction.

"And I shall dwell amongst them...": Exodus 25:8

"The mother of children": Psalms 113:9

"Congregation of Israel": *Shir HaShirim Rabbah* to Song of Songs 1:4, a.f.

As explained in the *Zohar*: *Tikunei Zohar* 26 (71b)

"And G-d will be King over all the earth...": Zechariah 14:9

Moses was drawn out of the sea...by the daughter of Pharoah: Exodus 2:10

"The fifty gates of understanding": *Rosh HaShanah* 21b; *Zohar* 2:115a, 3:216a

"And you shall sanctify the fiftieth year...": Leviticus 25:10

The "Hebrew slave" who, when not willing to part from his master: Exodus 21:6

"Forever"...is interpreted...to mean "till the Jubilee year": *Kidushin* 21b

"Who is wise? He who knows his place": cf. *Avot* 6:6

"Fifty years old to counsel": *Avot* 5:25

At the end of the book of Job, G-d confronts Job with fifty queries: Job 38, 39

Its daily experience of "the exodus from Egypt": *Tanya*, ch. 47

"Hear O Israel, the L-rd is our G-d, the L-rd is One": Deuteronomy 6:4

"To hear"...means "to understand": *Sha'ar HaYichud*, ch. 1; Commentary of R. Hillel of Poritch *ad. loc.*

"Her Husband is known in the gates": Proverbs 31:23

G-d, the "husband" of every Jewish soul, is known...by each soul...: *Zohar* 1:103ab; *Tanya*, introduction, ch. 24

מצרים, "Egypt," means "straights" or "confines": *Likutei Torah (Arizal)* to Genesis 40:1

"From my flesh I see G-d": Job 19:26. This verse is the proof-text and springboard for the many explanations of Divine phenomena in *Chassidut* based on empirical observations of the palpable world.

"And you shall count for yourselves from the day after the Sabbath...": Leviticus 23:15-16

Fifty thousand Jubilee periods...of continuous ascent of all reality...: *Sefer HaTemunah*, Introduction to *Gimel* (pp. 27-31); Commentary of Rabbi Bachya ben Asher to Numbers 10:35; *Likutei Torah* 3:52c

Samech

"Their end is enwedged in their beginning and their beginning in their end": *Sefer Yetzirah* 1:7

"The endless cycle": Ecclesiastes 3:11

G-d's Transcendent Light (*sovev kol almin*): *Zohar* 3:225a

"He is equal and equalizes small and large": *Piyut "VeChol Ma'aminim,"* Liturgy for *Rosh HaShanah*

The attribute of "equanimity" (מדת ההשתוות) as taught by the Ba'al Shem Tov: *Tzava'at HaRibash* (ed. Kehot) 2

"I place G-d before me always": Psalms 16:8

The saying of the Sages...pertains only to...: *HaYom Yom*, 30 *Sivan*

"Who is wealthy? He who is happy with his portion": *Avot* 4:1

"The wheel within the wheel": Ezekiel 1:16

"She has fallen and shall not rise, the virgin of Israel": Amos 5:2

"As I have fallen, so surely shall I rise": Michah 7:8

The initial *tzimzum* of G-d's Infinite Light: *Etz Chaim*, etc., beginning; *Mystical Concepts*, ch. 2

"Vanity of Vanities, says Kohelet...": Ecclesiastes 1:2

"The end of the matter, all has been heard...": Ecclesiastes 12:13

The impression (רשימו) of Divine Light "left over" within the vacuum: *Etz Chaim*, etc., beginning; *Mystical Concepts*, ch. 2

The "Soul of the universe": cf. *Midrash Tehilim* 103:5

"The *tzadik* is the foundation of the world": Proverbs 10:25

"All of your nation are *tzadikim*, forever they will inherit the earth": Isaiah 60:21

All souls are in essence equidistant (equally close) to G-d: *Tanya*, ch. 32

All "large letters" in the Bible relate to the level of Divinity: *Likutei Hagahot leSefer HaTanya*, p. 89 (quoted in *Sod HaShem Lireiav*, p. 188)

"The end of deed [rose up] in the beginning of thought": R. Shelomo Al-Kabetz, *Piyut "Lecha Dodi,"* Shabbat night liturgy

The engraved letters of the "tablets of covenant"...penetrated through the tablets "from side to side": Exodus 32:15

"Rabbi Chisda said, 'the *mem* and *samech* of the tablets stood by miracle'": *Shabbat* 104a

These two letters are the secret of the two levels of the future revelation: *Likutei Levi Yitzchak* 1, p. 5; *Sefer HaArachim, Samech*, col. 238

"The future to come" is a...higher revelation than that of "the coming world": In the writings of the Arizal it is explained that "the coming world" corresponds to the level called *Tevunah*, whereas "the future to come" corresponds to the level called *Ima Ila'ah*, which is higher.

"No eye has seen it, G-d, except Thee": Isaiah 64:3

The union of the ׳י of איש, "man", and the ׳ה of אשה, "woman": *Sotah* 17a

"Generation goes and generation comes...": Ecclesiastes 1:4

"You shall be for Me a desired earth": Malachi 3:12

"In the future G-d will make a dance for the *tzadikim*": *Ta'anit* 31a

The dance of the maidens of Israel on...the fifteenth...day of Av: *Ta'anit* 26b

Ordination...permits the student to judge independently: Deuteronomy 34:9; *Mishneh Torah, Sanhedrin* 4:1

The secret of his "hand": See discussion on the *yud*, Souls-level of its Name.

"And G-d said to Moses, 'Take unto you Joshua the son of Nun...' ": Numbers 27:18-23

"And Joshua the son of Nun was full of the spirit of wisdom...": Deuteronomy 34:9

Initially, Joshua's name was Hoshea: Numbers 13:16

The juxtaposition of the two letters ס״ע is read סמנים עשה, "make signs": *Shabbat* 104a

The teaching process begins with the contraction (*tzimtzum*) of the teacher's relatively "infinite" brilliance of mind...: *Sefer HaMa'amarim 5678*, p. 1

In the Temple service, before offering a sacrifice...: Leviticus 1:4

The secret of sacrifice in Torah is the elevation of Worlds...: *Zohar* 1:64b-65a; *Tanya*, ch. 34

"The mystery of the sacrifice ascends to the mystery of the Infinite": par. *Zohar* 1:65a

Michael..."offers" the souls of the *tzadikim*...: *Tosefot, Menachot* 110a, citing the Midrash; *Chagigah* 12b and *Chidushei Agadot* (R. Shmuel Eidels) *ad. loc.*; cf. *Bamidbar Rabbah* p. 249; *Zohar* 1:80a; *Zohar Chadash* 24b

טבע, "nature," means "to drown": *BeSha'ah SheHikdimu 5672* 278

"Though he falls he shall not be utterly cast down...": Psalms 37:24

"G-d supports all the fallen and raises up all that are bent over": Psalms 145:14

Mercy, the most essential attribute related to the Name *Havayah*: *Zohar* 3:65a

"You open Your hand...": Psalms 145:16

"Nullification in sixty" (בטול בששים): *Shulchan Aruch, Yoreh Deah* 98:1

"Sleep is one-sixtieth of death": *Berachot* 57b

"Dream is one-sixtieth of prophecy": *Berachot* 57b

"Fire is one-sixtieth of hell": *Berachot* 57b

"Honey is one-sixtieth of manna": *Berachot* 57b

"Shabbat is one-sixtieth of the World to Come": *Berachot* 57b

"Sixty ten-thousands" (ששים רבוא) of souls: *Shir HaShirim Rabbah* 6:15.

Each of these...soul-roots further divides...: *Tanya*, ch. 37

"Ones," "tens," "hundreds," "thousands," and "ten-thousands": In Hebrew there are unique terms for each of these five categories, not as in English, where only the first four categories possess unique terms.

The five levels of the soul: *Bereishit Rabbah* 14:9; *Devarim Rabbah* 2:37; *Zohar* 1:81a, 206a; *Etz Chaim* (*Shaar HaAkudim*) 5; *Sefer HaMa'amarim 5701*, p. 82 ff

King Solomon possessed sixty heroes: Song of Songs 3:7

The sixty tractates are the secret of the "sixty queens": *Shir HaShirim Rabbah* to Song of Songs 6:8

The "sixty queens": Song of Songs 6:8

"One is my dove": Song of Songs 6:9

"May G-d Bless you and guard you...": Numbers 6:24-26

The Priestly Blessing recited daily in the Temple service: *Mishneh Torah, Tefilah* 14:9

G-d's Ineffable Name...was pronounced as is written: *Mishneh Torah, Tefilah* 14:10

One does not look at the hands of the *kohanim* **while they are blessing...:** *Mishneh Torah, Tefilah* 14:7

The custom of not looking at a rainbow: *Chagigah* 16a

Thirty bones in the anatomy of each hand: *Ohalot* 1:8

In the first account of creation: Genesis 1:1-2:3

In the second account: Genesis 2:3 ff

"Which surrounds": Genesis 2:11

"And a fountain from the House of G-d shall flow forth....": Joel 4:18

Ayin

"The land which G-d your G-d seeks...": Deuteronomy 11:12

"End enwedged in beginning": *Sefer Yetzirah* 1:7

The primary revelation of supernatural Providence is in *Eretz Yisrael*: See *Igeret HaKodesh* 14

The Jew...is commanded to realize a "part"...of the sanctity of *Eretz Yisrael*...: *Likutei Sichot*, vol. 2, p. 621

The second city to be conquered by Joshua was Ai: Joshua 8:1-2

Jericho, the first city to be conquered: Joshua 6

The origin of the sense of smell is in *keter*: *Mevo Shearim*, 3:2:2-3

"Why is it called *eretz*, for it wills to do the Will of its Creator": *Bereishit Rabbah* 5:7

Sight is the first conscious sense, corresponding to the *sefirah* of *chochmah*, "wisdom": *Zohar* 1:26b; *Igeret HaKodesh* 14

Coveting is the spiritual blemish of the sight of the eye: *Likutei Moharan* 1:54

"Rise, sanctify the people...": Joshua 7:13

"The Eye of G-d is on those who fear Him": Psalms 33:18

"The Eyes of G-d are on the *tzadikim*": Psalms 34:15

Fear of G-d refers...the *sefirah* of *malchut*: *Zohar* 3:81b; 1:112ab; *Tikunei Zohar* 33 (77a), a.f.

The *sefirah* of *malchut*...likened to the woman of valor: *Zohar* 3:42b, 178b, a.e.

"The woman who fears G-d, she shall be praised": Proverbs 31:13

***Malchut* is constructed and directed by the five "mights":** *Etz Chaim* 34; *Likutei Torah* 4:31a

The "male figure": the *partzuf* of *Z'eir Anpin*

Corresponding to the six emotive attributes of the heart: primarily the sixth, *yesod* ("Foundation"), the property of truth and faithful devotion in the service of G-d (the level of *tzadikim,* in the verse "The Eyes of G-d are on the *tzadikim*")

The singular eye...possesses a hidden reference to the "ever open eye"...: עיינא פקיחא; see *Torah Or* 117a

"There is no left in the Ancient One, all is right": *Zohar* 3:129a

The three stages of service: submission, separation and sweetening: *Keter Shem Tov* (ed. Kehot) 28, 160, 302; see Introduction, section of this name.

His most fundamental...teaching in regard to "particular Divine Providence": See *Likutei Sichot,* vol. 8, p. 276 ff

The perfectly humble one (Moses): Numbers 12:3

Integrating the secrets of the Law (Divinity): See discussion of the form of the *nun.*

The days...each of which receives its...blessing from the previous Shabbat: *Zohar* 2:63b, 88a; *Cf.* also *Benei Yissachar* p. 2

Shammai says...Hillel says...: *Beitzah* 16a

"Bless G-d day by day": Psalms 68:20

"The humble shall increase joy in G-d": Isaiah 29:19

The joy of the humble in serving G-d is due to their sense of the infinite, undeserved, merit...: See R. Dov Ber of Lubavitch, *Ma'amar VeYasufu Anavim BeHavayah Simchah*

The dance of the *tzadikim* in "the future to come": *Ta'anit* 31a

The mouth...expresses the will of the "goodly" eye to connect to other souls through "goodly" speech: *Likutei Moharan* 54

"The good of eye, he shall be blessed": Proverbs 22:9

The Sages read: "he shall bless": *Sotah* 38b

"And the man Moses was very humble...": Numbers 12:3

"...in all of My house is he trustworthy": Numbers 12:7

"The humble shall increase joy in G-d": Isaiah 29:19

"Fountain of wisdom": This is the name of a book ascribed to Moses.

"There is no 'water' but Torah": *Bava Kama* 17a

"...and Israel shall dwell secure, alone the eye of Jacob...": Deuteronomy 33:28

"Behold, I give before you today blessing and curse": Deuteronomy 11:26

"Behold, I have given before you today life and good...": Deuteronomy 30:15

The initial letters of יחוד, ברכה, קדושה: *Tikunei Zohar* 70 (128a), 3rd section (140a); *Torah Or* 25a

"The good of eye, he shall be blessed": Proverbs 22:9

"Don't read 'shall be blessed' but 'shall bless' ": *Sotah* 38b

His Providence over Israel is much more apparent than that over the rest of nature: See *Igeret HaKodesh* 14

"G-d is my shepherd, I shall not lack": Psalms 23:1

The three levels of Providence discussed above: in the introduction to the *samech*

"Enclothed" in seven eyes of Providence: See in the discussion of the Number-dimension of the *zayin*.

"Your eyes are as doves": Song of Songs 1:15

The ultimate expression of their love...is their tireless gazing...: *Likutei Torah* 5:14b

"He shall never slumber nor sleep, the Guardian of Israel": Psalms 121:4

The "ever-open eye" of the "Ancient One": See the introduction to the *ayin*.

"And you shall walk in His ways": Deuteronomy 8:6, 19:9, 26:17, 30:16

The prayer of silent devotion, corresponding to...the world of Emanation: *Pri Etz Chaim, Sha'ar HaAmidah*

"Heart Above and eyes below": *Shulchan Aruch, Orach Chaim* 95:2; *Shulchan Aruch HaRav* 95:3

"He is all"..."all is He": *Likutei Diburim* 36 (p. 1322)

Noah's seventy descendants: Genesis 10 and 11

The collapse of the Tower of Babel: Genesis 11:1-9

Our sacrifice of seventy oxen during the festival of *Sukot*: Numbers 29:12-34

The innate...force...is ever being reduced while...their essence is being sustained: *Sukah* 55b

"Then will I transform to peoples a clear tongue...": Zephaniah 3:9

"The days of our years are in them seventy years...": Psalms 90:10

"G-d will answer you in the day of distress...": Psalms 20:2

To correspond to the seventy cries of a deer during labor: *Zohar* 3:249b

"Her womb is narrow": *Eruvin* 54b; *Yoma* 29a

The seventy souls of Israel, the descendants of Jacob: Exodus 1:1-5

The seventy elders upon whom descended the spirit of Moses: Numbers 11:24

The seventy Sages of the Sanhedrin, the Supreme Court of Israel: *Sanhedrin* 1:6

"Seventy wolves around a sheep": *Pesikta Rabati* 9:2; *Esther Rabbah* 10:11; *Midrash Tanchuma, Toldot* 5

On *Shmini Atzeret*...one ox...was offered: Numbers 29:35-36

One ox, symbolizing Israel: *Sukah* 55b

The "prince" of the Sanhedrin: *Horiot* 4b; *Tosefot* to *Sanhedrin* 16b

These years were given him by Adam: *Zohar* 1:91b

Adam is an acronym for םדא, דוד, חישמ, Adam, David, *Mashiach*: *Sefer HaGilgulim*, ch. 62; *Torah Or* 46d

David's seventy years were given him by Abraham...: *Zohar* 1:168a

Abraham, who lived five years less than his son Isaac: Genesis 25:7, 35:28

Jacob who lived twenty-eight years less than Abraham: Genesis 47:28, 25:7

Joseph who lived thirty-seven years less than Jacob: Genesis 50:26, 47:28

The deer cries out "seventy voices" in labor: *Zohar* 3:249b

When one completes the rectification of one of the levels of his soul: *Sha'ar HaYichudim* on the verse נפשי אויתיך בלילה

The seventy years of the Babylonian exile: 2 Chronicles 36:21

G-d possesses seventy Names: *Bamidbar Rabbah* 14:24

"...for no man shall see Me and live...and My Face shall not be seen": Exodus 33:20-23

The seventy faces of Torah: See *BaMidbar Rabbah* 13:15.

49...gates of understanding: *Rosh HaShanah* 21b

"And You have made him less just a little than G-d": Psalms 8:6

The last day of Moses' life, his 120th birthday: Deuteronomy 31:2

He achieved the fiftieth gate and perceived the "wondrous face": *Shnei Luchot HaBrit* 369ab; *Likutei Torah* 3:12a

"When wine enters in, the secret goes out": *Eruvin* 65a

The *Kiddush* on Shabbat over wine consists of seventy words: See *Sidurei HaArizal; Sha'ar HaKolel* 18:4

The birth pangs of *Mashiach*: *Sanhedrin* 98b

Pei

***Da'at* is the power of union and communication:** See *Tanya*, ch. 3; *Igeret HaKodesh* 15

"...and Adam knew his wife Eve": Genesis 4:1

"*Da'at* is concealed in the mouth": *Zohar* 2:123a

The reader must see each and every letter of the Torah scroll: *Shulchan Aruch, Orach Chaim* 139:3: "...it is forbidden to read even one letter not from what is written..."

"There is no good other than Torah": *Avot* 6:3; *Berachot* 5a

"Let there be light": Genesis 1:3

Were subsequently seen, by His "Eyes," "to be good": Genesis 1:3-4

"You are my witnesses, says G-d": Isaiah 43:10

"G-d's testimony is within you": 1 Samuel 12:5

With closed eyes...: *Berachot* 13b: "one passes his hands over his face"; Rabbi Asher (the *Rosh*), *ad. loc*: "over his eyes."

"Hear, O Israel, G-d is our G-d; G-d is one": Deuteronomy 6:4

The *ayin* of the first word...and the *dalet* of the last word...are large letters: See *Minchat Shai* to Deuteronomy 6:4.

Together they spell the word עד, "witness": *Ba'al HaTurim* to Deuteronomy 6:4

"The heart of the wise informs his mouth": Proverbs 16:23

"The words of the mouth of the wise find favor": Ecclesiastes 10:12

The "gift" to the holy mouth is grace: *Sefer Yetzirah* 4:14

"There is no 'good' other than Torah": *Avot* 6:3; *Berachot* 5a

The "male figure": the *partzuf* of *Z'eir Anpin*

The "female figure": the *partzuf* of *Malchut*

The white space within the *pei* forms a hidden *beit*: *Mishnat Soferim* (in *Mishnah Berurah* 36)

The phonetic group, בומ"פ, the letters of the lips (the labials): *Sefer Yetzirah* 2:3

"All exiles are called by the name Egypt for they cause distress to Israel": *Vayikra Rabbah* 13:4

"Behold the people of the Children of Israel are more...": Exodus 1:10

"But the more they afflicted them the more they multiplied": Exodus 1:12

"You have broken the teeth of the wicked": Psalms 3:8

The soul is called מדבר, "a speaker": *Torah Or* 3d; *Sefer HaMa'amarim 5703*, p. 162, a.f.

Onkelos: the standard Aramaic translation of the Pentateuch, written by the Roman convert, Onkelos

"...and man became a living soul": Genesis 2:7

The thirty-two teeth of the mouth actually correspond...: *Ma'marei Admur HaZaken 5562*, p. 139 , a.e.

The thirty-two Pathways of Wisdom: *Sefer Yetzirah* 1:1

The thirty-two times G-d's Name *Elokim* appears in...creation: Genesis 1:1-2:3

"You have made all of them with wisdom": Psalms 104:24

An *alef*...whose form splits into ייו: *Sidurei HaArizal*, beginning of the *Amidah*

"I will teach you wisdom": Job 33:33

"...in all of My house he is faithful...": Numbers 12:7-8

"The Divine Presence speaks from the throat of Moses": See *Zohar* 3:232a

"Eighty years old to might": *Avot* 5:25

"The death of the kiss": Deuteronomy 34:5; Rashi *ad loc.* (from *Moed Katan* 28a); *cf.* Rashi to Numbers 20:1

"He shall kiss me with the kisses of His mouth...": Song of Songs 1:2

The new...dimension of Torah that will be revealed...by *Mashiach*...: Rashi to Song of Songs 1:2

"Year," שנה, the general term for time in *Sefer Yetzirah*: 3:3 ff

"Blessed is He who said...and the world came into being...": Daily morning liturgy

Korach...speaking against the true prophet, Moses: Numbers 16

"Measure for measure": *Shabbat* 105b; *Nedarim* 32a; *Sanhedrin* 90a, etc.

The mouth of the earth opened up to swallow him...: Numbers 16:32

"Moses is true and his Torah is true": *Midrash Tanchuma, Korach* 11

The mouth of the snake in the garden of Eden: Genesis 3:1 *et seq.*

The mouth of the ass of Balaam: Numbers 22:28-30

"The power of the Jew is in his mouth": *Mechilta* and Rashi to Exodus 14:10: "they took to the art of their forefathers [prayer]"; Rashi to Numbers 20:16: "we cry out and are answered"; Rashi to Numbers 22:4 (regarding Moses): "his power is only in his mouth." *Zohar* 3:232: "Israel's power is not in eating and drinking like other nations, rather their power is in their voice."

Balak, the king of Moab, in fear of the approaching camp of Israel...: Numbers 22:4; *Rashi, ad loc.*; *Midrash Tanchuma, Balak* 3; *Bamidbar Rabbah* 20:4, *et al.*

Balaam is the evil counterpart of Moses: See *Sifrei* to Deuteronomy 34:10

Balaam...to know the moment...that G-d allows His attribute of anger to express itself daily: *Sanhedrin* 105b; *Berachot* 7a

Those days...G-d did not allow His anger to express itself at all: *Sanhedrin* 105b; *Berachot* 7a

Every negative property has its positive counterpart: Ecclesiastes 7:14: "For G-d made one opposite the other."

"There is no place void of Him": *Tikunei Zohar, Tikun* 57 (91b)

His words never leave His mouth: *Bava Metzia* 86a

For the sake of learning Torah one may leave the *sukah*: *Shulchan Aruch, Orach Chaim* 640:7; *Mishnah Berurah* 640:35

"His mouth never ceased from speaking words of Torah": *Bava Metzia* 86a

The forty-two journeys of the camp of Israel in the desert: Numbers 33:1-49

"By the Mouth of G-d they camped and by the Mouth of G-d they travelled...": Numbers 9:23

"The days of our years are in them seventy years...": Psalms 90:10

The eighty years Joseph ruled over Egypt: Genesis 41:46 and 50:22

"And Solomon had seventy thousand bearers of burdens...": 1 Kings 5:29

"...look unto the rock from which you were hewn...": Isaiah 51:1-2

"Abraham called the Temple site 'mountain' ": *Pesachim* 88a

David...was unable himself to build the Temple: 2 Samuel 7

The practice of witchcraft, most severely forbidden by Torah: Exodus 22:17; Deuteronomy 18:10

Eighty witches were "caught" by eighty pupils of Shimon Ben Shetach...: *Sanhedrin* 45b

Eighty thousand Roman soldiers blew horns...: *Y. Ta'anit* 4:5

Due to the blemish of the...covenant...between the Jewish People and G-d: Bar Kochba erred in that he was impressed with his own military prowess and ceased to rely on G-d. (*Y. Ta'anit* 4:5)

After each judge rose up..."the earth was quiet" for a period of time: Judges 3:11, 30, 5:31, 8:28

"And the earth was quiet for eighty years": Judges 3:30

"G-d will give His people might...": Psalms 29:11

"Eighty years to might": *Avot* 5:25

Forty years of the Kingdom of *Mashiach*: *Sanhedrin* 99a

"Peace without end": Isaiah 9:6

"Eighty pairs of kohanite brothers were married to...": *Berachot* 44a

"Eighty thousand young men all called Aaron went after his bier...: *Kalah* 3

Aaron made peace between...man and wife: *Kalah* 3

The "sixty queens"..."eighty concubines": Song of Songs 6:8

The "eighty concubines" correspond to the eighty tractates of *Baraita*: *Shir HaShirim Rabbah* to Song of Songs 6:8

The "one dove": Song of Songs 6:9

"The ingathering"...will be in the merit of the learning of Mishnah: *Vayikra Rabbah* 7:3; *Pesikta Rabati* 16:17

"Numberless maidens": Song of Songs 6:8

"Numberless maidens"—individual laws: *Shir HaShirim Rabbah* to Song of Songs 6:8

Eighty ten thousands below the age of twenty: *Shir HaShirim Rabbah* 6:14

Moses, whose "weight" equals that of all the...adult souls of Israel: *Midrash Tanchuma, Beshalach* 10

At the time of the Exodus...Moses...was eighty years old: Exodus 7:7

"Eighty years old to might": *Avot* 5:5

"The Mouth of might": The commandments which G-d gave through Moses are commonly referred to in Rabbinic literature as coming מפי הגבורה, lit. "from the mouth of might."

Moses initially possessed a speech impediment: Exodus 4:10 and Ibn Ezra *ad loc.*

"I will be with your mouth": Exodus 4:12

"I am G-d your G-d...": Exodus 20:2

"Torah and the Holy One Blessed Be He are One": *Zohar* 1:24a

"Life for those who find them": Proverbs 4:22

"Don't read 'for those who find them' but 'for those who say them with their mouth' ": *Eruvin* 54a

Tzadik

"The *tzadik* lives by his faith": Habakkuk 2:4

"The *tzadik* is the foundation of the world": Proverbs 10:25

The Divine "image" in which G-d created man: Genesis 1:27

The *tzadik* of צלם corresponds to the three conscious levels of soul...: *Mevo Shearim* 5:1:13; *Likutei Torah* 4:36c

The three conscious levels of soul...the two transcendent levels of the soul: *Zohar* 1:81a, 206a; *Bereishit Rabbah* 14:9; *Devarim Rabbah* 2:37; *Likutei Torah* 4:93c; *Sefer HaMa'marim 5701*, p. 81 ff, a.e.

As discussed in the letter *hei*: in the discussion of the Soul-aspect of its Number

"The *tzadik* lives in his faith": Habakkuk 2:4

"Living in one's faith" means experiencing greatest joy in one's service of G-d: *Tanya*, ch. 33

"Man is the tree of the field": Deuteronomy 20:19

Tiferet...is the origin of *yesod*: *Zohar* 1:16b

The secret of the "middle line": *Tikunei Zohar*, Introduction

"The body and the *brit* are considered one": See *Tikunei Zohar* 69 (107a) גופא וברית = חיות

The twelve (simple) letters...correspond to the twelve months of the year: *Sefer Yetzirah* 5:2; also, each month relates in particular to a specific "sense" in the soul: *Sefer Yetzirah* 5:1

The letter *tzadik* is the letter of the month of *Shevat*, whose "sense" is that of "eating": *Sefer Yetzirah* 5:1 (ver. Arizal 5:10)

Tu B'Shevat is the New Year of Trees: *Rosh HaShanah* 1:1

The "king of trees" is the palm tree: *Or HaSechel* (R. Avraham Abulafia)

"The *tzadik* will flower like a date palm": Psalms 92:18

The 288 fallen sparks: *Etz Chaim* 18:1; *Torah Or* 27d

Elevated by...the *tzadik* in...the act of eating: *Tanya*, ch. 7

"In all your ways know Him": Proverbs 3:6

"The *tzadik* eats to the satisfaction of his soul": Proverbs 13:25

The "righteous *kohen*" is the future companion of *Mashiach*: *Sukah* 52b

The "point" of creative lifeforce "enwedged" in every created being: *Sha'ar HaYichud VeHaEmunah*, ch. 1

"The power to actualize potential ever present within the actualized": See the introduction to the *kaf*.

The two dimensions of form and matter present...in all created reality: *Mishneh Torah*, *Yesodei HaTorah* 2:3; *Moreh Nevuchim* throughout; *Shemoneh Perakim*, ch. 1; *Igeret HaKodesh* 15; *Likutei Torah* 4:72b

"The *tzadik* decrees and the Holy One Blessed Be He realizes": *Shabbat* 59b

"The foundation of the world": Proverbs 10:25

The "Congregation of Israel": *Shir HaShirim Rabbah* to Song of Songs 1:4, a.f.

The great *tzadik*...enlivens all of the souls of his generation: *Tanya*, ch. 2

All prayers are elevated to G-d by his prayer: *Likutei Moharan* 1:2

The fifty...gates of understanding: See *Rosh HaShanah* 21b

Each soul relates...to one of the fifty gates: *Sha'ar HaKavanot*, *Sefirat HaOmer*

The Divine 'Nothing' is the source of life flow of Israel": *Shabbat* 156a

"*Aba* dwells in *Atzilut*": See *Etz Chaim* 3:1, 47:2, etc.; *Tikunei Zohar* 6; *Torah Or* 75a; *Sefer HaMa'amarim 5700*, p. 59 in note

"The two companions that never part": *Zohar* 3:4a

"As mother, daughter": Ezekiel 16:44

"*Aba* founds daughter": *Zohar* 3:248a

The root אצל means "near": *Ma'amarei Admur HaZaken 5566*, p. 203; *Sefer HaMa'amarim 5666*, p. 6

The root אצל means "emanation": as in Numbers 11:17; *Pardes Rimonim* 16:1

The term used by Onkelos to translate the word תהו: Genesis 1:2

"A man who knows hunt, a man of the field": Genesis 25:27

"For hunt was in his mouth": Genesis 25:28

Esau would "hunt" (deceive) his father Isaac: Rashi to Genesis 25:28. *Cf. Bereishit Rabbah* 63:10: " 'a man who knows hunt'—he would deceive people."

Isaac himself would hunt for fallen Divine sparks trapped in...Esau: *Torah Or* 20c

These sparks were actually great souls: *Torah Or* 20c

"His hand was holding the heel of Esau": Genesis 25:26

"Great artist": *Berachot* 105a

This is the work of the "lower *tzadik*," Benjamin: *Zohar* 1:153b; *Torah Or* 80d; *Ma'amarei Admur HaZaken 5566*, p. 330

Benjamin was the only son of Jacob to be born in the land of Israel: Genesis 35:18

The right side, *chesed*: *Tikunei Zohar*, introduction

In Jacob's blessing of Benjamin he likened him to "a preying wolf": Genesis 49:27

Rashi comments: *ad loc.*

The account of "the concubine of Givah": Judges 21

"The end"..."enwedged in the beginning": *Sefer Yetzirah* 1:7

The "*tzadik* is the foundation of the world": Proverbs 10:25

"And you go to the end...": Daniel 12:13

כפרה, "atonement," the cleansing of the soul from all impurity...: See *Igeret HaTeshuvah*, ch. 1.

The "higher *tzadik*," personified in Torah by Joseph: *Zohar* 1:153b; *Torah Or* 80d; *Ma'amarei Admur HaZaken 5566*, p. 330

"Run and return": Ezekiel 1:14

"The passion of *tzadikim* is exclusively good": Proverbs 11:23

"A mighty tower is the Name of G-d, into it runs the *tzadik* and is exalted": Proverbs 18:10

The "mighty tower"...is the secret of *malchut*: *Zohar* 3:164a, 1:74b

The powers of consciousness divide into...מוטבע...מורגש...מושכל: *Pardes Rimonim* 12; *Torah Or* 108a

"At the age of ninety one bends over": *Avot* 5:22

At the age of 100...one "disappears from the world": *Avot* 5:22

"There are ninety-one days and seven-and-a-half hours from season to season": *Eruvin* 56a

A "quarter" is the secret of *chochmah*: *Likutei Torah* 3:67a ff

Chochmah corresponds to *Atzilut* in general: *Sha'arei Kedushah* 3:1-2; *Mevo Shearim* 6:2:1; *Mystical Concepts*, ch. 4, section 2

The Arizal instructs one to say before prayer: *Pri Etz Chaim* 5:1; *Sha'ar HaKavanot* p. 2

"You shall love your fellow Jew as yourself": Leviticus 19:18

At the birth of Isaac, Sarah...was ninety years old: Genesis 17:17

"And Sarah laughed inside herself": Genesis 18:12

"G-d has made laughter of me; all who hear shall laugh with me": Genesis 21:6

Ninety, the age of Sarah...one hundred, the age of Abraham at Isaac's birth: Genesis 17:17, 21:5

Abraham also laughed when told by G-d of Isaac's birth-to-be: Genesis 17:17

When King David brought the ark...to Jerusalem: 2 Samuel 6:12-19

He appointed ninety thousand elders to dance joyously before the ark: *BaMidbar Rabbah* 4:21

One's requirement to say ninety "amens," four *kedushot*...: One hundred blessings: *Bamidbar Rabbah* 18:21; *Menachot* 43b; *Mishneh Torah, Tefilah* 7:14; *Shulchan Aruch, Orach Chaim* 46:3

"All goes after the beginning": *Pirkei d'Rabbi Eliezar* 42

"All that Sarah tells you, listen to her voice": Genesis 21:12

"Sarah is greater than Abraham in prophecy": *Shemot Rabbah* 1:1

"The people who are a *tzadik* shall come, those who guard their faith": Isaiah 26:21

"Those who guard the saying of...'amen' daily": *Shabbat* 119b

Kuf

"There is none holy as G-d": 1 Samuel 2:2

The letter *kuf* **stands for holiness:** *Shabbat* 104a

"He is grasped within all worlds, yet none grasps Him": *Zohar* 3:225a

"Hunts" for fallen sparks: See discussion of the Worlds dimension of the name of the *tzadik*

"...and Adam called the name of his wife Eve...": Genesis 3:20

"Her feet descend into death": Proverbs 5:5

Even within the...dead corpse a spark of life remains hidden: called קיסטא דחיותא and הבל דגרמיה.

Abel, the second son of Adam and Eve...: Genesis 4:8

The nineteen-year cycle of the moon in relation to the sun: *Mishneh Torah, Kidush HaChodesh*

The moon represents the female: *Zohar* 1:16b

The secret of the *sefirah* **of** *malchut:* *Zohar Chai, Yitro* 40b

The sun represents the male figure: *Zohar* 3:12a

The *sefirah* **of** *yesod:* *Zohar* 1:33a

Personified by Adam: *Tikunei Zohar* 69 (116b)

"The woman of valor is the crown of her husband": Proverbs 12:4

"...He has set an end to darkness": Job 28:3

"Her feet descend into death": Proverbs 5:5

"Death will be swallowed up forever": Isaiah 25:8

The three impure *kelipot:* *Etz Chaim* 49:2 ff; *Tanya*, ch. 6; *Mystical Concepts*, ch. 10

"Suck" life force from the "excess products" of *kedushah:* *Likutei Torah* 3:56c

Eve...added to G-d's command not to eat of the tree of knowledge...: *Sanhedrin* 29a

Even an Israelite is considered "foreign"...: See, *inter alia*, Leviticus 22:10; Numbers 1:51, 3:10, 38, 17:5, etc.

"...and the impure spirit I will make pass away from the earth": Zechariah 13:2

The Will of G-d...decrees upon it to descend, against its own initial will, into a physical body: *Avot* 4:22; *Midrash Tanchuma, Pekudei* 3

The soul's mission below...rectification, clarification, of its body...: *Tanya*, ch. 37

The soul's initial state...is transformed into a state of willingness...: *Avot* 4:22: "Against your will you are born, but against your will you die."

Seven spiritual heavens: *Chagigah* 12b

The three "crowning borders" of the ark: Exodus 25:11

Table: Exodus 25:24

And inner altar: Exodus 30:3

They symbolize "the crown of Torah," "the crown of Kingdom" and "the crown of *kehunah*," respectively: *Yoma* 72b

"Throw a stick, and it will fall to its source": *Bereishit Rabbah* 53:15; Rashi to Genesis 21:21

"Returning light"..."straight light": *Etz Chaim* 39:14; see introduction to *zayin*

"He is grasped within all worlds, yet none grasps Him": *Zohar* 3:255a

"Touching" and "not touching": *Y. Chagigah* 2:1

A Divine Name in Kabbalah, לקי: Prayer cited at the beginning of standard editions of *Etz Chaim* (4b)

"For Your salvation do I hope, G-d": Genesis 49:18

The monkey is the intermediate state between animal and man: *Etz Chaim* 42:1

So do there exist intermediate states between...: *ibid.*

The descendents of Cain "degenerated" into monkeys: *Sanhedrin* 109a (regarding one of three groups of the דור הפלגה; *Bereishit Rabbah* 23:6 (regarding the דור אנוש)

"Vanity of vanities said Kohelet, vanity of vanities, all is vanity": Ecclesiastes 1:2

The minimal level of plurality is two: *Cf. Yoma* 62b; discussion of the Worlds dimension of the number of the *beit.*

These seven vanities refer to seven periods...through which one passes in life: *Kohelet Rabbah* 1:2

The Torah of this world...is itself considered "vanity" relative to the inner truth of the Torah: *Kohelet Rabbah* 11, 2

In truth, from G-d's perspective, the *tzimtzum* is not real: *Sha'ar HaYichud VeHaEmunah*, ch. 7; *Likutei Sichot*, vol. 15, p. 470 ff

The soul of Israel, the true "man": *Yevamot* 61a

"There is no place vacant of Him": *Tikunei Zohar*, *Tikun* 57 (91b)

This world...is "the world of deceit": *Cf. Tanya*, ch. 6.

"For the thing is very close to you, in your mouth and in your heart to do it": Deuteronomy 30:14

The *hakafot* of *Simchat Torah*: *Shulchan Aruch*, *Orach Chaim* 664:1

"Open to me an opening as the eye of a needle...": See note at end of Introduction.

"I and he cannot dwell together": *Sotah* 5a

"Then Esther the queen, the daughter of Avichail...": Esther 9:29

Rashi interprets: *ad loc.*

Amalek, the ancestor of Haman: Esther 3:1; *Soferim* 13:6 and *Nachalat Yaakov ad loc.*

Amalek...the "arch enemy" of Israel: Exodus 17:16; *Torah Or* 84b ff; *Sefer HaMa'amarim 5680*, p. 296 ff; *Sefer HaMa'amarim 5681*, p. 1 ff

"The elephant entering the eye of a needle": *Berachot* 55b; *Bava Metzia* 38b

The month of *Adar*, whose letter...is the *kuf*...: *Sefer Yetzirah* 5:1-2

"Turn over": Esther 9:1

"One who sees an elephant in his dream...": *Berachot* 56b

"How great are Your deeds, G-d; very deep are Your thoughts": Psalms 92:6

Our acceptance of the yoke of Torah with infinitely firmer conviction...: *Shabbat* 88a

The life span of an eagle is said to be 100 years: Commentary of R. David Kimchi to Psalms 103:5

"May my youth be renewed like an eagle": Psalms 103:5

"A youth will die at the age of 100": Isaiah 65:20

Before the flood man became liable to punishment only at the age of 100: *Bereishit Rabbah* 26:2

The eagle...corresponds to the *sefirah* of *tiferet*: *Tikunei Zohar* 70 (133b)

The third of the four faces of the "chariot": Ezekiel 1:10

"Youth of Israel": Hosea 11:1: כי נער ישראל

"...at the age of 100 one is as though dead...": *Avot* 5:22

עולם, **"world," from** העלם, **"concealment":** sources cited in *Mystical Concepts*, ch. 4, note 10

Isaac was miraculously born to Abraham at the age of 100: Genesis 21:5

"Abraham was one": Ezekiel 33:24

To "pass on" the Soul to his descendents forever: *Cf. Sefer HaKuzari.*

The...*kuf* **stands for the 100 years of his father Abraham:** *Bereishit Rabbah* 53:7; *Midrash Tanchuma, Korach* 12

The...*yud***...stands for the ten trials Abraham stood through...:** *Avot* 5:3

"Go to you": Genesis 12:1

Upward travel to reach the source of the soul above: *Likutei Sichot*, vol. 1, p. 17

The downward journey of the soul to earth to enter a body: *Zohar* 1:77a; *Likutei Sichot*, vol. 1, p. 15 ff

"And you shall teach them to your children...": Deuteronomy 6:7-8

The age of Abraham when told "go to you": Genesis 12:1, 4

The number 100 represents perfection and completion: See *Kuntres 20 Marcheshvan 5748*, note 66

"The elephant in the eye of the needle": *Berachot* 55b; *Bava Metzia* 38b

The *yud* **is the letter of the month of** *Elul***...:** *Sefer Yetzirah* 5:2

"Ten intangible *sefirot* **and 22 letters of foundation":** *Sefer Yetzirah* 1:2

The "32 pathways of wisdom": *Sefer Yetzirah* 1:1-2

Dan, the "lowest" of the tribes: Rashi to Exodus 35:34

100 is the number of blessings to be said daily: *Menachot* 43b

Reish

The four New Years: *Rosh HaShanah* 1:1

The amorphic "matter" from which...every letter is formed is the secret of the letter *hei***:** *Igeret HaKodesh* 5

In script, every letter begins from a point, the secret of the letter *yud***:** *Likutei Moharan*

The Divine chariot of Ezekiel: Ezekiel 1:10

"The beginning of wisdom is the fear of G-d": Psalms 111:10

The inner experience...to arouse...insight...is..."selflessness": See at length *Sha'ar HaYichud*, ch. 1 and the commentary of Rabbi Hillel of Poritch *ad loc.*

"The Cause of all causes": *Mishneh Torah, Yesodei HaTorah* 1:1; *Zohar* 1:22b

The...Divine wisdom is the "nothing"...between the two states of "something": *Sha'ar HaYichud*, ch. 2; commentary of R. Hillel of Poritch *ad loc.*

"You have made all in wisdom": Psalms 104:24

"Made" refers...to the process of rectification and clarification: Rashi to *Bereishit Rabbah* 11:7

The *Zohar* paraphrases this verse: בחכמה אתבררו; see sources cited in English Translation of *Igeret HaKodesh* 26, note 82.

"Poverty causes man to lose possession of his own *da'at*...": Cf. *Eruvin* 41b.

"He blew into his nostrils the breath of life...": Genesis 2:7

"A speaking spirit": Onkelos to Genesis 2:7

Two great Chassidim...: *Sefer HaMa'amarim 5708*, pp. 260; *Toldot Yitzchak Isaac*, p. 83

"The concealed things are to G-d our G-d...": Deuteronomy 29:28

Amalek, the archenemy of Israel...: Exodus 17:16; *Torah Or* 84b ff; *Sefer HaMa'amarim 5680*, p. 296 ff; *Sefer HaMa'amarim 5681*, p. 1 ff

Amalek...wishes to disassociate...the letters י"ה from...the letters ו"ה: Rashi on Exodus 17:16: "The Holy One, blessed be He, swears that his Name will not be complete [i.e. the first two letters separate from the second two]...until the name of Amalek be entirely blotted out." *Pesikta Rabbah, Parshat Zachor*; *Midrash Tanchuma, Ki Tetzei*

This is the secret of drawing Shabbat into the six days of the week: since on Shabbat one's main preoccupation in Torah-study should be the esoteric aspect of Torah, whereas during the week it should be the exoteric.

" 'There were two men in one city, one rich and the one poor...' ": 2 Samuel 12:1-7

"There is none rich but in knowledge and there is none poor except in knowledge...": *Nedarim* 41a

King David is the secret of *malchut*: *Zohar* 3:302b, etc.

"The poor man had not all": 2 Samuel 12:3

The two days of *Rosh Hashanah*: *Shulchan Aruch, Orach Chaim* 600

The two days of *Rosh Hashanah*...correspond...to the "depth" of *keter*...and the "depth" of *chochmah*: See *Sidurei HaArizal*, Psalm added before the blessings before the morning recitation of the *Shema*.

The ten days of *teshuvah*...are the secret of the ten "depths" of the ten *sefirot*: *Likutei Torah* 4:39b

Rosh Hashanah will remain two days even in the future: *Beitzah* 5ab; *cf. Y. Eruvin* 3:9; *Sotah* 48b; *Mishneh Torah, Kidush HaChodesh* 5:7; *Zohar* 3:231a; *Pri Etz Chaim, Sha'ar Rosh HaShanah* 4; *Tosefta Rosh HaShanah* 1:10.

The two days of the other holidays observed only in the Diaspora: *Beitzah* 4b; *Mishneh Torah, Yom Tov* 1:21; *Shulchan Aruch, Orach Chaim* 496:1, 3

The soul of Israel comes from the wisdom of G-d: *Tanya*, ch. 2

On the first day of *Rosh Hashanah*...Adam and Eve were created: *Rosh HaShanah* 8a, 10b, 27a; *Avodah Zarah* 8a; *Tosefot, Avodah Zarah* 8a, *s.v.* לתקופת

G-d intended the fulfillment...to take place the next day: *Pri Etz Chaim, Rosh HaShanah* 1; *Or HaTorah, Bereishit*, pp. מור־מט; *cf. Bereishit Rabbah* 18:6; *Biurei HaZohar (Tzemach Tzedek)*, pp. 15-17.

"...and fill the earth and conquer it and rule...": Genesis 1:28

"For My thoughts are not your thoughts...": Isaiah 55:8-9

"Seek G-d while He may be found...": Isaiah 55:6-7

Which...refer to the ten days of *teshuvah*: *Rosh HaShanah* 18a; *Mishneh Torah, Teshuvah* 2:6

"Lift up the head of the Children of Israel": Exodus 30:12

So long as a man possesses up to 199 *zuz*...: *Peah* 8:8

"The thousand is to you Solomon...": Song of Songs 8:12

The "thousand lights" which shine inwardly...outwardly: *Pelach HaRimon* 1:58a ff

"The sun is charity": Malachi 3:20

"And from the children of Issachar...": 1 Chronicles 12:33

Our mother Leah...merited to give birth to Issachar: Genesis 30:14-18

"The secret of impregnation": *Bereishit Rabbah* 72:5. This is the secret of the fixing of the Jewish calendar, with an additional 13th, "pregnant" month added seven times within the lunar-solar cycle of 19 years.

The tribe of Issachar...possessed 200 heads of the Sanhedrin: *Bereishit Rabbah* 72:5, 98:12

"If there is no *da'at* there is no *binah*...": *Avot* 3:17

"The mother of children is happy": Psalms 113:9

Even on days of mourning one is conscious that in the future...: *Mishneh Torah, Ta'aniot* 5:19

The *tzimtzum* of the Infinite Light took place in its middle point...: *Etz Chaim*, beginning

The letters האמנתיו: See R. Meir Leibush (Malbim), *Ayelet HaShachar*.

"There is no king without a people": *Kad HaKemach, Rosh HaShanah* 70:1

Shin

The letter *shin* appears engraved on both sides of the head-*tefilin*: *Shulchan Aruch, Orach Chaim* 32:42

On the right side...the *shin* possesses three heads...: *Shulchan Aruch, Orach Chaim* 32:42

"The flame bound to the coal": *Sefer Yetzirah* 1; *Kuzari* 4:27

"I am G-d, I have not changed": Malachi 3:6

Relative to G-d's Essence absolutely no change has occurred...: *Sha'ar HaYichud VeHaEmunah*, ch. 7

The changeless Essence is...The power of change...: *Sha'ar HaYichud Ve-HaEmunah*, ch. 6

"As mighty as death is love...the flame of G-d: Song of Songs 8:6

The love of Israel: Leviticus 19:18; *Mishneh Torah, Deiot* 6:3; *Shulchan Aruch, Yoreh Deah* 228

The love of Torah: See *Sefer HaArachim*, vol. 1, col. 612 ff.

The love of G-d: Deuteronomy 6:5; *Mishneh Torah, Yesodei HaTorah* 2:1, *Teshuvah* 10:3

The love of the Land of Israel: *Ketubot* 110b ff

"The Land of Israel will in the future spread...": See *Pesikta Rabati, Shabbat veRosh Chodesh* 2; *Yalkut Shimoni, Yeshaya* 503; *Sifrei* to Deuteronomy 1; *Shir HaShirim Rabbah* 7:10.

In *Sefer Yetzirah*, the *shin* is the letter of fire: 3:3

The eight synonyms for beauty in Hebrew: corresponding to the eight *sefirot* from *binah* (the mother) to *malchut* (the daughter). Each relates to a different aspect of beauty. See note on the introduction to *tet*.

"And Noah found grace in the eyes of G-d": Genesis 6:8

Rabbi David Kimchi in *Sefer HaShorashim*: s.v. איש

In *Sefer Yetzirah* **the** א **stands for** אויר, **"air":** 3:3

Mashiach, **whose anti-being, the snake:** *Erkei HaKinuyim, s.v. Mashiach*

Noah, the tenth...generation from Adam: Genesis 5

"Noah was a *tzadik***":** Genesis 6:9

The *shin* **is referred to as "the letter of the fathers":** *Zohar* 1:2b; *Tikunei Zohar* 51 (86b)

The four-headed *shin* **of the future...corresponds...to the four matriarchs:** *Levush, Orach Chaim* 32:43

The three divisions of the Jewish people...: *Shabbat* 88a

The fourth *vav,* **corresponding to the righteous converts...:** The fourth leg of the chariot is David, descendant of Ruth the convert.

Their special role and unique merit in the bringing of *Mashiach*: *Likutei Moharan*

The union of *yesod* **and** *malchut*: *Zohar* 3:69a

Yesod **and** *malchut,* **personified by Joseph and David:** *Zohar* 3:26a, 2:101a

"*Tzadik,* **the foundation of the world":** Proverbs 10:25

The...origin...of King David, Ruth the Moabite: Ruth 4:21-22

The archetype righteous convert: as the laws of conversion are derived from the story of hers.

*Shin...***begins the word** שקר, **"lie":** *Shabbat* 104a; *Zohar* 1:2b

"No lie can endure if not based on truth": Rashi to Numbers 13:27: "Any lie that does not have a little truth in it at the beginning will not endure in the end."

The secret of the Exile of the *Shechinah*: *Shabbat* 104a

"False is grace": Proverbs 31:30

"The grace of place is on one who inhabits it": *Sotah* 47a

"He is the Place of the world yet the world is not His place": *Bereishit Rabbah* 68:10

G-d's Transcendent Light which "surrounds all worlds": *Zohar* 3:225a

The three lines, or columns, in...*Atzilut*: *Siddur Im Dach* 14b

The three lower worlds of Creation, Formation, and Action: *Mystical Concepts,* ch. 4, section 2

The secret of the Name Tzevakot: *Torah Or* 60a ff

The seven Divine Names...which we are forbidden to erase: *Mishneh Torah, Yesodei HaTorah* 6:2

"He is a sign is His hosts": *Zohar* 1:6a, 3:286b

The...Immanent Light which "fills all worlds": *Zohar* 3:225a

"And it was in that very day that all of the Hosts of G-d...": Exodus 12:41

Leaving Egypt symbolizes leaving all states of...confinement: *Tanya*, ch. 47

"And you shall teach them diligently to your children": Deuteronomy 6:7

שנה...is the term used for time in general: *Sefer Yetzirah* 3:4

The "breaking of the vessels": *Mystical Concepts*, ch. 7

The scarlet hue of שני...used in the clothing of the *kohanim*: Exodus 28:4-5

In the time of exile "I am asleep...": Psalms 126:1; *Torah Or* 28c

"I am asleep...": Song of Songs 5:2

When Choni HaMaagel slept for seventy years...: *Taanit* 23a

"He does not slumber nor sleep": Psalms 121:4

"...and you shall teach them to your children": Deuteronomy 6:7

"Your children" means "your students": *Sifrei* to Deuteronomy 6:7

"A sharpened arrow": Proverbs 25:18

"A sharp sword shines flashes of lightning": Nahum 3:3: ולהב חרב וברק חנית.

The Torah he was taught in the womb...: *Nidah* 30b

משנה, the "viceroy"...from the root "two": See the discussion of the Soul-level of the Number of *beit*

"The one of the nation": Genesis 26:10; see Rashi *ad loc.*

"Thirds [in command]": Exodus 14:7

Both Joseph and Mordechai served as viceroys: Genesis 41:43-44; Esther 10:3

Joseph's first born son, Menashe: Genesis 41:51

The Midrashic account of G-d as (the King) taking counsel...: *Bereishit Rabbah* 8:7; *Ruth Rabbah* 2

"Double loaves": Exodus 16:22

The two challah-loaves...at the Shabbat meal: *Shabbat* 117b; *Shulchan Aruch, Orach Chaim* 274:1

The double portion of manna: Exodus 16:22

"I am G-d, I have not changed": Malachi 3:6

"Peace"...a name of G-d: Shabbat 10b; Bamidbar Rabbah 11:7

מזוזת (*mezuzot*, as written in the chapter of *Shema*): Deuteronomy 6:9, whereas in Deuteronomy 11:20 it is written "full"; i.e. with a *vav* between the two *zayins*.

זז מות, **"death is made to move away":** Zohar 3:300b

Its blessing: "...to fix a *mezuzah*": Shulchan Aruch, Yoreh Deah 289:1

"G-d shall guard your going out and your coming in": Psalms 121:8

On the outside of the scroll...is written the name Shakai: Shulchan Aruch, Yoreh Deah 288:15

"The guardian of the doors of Israel": Zohar 3:266

"He has set an end to darkness": Job 28:3

Samson took three hundred foxes...: Judges 15:1-6

King Yoshiyahu...was killed...in battle with Pharoah Necoh...: 2 Kings 23:29; 2 Chronicles 35:19-24; Eichah Rabbah 1:61

King Yoshiyahu...referred to as "the Mashiach of G-d": Lamentations 4:20

The temporary disappearance of the "moon" of Israel: See the discussion of the Soul-level of the Number-dimension of *lamed*.

In the days of the Judges...: Tana d'vei Eliahu Zuta 8

For three hundred years the people were "asleep" in the land of Israel: Tana d'vei Eliahu Zuta 8: שלש מאות שנה עבדו ישראל ע"ז בימי שפוט השופטים

"Work salvations in the midst of the land": Psalms 74:12

Rabbi Meir taught three hundred parables of foxes: Sanhedrin 38b

King Solomon spoke three thousand parables...: 1 Kings 5:12

The three hundred and ten worlds of the *tzadikim* in the World to Come: Midrash Tehilim 31:6; Zohar 2:166b; Uktzin 3:12

"To give inheritance to those that love Me": Proverbs 8:21

Three hundred first-born Levites in the desert: Berachot 5a

Gideon...chose three hundred men to fight with him...: Judges 7:4-8

"Three hundred *halachot* concerning 'a mighty bright spot' ": Sanhedrin 68a

"A mighty bright spot": Leviticus 13:1-28

"Three hundred *halachot* concerning 'you shall not let live a sorceress' ": *Sanhedrin* 18a

"You shall not let live a sorceress": Exodus 22:17

"Three hundred *halachot* concerning 'the tower soaring in air' ": *Chagigah* 15b, *Sanhedrin* 106b

"The tower soaring in air": See notes to the *Lamed.*

" 'Is not My word like fire?' says G-d...": Jeremiah 23:29

A "broken heart": Psalms 51:19

The broken pieces of *Tohu*...: See *Mystical Concepts,* ch. 7.

"Three hundred *halachot* concerning 'and the name of his wife was Meheitavel' ": *Zohar* 1:145b

"The name of his wife was Meheitavel": Genesis 36:39; 1 Chronicles 1:50

The death of the first seven kings of Edom: Genesis 36:31-39

As expounded by the Arizal: See sources cited in *Mystical Concepts,* ch. 7.

"And the earth was *tohu* and *vohu*...": Genesis 1:2

Which...refers to the spirit or soul of *Mashiach*: *Bereishit Rabbah* 2:4

The "waters of Torah": *Derech Eretz Zuta* 8; *Midrash Tanchuma, Vayakhel* 8: "Torah is compared to water."

The "waters of *teshuvah*": *Bereishit Rabbah* 2:4: "*teshuvah* is compared to water."

Tav

"The *tav* makes an impression on the Ancient of Days": *Zohar* 3:128b; *Or HaTorah, Toldot* 153b

"The Ancient of Days": Daniel 7:9

"The Ancient of Days" refers to the sublime pleasure...: *Zohar* 3:101a; *Likutei Torah* 3:52b, 29a; *Or HaTorah, Lech Lecha,* p. 673a

"Kingdom of the Infinite One, Blessed be He": See *Likutei Torah* 3:51d.

"There is none like unto Him": Sabbath liturgy; see Isaiah 40:18; Lamentations 2:13

This faith passes in inheritance from generation to generation...: *Cf. Shimusha Rabba* 22.

"Your Kingdom is the Kingdom of all worlds": Psalms 145:13

Worlds—generations: from commentary of the Arizal on *Sefer Yetzirah*—the *tav* represents the channel from *yesod* (space or worlds) to *malchut* (time or generation).

The...true faith...the soul of our first father, Abraham: See *Avot d'Rabbi Natan* 33.

"The first of all believers": ראש לגרים (*Sukah* 49b); תחילה לגרים (*Chagigah* 3a)

Abraham's purchase of the Cave of Machpelah: Genesis 23:16

"Four hundred worlds of pleasure": *Zohar* 1:123b; *cf. Torah Or* 24c.

G-d's seal...is truth: *Shabbat* 55a; *Bereishit Rabbah* 81:2; *Sanhedrin* 64a; *Yoma* 69b

The three last words in the account of creation: ברא אלקים לעשות: Genesis 2:3

The beginning, middle and end of the *alef-beit*: *Shabbat* 55a in Rashi; *Devarim Rabbah* 1:10

Divine paradox: *Cf. Responsa of Rabbi Shlomo ben Aderet* 418.

"The final end of knowledge is not to know": *Bechinat Olam* 13:45, explained at length in *Sefer HaMa'marim 5670* p. 126 ff.

The infinite "treasure-house" of simple faith...innate in...Israel: *Cf. Tanya*, ch. 18-19; *Torah Or* 111a ff.

"All follows the seal": *Berachot* 12a

The secret of "returning light": אור חוזר: *Torah Or* 5a, 33a; *Likutei Torah* 5:17c

Around the inner Sanctuary...were constructed many תאים, "cells": Ezekiel 40:7, 16; explained in *Biurei HaZohar (Tzemach Tzedek)* p. 28a

These "cells" were without windows: Ezekiel 40:16

These "cells" reveal the level of "He places darkness...": *Biurei HaZohar (Tzemach Tzedek)* p. 28a

"He places darkness His concealed place": Psalms 18:12

"Torah is the impression of Divinity, Israel is...": *Ma'amar HaShiflut Ve-HaSimchah*, p. 32a, quoting Rabbi Shneur Zalman of Liadi citing "ancient sources"

Submission...separation...sweetening: *Keter Shem Tov* 28, 160, 302.

"Silence"..."circumcision"..."speech": *Keter Shem Tov* 28

Chashmal: The secret word of Ezekiel's vision of the "Divine Chariot" (Ezekiel 1:4)

Torah is the secret of separation between good and evil: *Sha'ar HaMitzvot, VeEtchanan; Shulchan Aruch HaArizal, kavanot of Talmud Torah* 2; *Igeret HaKodesh* 26

"Israel" is an acronym for..."There are six hundred thousand...": *Megaleh Amukot, VeEtchanan* 186

These "worlds" were created and subsequently destroyed...: *Bereishit Rabbah* 3:9; see also *Shabbat* 55a: תיו—תיו תחי' תיו תמות—the latter aspect referring to the shattering of *Tohu*.

These worlds were spiritual, not physical...: *Etz Chaim* 2:1; cf. Ramban on Genesis: שתתהו היולי ראשונה.

Just law on earth is actually the reflection and impression of...: *Sefer HaMa'amarim 5666*, p. 426 ff.

The nine "vessel" letters beginning from *nun*: See the discussion of the Worlds-level of the Form-dimension of the *nun*.

Dan also denotes a camp of three tribes: Numbers 2:25-31

The camp of Dan was situated to the north: Numbers 2:25-31

Dan assumed the responsibility to return...losses: *Y. Eruvin* 5:1

He found and returned lost souls...: *Likutei Sichot*, vol. 1, p. 103-4; cf. *Likutei Torah* 3:91c, 4:33a.

"Dan shall judge his people as one of the tribes of Israel": Genesis 49:16

"One of the tribes of Israel" refers to the tribe of Judah: Ramban to Genesis 49:16

"The end is enwedged in the beginning": *Sefer Yetzirah* 10:7

The two chief craftsmen were from the tribes of Judah...and Dan: Exodus 31:2-6

"To Your salvation I hope, G-d": Genesis 49:18

The evil powers of the north: from Jeremiah 1:14

The closing of the "open north side": See *Yahel Or*, p. 261

The secret of reincarnation: Cf. *Emek Hamelech, Sha'ar Olam HaTohu*, ch. 54: תיו relates to both *tohu* (past lives) and *tikun* (present life); explained in *Biurei HaZohar* (*Tzemach Tzedek*) p. 26 ff.

"No one is wise but the master of experience": See *Akeidat Yitzchak* 14.

"One cannot understand the law unless one has stumbled over it": *Gitin* 43a

The resurrection...depends on...consciousness of G-dliness in the present: *Biurei HaZohar (Tzemach Tzedek)* p. 26 ff.

G-d's Name of Kingdom, the "reading" of the Name *Havayah*: Exodus 3:15 and Rashi *ad loc.*; sources cited in *Sefer HaLikutim (Tzemach Tzedek)*, s.v. אדנ״י.

"Dan shall judge his people as one, the tribes of Israel": Genesis 49:16

Refers to the One Above, blessed be He: as in the verse "The L-rd is our G-d, the L-rd is *One*"

"The law of *malchut* is law": *Gitin* 10b

Self-consciousness and ego are the expression of...*malchut*: Self-consciousness is expressed by the word אני, "I." R. Yosef Giktilia, *Sha'arei Orah* 1; *Pardes Rimonim, Sha'ar Erkei HaKinuim, s.v.* אני, based on the *Zohar*.

"Your Kingdom is the kingdom of all worlds": Psalms 145:13

To transcend its own finite ego and subdue itself...something "beyond,"...which is infinitely deeper in essence than anything I am capable of comprehending: The word אני can be transposed to read אין, "nothingness," complete self-nullification. *Etz Chaim, Sha'ar Derushei Avia,* end of ch. 1; *Likutei Torah* 3:18c.

"G-d set a mark upon Cain, lest any finding him should kill him": Genesis 4:15

"He scribbled on the doors of the gate...": 1 Samuel 21:13-14

***Nun*, the fiftieth "unintelligible" gate of understanding:** *Rosh Hashanah* 21b; *Zohar* 2:115a, 216a

Each and every part of creation sings...to the Creator: Each creature's song is listed in the Midrash *Perek Shirah*.

"Verily, in accordance with my impression shall the Almighty answer me": Job 31:35

Rashi explains: *ad loc.*

"And that man was perfect and upright...": Job 1:1

"And G-d said to him, 'go through the midst of the city...' ": Ezekiel 9:4-6

"*Tzadikim* in their death are called alive...": *Berachot* 18a

"*Teshuvah*"..."prayer"..."Torah"...in correspondence with the three patriarchs: Abraham represents *teshuvah*: cf. *Chagigah* 3a; *Sukah* 49b; Isaac represents prayer: see Genesis 24:63; Jacob represents Torah: *Midrash Tanchumah, VaYishlach* 9; *Yoma* 28b; *Midrash Tanchuma, Toldot* 2.

The fourth "foot of the chariot," King David, *malchut*: *Zohar* 1:248b, 3:262b; *Meorei Or* 1:84; *Likutei Sichot*, vol. 7, p. 301

"The advantage of light which shines from darkness": Ecclesiastes 2:13; *cf. Zohar* 3:47b.

The final letter of the account of creation: Genesis 2:3

"To do," as interpreted by the Sages—"to rectify": See commentary of Rashi to *Bereishit Rabbah* 11:7.

The final letters of the last three words of creation: Genesis 2:3

The final three letters of the beginning of creation: Genesis 1:1

"We came to your brother Esau and he also is coming to meet you...": Genesis 32:7

His four hundred men represent four hundred fallen sparks...: *Cf. Likutei Torah (Arizal),* end of *Vayishlach.*

Esau is called "a man of the field": Genesis 25:27

Through the merit accumulated by Jacob...he possessed the power to subdue Esau and his four hundred men: *Cf.* Rashi on Genesis 32:5.

The four hundred men of David: 1 Samuel 22:2, 25:13

David...is the rectification of the "red one,"...Esau: *Pardes Rimonim, Sha'ar HaGavanim*

The Covenant Between the Pieces: Genesis 15:13

The four hundred years actually began from the birth of Isaac: *Seder Olam* 3; Rashi to Genesis 15:13, Exodus 6:18-20 and 12:40

Only for the last eighty-six years...were the Jews subjected to most oppressive slavery: i.e., from Miriam's birth. *Shir HaShirim Rabbah* 2:4; *Midrash Tanchuma* (ed. Buber), *Bo* 7; *Pesikta Rabati* 15:11

Abraham purchased the Cave of Machpelah...for four hundred *shekel*: Genesis 23:15-17

Four pairs of "living" souls...are buried in the Machpelah: *Eruvin* 53a

"Tzadikim in death are considered living": *Berachot* 18a

"Her husband is known in the gates": Proverbs 31:23

The fifty gates of understanding: See *Rosh HaShanah* 21b

"If there is no knowledge there is no understanding": *Avot* 3:21

The "one hundred gates" of Isaac: Genesis 26:12

"He said much but did not even a little": Rashi to Genesis 15:18-21

"The evil eye": *Bereishit Rabbah* 58:7

The land of Israel...is four hundred *parsah* by four hundred *parsah*: *Megilah* 3a

The land of Israel...whose microcosm is the Cave of Machpelah: *Zohar* 1:128b

Every *parsah* is four *mil*: *Pesachim* 93b

A *mil* being approximately a kilometer: derived from *Shulchan Aruch, Orach Chaim* 261, *Yoreh Deah* 69.

The land of ten nations to be inherited only in the future: *Bereishit Rabbah* 44:23

"Four hundred worlds of Divine pleasure": *Zohar* 1:123b

The seven metals of the Torah: *Ma'aseh Torah* 11

The "land of the living": Psalms 116:9

"Trees of life": *Cf.* Genesis 2:9.

"The whole earth is full of His glory": Isaiah 6:3

"Blessed be the glory of G-d from His place": Ezekiel 3:12

"His place" being the land of Israel: *Cf. Targum* to Ezekiel 3:12; *Midrash Tehillim* 68:4.

Are all, in essence, one and the same: *Zohar* 3:73a; *Bamidbar Rabbah* 23:5, 7

These four...correspond to the four pairs of the Machpelah: *Eruvin* 53a; *Meorei Or* 40, 43; *Torah Or* 15d; *Or HaTorah, Chayei Sarah* p. 777a.

Abraham and Sarah, in their...work to bring all peoples to recognize the unity of G-d: *Bereishit Rabbah* 39:14: "Anyone who brings in a heathen and converts him is as if he created him.... Abraham converted the men and Sarah the women."

"The choice of the fathers": *Bereishit Rabbah* 76:1

"General soul" of Israel: since we are called "the children of *Israel*." *Cf. Bava Metzia* 81a; *Bava Batra* 58a; *Zohar* 1:35b, 2:111a, 275b.

Jacob and Leah, whose love...was primarily at the level of mind: *Etz Chaim* 37; *Torah Or* 22d-23a

The birth of Issachar, the master of Torah: *Eruvin* 100b; *Bereishit Rabbah* 98; *Pesikta Rabati* 47

"The keepers of the garden": Genesis 2:15

Its secret...to be fully revealed by the *Mashiach*: See *Shechinah Beineihem*, p. 138-40

***Mashiach*, who will complete the rectification of Adam and Eve's sin:** *cf. Tanya*, ch. 36.

"All was from the earth and all returns to the earth": Ecclesiastes 3:20; Genesis 3:19

"I am first and I am last...": Isaiah 44:6

The..."one hundred gates": Genesis 26:12

The holy land is the physical context of the "dwelling place for G-d below": See 1 Kings 8:27; *cf. Midrash Tanchuma, Naso* 16 (ed. Buber 24).

The "dwelling place for G-d below": *Midrash Tanchuma, Naso* 16 (ed. Buber 24)

His seal is truth: See note on introduction, above.

"There is no truth but Torah": *Y. Rosh HaShanah* 3:8

Bibliography

Bibliography

Abudraham (אבודרהם), R. David Abudraham (?-1340). Commentary on the liturgy.

Abulafia, Rabbi Avraham (1240-after 1291). Kabbalist.

A Chapter in the Service of G-d, R. Yitzchak Ginsburgh (author of the present work).

R. Aharon, quoted by R. Moshe Botaril (*q.v.*).

Akeidat Yitzchak (עקידת יצחק), R. Yitzchak Aramah (1420-1492). Sermons.

AlKabetz, R. Shlomo (1505-1584). Kabbalist.

Avodah Zarah (עבודה זרה), tractate of the Talmud.

Avot (אבות), tractate of the Talmud.

Avot d'Rabbi Natan (אבות דרבי נתן), tractate of the Talmud.

Ayelet HaShachar (אילת השחר), R. Meir Leibush ben Yechiel Michel (Malbim, 1809-1879). Hebrew grammar.

Ba'al HaTurim (בעל הטורים), R. Yaakov ben Asher (1269-1343). Commentary on the Torah.

Bach (ב"ח = בית חדש), R. Yoel Sirkes (1561-1640). Halachic commentary on the Code of R. Yaakov ben Asher.

R. Bachya ben Asher (?-1340). Kabbalist.

Bad Kodesh (בד קדש), R. Dov Ber of Lubavitch (1773-1827). Chassidic discourse.

Bamidbar Rabbah (במדבר רבה), Midrash to the book of Numbers.

Bava Batra (בבא בתרא), tractate of the Talmud.

Bava Metzia (בבא מציעא), tractate of the Talmud.

Bava Kama (בבא קמא), tractate of the Talmud.

Bechinat Olam (בחינת עולם), R. Yedayah HaPenini (?-c. 1315). Philosophy and ethics.

Bechorot (בכורות), tractate of the Talmud.

Beit HaMidrash (בית המדרש), Aaron Jellinek. Collection of obscure and rare Midrashim.

Beit Yosef (בית יוסף), R. Yosef Karo (1488-1575). Halachic commentary to the Code of R. Yaakov ben Asher.

Beitzah (ביצה), tractate of the Talmud.

Ben Adret, R. Shlomo (1235-1310). Halachic authority.

Benei Yissachar (בני יששכר), R. Tzvi Elimelech of Dinov (1783-1841). Chassidic teachings.

Ben Porat Yosef (בן פורת יוסף), R. Yaakov Yosef of Polnoye (1704-1794). Chassidic teachings.

Berachot (ברכות), tractate of the Talmud.

Bereishit Rabbah (בראשית רבה), Midrash to Genesis.

Besha'ah Shehikdimu 5672 (בשעה שהקדימו תרע״ב), R. Shalom Dov Ber of Lubavitch (1860-1920). Series of Chassidic discourses.

Biurei HaZohar (Mittler Rebbe) (באורי הזהר-אדמו״ר האמצעי), R. Dov Ber of Lubavitch (1773-1827). Chassidic commentary to the *Zohar*.

Biurei HaZohar (Tzemach Tzedek) (באורי הזהר-אדמו״ר הצמח צדק), R. Menachem Mendel of Lubavitch (1789-1866). Chassidic commentary to the *Zohar*.

Chagigah (חגיגה), tractate of the Talmud.

Chanah Ariel (חנה אריאל), R. Yitzchak Isaac of Homil (c. 1770-1857). Chassidic discourses.

Chasidic Masters, R. Aryeh Kaplan (1934-1983). Translation of and commentary to excerpts of many of the works of the early Chassidic Rebbes.

Chayei Olam HaBa (חיי עולם הבא), R. Avraham Abulafia (1240-after 1291). Kabbalistic Meditation.

Chidushei Agadot (חדושי אגדות), R. Shmuel Eidels (1555-1631). Commentary on the Talmud.

Chulin (חולין), tractate of the Talmud.

Commentary to Sefer Yetzirah (פרוש לספר יצירה), R. Avraham ben David (c. 1120-c. 1197).

Commentary to Sefer Yetzirah (פרוש לספר יצירה), R. Eliahu of Vilna (the Vilna Gaon, 1720-1797).

Commentary to Sefer Yetzirah (פרוש לספר יצירה), R. Eliezar of Worms (?-c. 1055).

Commentary to Sefer Yetzirah (פרוש לספר יצירה), R. Moshe Botaril (14th-15th cent.).

Commentary to Sefer Yetzirah (פרוש לספר יצירה), R. Saadia *Gaon* (892-942).

Commentary to Sha'ar HaYichud (פרוש לשער היחוד), R. Hillel of Poritch (1795-1864).

Commentary to the Mishnah (פרוש למשניות), R. Moshe ben Maimon (Rambam, 1135-1204).

Commentary to the Zohar (פרוש לזהר), R. Moshe Zacuto (1625-1698).

Derech Chaim (דרך חיים), R. Dov Ber of Lubavitch (1773-1827). Chassidic teachings.

Derech Eretz Zuta (דרך ארץ זוטא), tractate of the Talmud.

Derech Mitzvotecha (דרך מצותיך), R. Menachem Mendel of Lubavitch (1789-1866). Chassidic discourses on the *mitzvot*.

Devarim Rabbah (דברים רבה), Midrash on Deuteronomy.

Eichah Rabbah (איכה רבה), Midrash on Lamentations.

R. Eliahu the Elder, quoted by R. Moshe Botaril (*q.v.*).

Emek HaMelech (עמק המלך), R. Naftali Bacharach (1st half of 17th cent.). Presentation of Lurianic Kabbalah.

Erachin (ערכין), tractate of the Talmud.

Erkei HaKinuim (ערכי הכינויים), R. Yechiel Halperin (1660-1747). Encyclopedia of Kabbalistic terms.

Eruvin (ערובין), tractate of the Talmud.

Esther Rabbah (אסתר רבה), Midrash to the book of Esther.

Etz Chaim (עץ חיים), R. Chaim Vital (1543-1620). Presentation of Lurianic Kabbalah.

Gaon, R. Saadia (892-942). Halachic authority and Philosopher.

Gitin (גיטין), tractate of the Talmud.

Gur Aryeh (גור אריה), R. Yehudah Liva (1512-1609). Supercommentary to Rashi (*q.v.*) on the Torah.

Haggadah (הגדה), the text of the home liturgy for the first night of *Pesach*. Cf. Liturgy.

Hakdamah LeDerech Chaim (הקדמה לדרך חיים), R. Hillel of Poritch (1795-1864). Introduction to *Derech Chaim* of R. Dov Ber of Lubavitch (*q.v.*).

Handbook of Jewish Thought, R. Aryeh Kaplan (1934-1983). Compendium of Jewish Dogma.

HaTamim (התמים), Lubavitch journal, published 1935-1938.

HaYom Yom (היום יום), R. Menachem Mendel Schneersohn of Lubavitch (b. 1902). Compendium of Chassidic lore.

Hilchot Talmud Torah (הלכות תלמוד תורה), R. Shneur Zalman of Liadi (1745-1812). Laws of Torah study.

Horiot (הוריות), tractate of the Talmud.

Igeret HaKodesh (אגרת הקדש), R. Shneur Zalman of Liadi (1745-1812). Fourth section of *Tanya*.

Igeret HaTeshuvah (אגרת התשובה), R. Shneur Zalman of Liadi (1745-1812). Third section of *Tanya*.

Igrot Kodesh Admur HaRayatz (אגרות קדש אדמו"ר הריי"ץ), Collected letters of R. Yosef Yitzchak of Lubavitch (1880-1950).

Imrei Binah (אמרי בינה), R. Dov Ber of Lubavitch (1773-1827). Chassidic discourses.

Imrei Kodesh (אמרי קדש), R. Uri of Strelisk (1757-1826). Chassidic teachings.

Imrei Shefer (אמרי שפר), R. Avraham Abulafia (1240-after 1291). Kabbalah.

Introduction to Mathematical Structure in Torah, R. Yitzchak Ginsburgh (author of the present work).

Kad HaKemach (כד הקמח), R. Bachya ben Asher (?-1340). Ethics and Philosophy.

Kalah (כלה), tractate of the Talmud.

Kedushat Levi (קדושת לוי), R. Levi Yitzchak of Berdichev (1740-1809). Chassidic teachings.

Kehilat Yaakov (קהילת יעקב), R. Yaakov Tzvi Yallish (?-1825). Encyclopedia of Kabbalistic terms.

Kelalei HaTuma'ah (כללי הטומאה), R. Eliahu (the Vilna *Gaon*) (1720-1797). Laws of Impurity.

Kelim (כלים), tractate of the Talmud.

Keter Malchut (כתר מלכות), R. Shlomo ibn Gabirol (c. 1021-c. 1058). Liturgical Poem.

Keter Shem Tov (כתר שם טוב), R. Aaron of Opt. Compendium of Chassidic teachings of R. Yisrael Ba'al Shem Tov (1698-1760).

Ketubot (כתובות), tractate of the Talmud.

Kidushin (קדושין), tractate of the Talmud.

Kitzur Shulchan Aruch (קצור שלחן ערוך), R. Shlomo Ganzfried (1804-1886). Abbreviated *Shulchan Aruch*.

Kohelet Rabbah (קהלת רבה), Midrash to Ecclesiastes.

Korban HaEdah (קרבן העדה), R. David Frankel (1707-1762). Commentary to the Jerusalem Talmud.

Kuntres 20 Marcheshvan 5748 (קונטרס כ' מרחשון תשמ"ח), R. Menachem Mendel Schneersohn of Lubavitch (b. 1902). Chassidic discourse.

Kuntres Acharon (קונטרס אחרון), R. Shneur Zalman of Liadi (1745-1812). Fifth section of *Tanya*.

Kuntres HaAvodah (קונטרס העבודה), R. Shalom Dov Ber of Lubavitch (1860-1920). Chassidic discourse.

Levush Orah (לבוש אורה), R. Mordechai Yaffe (1530-1612). Supercommentary to Rashi (*q.v.*) on the Torah.

Likutei Amarim (לקוטי אמרים), R. Dov Ber (the *Maggid*) of Mezeritch (?-1772). Chassidic teachings.

Likutei Biurim (לקוטי ביאורים), R. Yehoshua Korf. Collection of commentaries on the *Tanya*.

Likutei Diburim (לקוטי דבורים), R. Yosef Yitzchak of Lubavitch (1880-1950). Chassidic teachings and lore. English translation by Uri Kaploun.

Likutei Hagahot leSefer HaTanya (לקוטי הגהות לספר התניא), collection of commentaries on the *Tanya*.

Likutei HaShas (לקוטי הש"ס), R. Yitzchak Luria (1534-1572). Kabbalistic dimensions of passages from the Talmud.

Likutei Levi Yitzchak (לקוטי לוי יצחק), R. Levi Yitzchak Schneersohn (1878-1944). Kabbalah.

Likutei Sichot (לקוטי שיחות), R. Menachem Mendel of Lubavitch (b. 1902). Torah lessons by the present Lubavitcher Rebbe *shlita*.

Likutei Moharan (לקוטי מוהר"ן), R. Nachman of Breslov (1772-1810). Chassidic discourses.

Likutei Torah (Arizal) (לקוטי תורה [אריז"ל]), R. Chaim Vital (1543-1620). Lurianic Kabbalah.

Likutei Torah (לקוטי תורה), R. Shneur Zalman of Liadi (1745-1812). Chassidic discourses.

Likutim Yekarim (לקוטים יקרים), R. Dov Ber (the *Maggid*) of Mezeritch, (?-1772). Chassidic teachings.

Liturgy: Most of the liturgy in the Jewish prayerbook dates back to the Men of the Great Assembly (אנשי כנסת הגדולה), and even later additions are considered to have been composed with Divine Inspiration. Therefore, the locutions and diction employed in these prayers is considered precise and authoritative.

Ma'amar Atah Echad (מאמר אתה אחד), R. Dov Ber of Lubavitch (1773-1827). Chassidic discourse.

Ma'amar HaShiflut VeHaSimchah (מאמר השפלות והשמחה), R. Yitzchak Isaac of Homil (c. 1770-1857). Chassidic discourse.

Ma'amar Marg'la BePumei d'Rava 5746 (מאמר מרגלא בפומיה דרבא תשמ"ו), R. Menachem Mendel Schneersohn of Lubavitch (b. 1902). Chassidic discourse.

Ma'amar Mayim Rabim 5717 (מאמר מים רבים תשי"ז), R. Menachem Mendel Schneersohn of Lubavitch (b. 1902). Chassidic discourse.

Ma'amar Ner Chanukah 5713 (מאמר נר חנוכה תשי"ג), R. Menachem Mendel Schneersohn of Lubavitch (b. 1902). Chassidic discourse.

Ma'amar VeYasfu Anavim BeHavayah Simchah (מאמר ויספו ענוים בהוי' שמחה), R. Dov Ber of Lubavitch (1773-1827). Chassidic discourse.

Ma'amarei Admur HaZaken (מאמרי אדמו"ר הזקן), general name for books of discources by R. Shneur Zalman of Liadi (1745-1812), published according to year.

Ma'aseh Torah (מעשה תורה), R. Eliahu (the Vilna *Gaon*) (1720-1797). Number associations.

Makot (מכות), tractate of the Talmud.

Mapah (מפה), R. Moshe Isserles. Halachic commentary to the *Shulchan Aruch*.

Maor Einaim (מאור עינים), R. Menachem Nachum of Chernobyl (1730-1798). Chassidic teachings.

Matzat Shemurim (מצת שמורים), R. Natan Shapiro (?-1623). Kabbalistic dimensions of *mezuzah, tzitzit, tefilin* and morning blessings.

Mevo Shearim (מבוא שערים), R. Chaim Vital (1543-1620). Lurianic Kabbalah.

MeAm Loez (מעם לועז), R. Yaakov Culi (1689-1732) and others. Commentary on the *Tanach*.

Meditation and Kabbalah, R. Aryeh Kaplan (1934-1983). History and translation of source material.

Mechilta (מכילתא), Halachic Midrash to the book of Exodus.

Megaleh Amukot (מגלה עמוקות), R. Natan Neta Shapiro (?-1633). Kabbalistic commentary to the Torah.

Megilah (מגילה), tractate of the Talmud.

Menachot (מנחות), tractate of the Talmud.

Menorat HaMaor (מנורת המאור), R. Yisrael Al Nakawa (?-1391). Ethics.

Meorei Or (מאורי אור), R. Meir Poppers (?-1742). Encyclopedia of Kabbalistic terms.

Metzudat David (מצודת דוד), R. Yechiel Hillel Altschuler (18th cent.). Commentary to the Prophets and Writings.

Midrash Mishlei (מדרש משלי), Midrash on the book of Proverbs.

Midrash Tanchuma (מדרש תנחומא), Midrash on the Five Books of Moses, arranged by Torah-portion.

Midrash Tehilim (מדרש תהלים), Midrash on Psalms.

Minchat Shai (מנחת שי), R. Yedidiah Shlomo Rafael of Nortzi (17th cent.). Compendium of variant readings in the *Tanach*.

Mishnah Berurah (משנה ברורה), R. Yisrael Meir of Radin (1839-1933). Halachic commentary on the first part of the *Shulchan Aruch*.

Mishnat Chassidim (משנת חסידים), R. Emanuel Chai Riki (1688-?). Kabbalah.

Mishneh Torah (משנה תורה), R. Moshe ben Maimon (1135-1205). Early codification of the Oral Torah.

Moed Katan (מועד קטן), tractate of the Talmud.

Moreh Nevuchim (מורה נבוכים), R. Moshe ben Maimon (1135-1205). Philosophy.

Mystical Concepts: *Mystical Concepts in Chassidism*, R. Jacob Imanuel Schochet (contemporary). Basic introduction to Kabbalistic concepts.

Nachalat Yaakov (נחלת יעקב), R. Yaakov Noimberg. Commentary to *Soferim* (*q.v.*).

Nedarim (נדרים), tractate of the Talmud.

Nidah (נדה), tractate of the Talmud.

Ohalot (אהלות), tractate of the Talmud.

Onkelos (אונקלוס), Aramaic translation of the Five Books of Moses by Onkelos, the 2nd century convert.

Or HaSechel (אור השכל), R. Avraham Abulafia (1240-after 1291). Kabbalistic Meditation.

Or HaTorah (אור התורה), R. Menachem Mendel Schneersohn of Lubavitch (1789-1866). Chassidic discourses, arranged according to Torah-portion, books of the *Tanach*, etc.

Otzar HaChaim (אוצר החיים), R. Yitzchak Yehudah Yechiel of Komarna (1806-1874). Exposition of the 613 commandments as they are alluded to in the 620 letters of the Ten Commandments.

Otzar HaShem (אוצר השם), R. Moshe ben Yaakov (1070-1140?), author of commentary to *Sefer Yetzirah*.

Pardes Rimonim (פרדס רמונים), R. Moshe Cordevero (1522-1570), systematization of pre-Lurianic Kabbalah.

Peah (פאה), tractate of the Talmud.

Pelach HaRimon (פלח הרמון), R. Hillel of Poritch (1795-1864). Chassidic discourses.

Perek BeAvodat HaShem (פרק בעבודת השם), R. Yitzchak Ginsburgh (author of the present work). Chassidic discourse.

Perek Shirah (פרק שירה), see glossary.

Peri HaAretz (פרי הארץ), R. Menachem Mendel of Vitebsk (c. 1730-1788). Chassidic teachings.

Perush Yonatan (פרוש יונתן), R. Shlomo Zalman Netter of Jerusalem. Commentary to *Targum Yonatan* (q.v.).

Pesachim (פסחים), tractate of the Talmud.

Pesikta d'Rav Kahana (פסיקתא דרב כהנא), a Midrash.

Pesikta Rabati (פסיקתא רבתי), a Midrash.

Pesikta Zutrata (פסיקתא זוטרתי), a Midrash.

Pirkei d'Rabbi Eliezar (פרקי דרבי אליעזר), a Midrash.

Pirush HaMilot (פירוש המלות), R. Dov Ber of Lubavitch (1773-1827). Chassidic discourses.

Piskei Maharai (פסקי מהר"י), R. Yisrael Isserlein (c. 1390-1460). Halachic decisions.

Pri Etz Chaim (פרי עץ חיים), R. Chaim Vital (1543-1620). Lurianic Kabbalah.

Rambam: R. Moshe ben Maimon (1135-1204). See also Glossary.

Ramban: R. Moshe ben Nachman (1194-1270). See also Glossary.

Rashi: Rabbi Shelomo Yitzchaki (1040-1105), author of classic and fundamental commentaries on the *Tanach* and Babylonian Talmud.

Raziel HaMalach (רזיאל המלאך), early Kabbalistic work, given to Adam by the angel Raziel.

Recanati (רקנטי), R. Menachem Recanati (13th-14th cent.). Commentary on the Torah.

Reishit Chochmah (ראשית חכמה), R. Eliahu diVidas (16th cent.). Ethics based on Kabbalah.

Rosh HaShanah (ראש השנה), tractate of the Talmud.

Ruth Rabbah (רות רבה), Midrash to the book of Ruth.

Sanhedrin (סנהדרין), tractate of the Talmud.

Seder HaYom (סדר היום), R. Moshe Machir (16th cent.). Rules of conduct, etc.

Seder Olam (סדר עולם), Chronological Midrash.

Sefer Ba'al Shem Tov (ספר בעל שם טוב), R. Natan Neta of Kalbiel. Collection of teachings of the Ba'al Shem Tov (1698-1760).

Sefer Chachmoni (ספר חכמוני), R Shabtai Donolo (913-after 982). Commentary to *Sefer Yetzirah*.

Sefer Chareidim (ספר חרדים), R. Eliezar Azkari (1531-1600). Ethics and Conduct.

Sefer HaArachim (ספר הערכים), R. Yoel Kahan (contemporary). Encyclopedia of *Chabad Chassidut*.

Sefer HaBahir (ספר הבהיר), early Kabbalistic work by R. Nechuniah ben HaKaneh (1st cent.). Translated into English by R. Aryeh Kaplan.

Sefer HaChakirah (ספר החקירה), R. Menachem Mendel of Lubavitch (1789-1866). Philosophic discourses.

Sefer HaCheshek (ספר החשק), R. Avraham Abulafia (1240-after 1291). Kabbalistic Meditation.

Sefer HaEchad (ספר האחד), R. Avraham ibn Ezra (1089-c. 1164).

Sefer HaGilgulim (ספר הגלגולים), R. Yitzchak Luria. Theory of Reincarnation.

Sefer HaKuzari (ספר הכוזרי), R. Yehudah HaLevi (c. 1080-c. 1145). Philosophy.

Sefer HaLikutim (ספר הלקוטים), encyclopedic collection of writings of R. Menachem Mendel Schneersohn of Lubavitch (1789-1866).

Sefer HaMa'amarim (ספר המאמרים), general name for books of discourses by various *Chabad* Rebbes, published by year. If followed by a year from 5643-5680, refers to discourses by Rabbi Shalom Dov Ber of Lubavitch (1860-1920); if by a year from 5680-5711, to discourses by Rabbi Yosef Yitzchak of Lubavitch (1880-1950); if by a year from 5711 on, to discourses by Rabbi Menachem Mendel of Lubavitch (b. 1902), the present Lubavitcher Rebbe *shlita*.

Sefer HaMa'amarim—Kuntresim (ספר המאמרים–קונטרסים), R. Yosef Yitzchak Schneersohn of Lubavitch (1880-1950).

Sefer HaMalchut (ספר המלכות), R. Avraham HaLevi. Printed as part of *Maor V'Shemesh* (מאור ושמש) by R. Yehudah Koryat.

Sefer HaShorashim (ספר השרשים), R. David Kimchi (1160-1235). Hebrew Grammar and Language.

Sefer HaSichot (ספר השיחות), Talks by R. Yosef Yitzchak Schneersohn of Lubavitch (1880-1950).

Sefer HaTemunah (ספר התמונה), Midrashic/Kabbalistic work by R. Nechuniah ben HaKanah (1st century).

Sefer Mitzvot Katan (ספר מצות קטן), R. Yitzchak of Korbeil (?-1280). *Halachah.*

Sefer Yetzirah (ספר יצירה), fundamental text of Kabbalah, containing teachings which dates back to Abraham and that was redacted by R. Akiva (2nd century).

Sha'ar HaEmunah (שער האמונה), R. Dov Ber of Lubavitch (1773-1827), Chassidic discourse.

Sha'ar HaGemul (שער הגמול), R. Moshe ben Nachman (1194-1270). Philosophy.

Sha'ar HaKavanot (שער הכוונות), R. Chaim Vital (1543-1620). Lurianic Kabbalah.

Sha'ar HaKolel (שער הכולל), R. Avraham David Lavut (1814-1890). Halachic commentary to the Prayerbook.

Sha'ar HaMitzvot (שער המצות), R. Chaim Vital (1543-1620). Lurianic Kabbalah.

Sha'ar HaPesukim (שער הפסוקים), R. Chaim Vital (1543-1620). Lurianic Kabbalah.

Sha'ar HaYichud (שער היחוד), R. Dov Ber of Lubavitch (1773-1827). Chassidic discourse.

Sha'ar HaYichud VeHaEmunah (שער היחוד והאמונה), R. Shneur Zalman of Liadi (1745-1812). Second section of *Tanya*.

Sha'ar HaYichudim (שער היחודים), R. Chaim Vital (1543-1620). Lurianic Kabbalah.

Sha'ar Ma'amarei Razal (שער מאמרי רז"ל), R. Chaim Vital (1543-1620). Lurianic Kabbalah.

Sha'arei Gan Eden (שערי גן עדן), R. Yaakov Kopel of Lipshitz (d. 1740). Kabbalah.

Sha'arei Kedushah (שערי קדושה), R. Chaim Vital (1543-1620). Lurianic Kabbalah.

Sha'arei Orah (שערי אורה), R. Yosef Giktilia (1248-1323). pre-Lurianic Kabbalah.

Shabbat (שבת), tractate of the Talmud.

Shavuot (שבועות), tractate of the Talmud.

Shechinah Beineihem (שכינה ביניהם), R. Yitzchak Ginsburgh (author of the present work), Chassidic/Kabbalistic dimensions of man-wife relationships.

Shekalim (שקלים), tractate of the Talmud.

Shem HaGedolim (שם הגדולים), R. Chaim Yosef David Azulai (1724-1806). Biography and Bibliography.

Shemoneh Perakim (שמונה פרקים), R. Moshe ben Maimon (1135-1204). Ethics.

Shemot Rabbah (שמות רבה), Midrash to Exodus.

Shever Yosef (שבר יוסף), R. Yosef Shlomo Del Mediga (1591-1656). Kabbalah.

Shimusha Rabbah (שמושא רבא). Gaonic work on the laws of *tefilin*, ascribed to R. Sar Shalom *Gaon* (9th century) and published in the Commentary of R. Asher (the "*Rosh*") to the Talmudic tractate *Menachot*.

Shir HaShirim Rabbah (שיר השירים רבה), Midrash to the Song of Songs.

Shivchei HaBa'al Shem Tov—A Facsimile of a Unique Manuscript (שבחי הבעש"ט), R. Yehoshua Mundshein. Comparative study of editions of *Shivchei HaBa'al Shem Tov*, with various other interesting material.

Shnei Luchot Ha'Brit (שני לוחות הברית), R. Yeshayiahu Horowitz (1560-1630). Kabbalah, *halachah*, ethics.

Shulchan Aruch (שלחן ערוך), R. Yosef Karo (1488-1575). The Code of Jewish Law. Arranged in four parts: *Orach Chaim, Yoreh Deah, Even HaEzer,* and *Choshen Mishpat*.

Shulchan Aruch HaArizal (שלחן ערוך האריז"ל), Kabbalah-based customs of R. Yitzchak Luria (1534-1572), arranged according to the *Shulchan Aruch*.

Shulchan Aruch HaRav (שלחן ערוך הרב), R. Shneur Zalman of Liadi (1745-1812). Update of the *Shulchan Aruch*.

Shulchan HaEzer (שלחן העזר), R. Yitzchak Tzvi Leibowitz. Compendium of Wedding Laws and Customs.

Sidurei HaArizal (סדורי האריז"ל), any of a number of prayerbooks arranged according to the teachings of R. Yitzchak Luria (1534-1572).

Siddur Im Dach (סדור עם דא"ח), R. Dov Ber of Lubavitch (1773-1827). Prayerbook with Chassidic commentary.

Sifra (ספרא), Halachic Midrash to Leviticus.

Sifrei (ספרי), Halachic Midrash to Numbers and Deuteronomy.

Sod HaShem Lireiav (סוד השם ליראיו), R. Yitzchak Ginsburgh (author of the present work). Chassidic/Kabbalistic teachings.

Soferim (סופרים), tractate of the Talmud.

Sotah (סוטה), tractate of the Talmud.

Sukah (סוכה), tractate of the Talmud.

Ta'anit (תענית), tractate of the Talmud.

Tamid (תמיד), tractate of the Talmud.

Tana d'vei Eliahu Rabbah (תנא דבי אליהו רבה), a Midrash.

Tana d'vei Eliahu Zuta (תנא דבי אליהו זוטא), a Midrash.

Tanya (תניא), R. Shneur Zalman of Liadi (1745-1812). Basic work of *Chabad Chassidut*.

Tanya b'tziruf Ma'arei Mekomot etc. (תניא בצירוף מארי מקומות וכו'), R. Aharon Chitrik (contemporary). *Tanya* with sources, cross-references and variant manuscript readings.

Targum: Targum Yonatan (תרגום יונתן), Yonatan ben Uziel (1st century). Aramaic translation/commentary to the Five Books of Moses and the Prophets.

Teshuvot uViruim (5734) (תשובות וביאורים–תשל"ד), R. Menachem Mendel Schneersohn of Lubavitch (b. 1902). Responsa.

Tikunei Zohar (תקוני זהר), R. Shimon bar Yochai (2nd century) and his school. Additions to the *Zohar*.

Toldot Yaakov Yosef (תולדות יעקב יוסף), R. Yaakov Yosef of Polnoye (1704-1794). Chassidic teachings.

Toldot Yitzchak Isaac (5747, תולדות יצחק אייזיק), R. Yochanan Gurary (contemporary). Biography of R. Yitzchak Isaac of Homil (c. 1770-1857).

Torah Or (תורה אור), R. Shneur Zalman of Liadi (1745-1812). Chassidic discourses.

Torat Chaim (תורת חיים), R. Dov Ber of Lubavitch (1773-1827). Chassidic discourses, arranged according to Torah-portion.

Torat Shmuel (תורת שמואל), general name for books of discourses by R. Shmuel of Lubavitch (1834-1882), published by year.

Tosefot (תוספות), medieval commentary to the Talmud.

Tosefta (תוספתא), Talmudic material not included in the body of the Talmud, arranged by tractates and printed in the back of most editions.

Treatise on Resurrection, R. Moshe ben Maimon (1135-1204). Translated in English by Fred Rosner.

Tzava'at HaRibash (צוואת הריב"ש), collection of teachings of Rabbi Yisrael Ba'al Shem Tov (1698-1760).

Uktzin (עוקצין), tractate of the Talmud.

VaYikra Rabbah (ויקרא רבה), Midrash to Leviticus.

Y.: indicates Talmud *Yerushalmi* (see Glossary: "Talmud").

Yahel Or (יהל אור), R. Menachem Mendel of Lubavitch (1789-1866). Chassidic discourses on Psalms.

Yalkut Reuveni (ילקוט ראובני), R. Avraham Reuven Sofer (?-1673). Compendium of Midrashic and Kabbalistic commentary on the Torah.

Yalkut Shimoni (ילקוט שמעוני), R. Shimon Ashkenazi (14th cent.). Collection of Midrashic material.

Yevakesh Da'at (יבקש דעת), R. Yom Tov Lippman Heller (1579-1654).

Yevamot (יבמות), tractate of the Talmud.

Yoma (יומא), tractate of the Talmud.

Zevachim (זבחים), tractate of the Talmud.

Zohar (זהר), R. Shimon bar Yochai (2nd century) and his school. Basic work of the Kabbalah.

Zohar Chadash (זהר חדש), R. Shimon bar Yochai (2nd century) and his school. Additions to the *Zohar*.

Zohar Chai (זהר חי), R. Yitzchak Yehudah Yechiel Safrin of Komarna (1806-1874). Commentary to the *Zohar*.

Index

Index